W9-AUN-817

Principles of Corporate Renewal

Principles of Corporate Renewal

Harlan D. Platt

Ann Arbor
The University of Michigan Press

Copyright © by the University of Michigan 1998
All rights reserved
Published in the United States of America by
The University of Michigan Press
Manufactured in the United States of America
♾ Printed on acid-free paper

2001 2000 1999 1998 4 3 2

No part of this publication may be reproduced, stored in a retrieval system, or transmitted in any form or by any means, electronic, mechanical, or otherwise, without the written permission of the publisher.

A CIP catalog record for this book is available from the British Library.

Library of Congress Cataloging-in-Publication Data

Platt, Harlan D., 1950–
Principles of corporate renewal / Harlan D. Platt.
p. cm.
Includes bibliographical references and index.
ISBN 0-472-10838-7 (alk. paper)
1. Corporate turnarounds. I. Title.
HD58.8.P576 1998
658.1′6—dc21 97-38129
CIP

Dedicated to

The Turnaround Management Association

especially

Tom Allison, Gary Brooks, and William Hass,
who asked me to develop the ACTP certification program

Contents

Figures

Tables

Preface

Listening to Erich Mundinger, a vice president at American Finasco, tell the following story helped me to realize how misinformed mainstream America is about the study of corporate renewal:

> After explaining to the dean of a prominent college of business administration about his work with companies in financial distress, the following day he received an unexpected call from the chairman of the University's School of Psychiatry. The doctor inquired in an anxious voice if "he needed assistance treating his suicidal clients."

If nothing else, this book should introduce members of the academy and their students to a new field of study. It also should outfit students to restore troubled companies.

Since 1988, when I began to teach corporate renewal to business students and executives, I have learned to start each class by reciting the one ground rule for class discussion: "Express your views about any topic in any way but never ask me or a fellow student the *unfair question,* "What if it was you?" Layoffs, cutbacks, downsizing, severance benefits, and related topics are associated with human suffering and misery and invariably elicit the *unfair question* unless the rule is enacted. There is no satisfactory answer to the question. Although the human tragedy produced by layoffs is an important social issue, it diverts attention from the equally valid corporate renewal issue of whether the company and some of its jobs can be saved. I advise readers of this book to keep an open mind and avoid the diffidence that leads to inaction and eventual failure. An equally contentious but, in my opinion, more valid question is, "What if it was your family's small business?"

Corporate renewal is an old profession in a new garb. Resourceful entrepreneurs have always stood ready to acquire failed businesses and inject new money or ideas in an effort to transform detritus into treasure. Today the corporate renewal specialist no longer works or invests for him/herself but probably is an employee of a large consulting firm or a Big Six accounting firm. Factors responsible for this dramatic shift include the protection provided to debtors through modern bankruptcy laws and bankers' and other secured lenders' recognition that turnaround professionals can help them recover problem loans.

In the past decade, courses on corporate renewal have emerged from business schools, though each campus's course catalogue coins its own title, for example, Corporate Renewal, Turnaround Management, or Corporate Restructuring. Schools now are contemplating master's degrees in corporate renewal. Moreover, practitioners now earn a certificate from the Turnaround Management Association, the Certified Turnaround Professional (CTP) designation similar to the CPA or CMA designation in accounting, that documents their competency in management, finance, accounting, tax, and legal issues pertaining to corporate renewal.

This book, the first tome on corporate renewal, attempts to assemble and codify the topic's myriad issues. Some might prefer a different collection of topics or an emphasis on different issues, but hopefully there is enough common ground in this volume to satisfy everyone.

I want to thank the many turnaround managers and related professionals who have helped me to understand their fascinating world: Tom Allison, Gary Brooks, Ken Glass, Jack Stone, Baker Smith, Clyde Hamstreet, Dave Ferrari, Judge Paul W. Glennon, Sheldon Solow, Margaret Howard, Katherine Heidt, Grant Newton, Chuck Hofer, Robert Weisberg, Edward P. Collins, Les Brown, Barry Evans, Nikesh Arora, Vinesh Kochhar, Chris Ryan, Rick Mikels, Karen Mills, Carol Smith, Martha Kopatz, Dick Gorges, Shaun Donnellan, Greg Frasier, Amin Khoury, Brad Yount, Don Bibeault, Carl Youngman, Tom Hays, Lee Goldberg, Gerry Sherman, Alan Cohen, Bill Bruns, Michael Segal and many others too numerous to mention.

I owe a special debt of gratitude to Bob Lehmann, a former student now at Fidelity Investments, who helped me prepare the financial tables for the Global Foods Case. Also to Chris Ioannides, who worked on the Global tables at the last minute. I am grateful to the many students who read an early draft and found errors. And to Ellen McCarthy and Tanis Furst at the University of Michigan Press, who creatively and diligently helped me to shape the book.

Part 1

Basic Issues

CHAPTER 1

Introduction to Corporate Renewal

Today's headline reads, "Apple Posts Record $740 Million Loss, More Than Doubles Planned Layoffs" (Carlton 1996a: B6). Days earlier another headline read, "Massive Restructuring at Scotts to Include Cuts in Spending, Staff" (Murray 1996: B4). Hardly a day passes without a major company announcing a revitalization campaign.[1] These corporate crusades are labeled "corporate renewal," "turnaround management," or "crisis resolution,"[2] phrases so new to the business lexicon that they often are used interchangeably.

How do companies transform and revitalize themselves? These questions are explored in this book, the aim of which is to educate readers in how the new science of company transformation treats distressed companies to make them healthier and save jobs.

Chapter Organization and Content

This study of corporate renewal is arranged into three sections. This first chapter covers the field's basic issues, including the causes and consequences of business failure. Legal issues relating to bankruptcy are described in chapter 2, while techniques to measure corporate health are described in chapter 3. The fourth chapter examines ethical issues related to financial distress. These chapters ground the reader in the discipline.

The middle part of the book is labeled "implementation." The two chapters in this part examine issues related to turnaround management and crisis resolution. Chapter 5 discusses the methods and techniques of turnaround management. It presents a coherent plan to enable a company to assess its position and structure a response. Chapter 6 examines how a downsizing campaign is implemented and identifies its limitations.

The final part of the book discusses advanced issues. Advanced legal topics are presented in chapter 7, including a major assignment, preparing a plan of reorganization, for the reader to complete. Chapters 8 and 9 introduce, respectively, the related topics of reengineering and quality. Tax considerations (net operating loss carryforwards and debt forgiveness) and investment issues are presented in chapter 10. The final chapter, chapter 11, presents accounting issues including fresh-start accounting and ABC accounting. A glossary of terms appears at the end of the book.

Change and Survival

The impetus for change and transformation is survival. Global competition, deregulation, technological change, loss of national culture, and megastores all contribute to the buildup of enormous pressures on businesses. To survive, businesses are instituting a variety of changes including

- debt restructuring
- laying off both white- and blue-collar employees
- downsizing operations
- divesting subsidiaries and divisions
- reengineering
- establishing total quality management programs
- engaging in product renewal
- rightsizing their workforces
- filing for bankruptcy protection

Which strategies are necessary and appropriate and at what times is not well understood, either by those being impacted by the changes (managerial and nonmanagerial workers, labor unions, shareholders, and even some employers) or by inquiring observers (politicians and reporters). As a consequence, companies are chastised for taking actions that harm certain employees or current shareholders and not praised for preserving remaining jobs and keeping firms operating and competitive in a global marketplace.[3] The origin of this paradox is American society's unfamiliarity with the processes and potential for company renewal.

The Three Levels of Corporate Renewal

Corporate renewal draws upon three paradigms: corporate transformation, turnaround management, and crisis management.

1. Corporate transformation occurs when a company, even a healthy one, asks itself two questions:
   - What are we doing wrong?
   - What could we do better?
2. Turnaround management occurs when a company with a major problem has sufficient time and resources to find a solution.
3. Crisis management occurs when a troubled company approaches the end of its existence.

A combination of actions and strategies is recommended in each stage of the renewal process, as is described in table 1.1. Several actions recur in each stage, while others are limited to a single stage of corporate renewal. Actions recommended during turnaround management overlap some used during corporate transformation and others used during crisis resolution. Corporate transformation, turnaround management, and corporate renewal offer a range of management techniques providing benefits to every company.

Although these management practices may be grouped under the same legend, corporate renewal, each has a distinct objective. Corporate

TABLE 1.1. Actions Taken in Each Stage of Corporate Renewal

Action	Corporate Transformation	Turnaround Management	Crisis Resolution
Divest subsidiaries and divisions	X		
Reengineer processes	X		
Establish total quality management program	X		
Engage in product renewal	X		
Product review and expiration	X	X	
Rightsize the workforce	X	X	
Determine full product costs	X	X	
Reprice products	X	X	X
Establish new wage and benefits levels	X	X	X
Downsize operations		X	X
Restructure debt		X	X
Lay off employees		X	X
Improve working capital management		X	X
Extend or compose debts		X	X
Negotiate partial settlements with creditors			X
File for bankruptcy protection			X
Liquidate			X

transformation further advances a successful company and is an enriching activity. Turnaround management rehabilitates a troubled company and sets the stage for future achievement. Crisis resolution follows triage principles[4] to treat an emergency; it is an agonizing process geared to finding a way for the company to survive.

It is critical to know that corporate renewal has distinct stages and that different actions work best in each stage, but it is not important to identify exactly where a company lies along the corporate transformation/turnaround management/crisis resolution continuum. For example, a company that is current on its obligations but underperforms its industry counterparts is probably somewhere between the corporate transformation and turnaround management phases, and a company that has received a warning letter from its bank although its sales are strong may lie between the turnaround management and crisis resolution phases.

Turnaround management is the central element of corporate renewal. Table 1.1 shows that turnaround management overlaps more than 50 percent of the methods used in both corporate transformation and crisis resolution. Consequently, most of this book is devoted to turnaround management.

Numerous books have been written about turnaround successes and failures at specific companies (Scully 1987; Stein 1989; Hammer and Champy 1993). This book introduces techniques and methods relevant to any company. While case studies are an important adjunct to the study of corporate renewal, they are not a substitute. No company is a perfect template for all turnarounds. Each case possesses an infinite number of special situations and circumstances that nullify its general application in other situations.

Turnaround Management

Types of Turnarounds

Charles Hofer is viewed by many as the academic pioneer in the area of corporate renewal and turnaround management. His work continues to guide the science's intellectual evolution. In a 1980 study, he characterizes the nature of turnarounds as being either strategic or operating.

- A *strategic turnaround* attempts either to change the strategy for competing in the same business or to define how to enter a new business. Most strategic turnarounds focus on marketing, production, or engineering functions. One type of strategic turnaround

accepts the current market share; the other type seeks significant (at least 100 percent) additions to market share.
- An *operating turnaround* is concerned with increasing revenues, decreasing costs, or decreasing assets.

The three ingredients of operating turnarounds—increasing revenues, decreasing costs, and decreasing assets—are strategic actions as well. According to Hofer, "performance becomes a derivative of the strategy change. In operating turnarounds, the primary focus is on the performance targets to be achieved" (Hofer 1980: 20). Hambrick and Schecter described Hofer's duality as "doing different things and doing things differently" (Hambrick and Schecter 1983: 232). Schendel, Patten, and Riggs (1975) interpret Hofer's paradigm to mean that operating remedies involve plant expenditures and actions taken to become more efficient, while diversification, vertical integration, and divestment are strategic remedies.

The final type of turnaround is a financial restructuring, in which a firm with excess debt exchanges new shares of its equity for a portion of its outstanding debt or arranges for creditors to modify the terms of the debt by lengthening its maturity date or lowering its interest rate. Texas International, the subject of my book *The First Junk Bond* (1994), arranged three debt restructurings before it eventually failed. The outcome of financial restructurings depends heavily on the negotiating skills of participants.

Using a small sample of distressed companies, Hofer observed that a turnaround may fail if the wrong type (i.e., operating versus strategic) of changes are implemented. Turnaround managers have a predilection to adopt operating changes even though they may be inappropriate because

- there is a longer wait until strategic turnarounds yield any rewards
- "effective strategic moves are possible only at certain periods in an industry's evolution, unless a competitor slips or the firm has some unusual strategic resource that it has thus far failed to utilize" (Hofer 1980: 30)

Hofer argues that if strategic change is necessary but unlikely to succeed, liquidation is preferred to an unsuccessful operating turnaround.

Hofer explains that the choice among cost-cutting, revenue-enhancing, and asset-reducing operating turnarounds depends upon how close the firm is to its break-even point, as seen in figure 1.1. Firms barely

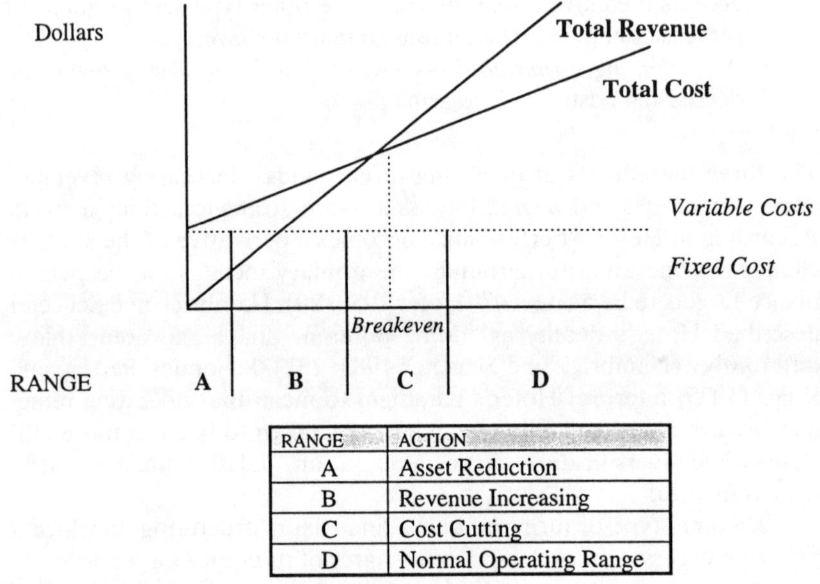

RANGE	ACTION
A	Asset Reduction
B	Revenue Increasing
C	Cost Cutting
D	Normal Operating Range

Fig. 1.1. Hofer's operating turnaround decision graph

covering their variable costs, in range A in figure 1.1, are operating in the shut-down region where revenues are insufficient to make a contribution to fixed costs (see the break-even discussion in chap. 3). They should dispose of assets (i.e., shut down). Revenue-enhancing strategies are followed in range B to give the firm enough of a boost, to first break even and later achieve positive cash flow. Firms in range C, the cost-cutting interval, need less overall improvement to reach their break-even. Firms in this range may also adopt revenue-enhancing strategies. Successful companies operate in range D. This is the target range for the distressed company.

Stages in a Turnaround

There are several distinct turnaround stages. Probably the first, and certainly the best, description of turnaround stages appears in Bibeault's Ph.D. dissertation, which he later adapted into a best-selling book.[5] His characterization of the five turnaround stages is especially sharp because it combines his scholarly pursuits and his personal corporate turnaround experiences. Bibeault's stages are described in table 1.2. Bibeault's prototype is simple yet inclusive: agree to attempt a turnaround, identify issues, perform triage, evaluate, and return to normalcy.

Unlike Bibeault, who studied turnaround managers, Richard C. Hoffman (1989: 46–66) surveyed seventeen major studies of the turnaround process. His summary reshuffles Hofer's types of turnarounds and Bibeault's turnaround stages into a new set of three turnaround stages encompassing the five generic strategies seen in table 1.3. Hoffman's condensation is especially useful because it combines stages and strategies in a single model.

Hofer's, Bibeault's, and Hoffman's prescriptions are generalizations and do not apply in all situations. Disparities between cases result both from the idiosyncrasies of practitioners and from unique aspects of particular companies and industries. By understanding these turnaround management frameworks, practitioners learn to consider their options. Yet other issues may arise to circumvent the turnaround manager's success.

TABLE 1.2. Bibeault's Stages of a Turnaround

Stage	Description	Actions
1	Management change stage	1. The board of directors or senior management decides a transition is necessary. 2. The turnaround agent, either internal or external, is selected and given some degree of authority.
2	Evaluation stage	1. The nature and extent of problems are diagnosed. 2. The type of turnaround, strategic or operational, is chosen. 3. An action plan is prepared.
3	Emergency stage	1. Companies on the brink of failing must do whatever is necessary to survive.
4	Stabilization stage	1. Immediate problems are resolved. 2. Plans are put in place to improve operating and strategic performance. 3. Results are evaluated for acceptability. 4. When results are insufficient, the liquidation, sale, or merger options are explored.
5	Return-to-normal-growth stage	1. Normal corporate operations.

TABLE 1.3. Hoffman's Turnaround Stages and Strategies

Stage	Strategies
1. Preparatory stage	1. Restructure leadership, organization, and culture
2. Short-term-fix stage	2. Cost reduction
	3. Asset redeployment
	4. Selective product/market strategies
3. Growth stage	5. Repositioning strategies

John Argenti (1976) notes three types of failed companies:

Type 1—startup companies with inadequate resources
Type 2—rocket companies that start out successful but then fail
Type 3—older firms whose problems have taken years to surface

He argues that there are vast differences in the managerial, financial, and operating issues confronting startup, rocket, and older firm failures. The turnaround manager adjusts his/her choice of tactics to the type of failure. Other turnaround differences arise due to preexisting management issues. Bibeault's 1982 survey of eighty-one CEOs at companies engaged in turnarounds exposed an extensive list of factors confronting the turnaround manager, including, in order of importance, the following:

1. One-man rule (44 percent)
2. Lack of managerial depth (22 percent)
3. Management succession problems (13 percent)
4. Inbred bureaucratic management (11 percent)
5. Unbalanced top management team (6 percent)
6. Nonparticipative board (3 percent)
7. Weak finance executive (1 percent)

No single action plan adequately confronts this medley of management issues.

Best practices in one industry may be ineffectual in another. On the other hand, illustrious turnaround specialists, such as Sandy Sigoloff or Al Dunlap, apply their skills across industries with equal success (Collins 1996).

Finally, the turnaround manager may be inhibited from taking the right action by a board of directors' reluctance to surrender control. Many turnaround managers believe that the critical juncture in any case is when their service contract is negotiated, in particular the stipulations concerning who will exercise corporate control. But turnaround management is both an art and a science, and its practice does not follow a strict outline or process.

The Failure Record

The federal government collects no business failure or corporate distress data. Instead, the Dun & Bradstreet Corporation (D&B), a private firm, dominates this field, which it pioneered in the 1920s. Over ten million companies are monitored by its National Business Information

Center. D&B publishes several failure reports: *Weekly Business Failures, Monthly Business Failures, Quarterly Business Failures,* and *Business Failure Record* (the annual survey). Some are distributed free of charge upon request.[6]

D&B defines failures as companies whose creditors suffer financial losses when the businesses either close voluntarily or initiate court proceedings (Dun & Bradstreet 1995). D&B's failure statistics exclude distressed companies seeking to compromise or extend creditor obligations as well as thousands of companies that, though unable to earn economic profits, repay creditors before closing. D&B's data reflects legalistic outcomes such as bankruptcy and liquidation rather than situations resolved out of court.

Clearly, the D&B definition is too broad. For example, Bruce Kirchoff (*Fortune* 1993: 21) examined data on 814,000 start-up firms for whom a 62 percent failure rate had been reported by the Small Business Administration during their first six years of existence. He found that 26 percent of the D&B failures actually had changed owners or switched their organizational form from a partnership to a corporation. Other companies had ceased to exist after the owner retired. Kirchoff's corrected failure estimate was 46 percent.

Although statistics on corporate renewal are absent from the D&B data, on occasion that information does emerge from surveys conducted by various analysts. Because surveys can be criticized for being infrequent, asking nonstandardized questions, and phrasing questions imperfectly, the preponderance of information describing the causes of business failure is drawn from D&B's data.

Failure Rates

Perhaps the most interesting D&B observation concerns the enormous swings observed historically in the national failure rate (i.e., the number of failures out of every 10,000 companies).[7] Annual failure rates are listed in table 1.4 and are illustrated for the period 1927–93 in figure 1.2.[8] Three primary factors explain failure rate variability:

1. economic conditions
2. age distribution of companies
3. partiality of bankruptcy laws to debtors

Economic conditions is the single most important factor determining the rate of corporate failure. However, which economic factor most affects corporate health changes at various times. Among the key economic agents are

- level of interest rates
- rate of inflation
- overall economic activity (e.g., the rate of change in gross domestic product)
- level of imports and exports
- value of the dollar.[9]

The economy's impact on failures is vividly revealed in figure 1.2. The worst failure year, 1932, when 154 out of every 10,000 companies failed, occurred in the midst of the Great Depression. The onset of the

TABLE 1.4. Failure Rate of U.S. Corporations and the Percentage Change in Real Gross Domestic Product[a]

Year	Failure Rate	% Change in Real GDP	Year	Failure Rate	% Change in Real GDP	Year	Failure Rate	% Change in Real GDP
1927	106	−0.11%	1950	34	7.97	1973	36	5.75
1928	109	0.58	1951	31	8.99	1974	38	−0.63
1929	104	6.24	1952	29	4.06	1975	43	−0.59
1930	122	−10.95	1953	33	3.62	1976	35	5.59
1931	133	−8.39	1954	42	−0.72	1977	28	4.85
1932	154	−17.41	1955	42	5.37	1978	24	5.01
1933	100	−1.91	1956	48	1.94	1979	28	2.90
1934	61	8.30	1957	52	1.90	1980	42	−0.26
1935	62	8.97	1958	56	−0.49	1981	61	2.45
1936	48	12.18	1959	52	5.13	1982	88	−2.16
1937	46	5.02	1960	57	2.13	1983	110	4.03
1938	61	−5.34	1961	64	2.62	1984	107	6.82
1939	70	7.88	1962	61	6.03	1985	115	3.72
1940	63	7.83	1963	56	4.29	1986	120	3.37
1941	55	13.84	1964	53	5.83	1987	102	2.89
1942	45	11.45	1965	53	6.36	1988	98	3.80
1943	16	11.66	1966	52	6.45	1989	65	3.37
1944	7	6.70	1967	49	2.63	1990	74	1.22
1945	4	−1.72	1968	39	4.72	1991	107	−0.97
1946	5	−13.63	1969	37	3.02	1992	110	2.72
1947	14	−1.22	1970	44	0.03	1993	109	3.48
1948	20	3.69	1971	42	3.85	1994	86	3.48
1949	34	0.38	1972	38	5.43			

Source: Dun & Bradstreet (1995); *Data Disk* (1996)

[a]Failure rate is the number of failures out of every 10,000 firms.

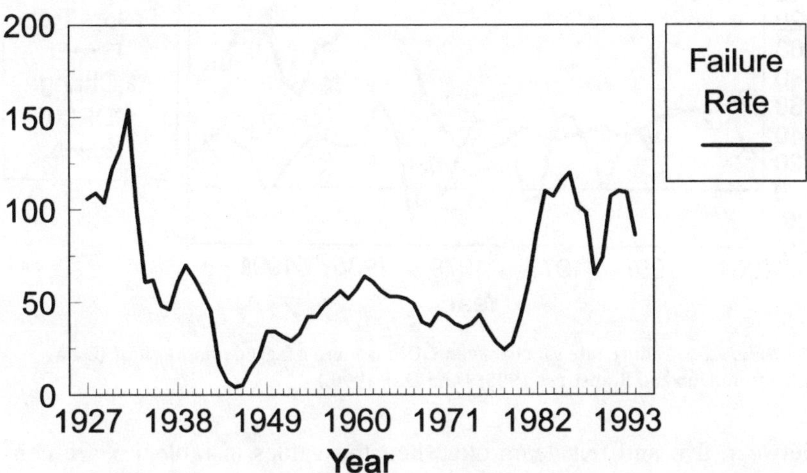

Fig. 1.2. Failure Rate 1927–93. (Data from Dun and Bradstreet 1994.)

depression in 1929 did not cause failures to accelerate immediately because other factors exerted influence on company health. A delayed reaction is consistent with D&B's belief (Dun & Bradstreet 1995: 1) that "the total level of business failure is often a lagging indicator of economic conditions in a particular industry or region." Evidence in figure 1.3 comparing the failure rate to the rate of change in the gross domestic product supports this hypothesis.[10]

The failure rate plunged to a historic low, four out of every 10,000 firms, in 1945, toward the end of World War II. For companies, that year was the "best of times and the worst of times." Mobilization and conscription for the war effort caused shortages and output restrictions, but the economy was going full blast. Virtually anything that a company could produce was sold for a profit. Firms that failed in 1945 probably suffered from either fraud or gross incompetence.

Failures rose again during the Reagan years (1980–88) and continued high through 1996. Ironically, the economy was relatively strong throughout this period, but rapid economic growth coupled with high failure rates is not unusual. A similar combination occurred just prior to the Great Depression. In both eras, vast numbers of entrepreneurs emerged, creating a rush of new companies.

D&B documents a monotonically higher failure rate for new companies less than four years old, between four and five years old, and

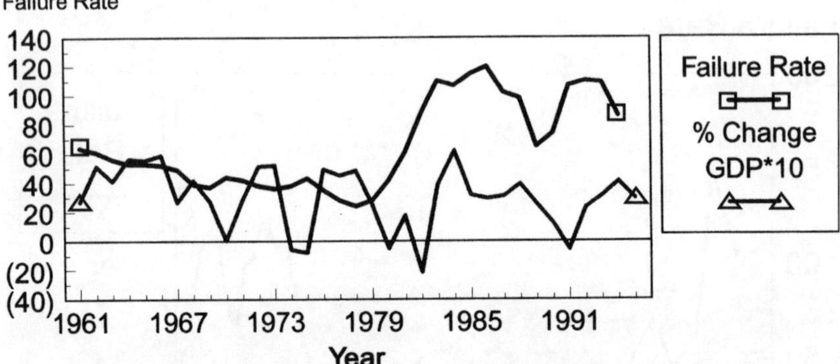

Fig. 1.3. Failure rate vs. change in GDP: Is there a lagged relationship? (Data from Dun and Bradstreet 1995; *Data Disk* 1996.)

between five and ten years old when the values in table 1.5 are converted into single years by dividing by three, two, and five respectively. Companies less than three years old are the most likely to fail; in 1985, for example, they were nearly twice as likely to fail *per year* as firms between six and ten years old and were almost three times more likely to fail than firms between four and five years old, as seen in table 1.5. The comparison is less dramatic for 1994. Factors contributing to the higher failure rate among newer companies include

- insufficient bank and trade financing arrangements
- inadequate managerial ranks
- lack of an independent board of directors[11]
- meager retained earnings
- dependence on a single product line
- operations in a single region of the country

TABLE 1.5. The Age Distribution of Failures

	Percentage of All Business Failures		Cumulative Failure Percent	
Age of Business	1994	1985	1994	1985
< 4 years old	24%	40%	24%	40%
4–5 years old	15%	16%	40%	50%
6–10 years old	27%	24%	67%	80%
> 10 years old	33%	20%	100.0%	100%

Source: Dun & Bradstreet (1994; 1984)

Consequently, the age distribution of companies is an important determinant of the overall failure rate.

Consider the two years 1994 and 1985: in 1994, 86 out of 10,000 firms failed; by contrast, 115 out of 10,000 firms failed in 1985. One explanation for 1994's lower failure rate is that relatively fewer new firms failed in 1994: 24 percent of failures were less than three years of age in 1994 versus 40 percent in 1984, as seen in table 1.5. Other factors may explain this phenomenon, but there simply may have been relatively fewer new firms in 1994 owing to the lower rate of economic growth in the early 1990s. Economic prosperity breeds new firms, some of which fail, leading to a higher failure rate.

Frank Knight, a celebrated 1930s Harvard economist, described capitalism as a wellspring of "creative destruction" in which new firms drive out (i.e., bankrupt) older firms. The truth of this statement is unquestioned, but what Professor Knight omitted is that many new firms fail themselves. Without failure an economy stagnates.

Bankruptcy laws (surveyed in chap. 2) have evolved over the past two hundred years, reflecting changes in society's mores and ethics. The legal process historically has favored creditors. Society's sympathies recently have shifted to favor debtors, and bankruptcy laws have been modified to reflect this new mood. Today, creditors are barred from seizing assets, old debts are expunged after reorganization, and neither the debtor nor his/her children are incarcerated.

Revisions in legal statutes and judicial sentiments have influenced businesspeople's behavior and the associated rate of corporate failure. Fewer firms file for bankruptcy court protection when laws favor creditors and the recovery of financial obligations (Platt 1989; Platt and Platt 1994).[12] The most recent major bankruptcy law, enacted in 1978, is more liberal to debtors and appears to have encouraged more firms to seek in the courts an escape from their legal obligations. The failure rate rose after the passage of this legislation, as seen in table 1.4, though other factors may have contributed to the rising failure rate.[13]

Survey Results

Dun & Bradstreet

While gathering failure rate information over the years, D&B also compiled information describing the underlying causes of individual business failures.[14] Although D&B's research method was imperfect,[15] their investigation nevertheless produced unsurpassed longitudinal data, 1965–93, on the causes of business failure. Modifications to the survey questions across thirty-eight years complicate the task of comparing these results. This difficulty notwithstanding, table 1.6 compares the first, 1965, and last, 1993, D&B surveys. Over that period there is a sharp drop in the incidence of failure caused by avoidable issues such as excessive assets or accounts receivable. Might modern businesspeople be better educated then their 1960s counterparts as a result of having attended business schools? It also appears that more companies now fail because of the impact of domestic and international competition on gross margins (see the excessive operating expense category in table 1.6).

Buccino

In 1991, Buccino & Associates, a major turnaround firm, conducted its own study to determine the causes of business failure (ABI Bankruptcy Reform Study Project 1995). Unlike the D&B approach, which relied on the opinions and observations of its own agents, Buccino sought information from over 10,000 crisis managers, bankruptcy and workout attorneys, workout bankers and lenders and CEOs of the 1,000 most publicly held U.S. companies. They received 1,335 responses, 87 percent of which reported that failure resulted from internal corporate factors. The three most common internal mistakes mentioned were

TABLE 1.6. D&B's Evidence on the Causes of Business Failure

Cause of Failure	1965	1993
Neglect	3.8%	3.9%
Fraud	1.8%	3.8%
Disaster	1.2%	6.3%
Economic factors		
Insufficient profits	Not asked	11.6%
Industry and competitive weakness	21.0%	22.3%
Inadequate sales	40.7%	2.2%
Inventory difficulties	5.1%	Not asked
Other		1.7%
Finance causes		
Excessive operating expense	13.3%	40.5%
Too much debt	Not asked	3.6%
Insufficient capital	Not asked	3.2%
Strategy causes		
Excessive fixed assets	4.1%	0.2%
Accounts receivable difficulty	9.0%	0.8%
Lack of experience	Included elsewhere	0.6%

Source: Dun & Bradstreet (1965; 1993)

1. Ineffective management
2. Undercapitalization
3. Excessive leverage

These results are quite different from D&B's. Ineffective management is not even a category in the D&B survey,[16] and items two and three only account for 6.8 percent of all failures in the last D&B survey (see table 1.3).

The remaining 13 percent of Buccino's respondents identified external factors as the source of troubles, with

- economic conditions
- industry weakness
- labor matters
- legislative issues

being the most important. These results are similar to those of D&B's survey.

Bibeault

Donald Bibeault wrote a Ph.D. dissertation on corporate turnarounds that he later turned into a best-selling book (Bibeault 1982). One part of his doctoral thesis involved an extensive questionnaire returned by eighty-one corporate presidents.[17] Although Bibeault's results are older then either D&B's or Buccino's, they are especially interesting because of his personal work experience with troubled companies. Bibeault's classic inquiry posed piercing questions not covered in other surveys and still provides valuable insights into why businesses fail.

Bibeault investigated the impact of organizational structure on corporate failure. He found that a disproportionately high number of distressed companies had centralized managements, while a surprisingly small share had managements decentralized around either products or geographic regions.[18] The conclusion is that centralized managers are too distant from the source of difficulties to promptly recognize and repair them. Centralized management can work more smoothly in the modern era, provided that adequate accounting, financial, and production information systems and control mechanisms are established. An additional advantage of decentralization is that management can structure rewards systems to fit the needs of particular plants, workers, and regions. Bibeault's other finding that over 40 percent of centrally managed distressed companies become decentralized across product line structure when they rebound from their difficulties[19] reinforced his observations about the impracticality of centralized management.

Bibeault also found that distressed companies lack adequate control systems in the areas of budgets (37 percent rank this as number one), product costing (25 percent), responsibility accounting (15 percent), and asset accounting (15 percent). These results affirm his findings regarding decentralized and centralized management styles.

Finally, the Bibeault study clearly articulated those managerial actions and infractions that cause businesses to fail. The number one offender was autocratic management, identified in 44 percent of cases. Other managerial issues related to corporate distress include lack of managerial depth, management change problems, and inbred bureaucratic management. Some of these obstacles are more common to small businesses, but they also afflict the biggest companies.[20]

Small Business Failures

The U.S. Small Business Administration (SBA) prepared a special report highlighting the special risks of small firms (1990). Among these risks are

- lack of geographic diversification
- lack of product diversification
- inadequate capitalization
- lack of resources to withstand economic downturns
- inadequate management skills
- expansion into new products or regions

While many of these also impact larger firms, they are especially troublesome for small businesses.

Measuring Performance: Net Income and Cash Flow

The two principal concepts used to measure a firm's performance over a specified time period are net income and cash flow. Although both examine the same company over an equal time period, they are substantively different, and each has its own special use. Corporate renewal specialists focus on cash. For them cash flow is the ultimate gauge of corporate health. Net income, the other standard, calibrates the economic merit of a business enterprise. It is more commonly employed in general investment analysis.

Because the two performance measures rely on alternate accounting conventions and methodologies, they report corporate transactions differently. The factors with the biggest impact are

- net income derived on the income statement with accrual accounting methods
- cash flow determined with cash accounting methods using the income statement, the balance sheet, and the impact of exchange rates

Accrual and cash accounting recognize revenues and costs at different moments. Accrual accounting acknowledges revenues during the period in which the product is delivered or the service is rendered and expenses during the period in which materials are received or services obtained. It pays no heed to when cash is actually exchanged. In contrast, cash accounting recognizes transactions at the time that cash is exchanged.

Charter Company may be the best example of how accrual and cash accounting methods provide asymmetric corporate information (Platt 1985: 21). Immediately before filing a bankruptcy petition in 1983, Charter reported $50 million of net income (using accrual accounting); meanwhile, it had negative cash flow of about $85 million. According to the net income number, the company's economic activity was successful: its revenues exceeded its costs. However, each month Charter paid out more cash than it took in. Its bankruptcy was caused by a lack of cash. Charter would have had ample cash had it been possible to instantaneously settle all the transactions from its net income calculation, but, as with most businesses, Charter's cash receipts lagged their transaction dates.

Both performance measures provide beneficial information. In corporate renewal, net income is less relevant than cash flow since the primary concern is to preserve the enterprise while solutions are found for its complex problems. As in the Charter Company example, cash solves problems that net income only promises to address.

Deriving Cash Flow

The quick method for estimating cash flow is to add to net income all noncash charges such as depreciation, amortization (such as goodwill), and depletion.

Quick cash flow = Net income + noncash charges

In practice, this calculation is widely used, but it is basically unsatisfactory since it excludes other factors impacting corporate cash flow. By only including certain items, quick cash flow generally appears more positive than net income since noncash charges are usually positive. However, as in the Charter Company discussion above, total cash flow may not be better than net income.

The statement of cash flow describes the net cash generated by a company from all its sources and uses. A statement of cash flow, as seen in table 1.7, has four major components: operating activities, investing activities, financing activities, and the effect of exchange rates on cash. Operating activities include the cash effects of all day-to-day business, including both income statement (profit and loss) and balance sheet (changes in working capital) transactions. Investing activities include the cash effect of the firm's capital and financial investments. Debt and equity funding decisions (both sales and purchases) are reflected in the financing activities category. Finally, cash flow includes the effect of exchange rates on cash and is especially important for firms with exposure to international currencies.

TABLE 1.7. The Cash Flow Statement

Activities	Major Elements	Components
Operating activities		
	Income from continuing operations	
	Adjustments to reconcile net income to net cash	
		Depreciation, amortization, and depletion
		Deferred income taxes
		Change in inventory
		Change in receivables
		Change in accounts payable
	Discontinued operations including change in net assets	
Investing activities		
	Net capital expenditure	
	Investments	
	Proceeds from investments	
Financing activities		
	Borrowings	
	Reductions in debt	
	Stock transactions	
Effect of exchange rate on cash		

The derivation of cash flow actually begins with the alternate measure of corporate performance, net income from continuing operations, as the initial item in the operating activity category. Then quick cash flow adjustments are input to the calculation, and these are joined by adjustments from the balance sheet—changes in taxes, inventories, receivables, and payables—that affect cash flow. Companies gain cash by accumulating deferred taxes and accounts payable and by reducing inventories and receivables. The sum of these factors estimates cash flow from continuing operations. When the cash effect of discontinued operations is added in, that estimate provides the cash flow effect of operations.

Investing, financing, and exchange rate factors affecting cash flow are derived next. Companies in financial distress have few investing opportunities, though they may have to break preexisting contracts committing the firm to expenditures that are no longer necessary. They may face significant refunding requirements, including mortgage and other secured debts, sinking fund obligations (i.e., an annual repayment schedule for a bond), and bank debt repayments. Combining operating results with financing and investing flows gives a clear picture of how the firm reaches its current cash position.

Insolvency

Insolvency perhaps is the most commonly uttered but the least well-understood word in the corporate renewal vernacular. There are four related but contrary definitions of insolvency. The most common phrase is "insolvent in a bankrupt sense," which means that the company has negative net worth (i.e., its liabilities exceed its assets). Technical insolvency occurs when a firm violates an indenture covenant, generally in connection with a bond or a bank loan. A technically insolvent firm is probably not insolvent in a bankruptcy sense. Economic insolvency describes a firm whose obligations exceed the present value of its future cash flows; it will never earn enough to repay all of its creditors. Finally, a company is equitably insolvent if it has too little capital to conduct its business. The precise measurement of equitable insolvency is somewhat ambiguous. The concept is employed in fraudulent actions (see the section on fraudulent conveyances in chap. 2) seeking to recover monies lent in a leveraged transaction.

CHAPTER 2

Understanding Bankruptcy Law and Its Application

A Short Overview of Chapter 11

Bankruptcy is a complex process. Every corporate bankruptcy involves a multitude of factors that precipitated the failure, important legal issues, diverse creditors, and strategic objectives. Nonetheless, the following procedures are followed in every case.

I. A company files for Chapter 11 bankruptcy protection.
II. The automatic stay provision is decreed, protecting corporate assets from seizure by creditors.
III. A committee of unsecured creditors is formed by the U.S. trustee; additional committees may be created.
IV. The debtor informs creditors about relevant matters at the 341 meeting.
V. Executory contracts are assumed or rejected by the debtor.
VI. A plan of reorganization is crafted by the debtor.
VII. A vote on the plan is taken by all parties in interest.
VIII. If the plan is approved:
  a. Debts and obligations are discharged.
  b. New securities, debt and equity, are created.
  c. A new company emerges.
IX. If the plan is not approved, the proponent makes revisions, new plan proponents step forward, or the case is converted into a liquidation.

This chapter explains the bankruptcy process in detail. Some students object to studying bankruptcy laws, reasoning that they can hire an attorney when the need arises. But the threat of bankruptcy is probably the turnaround manager's most forceful stratagem, and managers must understand the conditions and the outcomes of bankruptcy law.

U.S. Bankruptcy Laws[1]

Historical Overview

Nonrepayment of debts is an ancient problem. A biblical injunction is, "Every seventh year you shall practice forgiveness of debts." But before the advent of bankruptcy laws, punishments for nonpayment of debts ranged from physically harming a debtor to breaking a merchant's selling bench.[2] The word *bankruptcy,* in fact, is derived from the Italian *banca,* meaning bench, and *rupta,* meaning to break. Roman debtors were protected from bodily harm if their assets were assigned to creditors. Similarly, English debtors remaining in their homes or in religious sanctuaries had their assets seized but were not prosecuted. The inviolability of a person's home is still recognized by modern collection laws through homestead provisions that safeguard principal dwelling places against seizure by creditors.[3]

A bankruptcy law is a system of jurisprudence that details how an insolvent debtor's assets are to be collected and distributed to multiple creditors. The original objective of bankruptcy laws was to restore creditors' funds, and little concern was devoted to how those practices affected debtors. That system encouraged debtors to

- conceal assets from creditors
- spend remaining assets in last-ditch attempts to achieve solvency

Creditor-favoring bankruptcy laws not only gave inefficient signals to businesses concerning resource utilization but also magnified the inherent distrust between creditors and debtors.

England codified the first modern bankruptcy law in 1542; it treated bankruptcy as a criminal offense punishable by debtor's prison or even death. Under English law, creditors held the exclusive right to file a bankruptcy petition, but debtors could avoid prosecution by agreeing to emigrate to the colonies. The large contingent of debtors in the American colonies accounts for the prodebtor prejudice of U.S. bankruptcy laws.

By 1705, English law allowed debtors to discharge debts in bankruptcy. Debt discharge allows debtors to resume an active economic role in society whether or not old creditors are repaid. Modern American bankruptcy law discharges virtually all corporate debtors except executory contracts assumed after a plan of reorganization is confirmed; individuals filing plans of reorganization are not discharged from taxes, alimony, or child support.[4] Companies liquidating their assets are not discharged from past debts in order to forestall the sale of shell corporations with sizable tax losses and no debts.[5]

The American Experience

Article I, Section 8 of the U.S. Constitution reads, "The Congress shall have power to establish . . . uniform laws on the subject of bankruptcies throughout the United States." This clause gives Congress the sole and exclusive power to devise bankruptcy laws.[6] At times, Congress has been reluctant to exercise this authority. Until the Bankruptcy Act of 1898, America enacted interim bankruptcy laws during economic crises, as seen in table 2.1.[7] The 1898 legislation was extensively amended (the Chandler Act) during the Great Depression to include

TABLE 2.1. Major U.S. Bankruptcy Legislation

Law	Motivation for Drafting	Major Contribution
Bankruptcy Act of 1800 (repealed in 1803)	Failures due to land speculation	Provided for some debt discharge
Bankruptcy Act of 1841 (repealed in 1843)	Economic depression in 1837	Added voluntary bankruptcy and debt discharge after all assets were distributed
Bankruptcy Act of 1867 (repealed in 1878)	Failures due to the Civil War	Added some corporate relief
Bankruptcy Act of 1898 (called the Act)	Land speculation in the West	Protected companies from creditors. "Equity receiverships" reorganized companies, but not efficiently. Stopped sending debtors to prison
Chandler Act of 1938 amending the Act		Chapter 11 created to reorganize business
Bankruptcy Reform Act of 1978 (called the Bankruptcy Code)[a]	Criticism that after 80 years the law was antiquated	Simplified reorganization for both individuals and corporations
Bankruptcy Amendment Act of 1984 amending the code		Limits use of bankruptcy to end labor contracts
Bankruptcy Amendment of October 22, 1994		Unsecured creditors may elect trustee in Chapter 11 cases

[a]Tax issues such as tax loss carryforwards are addressed in the Bankruptcy Tax Act of 1980.

business reorganizations (Chapters 10 and 11). In lieu of a national bankruptcy law, creditor/debtor issues are governed by state or federal collection laws or state insolvency laws. Collection law permits "a first come, first served" allocation of assets to creditors, while bankruptcy law promotes a distribution among creditors.

The novel principle of debtor reorganization was pioneered in American bankruptcy laws. Reorganization allows a debtor to compromise (partially repay) or extend its debts and emerge as a new enterprise.[8] Subtle name changes may disguise the history of the bankrupt company; for example, Braniff Airways, Inc., filed for bankruptcy in 1983, reemerged as Braniff, Inc., in 1984, refiled for bankruptcy in 1989, emerged as Braniff International Airlines in 1991, and liquidated in 1992. At a minimum, reorganization saves the firm's goodwill, which otherwise is lost in a liquidation; in addition, it attempts to produce a viable sustaining business, creating profits and employing people. The Bankruptcy Act of 1898 first sanctioned a limited form of reorganization, "equity receivership," but the Chandler Act in 1938 created reorganization as we know it today.

The Bankruptcy Process

The ninety-four U.S. Bankruptcy Courts, one for each U.S. District Court region, supervise corporate, farm, and personal bankruptcy petitions. Each court has a chief judge and several associate judges. Companies file bankruptcy petitions in districts where they do business or have assets; however, companies operating in several states may select among courts.[9] Technically, once a corporation has filed a bankruptcy petition in a court, related corporations may file in the same court. Court-shoppers (a.k.a. forum shoppers) may seek judges known to encourage business perpetuation or to rule in particular ways on questions of law.[10]

Eastern Airlines, a Miami-based airline that filed for bankruptcy in the Southern District Court of New York in 1989, is a firm that went court-shopping. Creditors objected to the filing location because of that court's reputation as sympathetic to management; however, creditors were overruled since Eastern's premier travel center, the Ionosphere Club, was chartered in New York. The choice of districts was critical to the final outcome of the case. Judge Burton Lifland authorized Eastern to continue operating even though revenues failed to cover operating expenses, resulting in negative operating income, also called earnings before interest and taxes (EBIT). After several years, nearly all corporate assets had been consumed and Eastern was liquidated.

The Bankruptcy Code has eight chapters corresponding to the

seven odd numbers ranging from one to thirteen and also the number twelve. Common references to companies filing Chapter 11 or Chapter 7 petitions actually refer to specific sections of the Code dealing either with business reorganization or liquidation. The principal chapters of the Code are described in table 2.2. Both corporations and individuals may use Chapter 7 liquidations. Many attorneys call them straight bankruptcies. In liquidation, all of a company's assets are sold and the proceeds are given to creditors, generally after paying administrative costs. After liquidation, corporations cease to operate. Overall, more companies liquidate than reorganize (for example, there were 29,689 liquidations and 12,508 reorganizations in 1994), but most of these liquidations are modest-sized firms (*1995 Bankruptcy Yearbook & Almanac* 1995).[11] Large companies, especially those listed on stock exchanges, generally reorganize. When a company listed on a major stock exchange liquidates, the motivation usually is not to end a failed business enterprise but instead is a response to favorable tax laws.

After an individual liquidates in Chapter 7, creditors commonly receive no payments, chiefly because after the date of the petition the debtor's earnings are excluded from the bankruptcy estate. Credit card companies and other personal account vendors treat these losses as a cost of doing business. The individual is restricted for a period of seven years from filing for either Chapter 7 or Chapter 11 again (Shuchman and White 1995).[12] Consequently, the person is a good candidate for new credit, once he or she leaves bankruptcy, since it is unlikely that the person will file for bankruptcy again, at least for seven years. On the other hand, people's credit history references their bankruptcy filing, which may negatively influence future credit or even employment decisions and deter persons from abusing the bankruptcy system.

Few municipal bankruptcies have occurred since the Great Depression; Orange County, California, filed in 1995 for protection under Chapter 9 of the Bankruptcy Code as a result of billion-dollar losses in derivatives trading. Most cases of municipal distress are symptomatic of either

TABLE 2.2. Chapters in the Bankruptcy Code

Chapter Number	Content
1, 3, and 5	Administrative rules and procedures
7	Liquidations
9	Municipal bankruptcies
11	Corporate reorganizations
12	Family farm bankruptcies
13	Individual payment plans

extravagant spending or inadequate taxation. Remedies for both afflictions exist outside the bankruptcy court.[13]

Corporate reorganization, or Chapter 11, is a shield employed by

- failed companies with excessive debt or imbalanced costs, such as Continental Airlines or Gillette Properties, the owners of the Vail Ski Resort
- healthy companies with singular problems, such as Texaco, which lost a lawsuit to a competitor, or A.H. Robbins (the Dalkon Shield provider)

to stave off creditors while searching for solutions to their specific difficulties. Individuals with debts in excess of $1 million are eligible to file a Chapter 11 petition. On average, companies spend about two years in Chapter 11 (Altman 1995). During that time, creditors and debtors negotiate a claim's settlement, called a plan of reorganization. Prepackaged bankruptcies, a recent phenomenon, accelerate the bankruptcy process by obtaining prior creditor approval for a reorganization plan.[14] Fast-track bankruptcies are another recent development to expedite cases moving through the courts. After completing a Chapter 11, a debtor may not receive a debt discharge from a Chapter 7 petition for seven years,[15] although a current Chapter 11 case may be converted into a Chapter 7 if payments promised under the plan are not made.

The code added Chapter 12, family farm bankruptcies, in 1986. The impetus for the change was a realization that family farms are too indebted to qualify for Chapter 13 (individual bankruptcy) and that Chapter 11 is too elaborate for this single-asset problem. The farmer's debts must not exceed $1.5 million and 80 percent of debts (excluding the family home) must be farm debts. The aim of Chapter 12 is to let the farmer keep his/her land. The debtor must file a plan of reorganization within ninety days of the bankruptcy petition. The farmer is given three years in which to repay as much debt as possible.

Only individuals are eligible for Chapter 13 bankruptcy; in contrast, a person may also file a Chapter 7, Chapter 11, or a Chapter 12 petition. To qualify for Chapter 13, the person must have regular income and secured debts of less than $750,000 and unsecured debts less than $250,000. In a Chapter 13 plan of reorganization, no one, including unsecured creditors votes on the plan, and secured creditors have limited rights. The plan of reorganization is due within fifteen days of the Chapter 13 filing. The debtor has three years (though the court often extends this period to five years) to repay creditors after which most remaining debts are discharged. The person may not file a Chapter 7 petition for seven years. In 1994, 249,877 persons filed for Chapter 13 bankruptcy. A decade earlier, 93,221 persons filed Chapter 13 petitions.

All properties remain with the debtor after a Chapter 13 filing. In contrast, with Chapter 7, the individual keeps only

- limited portion of home equity
- cash value of insurance policies
- pensions qualifying under Employee Retirement Income Security Act (ERISA)
- some personal property such as furniture
- tools of his/her trade (*Nolo's Little Law Book* 1996)

Liquidation and reorganization provide for different treatment of past-due taxes. Additional tax-treatment differences arise between individual filers and corporations and partnerships. Corporate taxes are discharged in Chapter 11, in the same fashion as are other debts; in a Chapter 7, no corporate debts, including taxes, are discharged. The principal reason for this difference is to impede the purchase of empty corporate shells after liquidation that could be used to reduce the purchasers' tax liabilities. Individual taxes are not discharged in either Chapter 7 or Chapter 11 bankruptcy but may be discharged in Chapter 13.

The Lineup In Bankruptcy

A bankruptcy involves three principle groups:

1. court system
2. creditors
3. debtor

Each group contains a number of key agents. Interactions between and within these groups by the agents defines the outcome of the bankruptcy case.

The Court System

The key actors in the bankruptcy court are the bankruptcy judge, the U.S. Trustee, an appointed trustee (if appointed) and an examiner (if appointed). The president appoints bankruptcy judges to fourteen-year terms in local federal districts. Although the bankruptcy judge is officially a special assistant to the federal district court judge, in fact in bankruptcy cases the judge's authority is "virtually absolute" (Summers 1989). The overwhelming majority of judges are lawyers, though accountants and businesspeople have also sat on the bench. U.S. trustees are appointed by the U.S. attorney general for twenty-one geographic regions subdividing the country.

The bankruptcy commences with filing a petition in the court. The U.S. trustee

- organizes creditors' committees
- schedules the first (341) meeting of creditors and debtors
- appoints trustees or examiners

Trustees are assigned the task of running bankrupt companies or collecting payments from bankrupt individuals; a trustee is appointed in every Chapter 7, Chapter 12, and Chapter 13 and in those Chapter 11s where managerial malfeasance or incompetence is alleged and corroborated. Both charges are difficult to prove. As a result, few trustees are appointed in reorganizations. Otherwise the debtor (i.e., the company) serves as debtor in possession, with the same powers as a trustee though without compensation. Examiners investigate the conduct and competence of management;[16] they do not operate firms.

Persons (accountants, businesspeople, or lawyers) joining the panel of trustees in a district must demonstrate their qualifications and submit to an FBI investigation. They must have the trust, confidence, and respect of the U.S. trustee's office. In a busy district, a trustee is assigned upwards of forty cases per month, virtually all of which are Chapter 7s. Many of these are no-asset cases. When the estate lacks assets, the courts authorizes a minimal payment of approximately $50 to the trustee;[17] otherwise in a Chapter 7, the trustee is awarded a percentage of the asscts, up to 3 percent of what is distributed to creditors, while in a Chapter 11 the trustee's salary is negotiated with the official creditors' committee, legally noticed, and submitted to the bankruptcy judge for approval.[18] Trustees willingly accept no-asset cases for several reasons:

- Expense recovery helps cover overhead expenses
- Trustee may become creditors' representative in other cases
- As public service
- To obtain major Chapter 11 trusteeship

Creditors

Creditors have a claim against the bankrupt estate. Claims are creditors' rights that supersede the rights of shareholders in bankruptcy. Claims are treated unequally in terms of receiving payment. In liquidation (and bankruptcy), there are four types of creditors:

1. fully secured creditors
2. partially secured creditors
3. unsecured creditors with priority
4. unsecured creditors without priority

A creditor is secured when a signed security agreement in proper form is noticed in the appropriate public record, that is, "perfected." The agreement must describe the assets used as security and note the amount of debt being secured.[19] If not filed, the security interest is avoidable and the creditor becomes unsecured. Creditors must file a copy of the agreement with their state under the Uniform Commercial Code (UCC) to perfect the agreement if it is personal property, a UCC-1 filing. Real property, motor vehicles, boats, airplanes, and other special items are treated separately. UCC-1 filings are effective in every state except Louisiana, which has its own (similar) form. If two creditors file UCC-1 documents against the same asset, the first creditor to file is usually superior to the other creditor. UCC is discussed more fully later in this chapter.

Claims in excess of the asset's value are general unsecured claims. Priority refers to the bankruptcy code's designation of seven categories of payment priority. Other claims are unsecured creditors without priority.

In liquidation, junior creditors receive payment only after senior creditors are fully reimbursed, and shareholders are paid only after unsecured claims are fully satisfied, in a manner referred to as the absolute priority rule (APR). The APR may give way to a relative priority rule in Chapter 11 reorganizations; that is, payments may follow but not adhere strictly to the APR.[20] Waiving the APR necessitates an agreement among all parties to the case. Creditors are either secured or unsecured. Secured claims are paid just after superpriority claims. Superpriority status is granted to claims involving money lent postpetition (after the bankruptcy) to finance the continuation of the enterprise.[21] Each secured claim may be listed as a separate class. The claims hierarchy established by the bankruptcy code is shown in table 2.3.

Using this hierarchy, the debtor proposes a classification of claims against the estate.[22] As long as the hierarchy in table 2.3 is not violated, the debtor can classify claims in any fashion to suit its needs, provided that similar claims are classified together. Within a priority level, claims can be separated, but the classes must contain claims that are similar to each other.[23]

Administrative expenses are mainly attorney, accountant, investment banker, and U.S. trustee fees and expenses of the creditors' committee, but they may also include expenses incurred to preserve the estate, such as new inventories or new taxes. General unsecured debt is a catchall category that includes unsecured nonpriority claims such as

- trade claims
- senior bonds
- junior bonds
- the excess portion of secured indebtedness.

The settlement paid to claimants in Chapter 11 cases depends on

- how well their attorneys bargain
- their security interest and relative seniority
- the estimated value of the corporation's assets

The best attorneys are very expensive and very busy. Attorney's fees in major bankruptcies may exceed several million dollars. Secured claim-

TABLE 2.3. Hierarchy of Claims in Chapter 11

Claim Category	Priority in Chapter 11
Superpriority liens (technically these are a subset of administrative expenses, but they may be elevated to the highest rank to encourage lenders to work with the debtor)	1
Secured claims (excess of claim over the value of the asset is a general unsecured claim)	2
Priority Claims Specified in the Bankruptcy Code	
Administrative expense	3
Claims against an involuntary bankruptcy from filing date until court puts company under supervision	4
Wage claims up to $4,000	5
Employee benefit claims within 180 days of the bankruptcy and up to $4,000	6
Farmers and fishermen with crops or fish held by revelers	7
Consumer deposits up to $1,800	8
Tax claims	9
Claims without Priority	
General unsecured debt (the plan may further differentiate these)	10
Equity Classes (claims without priority)	
Preferred stock	11
Common stock	12

ants with a perfected claim recover proportionately more than other classes, as seen in table 2.4. Similarly, senior notes receive a higher payout than junior notes. The equity classes receive, on average, hardly anything, as would be expected given the Bankruptcy Code's hierarchy of claims. Table 2.4 illustrates that lower classes usually receive some settlement before senior classes are entirely repaid, and this pattern of payments deviates from the APR. The APR applies in the absence of an agreement to the contrary reached by interested parties. Equity holders may receive something even though unsecured claims are not paid in full if unsecured creditors agree to that distribution. The principal reason unsecured creditors agree to partially repay equity holders is to obtain their approval of a plan of reorganization and avoid a cramdown (see discussion of the plan of reorganization later in this chapter). Another reason may be that senior management is a major equity investor and the plan, by providing for the equity class, is part of a strategy to retain senior management.

A newly bankrupt company is required to inform promptly the U.S. trustee of its twenty largest unsecured creditors.[24] With this information, a committee of creditors is formed, including representatives of the seven largest creditors and others authorized by the court.[25] The committee confers with the debtor throughout the case to determine its financial condition and may help the debtor draft a plan of reorganization. The committee may also

- investigate the debtor, the bankruptcy case, or matters related to the formulation of a plan
- participate in developing a bankruptcy reorganization plan
- advise other class members how to vote
- request that a trustee or examiner be appointed

TABLE 2.4. Payments to Bankruptcy Claims by Class of Claims

Claim Type	Dollars Paid per $1,000 of Claim
Secured loans[a]	$959
Bank debt	$896
Unsecured	$514
Convertible bonds	$338
Equity	$2.10[b]

Source: Betker (1991)

[a]Secured by physical property or other asset.

[b]Per share, hence not strictly comparable with the other figures.

Committee members have a fiduciary responsibility to nonmember creditors and must uphold a higher standard of behavior. For example, a committee member should not advance his/her own interest if in so doing the interests of similar creditors are harmed.

Additional committees are created if creditor interests are sufficiently diverse; for example, there might be one committee of secured creditors and one of unsecured creditors. Committee proliferation wastes the corporation's residual value since each committee hires its own professional advisers: lawyers, accountants, and investment bankers.[26] On the other hand, disagreements among committee members, arising from incompatible interests, may postpone the bankruptcy process by hindering the formation of a unified committee position. Delay is costly to creditors who must wait to receive a settlement. Moreover, in bankruptcy, interest is not paid on unsecured indebtedness and is paid on secured loans only when they are oversecured. However, "adequate protection" may be paid to protect a secured creditor against the diminution in value of his collateral or in some instances for the loss of use of collateral.[27] The Supreme Court ruled that periodic interest payments on secured claims during bankruptcy are not required; payments at confirmation are sufficient. Delay is costly to the company, as well, because management's time is consumed by non-value-adding legal wrangling, and it may be impossible to implement the company's strategic plan until the end of the bankruptcy.

Secured creditors hold a lien against a debtor's assets, possibly a building (for a mortgagee), accounts receivable (for a factor), or inventory (for a bank lender). Outside of bankruptcy, the secured creditor with a perfected lien (see the secured transactions discussion later in this chapter) may seize assets used as security when the debtor violates a contract provision. The Bankruptcy Code provides an "automatic stay," which prohibits all creditors from seizing any of the debtor's assets. The creditor may file a motion to lift the stay if it wishes to pursue foreclosure. It must prove that the debtor has

- no equity in the property
- no essential need for the property

In return for the stay, the use and sale of these assets is subject to court supervision. The stay also halts the accrual of interest on unsecured debt. Secured creditors, in recognition of their due-process rights, must be furnished adequate protection that preserves their claim on the asset and allows them to earn interest (though not necessarily receive it immediately). Adequate protection is not interest; instead, it assures that the value of the secured creditor's claim does not decline. The Code prohibits any early payments on debts incurred before bankruptcy.[28] The automatic stay begins when the bankruptcy petition is filed, not when the creditor is notified. In Chapter 12 and 13 bankruptcies, the automatic stay provision includes any co-debtor liable for a consumer debt.

Management

In Chapter 11, the bankrupt firm is referred to as the "debtor in possession," or DIP. Existing management runs the firm (and is itself commonly called the DIP) subject to limitations, unless a trustee is appointed. Trustees are appointed when there is evidence of malfeasance or mismanagement. Frequently, creditors have merely lost confidence in management, but that is not sufficient reason for a trustee to be appointed.

Bankruptcy is inhospitable to management, which must relinquish its absolute authority. For example, long-range decisions such as investments, acquisition, and divestitures must be submitted to the court, defended, and approved. Court permission is also required in the matter of obtaining credit, hiring bankruptcy professionals, or assuming/rejecting leases. Creditor committees may seek to prevent "wasteful expenditures," including executive salaries or corporate perks such as country clubs or private jets.[29] The DIP has freedom only regarding decisions conducted in the ordinary course of business.

Early in the bankruptcy, the U.S. trustee convenes the "341 meeting," called that because it is authorized by Section 341 of the Code. Here creditors are given an opportunity to interrogate the DIP. The meeting is conducted in federal court with management under oath to tell the truth. The meeting assists creditors, shareholders, and the trustee to identify assets, investigate disputed claims, and understand the financial condition and potential future of the debtor's business.

New CEOs are frequently hired before companies enter bankruptcy. The purpose of these changes is not window dressing to impress the bankruptcy court. Rather, these distressed companies are seeking leadership. Gilson reports that these changes continue in bankruptcy. Of those corporations retaining their original CEOs, more than half replace them during their stay in court (Gilson 1989).

Voluntary versus Involuntary Bankruptcy

Companies enter bankruptcy for two fundamental reasons:

- value of liabilities exceeds value of assets
- an overwhelming problem exists—a judgment or an impending lawsuit.

Companies may voluntarily petition the bankruptcy court for protection. The petition specifies whether they are seeking a Chapter 7 liquidation or a Chapter 11 reorganization. The debtor can convert a Chapter 7 case into a Chapter 11 proceeding or vice versa. The court can convert a Chapter 11 upon notice into a Chapter 7 (and vice versa) and would do so if the debtor were unable to develop a plan of reorganization.

The plan of reorganization must be filed in good faith. For example, the bankruptcy court is likely to dismiss the plan if property is transferred to the debtor immediately before the filing in order to utilize the automatic stay provision. Moreover, the Bankruptcy Amendment Act of 1984 limits the ability of companies to use bankruptcy to breach labor contracts. This tactic now faces a "balance of equities test," which mandates that all parties—creditors, shareholders, and unions—suffer proportionately.

Creditors may petition to have a company put into bankruptcy involuntarily. If the firm has more than a dozen creditors, an involuntary bankruptcy petition can be filed by any three creditors who in the aggregate are owed at least $10,000 more than any lien they hold on the debtor's property. If there are fewer than a dozen creditors, the company need be in arrears to only one.[30] If the debtor proves that it is current on its debt, the petition is disallowed.[31] Failing to disprove the allegation, the debtor can request that the case be converted into a voluntary Chapter 11.

Involuntary petitions arise when creditors believe that the debtor is dishonest or lacks the ability to manage the enterprise. Recently, the number of involuntary petitions has increased; in part this increase is because creditors can now obtain involuntary relief under Chapter 11 instead of having to resort to Chapter 7.

Initial Steps in a Chapter 11

The Code imposes on companies a rigid timetable of actions and events once they file a petition with the bankruptcy court.[32] Initial obligations are listed in table 2.5. While it appears that the tasks in table 2.5 are discharged by the external legal counsel or by the U.S. trustee, an inordinate amount of management's time is consumed preparing for the 341 meeting and gathering information for the various schedules. Managing a bankrupt company is really two jobs: the normal responsibilities of the CEO and overseeing the bankruptcy case.

Coincident with performing actions mandated by the Bankruptcy Code, the CEO pursues new financing to enable the firm to continue its operations. Companies need these funds in order to purchase new inventory and to give additional credit to customers. Normally these funds come from a bank line of credit, but once the debtor files for bankruptcy protection, the bank cuts off the line. Bank credit lines are normally secured by the debtor's accounts receivable and its cash holdings. In fact, while the bank line is still active, payments made by customers to the debtor go to the bank in partial payment of the firm's credit line (a portion of cash payments and all repayments of receivables). One source of cash to the bankrupt company is the funds securing the bank credit line. In order to use those monies, the debtor requests a cash collateral order from the court.[33] The judge may grant one for sixty days and will possibly extend it for up to 180 days. At that point the debtor needs DIP financing: a new credit line that may be given a superpriority status by the court, virtually eliminating any collection risk.[34] The cash collateral order allows the debtor to use cash as it is generated out of receivables instead of having this money go to the bank. As more of the funds go the debtor, the bank's security interest declines, which puts great pressure on the bank to become the DIP financier. Banks demand fees to become DIP lenders and will charge higher-than-normal rates of interest, and

TABLE 2.5. Early Steps Followed in Chapter 11

Mandated Action	Schedule	Purpose
Hold a 341 meeting	Within 40 days	Enables creditors to learn about the firm
File Schedule A: Statement of all liabilities of the debtor	Within 15 days	Schedule A1: Identifies creditors with priority status Schedule A2: Identifies creditors holding security Schedule A3: Identifies creditors with unsecured claims without priority
File Schedule B: Statement of all property of the debtor	Within 15 days	Identifies corporate assets
Prepare schedule of current income and expenses	Within 15 days	Documents current state of affairs
Prepare statement of financial affairs	Within 15 days	Documents current state of affairs
List debtors holding 20 largest unsecured claims	Within 15 days	Is used in forming creditor's committees; ex officio by vulture investors seeking to buy claims
Prepare alphabetical list of all creditors and their addresses	Within 15 days	Establishes matrix for notice mailing to creditors
Prepare monthly operating report to U.S. trustee	Within 15 days of month's end	Postpetition activity is reported on a cash basis

they monitor bankrupt creditors more closely, possibly daily, which raises their cost of servicing the loan.[35]

Following these preliminary actions, the bankruptcy case begins two discovery phases. The first discovery phase concerns legal issues. The second discovery phase is a search for value within the enterprise.

Discovery Phase 1: Legal Inquiries

Managers and owners of distressed companies may be provoked by circumstances to cross the moral line and behave unethically. These actions may reduce the debtor's asset value and may be construed as attempts to defraud some or all of the firm's creditors. Both the Bankruptcy Code and various state laws recognize such motives and sanction legal actions to recover assets for the benefit of all creditors.

Fraudulent Conveyance

A fraudulent conveyance is the sale or conveyance of assets in exchange for inadequate payment. There are two types of fraudulent conveyances: those involving intent and those viewed as constructive, or unintentional, fraudulent conveyances. An example of a fraudulent conveyance with intent is a company president selling his company car to his spouse at a price below its market value. An example of a constructive fraudulent conveyance is the below-market sale of a division of a distressed company in an effort to raise cash.[36] The presence or the lack of a moral taint distinguishes the two types of fraudulent conveyances.[37]

Unscrupulous managers doubtlessly regularly perpetuate undetected frauds in the ordinary course of business. But in bankruptcy, creditors who normally are virtually powerless to investigate a debtor's corporate transactions are represented by an accomplished legal counsel experienced and rewarded for unearthing acts of fraudulent conveyance.

A transfer is fraudulent if a creditor can prove it was made to hinder, delay, or defraud creditors. When the intent is questionable, a transfer can be shown to be fraudulent if

- too little was received in exchange
- the debtor was or became insolvent because of the transaction
- the debtor's capital was insufficient at the time of exchange

The Bankruptcy Code permits assets transferred by a fraudulent conveyance to be recovered within one year of the filing of the bankruptcy petition. These are called voidable transfers. State law may extend the recovery period. In practice, fraudulent conveyances are unearthed after a careful review of recent transactions by attorneys representing creditors.

The liquidation of Luria Steel and Trading presents an interesting example of a fraudulent conveyance. In that case, the counsel for the trustee, Sheldon L. Solow, discovered that season tickets to the Chicago Bulls' basketball games had been sold at face value (less than $2,000) as the bankruptcy neared.[38] He argued that the sale was a fraudulent conveyance and/or a preference (see the following section). The purchaser of the tickets did not contest the allegation and returned them. Normally, the original purchaser is reimbursed out of the new sale proceeds. Solow notified the Chicago Bulls, as a party of interest, of his intent to resell the tickets with a right of renewal. Chicago Bulls season ticket holders sign a one-year revocable license. Revocation occurs when tickets are scalped or the patron is rowdy. The Bulls disputed his plan and said the tickets, if sold, would not carry renewal rights. The judge agreed that the original sale was a fraudulent conveyance and ordered that the ticket buyer be given renewal rights like any other patron. The tickets sold at auction to a railroad for approximately $25,000.

Fraudulent conveyances are discovered in some but not all bankruptcies. They are a serious offense, especially if they involve intent and are not accidental. However, they are difficult to uncover. In many cases, records are incomplete; in other cases, burglaries of "valuable business records" suspiciously occur just after the bankruptcy filing. Unethical attorneys may advise clients to engage in fraudulent conveyances as their firms are failing. Similarly, they may encourage them to borrow as much money as possible.

A less obvious but potentially costly application of fraudulent conveyance statutes involves leveraged buyouts (LBOs). In an LBO, all of the equity is purchased with borrowed money. The transaction uses the proceeds of a loan to buy out old shareholders where the loan is secured by the assets of the corporation. The benefits derived from the loan do not accrue to the corporation, but the corporation's assets are encumbered in order to assure repayment. If the firm fails, the court may rule that the transaction was a fraudulent conveyance since assets (i.e., the proceeds of the loan) were transferred out of the firm before creditors of the pre-LBO company were paid off. If legal premise is accepted by the court, monies recoverable by the firm include money paid to old stockholders and fees paid to professionals, and LBO lender debts may be subordinated to other claims (Michel and Shaked 1990).

Preferences

A preference occurs when a creditor receives a payment that exceeds what it would have received from that debtor in a liquidation. Conceptually, the creditor receives more than a fair share of the debtor's assets. The Bankruptcy Code voids preferences within ninety days of the case's filing or within one year for transactions by insiders.[39] For example, a firm might agree to pay a particularly aggressive creditor's current bill.[40] The payment is unfair to other creditors if the firm making the payment is in financial distress. Had the firm first filed for bankruptcy protection, the questionable payment would have remained in the estate and would have been divided among all creditors. However, payments to a fully secured creditor are not preferential.

The Code says that a preference is a payment made by an insolvent company. The Code presumes that the debtor was insolvent for the ninety-day period preceding the bankruptcy filing. However, with evidence this presumption may be rebutted, and if it is, the burden shifts back to the debtor or trustee who is seeking to recover a payment. For payments made more than ninety days before bankruptcy, the Code uses a balance-sheet test to prove insolvency: if total assets exceed liabilities, the debtor is solvent. The test is performed using net book values.

Preferences are more common than fraudulent conveyances. They occur in the ordinary course of business. For example, a firm that pays a supplier on the first of the month and then files for bankruptcy on the second of the month potentially has created a preference. However, if the firm regularly pays this supplier on the first of the month, a preference is not created. The Code states that payments made in the ordinary course of business and those made in exchange for new goods are not preferences.

Deprizio Decisions

In 1989, in the *Levit v. Ingersoll Rand Financial Corporation* case, the First Circuit Court found that the preference recovery period should be extended to one year for a noninsider if an insider had guaranteed payment (as in cosigning a loan). These are called Deprizio issues. To limit the application of Deprizio cases, a 1994 amendment to Section 550 of the Bankruptcy Code protects noninsiders against preferences when a transfer benefits an insider (e.g., a guarantor). Nonetheless, the legal logic underlying the Deprizio decision still remains and may result in preferential recoveries from unsuspecting creditors (Epstein 1995).

Discovery Phase 2: The Search for Value

By now the bankrupt company has ascertained how much it owes and to whom. A creditors' list is compiled promptly because the publication of a bar date establishes the last day upon which a new claim can be filed. The bar date generally occurs ninety days after the 341 meeting in Chapter 7 or 13 cases, in fewer than ninety days in Chapter 12 cases, and as set by the court in Chapter 11 cases. Notice of the bar date is mailed to all known creditors; in large cases, the court may allow the bar date to be published in major newspapers. If the debtor lists a debt as disputed and the creditor misses the bar date, the claim is declared invalid. Creditors uncertain of their standing in a case and other less scrupulous individuals file claims (often inflated in value) in hopes that the claim will not be disputed. The bankruptcy judge invalidates unmeritorious claims identified by legal counsel.[41] An extreme example occurred in the 1990 Continental Airlines bankruptcy case. Class 14, *CAL Holding GVC,* filed a claim in the amount of $83 billion. The court allowed $545,000. A company's debts may also be contingent liabilities. For example, the bankrupt firm may be a defendant in a product liability lawsuit, and in the event that it loses the case it will have a debt. Whatever settlement is proposed for that claim is held in escrow pending the outcome of the liability case.

The debtor next determines both its liquidation and its enterprise values. Liquidation value equals the proceeds obtainable from a total liquidation of corporate assets. Enterprise value equals the firm's value as a going concern. Generally, both values are estimates provided by management. Unless the debtor's enterprise value exceeds its liquidation value, it is liquidated. Figure 2.1 presents the two alternate outcomes for a company in bankruptcy, with the decision between reorganization and liquidation depending on the relative size of the enterprise value. This bifurcation of companies creates an agency problem: management preserves its own job by biasing its value estimates (i.e., deflating estimated liquidation value and inflating estimated enterprise value) to insure that the debtor reorganizes. Creditors are the countervailing force to this agency problem. They stand ready to challenge attempts at reorganizing companies that should be liquidated. If creditors choose not to fight this battle, their bankruptcy recovery is likely to be diminished since companies with lower enterprise values than liquidation values are likely to have negative cash flow. Negative cash flow drains away assets and lowers the recovery value of creditors' claims. These creditors would have recovered more in liquidation.

New managers may succumb to pressures from the opposing direction. A new manager may feel no affinity to the old equity class but may hope to ingratiate him/herself with a new equity class to be drawn from creditors to be repaid with new stock. These managers may willfully underestimate enterprise value. A lower estimate of enterprise value

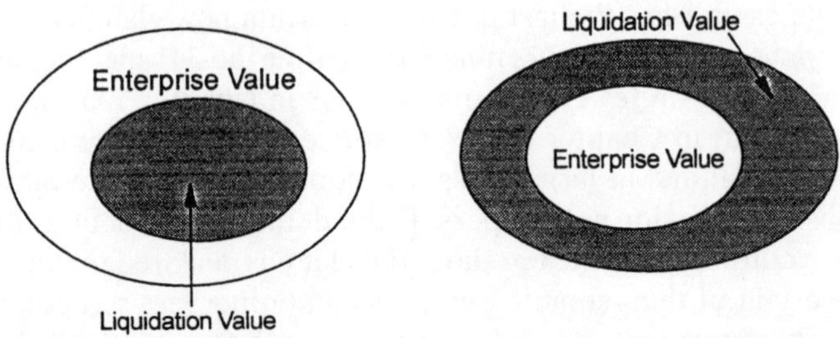

Fig. 2.1. Enterprise and liquidation value

reduces the amount of value available to be distributed in the reorganization plan and, if low enough, may result in no payment at all to old stockholders. The equity class is the countervailing force to this practice. Its advocates must dispute the enterprise value estimate. Historically, the SEC has supported shareholders on this issue, but in recent years the SEC has become passive.

Remaining Steps in a Chapter 11

At this point, the Code imposes a final set of obligations on the DIP. These are listed in table 2.6.

Executory Contracts

Executory contracts are unperformed or unfinished corporate obligations. Examples include store leases, employment agreements with key executives, and requirements contracts. Section 365 of the Code allows companies to assume (i.e., retain or assign) or reject executory contracts. The opportunity to reject unnecessary executory contracts is a critical element of permanent relief extended to distressed companies by

TABLE 2.6. Later Steps Followed in Chapter 11

Mandated Action	Purpose
Resolve executory contracts	Accept or reject unfinished corporate obligations
Prepare the disclosure statement	Disclose corporate history and summarize the plan of reorganization
Prepare a plan of reorganization	Describe how existing debts are to be resolved

Chapter 11.[42] Debtors want to delay the decision date for executory contracts; creditors anxious to know their fate request a court order setting a decision deadline.[43] Rejected contracts have a claim (unsecured) against the debtor for damages; however, there is a statutory limit on claims for rejected leases of real property.[44] Additional lease obligations are discharged. If leased space is released to a new tenant, the claim is correspondingly reduced. Executory contracts that are assumed remain in force. After bifurcating executory contracts into assumed and rejected categories, the firm is required to honor continuing lease obligations.

Special treatment is afforded certain categories of executory contracts: employee contracts and intellectual property licenses. Following the union busting/contract reneging tactic practiced first in 1983 in the Wilson Foods and then in the Continental Airlines bankruptcies, Congress drafted Section 1113 of the Code, which limits the ability of the DIP to reject collective bargaining agreements. Section 1113 requires negotiations with unions, prohibits employers from unilaterally altering employment agreements, and establishes a standard "balance of equities test" to apply to a motion to reject a contract.

The Disclosure Statement

The Code requires the debtor to prepare a document, called the disclosure statement, which sets out in a clear and concise manner the following information:

- causes of firm's distress
- the firm's past and current financial condition
- a summary of the plan of reorganization

The disclosure statement is a briefing book that educates the parties in interest in preparation for their voting on a plan of reorganization. The disclosure is to bankruptcy what a prospectus is to the field of investments.

A disclosure hearing is held in bankruptcy court before the document is widely circulated. Objections are expressed to the bankruptcy judge, and revisions are made before the document is distributed to all parties in interest. The disclosure and the plan of reorganization should be mailed out together.[45]

Claimants must read carefully both the disclosure statement and the plan of reorganization. If the disclosure promises an allocation of new securities to a particular class but the plan of reorganization does not mention the securities, the class receives nothing.

The Plan of Reorganization

The plan of reorganization is a critical document that describes how the debtor proposes to satisfy past obligations. Plans may exceed several hundred pages in length and may be quite technical and difficult to read.[46] The plan of reorganization and the disclosure statement are distributed to all parties in interest. The plan must include

- a listing of classes of claims
- classification of impaired and unimpaired classes
- equal treatment for claims in one class
- a narration of how the plan will be implemented

The Code grants an exclusive right to the DIP to submit a plan of reorganization during the first 120 days of a bankruptcy case. The court may extend the exclusive period repeatedly for additional days (usually 90 or 120 days). Consequently, in some cases, many years pass before a plan of reorganization is submitted.[47] When requesting delays, DIPs argue that they need more time to

- investigate the number, merit, and size of claims
- allow critical projects to develop so enterprise value achieves its potential
- have time to develop a plan of reorganization while managing the business

The 1994 amendments to the Code added new rules for small business cases. For these, the exclusivity period is one hundred days, and extensions are permitted only under "circumstances for which the debtor should not be held accountable."

If no plan of reorganization is submitted, the judge may eventually lose patience and allow other parties to submit competing plans of reorganization. Competing plans may be crafted by

- creditors' committee
- equity committee
- new investors who want to gain control of company.

A competing plan may incorporate the DIP's disclosure statement if it received court approval. The DIP is not restricted from issuing its own plan when the exclusive period ends, but various plans then compete. Competing plans have an additional nonstatutory requirement compared to that of the DIP: outsiders, since they are not members of the current management team, must convince the court that their plans rest on sound economic values. In contrast, the DIP must merely prove to the court that its plan is fair and feasible.

Concerns about the time and expenses squandered in bankruptcy cases have led some analysts to recommend limiting the duration of the exclusive period or the number of extensions granted. While these proposals are designed to motivate the DIP to file its plan earlier, they may instead promote the filing of more competing plans.

Plans of reorganization identify their proponents in their titles. For example, a plan might be described as

1. consensual plan (supported by management and all committees)
2. submitted by DIP
3. submitted by creditors' or equity committee
4. submitted by ABC Acquisition Company

A voting process determines which plan is confirmed.

Plans of reorganization are expensive to create. They range from $50,000 to several million dollars. Proponents of competing plans are at risk for this investment unless their plan is approved, in which case their expenses are paid by the estate. Examples of bankruptcies that had competing plans include Sunbeam/Oster, Inc. (Japonica Partners gained control in a contested battle); New Valley Corporation (formerly Western Union, Inc.), which saw several plans, as did America Air West, Inc. The high cost of preparing a reorganization plan partially explains why only one in ten bankruptcy cases ends in reorganization.

Drafting the Plan

The plan of reorganization organizes claims into classes. The plan proponent has limited discretion in how claims are organized. Essentially similar claims are put into the same class. The plan must not violate the Code's established priority of bankruptcy claims but need not provide equal treatment within a priority class. Mark Summers notes that the general unsecured category may be subdivided into several categories, one of which, claims under $500, might be paid out in full in cash, while other general unsecured claims might receive only a fraction of their debts.[48] The roster of claims is likely to include the following classes:

- secured creditors
- trade creditors
- unsecured creditors[49]
- equity interests

An important consideration in designing classes of claims is partitioning claims to facilitate plan approval during the voting process. For example, by putting secured creditors and unsecured creditors into different classes, the plan can propose greater repayment for the secured class and still be approved by both classes.[50] Unimpaired creditors are those whose legal, equitable, and contractual rights are unaffected by the plan. These classes are presumed to vote in favor of the plan. A small cantankerous group of creditors can be disposed of by placing them into an unimpaired class.

The key part of the plan of reorganization is how it proposes to treat each class of claims. The plan need not fully repay each class, though in cases where enterprise value substantially exceeds total liabilities full repayment is possible, as was the case with Texaco's bankruptcy. More often, most creditors receive partial repayment ranging from 95 to 100 percent for secured creditors, 30 to 60 percent for unsecured creditors, and 0 to 5 percent for equity holders. Much of the jockeying and associated delay in bankruptcy cases occurs because of disputes about how much each class of claims should receive. The Code provides little guidance about how value is to be allocated between claimants except for minimum amounts that must be paid. Dissenting creditors must receive at least as much as they would in a liquidation. If assets exceed liabilities, even creditors receive 100 percent. Secured creditors must get at least the value of their collateral, plus interest at an appropriate rate if payment is made over time.

Negotiations between classes are time consuming and therefore expensive. Some advocates have proposed eliminating these negotiations and replacing them with a formula that would clearly define the distribution of securities to various classes. For example, Lucian Bebchuk (*New York Times* 1993b) proposed an allocation scheme in which secured creditors would receive all the equity in a new debt-free company, while unsecured creditors and equity holders would receive only warrants. Such warrants can be exercised to acquire all the new equity at a cost equal to the secured creditors' old investment. If the warrant is exercised, the secured class is cashed out without any loss. The warrant given to old equity holders can also be exercised but at a price high enough to return money paid to secured creditors by unsecured creditors plus an amount equal to unsecured creditors' original investments. That is, if this second warrant is exercised, the unsecured class is fully repaid. These warrants will only be exercised if their holders believe that the new company's enterprise value is sufficient to warrant an additional investment of this size.

Under the current system, claims are not necessarily repaid with cash. Various combinations of securities and cash are tendered in satisfaction of claims, as seen in table 2.7. Cash typically is a scarce commodity. It is reserved to repay parties in interest who value cash highly or who have a dominant power position in the bankruptcy and demand cash payments. For example, banks are prohibited by law from holding equity in other companies and hence they place a special premium on cash.[51] When cash runs out, debt instruments against a newly reorganized company may be offered to former debt holders or to banks. When new debt runs out, equity securities or warrants on a new company may be issued. The sum of debt and equity securities equals the firm's enterprise value. The mix of securities creates a new capital structure.

Warrants (i.e., long-term options) are useful securities in bankruptcy cases where the value of debts greatly exceeds enterprise value.[52] In those cases, shareholders are entitled to little if anything in the reorganization but may be given warrants to receive their plan approval without reducing the allocation to other creditors. Warrants are awarded "out of the money"; that is, their immediate value is speculative and remains so until the price of the new equity rises to the warrant exercise price. In these cases equity holders are warned that they will receive nothing should the plan offering them warrants be rejected. This "carrot and stick" strategy is designed to persuade equity holders to approve the plan and avoid a cramdown. Sometimes former debt holders also demand warrants in addition to new bonds or equity. These warrants act as rewards in case the company is more successful than envisioned in the pro forma.

Some plans offer creditors two choices; for example,

1. 20 percent of their claim in cash paid immediately.
2. 50 percent of their claim paid in new restricted equity that cannot be resold for three years.

The principle behind this stratagem is to cash out reluctant creditors with minimal payments and to reward sympathetic creditors. However,

TABLE 2.7. Options to Satisfy Prior Claims

Payment	Typical Recipient
Cash	Banks and secured lenders
Debt on the reorganized company	Secured and unsecured lenders
Equity in the reorganized company	Unsecured lenders and equity holders
Warrants	Equity holders
Allocation of some corporate asset	Secured and unsecured lenders

this strategy may also indicate an attempt to disenfranchise ignorant or financially foolish creditors.

Voting on the Plan

All impaired classes of claims vote on the plan of reorganization (unless the class receives nothing in the plan, and then it is presumed to vote against the plan). If there are multiple plans, the classes vote on each plan, and more than one plan may be approved though the court will only confirm one plan. A class is unimpaired (ineligible to vote) if all of its legal and economic rights are restored. For example, an old debt instrument is unimpaired if it receives all back interest and a new debt instrument that has all the provisions of the original security. Another way to unimpair a class is to cash it out, that is, pay back interest and redeem the old security.

Votes are counted according to two criteria, first by the number of dollars, and second by the number of holders they represent. For a plan to be approved outside of the cramdown provision, it must receive consent *from each class* separately: by two-thirds of each class in dollar amount and half of each class in number. Votes not cast are not counted. Unimpaired classes are presumed to vote yes, while classes receiving nothing are presumed to vote no. Table 2.8 illustrates the voting procedure using a single class. Holder E, blocking combination 1 in table 2.8, causes the entire plan to be rejected by voting no, since without this holder the two-thirds acceptance rate in dollar amount cannot be achieved. Similarly, in blocking combination 2 in table 2.8, holders A, B, and C can block plan approval by voting no, since without their votes the half-in-number acceptance rate can not be achieved.

Vulture investors exploit the power to block approval of plans of reorganization, as described in table 2.8 by the column heading "Blocking Combination 1." Vultures attempt to buy up claims in bankruptcies at low prices and to profit either by receiving more than they paid in the

TABLE 2.8. Voting on a Bankruptcy Plan

Holder	Dollar Amount	Blocking Combination 1	Blocking Combination 2
A	$100,000		X
B	$200,000		X
C	$200,000		X
D	$100,000		
E	$300,001	X	
Total	$900,001		

plan of reorganization or by gaining control of the company. Holder E in the table (the vulture) has over one-third of the votes in that class; hence, no plan can be approved, except through a cramdown, without the consent of the vulture. The vulture must decide carefully which class of claims to buy up. Three possible vulture investing outcomes are shown in table 2.9. Clearly, the critical decision for the vulture investor is which class of claims to purchase. In several investing battles between Carl Icahn and Leon Black, Black bested Icahn by buying a higher class of claims and imposing his plan downward. Investors buying either too high or too low on the claims hierarchy miss the big rewards earned by acquiring a disproportionate total of a new firm's equity.

Evaluating the Plan (Fairness and Feasibility)

Following an affirmative vote on the disclosure statement and the plan of reorganization, the court holds a confirmation hearing. To be approved outside of the cramdown provision, a plan needs both creditor approval and court confirmation. The purpose of the confirmation hearing is to ensure that

- claims are classified properly
- the plan is fair and in the best interest of creditors
- the plan is feasible

Fairness, or the best-interest-of-creditors test, means that every impaired class of claims receives no less than it would receive in a liquidation. That

TABLE 2.9. Vulture Investing Outcomes

Class of Claims Purchased	Cost of the Securities	Possible Outcomes	Return on Investment
Buying securities too high up in the hierarchy	Expensive	• Claims are cashed out or unimpaired • Receive new debt securities	Positive but possibly low
Buying the right securities	Reasonable	• Receive new equity in an amount to control the company	Positive and possibly very high
Buying securities too low in the hierarchy	Inexpensive	• Receive warrants • Receive nothing	May be negative but if positive probably low

allocation is determined using the DIP's estimate of liquidation value. That definition of fairness does not preclude

- a class from receiving less than owed
- deviations from the APR

Deviating from the APR, Section 1129(b)(2)(B) of the Code, allows lower classes to receive partial payment before more senior classes are fully recompensed. This embodies a relative-priority concept. Deviations occur in order to more quickly reach a conclusion in a case by offering lower classes something, albeit little, in exchange for an affirmative vote on a plan. APR applies in cramdowns only. Creditors may consent to any sort of treatment outside of a cramdown.

Plans also must be feasible. If a plan is feasible then the company is not expected to return to bankruptcy court soon (usually at least three years). Some of the factors considered in determining feasibility are

- reasonableness of capital structure
- expected cash flows
- management's strengths and weaknesses
- availability of new and continuing credit

Several strategies that help achieve feasibility are

- creating a debt-free company (i.e., issue only new equity)
- utilizing payment-in-kind debt (i.e., debt paying interest by issuing more debt securities)
- issuing debt paying, no-cash interest for first three years

On occasions, senior creditors prefer that a company promptly return to bankruptcy. This deceitful strategy works as follows: in the original plan of reorganization, all new debt goes to senior creditors, junior creditors and possibly old equity holders get only new equity. After the second bankruptcy filing, equity holders (junior creditors in the original company) are completely excluded from the distribution of new securities.

Some plans classified as feasible do result in early returns to bankruptcy; for example, those of Braniff Airlines, Memorex, Crystal Oil, and Trans World Airlines. Few companies return to bankruptcy because of dishonest creditors, and most fail because of unforeseen events. The judge has the ability to reject a plan even if it has been accepted by all creditors.

Creditors may vote on multiple plans. More than one plan may be approved. However, only one plan is confirmed. Section 1129(c) of the Code says that in choosing between approved plans, the court must consider "the preferences of creditors and equity security holders."

The Cramdown

In the event that a plan of reorganization is not approved, the judge may ask the DIP (if the exclusive period is still in effect) or other plan proponents to resubmit a revised plan. After one (or several) no vote(s), plan proponents may ask the court to "cram down" their plan on dissenting classes. Basically, a cramdown means that the plan is confirmed even though it did not achieve the two-thirds margin in dollar amount and the one-half margin in number of holders.

A plan can be crammed down if it has been accepted by at least one class of impaired claims, does not discriminate unfairly (claims with similar legal rights are treated equally), and is fair and equitable. Fair and equitable has different meanings to secured and unsecured classes. To be fair to secured classes, a plan must immediately pay the value of their claim, measured by the value of their collateral, or allow them to retain their lien and receive deferred cash payments with a present value equal to the amount of their claim. To unsecured classes, fair and equitable means that they receive their claim in full, or, if they receive less than that amount, creditors junior to them will receive nothing at all. Hence, in a cramdown equity classes receive nothing. This requirement is the APR (Branch and Ray 1992: 15).

While negotiating a Chapter 11 plan, all parties probably tally the effects of a cramdown. These scenarios are used to pressure certain classes of claims to adopt less restrictive positions.

Confirmation and Consummation

The court confirms the plan if it

- complies with Chapter 11 of the Bankruptcy Code
- has been approved by each unimpaired class or the class is being crammed down
- has been filed in good faith
- pays all priority claims in full (possibly over time)
- pays all administrative expenses in cash
- does not result in the immediate reorganization or liquidation of the debtor

A confirmed plan is binding. All corporate debt is discharged upon confirmation, including debts not mentioned in the plan; the reorganized corporation is responsible for only those obligations listed in the plan. Individuals using either Chapter 7 or Chapter 11 are not discharged from taxes, child support, alimony, or debt incurred due to fraud.

After confirmation, the case leaves the court. After all the steps agreed to in the plan of reorganization have been completed and documented in court, the plan is said to be consummated.

Accelerating the Process

Fast-Track Bankruptcies

The Bankruptcy Reform Act of 1994 created a streamlined Chapter 11, fast-track bankruptcy for small businesses whose total secured and unsecured debts do not exceed $2 million and who are not primarily in the real estate business. The idea was pioneered by Judge A. Thomas Small, chief U.S. bankruptcy judge for the Eastern District of North Carolina. In fast-track bankruptcy, cases are accelerated by

- not necessarily creating a creditors' committee
- limiting the debtor's exclusive period to file a plan to one hundred days
- requiring all plans to be filed within 160 days
- authorizing a "conditionally approved" disclosure and holding a combined disclosure and plan confirmation hearing

While this innovation accelerates the process and curtails expenses on small bankruptcies, it offers no relief to larger cases.

Prepackaged Bankruptcies

The approval level essential in bankruptcy (two-thirds in dollar amount and one-half in number) is less than that necessary (often 90–95 percent) outside of bankruptcy to achieve a restructuring that changes a covenant or effects a debt-for-equity swap with creditors. With prepackaged bankruptcy, the company negotiates an out-of-court plan acceptable to at least half of its creditors owning two-thirds of its debt and then simultaneously submits a bankruptcy petition and a plan of reorganization. Since Crystal Oil filed the first prepack in 1986, they have proliferated. Compared with ordinary bankruptcy, prepacks are quicker, less expensive, less concerned with holdout creditors, and less likely to confront vulture investors. Compared with out-of-court workouts, prepacks retain the bankruptcy tax advantages discussed in chapter 9.

Workouts: An Alternative to Bankruptcy

A fundamentally sound company facing temporary creditor problems is not limited to a bankruptcy filing in order to continue operating. Bankruptcy is an expensive and time-consuming exercise. Altman (1984) observed that bankruptcy expenses, including investment bankers', accountants', and lawyers' fees, dissipate, on average, more than 5 percent of corporate assets during the two-year average time span that companies spend in bankruptcy. This dissolution of assets harms both the firm and its creditors. If the debtor and its creditors can agree to an out-of-court plan to repay, in full or in part, past-due obligations, these monies are saved. Not only are bankruptcy-related costs averted, but with a workout the company continues to employ most of its workers. Creditors are likely to cooperate if they believe the company is sustainable and that its survival will yield future profits for both the firm and its suppliers (Platt 1994).

Restructuring existing bonds is more problematic. The Trust Indenture Act of 1939 requires a unanimous vote of all holders to change the principal amount, interest, or maturity of debt. It is virtually impossible to get unanimous approval to make any change to a publicly held bond instrument. As a consequence, public debt is worked out rather than being restructured. A working-out is an arrangement, like a debt-for-equity swap or an exchange of one bond issue for another, offered to all holders but accepted only by some. Platt's (1994) study of Texas International's three bond-exchange offers is a source of detailed information on this procedure.

Comparing the Bargaining Power of Debtors and Creditors

The final form of the plan of reorganization and the recovery by various creditor groups compared to their allowed claims depends greatly on the relative bargaining powers of the debtor and the creditors.[53] In some respects, the Bankruptcy Code favors the debtor by providing a period during which the DIP has the exclusive right to propose a plan of reorganization. But the advantage created by that privilege gradually erodes as the bankruptcy judge grows less inclined to grant additional extensions to the exclusive period and as creditors start to exert their own power.

The debtor's power springs from two sources: detailed knowledge of the company and procedures mandated by the Bankruptcy Code. The sequence of the list in table 2.10 approximates the comparative importance of factors creating power. Creditors do not want to own or operate the businesses against which they have claims for several reasons:

1. Environmental liabilities may stick to the creditor and cost more than can be recovered in the bankruptcy.
2. Creditors want to avoid competing with their other customers.
3. Creditors are already running their own businesses.

Moreover, it is difficult on short notice to replace the current management team with persons as capable or with similar industry contacts. Even the business plan describing the firm's outlook and strategy is created with the current team's strengths and capabilities in mind.[54]

Unsecured creditors want the firm to exit from bankruptcy since until then their debts neither accrue nor receive interest payments. If the settlement offered to creditors is insufficient and they vote against a plan, management (as long the exclusive period is still in force) resumes its dialogue with creditors and tries to formulate a new plan. In actual or feigned frustration, the DIP may suggest liquidating the firm to persuade junior creditors to support its reorganization plan, since they are likely to suffer financially in Chapter 7. Cramdowns are an expensive solution to a stalemate, as all bankruptcy participants know, and may appeal only to senior creditors.

TABLE 2.10. Debtor's Sources of Power

Source	Explanation
1. Exclusivity	Creditors are restricted from submitting a plan of their own until the court removes the debtor's exclusive
2. Objective	Creditors do not want to own or operate the business
3. Threat of liquidation	Most creditors get less in a liquidation
4. The business plan	Negotiations are shaped by the business plan, which is controlled by the DIP
5. Time	Unsecured claimants do not receive or accrue interest until the plan of reorganization is consummated
6. Key man	It may be impossible to replace management because of its relationship with workers, customers, or suppliers
7. Costs	A valuation hearing (part of the cramdown procedure) is expensive
8. Knowledge	Management may know things that it would not share with a buyer brought in by the creditors
9. Capital needs and sources	Management understands future capital needs and may know how to finance their acquisition

Source: Mikels (1994)

Events such as those depicted in table 2.11 reduce a debtor's powers. For example, when one attentive buyer accumulates the disparate claims of hundreds of junior creditors, that investor develops a keen interest in studying the company, its future, and available alternatives. The DIP's knowledge becomes less critical and consequently he/she is less powerful.

On the other side, creditors have substantial power of their own, as shown in table 2.12. Many of those derive from the threat of legal statutes in the Bankruptcy Code or in contract law being applied against the debtor. Businesspeople generally are law abiding; however, during periods of distress, company managers may participate in wrongdoing.

TABLE 2.11. Countervailing Forces Limiting the Debtor's Power

Force	Explanation
1. A willing buyer exists	Clarifies the value issue
2. Someone exists who could operate the business	Resolves the succession problem
3. Claims can be sold	One party can accumulate sufficient claims to become an active participant in the bankruptcy
4. If the stock trades publicly	The board of directors can be replaced

Source: Mikels (1994)

TABLE 2.12. Creditor's Sources of Power

Source	Explanation
1. Threat to search for preferences and fraudulent conveyances	Puts management on notice that its past deeds may be closely inspected
2. Personal guarantees	Banks may threaten to exercise the guarantee unless management compromises
3. Attacking the owner's assets	Ask how the owner of the firm was able to buy his/her home or car
4. Creditors can stop offering new credit	Suppliers can stop shipping if the DIP's plan is not favorable to creditors
5. The absolute priority rule	Allows certain creditors to demand 100% of their claim
6. Just say NO?	Creditors can turn down management's plan and request that the exclusive period not be renewed
7. Competing plans	Once the exclusive period expires, a creditor's plan can be prepared that describes a new management team

Source: Mikels (1994)

Anxiety about having their past deeds inspected improves the negotiating relationship once creditors question the debtor's financial history.

The Code gives each class of creditors the power to veto any plan and requires that creditors receive as much from a reorganization as they would in a liquidation.[55] Creditors dissatisfied with management's plan of reorganization may produce their own plans, but the bankrupt estate is not responsible for paying the cost of producing a creditor's plan unless it is approved and consummated.

More advanced bankruptcy topics are covered in chapter 7, in particular, bargaining issues in plans of reorganization, the valuation of assets in bankruptcy, and ways to reform the Bankruptcy Code.

Secured Transactions[56]

The Uniform Commercial Code (UCC) was first enacted in 1957 and later modified (most recently in 1977) (*Uniform Commercial Code* 1991) to "simplify, clarify and modernize the law governing commercial transactions by imposing a common set of laws and procedures." Bailey and Hagedorn (1988: 8) summarize Article 9: "[it] provide[s] a simple and unified structure within which the immense variety of present-day secured financing transactions can be carried out with less cost and more certainty then under pre-Code law."

Every state except Louisiana has adopted the nine articles of the UCC displayed in table 2.13.[57] The turnaround manager is most concerned with Article 9, secured transactions, which considers the collateralization of loans and the perfection of loan agreements.

The secured-transactions problem concerns the lender's ability to

- protect (i.e., secure) a loan with collateral
- take (i.e., possess) the collateral should the debtor default or go bankrupt

TABLE 2.13. The Nine Articles in the UCC

1	General provisions
2	Sales
3	Commercial paper
4	Bank deposits and collections
5	Letters of credit
6	Bulk transfers
7	Documents of title
8	Investment securities
9	Secured transactions

Before the UCC, lenders devised numerous "security devices" or written instruments to achieve these goals. Each device had specific rules, sovereignty (between debtor, creditor, and third parties), and filing requirements that made the practice of doing business in multiple locations within the United States needlessly complicated. Article 9, as it applies to all secured transactions, replaces this regulatory quagmire. Rather than codify regulations for each type of security device, Article 9 addresses security interests in general. A security interest that conforms to Article 9's rules protects the lender's collateral in virtually every situation against pursuit by those who have purchased from or lent funds to the debtor.[58]

A secured transaction formally creates a security interest for the first party in the personal property of a second party. For example, a secured transaction occurs when

- the first party lends money to the second party with one of the second party's assets serving as collateral
- the second party buys an asset on credit from the first party and uses that asset as collateral.

If a third party lends money to enable the transaction, his/her security interest is called a purchase money security interest. Purchase money security interests are the most frequent secured transactions. Bailey and Hagedorn (1988: 5) note that to be official the secured transaction must be defined by an agreement that is consensual and in writing and that both parties must expect that a security interest is being created.

Collateral is property pledged to the secured party by the debtor. Article 9 has specific rules for various types of collateral primarily depending on how the collateral is used. The three broad categories of collateral are

- goods (movable items like automobiles or inventory)
- semi-intangibles (documents of title, checks, securities, or chattel paper)[59]
- intangibles (a right to payment for goods sold or leased and literary rights, copyrights, etc.)

Creation and Perfection of a Security Interest

The creation of a valid security interest is referred to as attachment. When a security interest is attached, the creditor can demand and receive the collateral from the debtor. Attachment is insufficient if other creditors assert that they have an interest in the collateral or if the collateral has been transferred to another party. Perfection, which goes one step beyond attachment, enables a security interest to be enforced against the debtor and most third parties.

A security interest is attached and therefore enforceable when

- there is an agreement between the debtor and the secured party giving a security interest
- value is given (i.e., consideration is received or a security interest is received for an earlier debt)
- the debtor has rights, such as ownership, in the collateral

A secured party gives value when it accepts a security interest in exchange for extending credit or for a preexisting debt. Ownership gives the debtor rights, but so too does a contract of sale identifying the goods according to UCC Article 2. Article 9 is indifferent to title or possession of title even though that is important outside the UCC.

To be perfected, a security agreement must be attached and have followed UCC guidelines for perfection. Perfection is accomplished in one of four ways:

1. automatically
2. by possession
3. by filing
4. by complying with a state certificate of title law

UCC rules overlap somewhat so that certain items are perfected in multiple ways. Automatic perfection applies mostly to semi-intangibles (purchase money, security interest of consumer goods, and certain assignments of account) provided that they are attached. Possession perfects a security interest in consumer goods, equipment, inventory, negotiable documents, chattel paper, or money, but not in accounts or general intangibles. Filing of a financing statement perfects all security interests except for money and instruments; it is the only method that works on accounts and general intangibles. Filing is the most prevalent method for obtaining perfection.[60] Certificate-of-title laws apply mostly to motor vehicles.

The logic of perfecting by filing is that third parties can review in a single location whether a security interest exists. Either a financing statement (a short document prepared to meet UCC requirements) or the security agreement itself is sufficient, provided that it contains the

- name of the debtor
- name of the secured party
- address of the secured party
- address of the debtor
- description of the collateral

and is signed by the debtor. Perfection continues for a period of five years and may be renewed. After the debt is repaid, a termination statement is filed.

What Happens When the Debtor Becomes Insolvent or Bankrupt

Perfection and attachment are especially meaningful if the debtor becomes insolvent. An insolvent debtor either restructures out of court (extension or composition) or files in court for bankruptcy protection. Neither action, of itself, harms a perfected security agreement; it is granted priority over any subsequent lien.

The Bankruptcy Code has several features pertaining especially to secured loans. First, there is the automatic stay provision. The code says that during the proceedings the "secured party may not collect the debt, obtain or enforce a judgment, make a setoff, repossess the collateral or perfect a security interest" (Bailey and Hagedorn 1988: 303). The secured creditor is restrained by these rules but not disenfranchised. His/her rights are exerted with a delay. Of course, if the collateral value is less than the obligation, a portion of the loan is unsecured.

Second, the Code requires a secured interest to turn over to the trustee any collateral in possession, even if perfected.[61] The trustee is responsible for locating and evaluating the size of the estate available to repay all creditors. Provided that the value of the collateral is sufficient, at the time of reorganization the secured party is granted full payment, back interest, and reasonable fees as specified in the security agreement.

Finally, security interests that are floating liens to finance accounts receivable and inventory and are to be repaid out of sales proceeds may have the appearance of a preference. The Code states that a perfected security interest in inventory or receivables may be a preference if the creditor's position has improved in the final ninety days. Only the extent of the improvement is a preference, and it may be recovered.

Bankruptcy Laws in Industrialized Countries

There is disagreement among industrialized countries as to which of two possible primary objectives of a bankruptcy code are most important:[62]

1. protection of the debtor until the business is reorganized
2. the liquidation of assets for the benefit of creditors

The United States and the United Kingdom each represent one of the extreme positions. The United States focuses on rehabilitating failed businesses; by contrast, the United Kingdom is concerned with maximizing the repayment of creditors (Franks and Torous 1993). Other industrialized nations fit along the spectrum between these two extremes. In this section, a comparison of the U.K. and U.S. bankruptcy systems is discussed first. Then bankruptcy laws in several other countries are examined. At the end of this section, two additional related topics are examined: bankruptcy in the European Union and bankruptcy among insolvent nations.

United Kingdom

The British bankruptcy system permits four types of reorganizations for insolvent firms:

1. liquidation
2. receivership
3. administrative receivership
4. administration

They are compared in table 2.14.[63] The British system is more rigid than that of the United States, where a company can easily move, once, from Chapter 7 liquidation to Chapter 11 reorganization or vice versa. By contrast, in the United Kingdom, only liquidators or administrators (never receivers) are appointed at companies without secured creditors. The liquidator's task is to sell off enough of the firm's assets to repay all its creditors.[64] Similarly, only an appointor, a secured creditor, has the statutory authority to appoint a receiver, who is responsible only for the specific asset owned by the appointor. After a receiver has repaid the appointor, residual assets are turned over to a liquidator. A company may have both a liquidator and a receiver, appointed by different creditors.

Unlike the liquidator, whose assignment is unequivocal, the receiver decides whether a distressed business is to be closed or maintained. Both the appointor and the receiver are linked inextricably by this decision since (as distinct from U.S. practices) the appointor is the only source of new funds required by the business. In addition, the receiver is personally responsible for corporate liabilities incurred after his/her appointment. As a consequence, few highly distressed businesses requiring new funds and liabilities are saved. The vast majority are liquidated. Liquidations also are encouraged by a concern to avoid new liabilities, and businesses often are sold in their entirety to existing management.

Administrators, as seen in table 2.14, joined the British bankruptcy profession in 1986. The legislation introducing administrators aimed to bridge the gap between the British and American systems (*Cork Report* 1982). The administrator is appointed by the company or by any creditor and, unlike receivers, is not personally liable for new debts, which removes a powerful disincentive against avoiding liquidation. Like the DIP in American bankruptcy practice, an administrator represents all creditors. Once the administrator is designated and approved, neither a liquidator nor a receiver may be appointed. However, creditors are permitted to oppose and check the administrator's appointment by appointing an administrative receiver instead. The negative strategy is highly effective: since 1986 fewer than 250 administrators have been appointed.

Like the DIP, administrators propose reorganization plans. At least 50 percent of all creditors must approve the plan. However, unlike the U.S. system, British creditors can vote to remove the administrator after voting against the plan.

TABLE 2.14. Types of Reorganizations in the United Kingdom

Type of Court Appointment	Must They Be an Insolvency Practitioner?	Are Requested By	Principal Responsibility Is To
Receiver	Yes	A secured creditor	The appointee (the specific creditor making the request)
Administrative receiver	Yes	Secured creditors	Preferential creditors, then the appointor, and then other creditors
Liquidator	No	Any creditor	All creditors in order of priority
Administrator	Yes	By the company or any creditor	All creditors

France

French bankruptcy laws are even more pro-debtor than those in the United States in that the creditor has no role in developing or voting on the plan of reorganization. The plan's architects are the debtor and a court official. Three outcomes are possible: continuation, fund-raising and asset sales, and liquidation. Given the limited creditor's role, reorganizations are common.

Germany

New German bankruptcy legislation, the Insolvency Act of 1994, becomes law on January 1, 1999.[65] The original German Bankruptcy Act of 1877 was closer to the U.K. system than to that of the United States: secured creditors were obligated to continue funding the business and debtors faced a rigid set of choices. Architects of the new German law adopted numerous provisions from U.S. Chapter 11, notably the concept of debt discharge,[66] the automatic stay, prompt bankruptcy filings to protect assets necessary in a reorganization, and a congress of creditors to choose between liquidation and reorganization.

Originally, German bankruptcy law made no provision for a distressed company to reorganize, and distressed firms first turned to their supervisory board (composed mostly of banks) for additional loans and advice. If that failed, they filed for bankruptcy protection, which afforded only two options: liquidation or extension of debts. To avoid liquidation, the company had to convince the court that at least 35 percent of creditor's claims would be repaid after an extension.

A plan of reorganization is proposed by the debtor or a court-appointed trustee under the new law, which requires approval from at least 50 percent of creditors in number and 50 percent in monetary amount. Unlike U.S. laws, the debtor must also approve. As with cramdowns in the United States, a plan can be confirmed without all creditors' approval.

Hungary

As a former member of the Soviet bloc, Hungary lacked a cohesive rehabilitative bankruptcy law until 1992. The new law recognizes both voluntary (when companies need ninety days of automatic stays) and compulsory bankruptcy (when companies have not fulfilled their obligations for thirty days). It was critically important that the new government "understood that bankrupt businesses should be given an opportunity to solve their problems using the modern techniques of reorganization, rescheduling, or proportional debt payment" (Aszodi 1995). As in the U.S. system, companies either go bankrupt, in which case they reorganize, or liquidate.

Italy

Italy has an antiquated national Bankruptcy Law, promulgated in 1942. Like bankruptcy legislation in the United Kingdom, Italian law lacks a reorganization chapter similar to U.S. Chapter 11; the closest approximation is controlled administration, providing an automatic stay for up to two years while the firm resolves its difficulties (Mazzei 1995).

Distressed Italian companies have three options, represented in table 2.15. Bankruptcy is for companies unable to pay their bills. The statutes preserve archaic customs such as confining the debtor to his/her residence. An official receiver manages the business while it is liquidated. Privileged creditors are repaid first, after which remaining creditors are paid in no special order.

A preventive agreement also can terminate an enterprise, but then bankruptcy is avoided and assets are sold off. With preventive agreement the debtor has three choices, described in table 2.16. The first two choices allow the debtor to sell the business and repay creditors; option two permits the enterprise to continue to exist after six months. The third choice resembles Italian bankruptcy.

TABLE 2.15. Italian Bankruptcy Options

Type of Action	Intended for	Who May File	Result
Bankruptcy	Insolvent debtors	• Creditors • The debtor • The public prosecutor	• A receiver manages the estate • Liquidation
Preventive agreement	Failing businesses not yet declared bankrupt	The debtor	Bankruptcy is avoided but firm goes out of business
Controlled administration	Debtors with a short-term liquidity problem	The debtor	• A receiver manages the estate • Delay of repayments for up to 24 months

Japan

Few distressed Japanese companies file bankruptcy. Instead, bankers or business partners may extricate firms by agreeing to indemnify creditors. With creditors satisfied, the concerns and interests of workers and equity holders become paramount in a corporate rescue.

Under formal Japanese bankruptcy law, there are three typical outcomes for distressed companies:

- liquidation
- composition
- rearrangement

Liquidation is the most frequent, with proceeds directed to repaying creditors according to a legal hierarchy of claims. The other two options restructure the business.

Mexico

In Mexico, bankruptcy is initiated by the debtor, creditors, the public prosecutor, or the judge. A trustee is appointed to manage each business in bankruptcy, but one, three, or five receivers (creditors) are appointed to watch over the trustee.

The priority of claims includes creditors with

- exclusive privilege (the DIP and employers)
- security
- special privilege (tax claims)
- common creditors due to business activities (trade creditors)
- common creditors based on civil law (judgment creditors)

TABLE 2.16. Options with Preventive Agreements

Option	Payment to Privileged Creditors	Payment to Other Creditors	Time Frame	Payment of Interest
1	100%	$\geq$40%	<6 months	None
2	100%	$\geq$40%	<6 months	On payments after more than 6 months
3	Assets are assigned to the creditors, who are repaid out of the proceeds			

Unlike U.S. laws, employees are treated as stakeholders in the bankruptcy and in fact are given top priority.

The case ends with the drafting of a settlement agreement; this may not reduce debt by more than 65 percent or delay repayment for more than three years. The settlement agreement meeting must be attended by at least 50 percent of creditors, at last 33 percent of whom must approve the agreement. Otherwise, the firm is liquidated.

The Netherlands

Dutch bankruptcy regulations are similar to the U.S. system. The law offers two options, bankruptcy and suspension of payments, that compare, with some differences, to U.S. Chapter 7 and Chapter 11, respectively. After repaying secured and preferred creditors, Dutch liquidations repay other creditors in proportion to their claims, while U.S. law follows the APR. Under suspension of payments, interest payments on unsecured obligations are halted, while in the United States all interest is deferred, and the maximum duration of a suspension of payments is one and a half years (though extensions are granted) (Koopmans 1994).

Many Dutch companies engage in debt restructurings. Management shares responsibilities with an adviser who pursues from the largest creditors a short-term reprieve from debt obligations. Obligations incurred after a meeting with creditors are paid in full. As work progresses on correcting the company's underlying difficulties, creditors, including tax authorities, are solicited to join a composition agreement.

Spain

Spain's antiquated bankruptcy laws are more than a century old. The law breaks firms into two groups: "bankrupt" firms that are totally insolvent and partially insolvent firms requiring a "suspension of payments proceedings."[67] Bankrupts are liquidated. Under a suspension of payments the debtor is protected from creditors but must submit a repayment plan on a date established by the judge. The voting procedure depends on the timing and amount of repayments, as seen in table 2.17.

Secured creditors in Spain are called privileged creditors, and their collateralized security is called a preferential credit. Even when a suspension-of-payments proceedings is initiated, privileged creditors may seize guaranteeing assets.

Switzerland

The Swiss Federal Code on the Collection of Debts and Bankruptcy was revised effective January 1997. The new law works through compositions and liquidations, but now, in a move toward the U.S. system, emphasizes "the restructuring nature of composition" (*Turnarounds & Workouts Europe* 1995b).

Bankruptcy in the European Union

Starting in 1980, legal scholars in Europe began to develop a convention for intermingling bankruptcy laws in the European Union countries. Several drafts have failed to obtain approval as the two sides – the unity approach (one bankruptcy law) and the territorialist approach (separate bankruptcies) – debate the future of bankruptcy in Europe (Lucheux and Passemard 1995).

Bankruptcy among Insolvent Nations

The International Monetary Fund (IMF) assists countries unable to meet their debt obligations; the list of countries that have defaulted or approached default is long. The IMF lends these countries additional funds on the condition that that they modify their behavior. Corrective monetary and fiscal policy measures are common, as are efforts to decrease tariffs and encourage free trade.

Ideas are circulating to replace this system with a bankruptcy-for-nations concept that would put the IMF out of the moneylending business altogether and refashion it into a bankruptcy court. The IMF would be "authorized to halt debt payments from bankrupt nations, oversee new borrowings from the private market, and approve a plan to pay off creditors" (Davis 1995). The new plan would simplify the bailout of countries such as Mexico, which required a $50 billion loan from the United States

TABLE 2.17. Voting Procedures under Spanish Law

Proportion of Debts Repaid	Timing of the Repayment	Proportion of Creditors Who Must Approve	Proportion of Dollar Amount of Debt That Must Approve Agreement
All	Less than 3 years	50%	60%
All	More than 3 years	50%	75%
Less than 100%	Less than 3 years	50%	75%

in 1995, or Korea, which borrowed $57 billion from the IMF in 1997. However, the plan increases the power of the IMF at the expense of individual countries and private lenders and is likely to be controversial.

Bankruptcy Laws in Emerging Countries

Bankruptcy laws worldwide contain broadly different provisions. One area of contrast concerns the rights of creditors relative to debtors. Certain countries elevate the interests of the creditor, while other countries adopt a pro-debtor stance. Creditors' main interest is in negotiating swift and just resolutions of their claims against a bankrupt estate. Debtors hope to have the necessary time to work out their problems. Bankruptcy laws favoring creditors may encourage companies to postpone a bankruptcy filing beyond hope of revival, which is a socially bad outcome. On the other hand, such laws may encourage financial institutions to lend, which is a worthwhile social result. Bankruptcy laws preferential to debtors promote out-of-court bankruptcy alternatives that result in highly discounted, but expeditious, settlements.

In Alan J. Lipkin's (1994: 39–46) comprehensive survey of bankruptcy laws in emerging countries, he observed a set of characteristics differentiating treatment of creditors and debtors. Table 2.18 describes five of these attributes. When a bankruptcy code contains several reorganization alternatives, one choice customarily is a rigid court-supervised transaction while the other is an out-of-court settlement. Such settlements provide debtors with better terms but also benefit creditors by accelerating the process. Automatic stay provisions inhibit creditors from seizing property used to secure loans and are a pro-debtor mechanism. Creditors favor the installation of trustees, since they lessen management's prerogatives. In some cases a trustee replaces management, while in other instances a trustee oversees management's decision-making with a focus on preserving creditors' assets.

A bankruptcy code favoring debtors may increase time spent in the courts.[68] A strongly pro-debtor bankruptcy code permits management to remain employed, secure new sources of credit, embark on new business ventures, and offer to repay creditors less than they are owed. When the average time elapsed for the bankruptcies in a country exceeds two years, the code is described as pro-debtor.

The bankruptcy codes surveyed by Lipkin also have unique features, such as how Singapore limits members of a bankrupt company's board of directors from serving on other company's boards or China's omission of a preference-transfer provision.

Lipkin also distinguishes between bankruptcy codes according to how they prioritize payments to creditors (see table 2.19). A code favoring creditors would put secured creditors at the top of the hierarchy. The APR is an extreme example of such favoritism. Three of Lipkin's six countries put the interest of secured creditors at the top of the hierarchy (a pro-creditor decision), while the other three countries put the interests of employees at the top of the list (a debtor-sensitive plan). Administrative claims in these countries receive a lower priority than in the United States.

TABLE 2.18. Major Provisions of Bankruptcy Laws in Emerging Countries

Country	Number of Reorganization Alternatives	Automatic Stay Provision	Is a Trustee Appointed?	Time Frame	Unique Feature
Argentina	2	No	Yes in one, no in other	More than 2 years	Favors debtors and allows lengthy stays
Brazil	2	Yes	Yes in one, no in other	Less than 2 years	Exchange rate set as of date of filing
China	1—government influenced	Limited	Yes	Less than 2 years	No preferential transfer provision
Indonesia	1	Only on the unsecured	Yes	Less than 2 years	Receiver keeps 15% of funds in a liquidation
Mexico	1	Yes	Yes	More than 2 years	Grave penalties for preferences and fraudulent conveyances
Singapore	1	Yes	No	More than 2 years	Directors may be barred from other boards

TABLE 2.19. Priority of Claims in Emerging-Country Bankruptcies

Claimant/Country	Argentina	Brazil	China	Indonesia	Mexico	Singapore
Employees	2	1	3		1	1
Government	3	2	4	2		3
Administrative	3	3	2	2	2	1
Secured creditors	1	4	1	1	3	2
Unsecured creditors	4	5	5	3		4

Questions

1. Fill in the following matrix:

	Who may file	Refiling restrictions
Chapter 7		
Chapter 9		
Chapter 11		
Chapter 13		

2. List the hierarchy of claims in a liquidation.
3. List the hierarchy of claims in a reorganization.
4. Comparing the two lists in questions 2 and 3, explain the movement of secured creditor's claims.
5. Define liquidation value and enterprise value.
6. Describe the voting requirements in a Chapter 11 case.
7. Compare the sources of power available to creditors and debtors.
8. Define UCC Article 9, perfection, and attachment.
9. Compare the U.S. and U.K. models of bankruptcy.

CHAPTER 3

Failure Prediction

In this chapter, we shall examine a number of techniques to measure corporate health and ways to predict company failure. Ratio techniques are the first failure-prediction methods discussed in this chapter. From ratio techniques we move into a discussion of financial and operating leverage, two alternative measures of corporate risk. Following that, early warning system (EWS) models are presented. Then, all of these methods are applied in an example of the performance of a corporate turnaround. At the end of the chapter, two other measures of performance and risk, sustainable growth rate and EVA, are examined.

Lenders, customers, suppliers, and stockholders are keenly interested in being warned before a company becomes financially distressed or, even worse, fails. These parties risk substantial financial losses and would have to endure innumerable hours of paperwork and meetings after receiving one of the following nasty surprises:

- nonpayment of a contractual obligation
- unfulfilled warranty services
- distressed debt restructurings
- formal bankruptcy filings

Their probable losses increase as their seniority position declines and their collateral value dwindles. Even when a formal bankruptcy filing is not an issue, expenses paid by institutions attempting to work out non-paying accounts may amount to 5 percent or even 10 percent of loan values (Platt 1993–94). Losses are even greater after a bankruptcy filing; Altman (1984) documents total bankruptcy costs ranging between 11 percent and 17 percent of firm value. These expenditures are dead-weight losses depleting assets that remain for creditors.

Companies should evaluate the creditworthiness of potential clients.[1] The least creditworthy should be rejected, while those on the border of high risk should be asked for deposits or other forms of security. Few firms allot sufficient resources to implementing failure-prediction techniques despite the tremendous financial losses they risk from distressed clients. Undercommitment to bankruptcy prediction results from

- excessive optimism or an unwillingness to acknowledge potential failure[2]
- unfamiliarity with advances in failure prediction and
- corporate organizations that delink lenders from the consequences of unsound loans

Instead of avoiding the costs of failure by predicting it, some financial firms treat failure as a nonzero probability risk and increase their fees to compensate for expected losses. This inferior strategy results in a higher cost structure and lower profits.

Not every failure is predictable. No single set of factors unfailingly predicts either corporate distress or bankruptcy. Yet there are compelling similarities between healthy enterprises, on the one hand, and unhealthy firms, on the other. The key to developing a feasible failure-prediction model is to understand these similarities and the reasons why a single model is insufficient.

A major reason why a single model cannot predict failure across all firms is the extent of differences among industries. These include special practices and regulations, idiosyncrasies in bankruptcy and common laws, and lending guidelines established by financial institutions. Although no single framework works for all, failure within particular populations of firms can be predicted with a reasonable degree of accuracy.[3] Examples of industry-specific bankruptcy-prediction models include those for savings and loan institutions, commercial banks, industrial corporations, oil and gas companies, and initial public offerings. Each group of companies has a unique set of predictors.

Failure prediction is not a modern idea. Lenders historically have tried to determine the quality of loan applicants, distressed bond buyers have pursued "money good" credits, and trade creditors have attempted to avoid shipping products to poor-risk clients, all with varying degrees of success. What is new is the application of scientific skills to the ancient art of failure prediction. Since 1965 academic research has extensively studied bankruptcy prediction, using EWS models. EWS models provide a quantitative assessment of company risk. These risk estimates play two roles in corporate renewal:

1. as analytical screens aiding the choice of investments, loans, or clients
2. to guide a turnaround by assessing the health of the distressed firm (Altman and LaFleur 1981; Platt and Platt 1991a).

In the first role, the EWS is employed to evaluate instantly hundreds or even thousands of companies, and poor performers are identified. In the second role, the corporate renewal agent measures the success or failure of corrective actions for a particular client firm by the quarter-to-quarter changes in the EWS model estimates.

Despite these innovations, some corporate renewal specialists eschew computers and statistical modeling techniques. Instead, they rely on more elemental methods such as financial-ratios analysis. Simple financial ratios provide keen insights similar to those produced by EWS models and have a powerful ability to predict bankruptcy.

Failure Prediction with Financial Ratios

Ratio analysis uses financial data from the balance sheet and the income statement.[4] These financial reports are presented below for Sutcliffe Industries in tables 3.1 and 3.2. Sutcliffe Industries began as a mop and broom company founded in 1972 by a penniless immigrant. Later it introduced a range of vacuums, electric brooms, and other household electrical instruments. Sutcliffe specialized in "time-saving" products and achieved excellent market reception until 1996, when low-priced products introduced by foreign competitors, along with the loss of two megastore contracts, led to its first major decline in sales. This decline came at a bad time. Sutcliffe had recently opened a new manufacturing facility built to relieve the three-shift-per-day, seven-day-per-week production schedule at the original facility. Sutcliffe's bankers insisted that an external consultant be hired as a prior condition to their renewing its credit line.

Sutcliffe's balance sheet is presented in table 3.1. The balance sheet shows the value of the firm's assets and claims against those assets as of December 31, 1995, and 1996. Most dollar values on the balance sheet are derived from book values, an item's historical cost. Market values appear only when they are readily known and lower than book values. Cash and accounts receivable are the two non-book-value items on the balance sheet. Omitting market values from the balance sheet may invalidate analysis if book values misrepresent true market values. Another potential problem with information contained on the balance sheet is that the data may not have been audited by the firm's accountants.

Striking a balance between economy and probity in the business community, audited financial statements are generally prepared annually, and unaudited statements are supplied during the other three quarters. The problem with unaudited statements is that companies, especially those in financial distress,[5] may succumb to the temptation to "play with the numbers." The best defense against fraud of this type is to rely on audited statements (see the financial/accounting frauds discussion in chapter 4); when that is impossible, as many assets and liabilities as possible should be spot-checked.

Both assets and claims on assets are presented, with items at the top of the table being more liquid than those entered further down. Liquidity refers to the speed with which something can or must be converted into cash. Current assets and current liabilities become cash or must be repaid within one year. Noncurrent assets are called fixed assets. Fixed assets include property, plant and equipment, and valuable deposits in the case of natural resource companies. Noncurrent liabilities are long-

TABLE 3.1. Sutcliffe Industries' Balance Sheet ($ in millions)

Assets	Dec. 31, 1995		Dec. 31, 1996	
Cash		$128		$27
Marketable securities		$43		$5
Receivables		$287		$172
Inventories		$302		$460
Total current assets		$760		$664
Gross plant and equipment	$689		$1,335	
Less depreciation	$300		$350	
Net plant and equipment		$389		$985
Total assets		$1,149		$1,649
Claims on assets	Dec. 31, 1995		Dec. 31, 1996	
Accounts payable		$198		$292
Notes payable		$182		$297
Accruals		$35		$26
Total current liabilities		$415		$615
Senior bond		$50		$355
Junior bond		$75		$75
Common stock		$95		$81
Retained earnings		$514		$523
Total claims on assets		$1,149		$1,649

term debts and equity. Long-term debts include secured obligations such as mortgages and unsecured obligations such as junk bonds. Equity is either common or preferred stock.

Sutcliffe's income statement is presented in table 3.2. The income statement contains four distinct measures of income, which are produced by progressively extracting additional cost items from revenues. These income measures are sometimes known by other names: gross income is called gross margin, net operating income is EBIT (earnings before interest and taxes), net income before taxes is EBT (earnings before taxes), and net income is EAT (earnings after taxes). Earnings per share (EPS), not shown in table 3.2, is calculated by dividing net income by the number of common shares. These data are utilized below in developing and discussing various ratios.

Types of Ratios

There are four principal types of ratios. Each ratio type provides specialized information about a particular aspect of the firm. Types of ratios and their function are listed in table 3.3. *Liquidity ratios* describe the firm's short-term indebtedness and provide insights into its ability to cover those obligations; in a word, these ratios describe solvency. *Leverage ratios* compare the amount of debt used by the firm to its assets; that is, leverage ratios depict indebtedness. *Activity ratios* contrast the firm's

TABLE 3.2. Sutcliffe Industries' Income Statement ($ in millions)

	Dec. 31, 1995	Dec. 31, 1996
Sales	$2,483	$1,375
Cost of goods sold	$1,061	$687
Gross profit	$1,422	$688
Less operating expenses		
General and administrative	$160	$165
Selling	$542	$404
Depreciation	$45	$50
Net operating income (EBIT)	$675	$69
Interest	$25	$58
Net income before taxes (EBT)	$650	$11
Taxes	$259	$2
Net income (EAT)	$391	$9
Dividends to common	$91	$0
Retained earnings	$300	$9

assets with its sales: these ratios denote efficiency. *Profitability ratios* compare the firms' profits to its investment, or returns.

Given that each type of ratio has a clear purpose, the question of which type of ratio is most important is not meaningful. However, the corollary question, "Which type of ratio best anticipates future cases of financial distress or bankruptcies?" can be answered. Liquidity ratios provide insights into distress or bankruptcy. Liquidity problems are the quickest route to trouble.[6] Leverage ratios mark firms likely to face a crisis in the future unless their debts are reduced. A firm unable to service its debts is likely to be shunned by other suppliers and lenders. Activity ratios identify firms that waste resources and fail to achieve their earnings potential. Finally, profitability ratios describe a firm's historical performance and may indicate impending failure.

Ratios may appear too high or too low because they deviate from historical values or because they vary from the industry average. Turnaround managers should always compare ratio calculations to both historical values (if available) and to industry values. Sometimes this is difficult because many companies operate in several industries. A turnaround manager operating within a company does not face this problem since divisional or subsidiary balance sheets break out values by company, but an external analyst must choose the larger industry in which the firm operates.

Liquidity Ratios

Three liquidity ratios are illustrated using Sutcliffe's data: the current ratio, the quick ratio, and the cash ratio. The three ratios are interrelated because the second ratio is the same as the current ratio without inventories, while the cash ratio removes receivables from the quick ratio.

The current ratio compares Sutcliffe's current assets to its current liabilities. The numerator includes those assets that can be converted into cash within a year, while the denominator includes claims

TABLE 3.3. Types of Ratios and Their Function

Type of Ratio	Descriptive Aim of Ratios
Liquidity ratios	Ability of firm to repay its short-term obligations
Leverage ratios	Amount of debt financing the firm
Activity ratios	Efficiency of asset utilization
Profitability ratios	Is the firm achieving sufficient returns?

of short-term creditors against Sutcliffe Industries. In 1996, the ratio was calculated as

$$\text{Current ratio} = \frac{\text{Current assets}}{\text{Current liabilities}} = \frac{\$664}{\$615} = 1.08$$

This current ratio shows that Sutcliffe's current assets are sufficient to repay all its short-term creditors 1.08 times over. Of course, Sutcliffe Industries is unlikely to sell all of its current assets in order to repay its creditors, and even if it did, there is no guarantee that it could sell assets at their book values. The calculation merely demonstrates that the firm would have enough to repay creditors if it were to be liquidated at book value. In 1995, the current ratio equaled 1.83. The substantial decline in the ratio in just one year is an indication of Sutcliffe's precarious financial condition. A simple rule of thumb is that a current ratio of 2.0 is an indicator of financial health. Sutcliffe Industries is sinking into a danger zone.

Although the current ratio is the best-known liquidity ratio, it is not used by some analysts because it includes all current assets at their book values. Inventories are most worrisome because their value is subject to rapid deterioration. In industries such as retail, fashion, entertainment, and technology, inventories depreciate so rapidly that the quick ratio is a better gauge of solvency. The quick ratio is derived by dividing current assets less inventories by current liabilities. For Sutcliffe this equals

$$\text{Quick ratio} = \frac{\text{Current assets} - \text{inventories}}{\text{Current liabilities}} = \frac{\$204}{\$615} = 0.33$$

The quick ratio suggests that in a liquidation in which Sutcliffe scrapped its inventories and then received book value for all of its other current assets, it would only be able to repay thirty-three cents on the dollar to its short-term creditors. This ratio is outrageously low. Moreover, it is far less than the quick-ratio value in 1995: 1.10. The crisis manager hired by Sutcliffe Industries notices that the quick ratio has fallen by 70 percent (i.e., 1.10 − (.33/1.10)) in 1996 while the current ratio only fell by 41 percent. This comparison tells the crisis manager that

1. Sutcliffe Industries' inventories are out of control
2. some of these inventories may not be salable

The most conservative solvency ratio is the cash ratio, which credits the firm only for its cash and marketable securities. For Sutcliffe Industries the cash ratio equals

$$\text{Cash ratio} = \frac{\text{Cash + marketable securities}}{\text{Current liabilities}} = \frac{\$32}{\$615} = 0.05$$

which is well below its 1995 value of 0.41. The cash ratio is especially useful to creditors when inventories are problematic and receivables are of doubtful quality or are already securing someone else's loan. The corporate renewal specialist considers the cash ratio's 88 percent decline to be a source of great worry. He/she knows that cash is the most precious asset as a crisis looms, because bankers are reluctant to advance new money to an ailing company.

Companies with robust current, quick, and cash ratios may nonetheless encounter solvency problems if their cash inflows and outflows are poorly coordinated throughout the year. For example, a firm whose sales are concentrated in the fourth quarter while its production is extended across the year (level production) may encounter a cash shortage before the advent of its selling season. Such surprises are minimized by preparing a cash budget that estimates monthly or weekly cash inflows and outflows.

Leverage Ratios

Leverage ratios describe a company's funding sources. Monies are raised either from owners via equity or are borrowed. As the proportion of monies raised from debt holders rises, the firm's interest costs rise, its equity cushion decreases, and equity holders may earn a higher return if the firm earns more on its investments than it pays its debt holders. As companies increase their relative use of debt, the interest costs of incremental funds generally rise because the firm is perceived as more risky. The source of the risk is twofold: first, there is an absolute increase in the amount of interest the firm is paying and hence a greater chance that it will be unable to make these payments; second, the equity cushion becomes a smaller share of the dollars invested in the firm, which means that each dollar of debt is protected by fewer dollars of equity. The higher returns earned on treacherous investments must justify their increased risk. Eventually, however, firms reach a subjectively determined debt capacity and are cut off from further access to debt funds.

There are two key leverage ratios: the debt-to-asset ratio (debt ratio) and the times interest earned (TIE) ratio. The first describes the proportion of invested funds raised from debt holders; the second compares the firm's earnings to its interest obligations. The debt ratio measures the amount of indebtedness relative to equity; TIE measures the firm's ability to service its debt. The debt ratio depends on balance-sheet data, while TIE uses income statement information.

The debt ratio is calculated for Sutcliffe Industries in 1996 as

$$\text{Debt ratio} = \frac{\text{Total debt}}{\text{Total assets}} = \frac{\$1{,}649 - \$523 - \$81}{\$1{,}649} = 63$$

Total debt equals the difference between claims on assets and net worth. In 1995, Sutcliffe's debt ratio was 47 percent. Moving from 47 percent financed by other people's money to 63 percent financed by debt resulted from financing the new plant with debt and from equity funds used to buy back shares from a disgruntled executive.

The debt ratio is bounded between zero and one, with zero indicating a firm funded entirely by owner's equity and one a firm using all debt financing (ignoring cases of negative equity). Some persons prefer the debt-to-equity ratio, which is calculated in 1996 for Sutcliffe Industries as

$$\text{Debt-to-equity ratio} = \frac{\text{Total debt}}{\text{Total equity}} = \frac{\$1{,}649 - \$523 - \$81}{\$523 + \$81} = 1.73$$

This debt-to-equity ratio says that Sutcliffe Industries uses \$1.73 of debt for each dollar of invested equity. The debt-to-equity ratio is bounded between zero and infinity (again ignoring cases of negative equity). Firms with zero debt-to-equity ratios are debt-free, while those with infinite debt-to-equity ratios have no equity funds. The debt ratio and the debt-to-equity ratio contain precisely the same information and are calculated as transformations of each other.

$$\text{Debt-to-equity ratio} = \frac{\text{Debt ratio}}{1 - \text{debt ratio}} = \frac{.63}{1 - .63} = 1.70$$

In 1995, Sutcliffe's debt-to-equity ratio was 0.89. Since the debt-to-equity and the debt ratio are transformations of each other, they are equally good; however, analysts usually adopt one ratio and stick with it to acquaint themselves with the meaning of movements in the ratios.

The TIE ratio is calculated as the quotient of EBIT and interest charges and describes the number of times that interest obligations can be paid out of current EBIT.

$$\text{TIE ratio} = \frac{\text{EBIT}}{\text{Interest charges}} = \frac{\$69}{\$58} = 1.19$$

EBIT, or operating income, tells how much money the firm makes before paying its financing costs. In 1995, Sutcliffe's ratio equaled 27.0. Another measure involves earnings before interest and taxes plus depreciation and amortization (EBITDA). A variant on the TIE is the EBITDA-to-interest ratio, which adds into the numerator both depreciation and amortization charges, two noncash items that reduce EBIT. The EBITDA variation is especially useful for capital-intensive companies whose depreciation charges greatly reduce operating income. There are other more sophisticated ratios, but for most applications the TIE is simple yet powerful.

Activity Ratios

Activity ratios measure the efficiency with which the firm employs its assets and inform managers when too many assets are doing too little work. Assets should not be sold off or retrenched at the outset of a crisis without first investigating activity ratios. These ratios help the turnaround manager learn which assets, if any, are superfluous.

Suitable ratios exist for every asset. The four most common are the inventory-turnover ratio, days sales outstanding, fixed-asset-turnover ratio, and total-asset-turnover ratio.

The inventory-turnover ratio is defined as

$$\text{Inventory turnover ratio} = \frac{\text{Sales}}{\text{Inventories}} = \frac{\$1{,}375}{\$460} = 2.99$$

The inventory-turnover ratio describes the number of times during the year the firm sells its inventory. In 1995, Sutcliffe's inventory turn was 8.22, but a sales slowdown and an unanticipated accumulation of inventories pummeled the ratio down to only 2.99. Companies selling expensive, high-margin items like pianos may have inventory-turnover ratios approaching 1.0 or even lower, while a firm that sells out its inventory every day has a turnover ratio of 365.0. The inventory turn reaffirms the crisis manager's initial conjecture that inventories are an obstacle.

Some analysts prefer to use cost of goods sold instead of sales in the inventory-turnover ratio because inventories are stated at cost in the balance sheet while sales are recorded at market prices. Using cost of goods sold produces a lower estimated turnover rate. But Dun & Bradstreet and other data vendors report the inventory-turnover ratio using sales, so in comparing a company's ratio to the industry average the sales-based ratio must be used.

Another concern with the inventory-turnover ratio is that sales in the numerator are gathered over the year, while in the denominator inventories are calculated at one point in time. This mixing of time-sensitive information can easily distort the ratio if the firm's sales are rising or falling rapidly or if sales are seasonal. This problem is avoided by averaging inventories over the year, quarter, or month.

Days sales outstanding (DSO) is calculated as

$$\text{DSO} = \frac{\text{Accounts receivable}}{\text{Sales / 365}} = \frac{\$172}{\$3.77} = 45.6$$

This is sometimes called the average collection period because the number 365 in the denominator converts annual sales to sales per day. DSO describes the number of days' sales tied up in receivables. Sutcliffe's DSO rose only from 42.2 in 1995 to 45.6 in 1996; that is, it is taking an extra 3.4 days on average to collect credit sales. Sutcliffe's DSO should be compared against its selling terms, however, which are net ten (full payment in ten days). Under this standard, its receivables policy is lax and worsening.

The fixed-asset-turnover ratio examines how well the firm uses plant and equipment and is calculated for 1996 as

$$\text{Fixed asset turnover} = \frac{\text{Sales}}{\text{Net fixed assets}} = \frac{\$1{,}375}{\$985} = 1.40$$

The sharp decline from 6.38 in 1995 in the fixed-asset-turnover ratio indicates that excess fixed assets resulting from plant expansion and decline in sales are among Sutcliffe's major problems. Fixed-asset turns must be compared cautiously between two virtually identical companies, because their net fixed assets may differ greatly if assets were acquired in different years, due to the dual effects of inflation and the use of historical costs on the balance sheet. Similarly, net fixed assets vary with different depreciation methods.

The total-asset-turnover ratio is almost identical with that for fixed assets except that it is calculated using total assets.

$$\text{Total asset turnover} = \frac{\text{Sales}}{\text{Total assets}} = \frac{\$1{,}375}{\$1{,}649} = 0.83$$

Compared with the 1996 value of 0.83, Sutcliffe's 1995 total asset turnover was 2.16. Total asset turnover has suffered a smaller percentage decline than the fixed asset turnover, reconfirming that Sutcliffe's major problem is fixed assets.

Profitability Ratios

There are two principal profitability ratios: the profit margin and the return on equity (ROE). Profit margin, calculated using information solely from the income statement, describes the profits earned per dollar of sale. ROE, combining income-statement and balance-sheet information, indicates the percentage return earned by investors.

The formula to calculate Sutcliffe's profit margin for 1996 is

$$\text{Profit margin} = \frac{\text{Net income}}{\text{Sales}} = \frac{\$9}{\$1{,}375} = 0.65\%$$

The year before, its profit margin was 15.74%. Sutcliffe Industries now earns less than one percent on its sales. The problem with this ratio is that it only says that something is wrong but does not provide the crisis manager with any insight.

Return on equity (ROE) is calculated as

$$\text{ROE} = \frac{\text{Net income}}{\text{Net worth}} = \frac{\$9}{\$523 + \$81} = 1.5\%$$

Sutcliffe's ROE has plunged from a spectacular 64.2% level in 1995 to a dreadful 1.5% level in 1996. Again, the crisis manager is only told that things are bad. Some analysts prefer to find the return on total assets because they object to the increase in ROE that results from leverage. However, in defense of ROE, the return on total assets is nothing more than the balance sheet equivalent of the profit margin, giving the percentage return on assets.

Financial and Operating Leverage

How risky is a company? Does it use too many machines or have too much debt? None of the ratios presented in the section above is designed to answer the question "how much is too much?" They are descriptive, not prescriptive. For example, the debt ratio describes the proportion of total assets derived from borrowed funds. In the case of Sutcliffe Industries, its debt ratio in 1996 is 63 percent. A 63 percent debt ratio is high and perhaps the firm should raise new equity by selling common shares. But that value judgment cannot be made without also looking at Sutcliffe's earnings. As it turns out, in 1996 Sutcliffe's ROE is low, 1.5 percent. Given that, the benefits of the high debt ratio are not apparent. However, in a good year, debt leverages ROE upwards as it did in 1995 to 64.9 percent for Sutcliffe Industries; then the advantage of high debt levels is obvious. But many ratios are too narrowly defined to answer independently the question, "is the ratio too high or low?"

Two other ratios present a more sweeping picture of the company's position: the degree of operating leverage (DOL) and the degree of financial leverage (DFL). These ratios weigh the impact of overall strategy. DOL evaluates the question "Is the company too capital (machine) intensive?" DFL considers the question "Does the company use too much debt?" The product of the two ratios is the degree of total leverage, DTL. DTL measures overall corporate risk: "Does the firm have too many machines and too much debt?"

$$DTL = DOL \times DFL$$

Steve Kaplan bifurcates troubled companies into those bothered by macroeconomic, industry, or operating troubles and those with too much debt. The former he calls economically distressed; the latter he refers to as financially distressed. The two leverage ratios provide good estimates of the risk of each type of distress.

Companies produce output using a mix of machines (i.e., capital) and people.[7] The decision to hire workers or to buy more machines is influenced by the cost of each input factor and by available technological choices. When labor unions raise wage rates, companies respond by automating their processes. When technological progress increases the throughput from machines, companies reduce their usage of labor time. Plants in distant locations or countries may employ different mixes of input factors because of cost, work rules, and environmental-law differences.

Input costs are either fixed or variable: Fixed costs are constant, while variable costs fluctuate.[8] Labor usually is thought of as a variable factor of production even though few companies treat labor as a variable cost item, laying off workers when they are not needed. For our purposes, assume that labor is a variable-cost input. Capital is unquestionably a fixed-cost item in the short run, even if it is leased. The advantage (disadvantage) of fixed costs is that when output rises (falls), fixed costs remain constant. Companies using more machines experience smaller changes in total costs as output fluctuates. They should earn more (less) operating profit than firms using relatively more labor when output increases (decreases).[9] Fixed costs are a benefit when output rises but a detriment when output falls.

When does a company employ too few workers or too few machines? The answer is related to the rate of change in the firm's EBIT compared with the rate at which its sales change. EBIT defines operating income—what the firm earns from its operations, ignoring financing costs. Companies that use more machines incur relatively more fixed costs and fewer variable costs. Since fixed costs are unchanging, these companies experience proportionately greater increases in their EBIT as sales increase. DOL measures this responsiveness by evaluating the income statement from sales down to EBIT. The calculation is shown for Sutcliffe Industries:

$$\text{DOL} = \frac{\%\,\Delta\text{ operating income}}{\%\,\Delta\text{ in sales}} = \frac{-90.0\%}{-45.0\%} = 2.00$$

The percentage-change calculation is made across the years 1995 and 1996 but could also be done with less precision using one, two, or three quarters of data. The DOL means that for each 1 percent change in Sutcliffe's sales, it experiences a 2 percent change in operating income. This DOL is relatively high, indicating that Sutcliffe Industries operates a production process intensively driven by machines.

DFL is calculated by moving down the income statement from EBIT to net income. DFL describes the responsiveness of Sutcliffe's net income to changes in its EBIT.

$$\text{DFL} = \frac{\%\,\Delta\text{ net income}}{\%\,\Delta\text{ operating income}} = \frac{-97\%}{-90\%} = 1.08$$

The calculation indicates that a 1 percent change in Sutcliffe's EBIT results in a 1.08 percent change in its net income. This is a low DFL. DFL is sensitive to the amount of interest subtracted from EBIT to get to net income. A firm with no debt has a DFL of 1.0; hence, the calculation reveals that Sutcliffe Industries is using little debt relative to its sales and net income even though it has a debt ratio of 63 percent. Sutcliffe Industries' major problem is not the use of debt. A shortcoming of DFL is that it is affected by the firm's financing decisions over the past twelve months, during which interest rates may have changed.

DTL is found by multiplying DOL times DFL, which in the case of Sutcliffe Industries equals 2.16. Each 1 percent change in sales results in a 2.16 percent change in net income. This is not an unreasonably high leverage rate. Fortunately for Sutcliffe Industries, its DFL is low, balancing its high DOL, otherwise it might have had a double-digit DTL.

Companies with high operating leverage that keep their DFLs low minimize risk while relying intensively on machines in their production process. In contrast, airlines are notorious for applying lots of capital equipment (airplanes) (high DOLs), financing the planes with debt (high DFLs), and having to manage sky-high DTLs. One needs to look no further to explain why so many airlines have failed. Similarly, companies with high DFLs should keep their DOLs as low as possible in order to minimize their DTLs. Pantalone and Platt (1987b) found that savings and loans (firms with high DFLs) with expensive office structures (operating equipment) are most likely to fail.

Failure Prediction Models

Beaver

In 1965, Beaver supervised the first bankruptcy-prediction study. His objective was to find empirical evidence that financial-ratio information is effective for predicting bankruptcy. Assembling a sample of seventy-nine failed and seventy-nine nonfailed firms over the period 1954–64, he employed a univariate methodology to test the predictive power of individual variables.[10] After comparing group means between distressed and nondistressed companies, he selected critical scores for thirty financial ratios. He applied those scores to another set of companies to determine which ratios, if any, could separate accurately the sample companies into survivors and failures. The results for several ratios were extraordinarily prescient. For example, the cash-flow-to-total-debt ratio only misclassified 13 percent of the sample of bankruptcy firms. A random selection process misses approximately 50 percent of the firms.

Since Beaver's work, dozens of bankruptcy-prediction, credit-scoring, and bond-default models have been tested. Beaver's inquiry spawned three related questions that subsequent researchers have addressed:

1. If one ratio works well by itself, can a group of ratios working together do better?
2. Should firms in different industries be combined in the same model?
3. Which statistical methodology should be used to estimate model parameters?

Many researchers have answered these questions. The consensus answer to the first question is yes: many ratios (properly chosen) predict bankruptcy better than one ratio. Prediction success rates in multivariate models often exceed 95 percent. The second question is answered yes and no: if there is enough data (normally the deficit is bankrupt-firm data), then industry models should be constructed, but there have been too few bankruptcies in most industries to break out industry-specific models. The third question is still unresolved, with various statistical methods vying for supremacy.

Altman

Not long after the publication of Beaver's work, Edward Altman (1968) shifted the science of failure prediction into the multivariate world. Unlike Beaver, who examined the power of a single ratio to predict incipient failure, Altman allowed a number of ratios to contribute to the prediction. Altman worked from a pragmatic perspective. His concern was to identify the set of ratios that best predicted failure, not to justify or prove a theoretical model. His results astonished the financial community. Even though he studied only thirty-three bankrupt firms and thirty-three nonbankrupt firms gathered over the period 1946–65, he correctly predicted 97 percent of those that survived and 94 percent of those that failed. Applications of Altman's work by other researchers generally have proved to be as highly prescient as the original study. The Altman *Z*-score, as it is known, appears in virtually every finance textbook and in numerous software packages and is recognized by most analysts on Wall Street.

The *Z*-score is derived using a statistical technique known as multiple-discriminate analysis, or MDA. MDA is similar to regression analysis except that, unlike regression, which seeks to minimize the squared deviations of a fitted line from the original values, MDA seeks to develop a function that minimizes the squared error within each group (bankrupt or nonbankrupt) while maximizing differences between groups. Altman's *Z*-score model takes the form

$$Z = (1.2X_1) + (1.4X_2) + (3.3X_3) + (.66X_4) + (1.0X_5)$$

where

$$X_1 = \frac{\text{Working capital}}{\text{Total assets}}$$

$$X_2 = \frac{\text{Retained earnings}}{\text{Total assets}}$$

$$X_3 = \frac{\text{EBIT}}{\text{Total assets}}$$

$$X_4 = \frac{\text{Market value of equity}}{\text{Book value of debt}}$$

$$X_5 = \frac{\text{Sales}}{\text{Total Assets}}$$

The numerical values are estimated coefficients, and the *X*s are the five financial ratios selected as best by Altman. *Z* is the value of the function. Note that estimated coefficient values do not convey by their size the importance of particular variables; coefficient size depends as well on the typical size of each variable.

Interpreting *Z* is tricky. Altman hit upon a straightforward approach. He evaluated the *Z*s for the sixty-six companies in his sample. Companies whose *Z*s exceed 2.99 never failed, while those with *Z*s below 1.81 always failed. He described these two values as his cutoff points. The area between 2.99 and 1.81 he called a zone of ignorance.[11] Companies with *Z*-scores in the zone of ignorance have an uncertain future; if their *Z*-score value is falling (rising) from one year to the next, then bankruptcy (survival) is more likely. Using these critical points, 95 percent of the companies in Altman's sixty-six-company sample are properly categorized as bankrupt or nonbankrupt in a follow-up evaluation exercise.

The bankruptcy risk of other companies is assessed using the Altman model by determining their *Z*-scores. For example, Sutcliffe Industries' income statement and balance sheets contain all the data necessary to solve for Altman's *Z*-score except for the market value of its equity (see table 3.4). Based on today's stock market quotations, Sutcliffe's market value of equity is $220 million. Sutcliffe's

TABLE 3.4. Applying Altman's *Z*-Score to Sutcliffe Industries

Variable	1996 Value	Coefficient	Product
Working capital/total assets	(664 − 615)/1,649 = 0.03	1.2	0.04
Retained earnings/total assets	523/1,649 = 0.32	1.4	0.45
EBIT/total assets	69/1,649 = 0.042	3.3	0.14
Market value of equity/book value of debt	220/(430 + 615) = 0.21	0.66	0.14
Sales/total assets	1,375/1,649 = 0.83	1.0	0.83
Z-score			1.60

Z-score is below Altman's bankruptcy cutoff point. Hence, the Altman model predicts that Sutcliffe Industries is likely to fail within the year.

Nonpublic companies whose common equity is not traded in a market are incapable of using Altman's original model specification since they lack information for one of the variables, X_4.[12] To surmount this obstacle, Altman (1983) reestimated the model and derived a Z' that included only variables that are accessible to nonpublic companies.[13]

$$Z' = (.717X_1) + (.847X_2) + (3.107X_3) + (.420X_4) + (.998X_5)$$

where X_1, X_2, X_3, and X_5, are as defined above and X_4 is defined as

$$X_4 = \frac{\text{Net worth (book value)}}{\text{Total liabilities}}$$

Altman computed different cutoff points for the Z' nonpublic firm model; firms with Z'-scores above 2.90 are expected to survive, while firms with scores below 1.23 are expected to fail. Firms in the middle range are in a zone of ignorance.

Treating Sutcliffe Industries as a privately held corporation, its Altman Z'-score is calculated as in table 3.5. Here, the Altman model predicts continued survival for Sutcliffe Industries, though the score is low in the zone of ignorance.

Finally, Altman, Haldeman, and Narayanan (1977) updated the original Z-score model using more current data (1969–75) more companies (fifty-three bankrupt and fifty-eight nonbankrupt) and after revising reported company data in accordance with six accounting issues[14] (see table 3.6). The new model's estimated parameters are proprietary and are unavailable except to clients of Zeta Services, Inc. It is known, however, that the new model incorporates seven variables. The new model is widely used in the financial community.

TABLE 3.5. Applying Altman's Z'-Score to a Privately Held Sutcliffe Industries

Variable	1996 Value	Coefficient	Product
Working capital/total assets	(664 − 615)/1,649 = 0.03	0.717	0.02
Retained earnings/total assets	523/1,649 = 0.32	0.847	0.27
EBIT/total assets	69/1,649 = 0.04	3.107	0.12
Net worth (book value)/total liabilities	(81 + 523)/1,649 = 0.37	0.420	0.16
Sales/total assets	1,375/1,649 = 0.83	0.998	0.83
Z'-score			1.40

Platt and Platt

Sample size is an important factor contributing to the value of a statistical model.[15] Larger samples have superior statistical properties. The number of publicly held companies resorting to Chapter 11 at any one time is not sufficient to create a large sample. A controversial aspect of Altman's major work is his including failed companies from many industries in an effort to enlarge his sample. While it is true that few individual industries have sufficient numbers of bankrupt companies to build industry-specific EWS models, an awkward complication arises when companies in many industries are combined to build a bankruptcy prediction model. Specifically, the *Z*-score model provides only a single version of the "correct" ratio values for all companies in all industries.[16] Since industry differences are ignored, the implication of the *Z*-score model is that firms in every industry should operate within the same financial bounds and have similar ratios. Observing the wide and persistent variation in average industry ratios across industries shows that this is patently incorrect and may explain the faulty projections when the model is applied to forecast solvency for companies not in Altman's original sample.[17] For example, in his own paper (1968), Altman obtains lower classification accuracy using the estimated model to predict solvency for companies not in the original sample: only 79 percent of nonbankrupt and 96 percent of bankrupt companies (84 percent overall) are correctly classified. In the original sample, in contrast, correct estimation rates are 97 percent and 94 percent (95 percent overall).

Platt and Platt (1990) resolved the multiple-industry problem by developing industry-relative ratios in order to put data from every industry on the same footing. An industry-relative ratio is defined as

$$\text{Industry-Relative Ratio} = \frac{\text{Company ratio}}{\text{Average industry ratio}}$$

TABLE 3.6. Variables in Altman, Haldeman, and Narayanan (1977)

Concept	Measure
Return on assets	EBIT/total assets
Stability of earnings	A ten-year trend in ROA
Debt service	EBIT/interest payments
Cumulative profitability	Retained earnings/total assets
Liquidity	Current ratio
Capitalization	Common equity/total capital
Size	Total tangible assets

Each industry-relative ratio compares a firm's ratio to the average ratio value across all the companies in that industry. Industry-relative ratios describe the firm's ratio as a percent of the average industry-ratio value. When the industry-relative ratio is greater (less) than unity, the firm has a ratio value larger (smaller) than the average firm in its industry. Consider the information on current ratios and industry-relative ratios for three companies in table 3.7.

Higher current ratio values are generally preferred since they indicate a greater ability to repay current obligations. On this basis, Airline A appears to be the most healthy of the three firms since it has the highest current ratio, 1.20, while Supermarket C emerges as the weakest since it has the lowest current ratio, 0.60. However, the airline and supermarket industries are totally dissimilar. Airlines have higher receivables than supermarkets since few airline and most supermarket customers pay with cash; supermarkets have high inventories (goods on their shelves) and accounts payables (money owed suppliers), while airlines have low inventories (just peanuts and magazines) but moderately high accounts payable (jet fuel), and airlines generally hold more cash than supermarkets. The average industry-current ratio column shows that the average airline has a higher current ratio than the average supermarket or computer manufacturer. The last column provides industry-relative ratios. It shows that *compared to firms in their own industries,* Airline A actually has a weak current ratio position, while Supermarket C has a relatively strong position. The airline's current ratio is only 66 percent as high as the average current ratio in its industry; Computer Manufacturer B's current ratio is exactly 100 percent of the average current ratio in its industry; and Supermarket C's current ratio is 120 percent of the average current ratio in its industry. Industry-relative ratios are more illuminating than company ratios alone.

After creating industry-relative ratios for the 114 companies in their sample (fifty-seven bankrupt and fifty-seven nonbankrupt) over the period 1972–87, Platt and Platt (1990 and 1991b) built an EWS model. Unlike Altman, they used a logit regression methodology instead of MDA. Logit regression, unlike MDA, allows individual coefficients to be subjected to rigorous statistical testing. As with Altman, pragmatism

TABLE 3.7. Current Ratios and Industry-Relative Ratios for Three Companies

Company	Ratio Value	Industry Average	Industry-Relative Ratio
Airline A	1.20	1.80	0.66
Computer manufacturer B	1.00	1.00	1.00
Supermarket chain C	0.60	0.50	1.20

superseded theory in Platt and Platt's work as they sought the best variables to predict failure. In a second paper, Platt and Platt (1991b) validated the superiority of the industry-relative framework compared to an unadjusted model. Their final model takes the form below. For simplicity, the industry component of the industry-relative ratios is not shown in the formula.

$$\text{Probability} = 1 \Big/ \left[1 + \exp - \left(-3.98 - 1.23 \frac{\text{Cash flow}}{\text{Sales}} + 2.36 \frac{\text{Total debt}}{\text{Total assets}} + 0.43 \frac{\text{Net fixed assets}}{\text{Total assets}} + 0.58 \frac{\text{Short-term debt}}{\text{Total debt}} - 6.11 \frac{\text{Cash flow}}{\text{Sales}} \times \%\,\Delta\,\text{industry output} + 7.61 \frac{\text{Total debt}}{\text{Total assets}} \times \%\,\Delta\,\text{industry output} - 0.007 \frac{\%\,\Delta\,\text{company sales}}{\%\,\Delta\,\text{industry output}} \right) \right]$$

Compared to MDA models, which are written linearly in their parameters, logit models are written exponentially (the symbol "exp" in the equation), and solving these equations also takes more effort. This complexity is the price to be able to test the statistical significance of each estimated parameter and to discard from the model any variable that is not a significant determinant of failure. The logit model does not solve for a *Z* but instead estimates the probability that the firm will fail. Probability estimates range between zero and one. Platt and Platt (1990) found that probabilities below 40 percent are not worrisome.

The Platt and Platt EWS model is solved in four steps:

1. multiply model coefficients (such as 1.23) times the industry-relative ratio
2. total the values in parentheses and add five[18]
3. take the log of the total and add one
4. take the inverse

Using the data for Sutcliffe Industries provided above, the Platt and Platt model is solved in table 3.8. Industry-average ratios are obtained from Robert Morris and Associates, COMPUSTAT, or the Internal Revenue Publication *Statistics of Income.* The Platt and Platt model predicts that Sutcliffe Industries has a 35 percent chance of failing. Their model is indifferent to probabilities below the 40 percent critical cutoff point. Hence, the Platt and Platt model, unlike the Altman *Z*-score model, maintains that Sutcliffe Industries is likely to survive the coming year. Of course, this prediction is nearing critical probability, and the company is advised to consider corrective action.

The column of industry-relative ratios in table 3.8 illustrates both how the Platt and Platt model operates and the severity of Sutcliffe Industries' problems. The Platt and Platt model compares company ratios to industry averages. When the industry-relative ratio is above (below) unity, Sutcliffe's ratio is larger (smaller) than the average value of the ratio in the industry. In two instances, Sutcliffe Industries' ratios are completely estranged from what is normal in its industry: in the growth-rate comparison (the industry-relative value is −30) and the net fixed assets to total assets comparison (the industry-relative value is 3.17).

TABLE 3.8. Applying the Platt and Platt EWS Model to Sutcliffe Industries

Variable	Coefficient	Sutcliffe's 1996 Variable Value	1996 Industry Variable Value[a]	Industry-Relative Ratios (IRR)	Product of Coefficient and IRR
Constant term	−3.98	*NA*	*NA*	*NA*	−3.98
Cash flow/sales	−1.23	(9 + 50)/1,375 = 0.043	.075	0.57	−0.70
Total debt/total assets	2.36	0.63	0.458	1.38	3.26
Net fixed assets/total assets	0.43	0.60	0.189	3.17	1.36
Short-term debt/total debt	0.58	(615 − 26)/ 1,019 = 0.58	0.314	1.84	1.07
(Cash flow/sales) × % Δ Industry output	−6.11			0.57 × .015 = 0.009	−0.05
Total debt/total assets ×% Δ Industry output	7.61		0.458	1.38 × 0.015 = 0.021	0.16
% Δ Company sales/% Δ Industry output	−0.007	−45.0	1.5	−30.0	0.21
Total					1.33
Total + 5.0					6.33
Logarithm					1.85
Logarithm + 1.0					2.85
Inverse					0.35
Probability					0.35

[a]These values are for the lumber products industry.

Clearly, a company whose ratio of net fixed assets to total assets is 317 percent of the level for the typical firm in its industry is either in a great deal of trouble or possesses knowledge unavailable to anyone else.

Platt, Platt, and Pedersen

Both the Altman *Z*-score and the Platt and Platt industry-relative model suffer from a shared objection: neither corrects for the effects of temporal distortions on variable values. Temporal distortions arise because data spanning many years must be combined in order to get enough companies with which to build an EWS model. The three studies discussed above used ten years (Beaver), nineteen years (Altman), and fifteen years (Platt and Platt) of data. Across so many years, the effects of inflation, interest-rate changes, and price changes cause similar values to have quite different meanings. The temporal distortion problem and its resolution resembles the solution to the industry differences problem discussed above.

Consider the effect of interest rates. Table 3.9 contains information using standard ratios for a company that does not appear to have undergone any changes in fifteen years. The regularly calculated debt-to-assets ratio in both years equals 0.45, implying that the firm is equally indebted in both years. But the prime interest rate has fallen precipitously in the intervening years. The dollar cost of debt drops from $68.85 per year to just $14.40 per year. This savings is not reflected in the debt ratio. If the analyst happens to include a TIE ratio in the formulation, some of the impact of interest-rate changes is captured, but the debt-to-asset ratio remains a distortion. A deflated debt-to-asset ratio is created by dividing the interest rate into the debt variable before the ratio is

TABLE 3.9. Data across Fifteen Years for One Company

	1980	1995
Debts borrowed at prime rate	$450	$450
Total assets	$1,000	$1,000
Debt/assets	0.45	0.45
Prime interest rate	15.3%	3.2%
Interest costs	$68.85	$14.40
Debt/interest rate/assets	2.94	14.06

created. The deflated ratio shows that the firm in 1995 (with a 14.06 value for the deflated ratio) is healthier than the firm was in 1980 (with a deflated ratio of 2.94).

Platt, Platt, and Pedersen (1994) examined thirty-five bankrupt and eighty-nine nonbankrupt oil companies. By selecting companies from the same industry, the industry-relative problem is a nonissue. The data covered the period 1982 to 1988, during which oil prices wildly fluctuated. Without correcting the temporal distortion problem, the EWS correctly classified 80 percent of bankrupt firms (90 percent overall); with deflated ratios, this percentage rose to 94 percent (95 percent overall).

Summary

The best scenario for building an EWS model is to use data on companies in the same industry and year. Few industries suffer enough failures, let alone in one year, to make this practical. The alternatives are clear. When combining data across widely disparate industries, consider developing industry-relative ratios; when the data span a number of years, consider how to deflate ratios.

Applying EWS Models in a Turnaround

As 1996 drew to a close, Herman Sutcliffe, the president and principal owner of Sutcliffe Industries, asked his son, Victor, the company's CEO, to come into his office. He had just read Victor's report describing a meeting with the company's lead banker. The report indicated that the banker had categorically refused to discuss with the members of the loan syndicate Sutcliffe Industrics' request to have its credit line increased beyond the current $300 million level. Before Victor had even taken his seat, Herman blurted out, "What the hell is the matter with the First National Bank? We've paid them every cent we've ever owed them, and on time too. They've always been good to us. Whenever we've needed money from them, they've always come through for us. And now they're saying no. I don't get it. We made money this year: $9 million! Now they're treating us like we're broke."

The father and son team had complementary skills. Victor handled the financial and accounting sides of the business, while his father managed strategy, marketing, and product development. This bifurcation of tasks suited the team well. Victor had earned an MBA in finance from a prestigious midwestern university. What his father lacked in formal education, he compensated for by person skills and a comprehensive grasp of the household-cleaning market. Now Victor was pressed to enlighten his father on the true financial condition of the business that he had built from scratch.

"The bank isn't looking at how much money we made," Victor told his father. "The problem is more complex than that. They're looking at our balance sheet and our sales report, and they don't like what they see. But what really set them off was the way we failed a computerized test dubbed the Altman *Z*-score. It alleges that we're likely to go bankrupt in 1997."

Herman was unable to camouflage his surprise. Sutcliffe Industries' recent stumble was all too present in his mind, but he had no idea that the excess manufacturing capacity and the decline in sales could cause its banker to lose faith in his company. He responded, "They're not the only bank around. Sales will rebound once Home Builders agrees to stock our products again. After that we'll get a new banker."

Victor knew the situation was far more serious than that. Time was running out for Sutcliffe Industries to make timely payments to its vendors. Without vendor and bank support, the company faced a liquidity crisis. Sutcliffe was still profitable, but the question was whether it could continue to pay its bills. With its cash ratio down to just 0.05 from 0.41 in 1995, Sutcliffe's cash position was low. Victor clarified the financial situation, then reported the bank's demand that, in Victor's words, "a restructuring expert be engaged to assist the company." In fact, the bank's message was far stronger, asking that an outsider assume control of the company.

The First National Bank provided Victor with a list of three firms it thought could assist Sutcliffe Industries.[19] Each firm had experience working with manufacturing companies facing problems similar to Sutcliffe's:

- superfluous capacity
- excess inventories
- cash shortfall
- family-run businesses with multigenerational employment
- inadequate marketing strategy
- low-cost foreign competition

Victor met by himself with representatives of the three firms. The principal topics discussed included

- turnaround management style/philosophy
- number and capability of available personnel
- estimate of how long it would take to fix the problem
- estimated engagement costs

In addition, each firm provided Victor with a list of client references. Victor called each referenced company's CEO for an opinion of the accuracy of information provided in the interviews. He also asked if the references were satisfied with the firm's performance. One firm's clients reported that while they were extremely pleased with the delicacy with which problems had been handled and resolved, all preliminary estimates provided by the consultants had been woefully optimistic. Another firm's clients reported that the crisis managers had requested/demanded equity in the troubled companies at a precarious moment during the workout. The third firm's clients were less than happy with the final outcomes. Victor compiled these accounts in table 3.10 and went in to see his father.

Herman listened to Victor and then suggested asking the bank for more names. Victor responded that there was insufficient time to continue searching and that most of the firms would have some problem anyway. Victor proposed retaining Firm 1 since it "would not hold up the family for equity and had a good national reputation." Herman reluctantly agreed, the contract was signed, and a retainer fee was paid.

Firm 1's personnel arrived at Sutcliffe Industries at 8:00 A.M. the next morning. The initial contact team was headed by Sue Worth. Sue had an MBA and had earned the designation of Certified Turnaround Professional (CTP) from the Turnaround Management Association. Her team included five others whose specialties were accounting, finance and vendor relations, operations, marketing, and liquidation. The team began by interviewing everyone working in the executive office complex. In the ensuing days the team visited manufacturing sites and talked with distributors and clients. At the end of the week, the team convened to prepare its internal reports and develop its action plan.[20] In addition to the problems catalogued above, the team uncovered additional issues:

1. Herman and Victor often circulated contradictory orders, and while they did not discuss their own disagreements, they would berate their confused employees for insubordination. In one instance, work was redone three times.
2. Products coming from foreign producers were technologically superior.
3. Home Builders removed Sutcliffe Industries from its approved-vendors list because of both pricing and product quality issues.
4. Some of Sutcliffe's inventory was obsolete and worthless.
5. Insufficient reserves had been taken against doubtful accounts.
6. Lax controls permitted the purchasing manager at the new plant

to abscond with several hundred thousand dollars in never-delivered materials and supplies.

7. Worker morale was low, wages were below average for the region, and absenteeism and quits were hurting production.

Sue was not surprised that her team had exposed problems unfamiliar to management. However, the number and severity of new issues arising in this case was unusually high. Sue scheduled a meeting with Herman and Victor for that afternoon to report her preliminary findings and to request authorization to attack the broader set of issues. Firm 1's internal policies required this interim consultation with the client to circumvent subsequent problems concerning the extent of the engagement and consulting fees. This meeting would be particularly difficult because Sue would be informing Herman and Victor of their roles in the problem. She postponed that issue for the end of the meeting. Until that moment both Sutcliffes accepted Sue's findings and complemented her on "uncovering things that we suspected but never knew." However, when she broke the news that employees throughout the company reported that father and son were part of the problem, they reacted defensively, with Herman ordering Sue to "pack it up." Victor kept a cooler head and told his father that the bank would not tolerate their throwing Firm 1 out at this time. Once Herman acknowledged this, he gave Sue an opportunity to present her most difficult proposal: that father and son relinquish their official duties but remain as her consultants while she assumed the role of interim CEO. "I can't promise you success," she said, "but if things work out, after I leave you'll remain the principal owners of this company and will be back in your old positions." The Sutcliffes had no choice but to accede. Throughout the turnaround, Sue ran Sutcliffe Industries; the Sutcliffes were frequently consulted, but these visits soon became perfunctory as Sue learned how few constructive ideas they could contribute.

Sue immediately informed the bank; the trustees of the publicly traded debt; the American Stock Exchange, where the common stock traded; and all vendors of her appointment as interim CEO. This proclamation was obligatory for a publicly traded company, but Sue hoped the

TABLE 3.10. Comparison of Crisis-Management Firms

Consulting Firm	Advantages	Disadvantages
1	Performed exceptionally well	More expensive and tardy than promised
2	Performed exceptionally well	Demanded stock or warrants
3	Less expensive	Performed poorly

news would create a small window of opportunity for change before creditors applied pressure to the cash-short company. Wall Street responded favorably, and the company's common stock rose fifty cents per share. The financial analyst on Sue's team facetiously recommended asking the bank to recalculate the Altman *Z*-score with the post-announcement higher equity value. Sue responded that this was not a far-fetched idea, since Firm 1 commonly relied on the Altman *Z*-score to track progress in distress cases where the client was not yet bankrupt.

Sue instructed her finance and accounting experts to build a spreadsheet program to calculate Altman *Z*-scores for use in monitoring Sutcliffe Industries' turnaround progress. The strategy was to establish target values for Altman *Z*-score variables that would return the firm to health within twelve months.

Because of her history of using EWS models in corporate renewal engagements, Sue warned the team to keep the target values realistic so the exercise would not be self-deluding and valueless. Sutcliffe Industries' various problems were assigned to particular team members who would decide what reasonably could be accomplished in one, six, and twelve months. Team members assigned tasks are detailed in table 3.11.

After the meeting, some team members pursued their mission at the company, and others worked out of Firm 1's offices, telephoning, visiting companies that bought or might buy Sutcliffe's products, and deliberating with the firm's attorneys. Sue's three-day deadline for initial EWS model inputs was achieved, but several analysts counseled her that their forecasts were preliminary and depended on competitors' responses, degree of vendor support, and reaction in the marketplace. Table 3.12 shows the preliminary estimates and associated solutions to Altman's *Z*-score for one, six, and twelve months.

The sales figure is the critical target projection. Sales are expected to jump 45 percent in the next twelve months, to $2 billion, still $483 million below 1995 sales. Sales lost to megastores such as Home Builders should be regained at the expense of a lower gross margin. This shows up in the weak EBIT response to the growth in sales. Receivables are targeted to grow both absolutely and as a percent of sales, as a means to spur new sales; doubtful accounts of $15 million are written off immediately. The targeted figure for inventories falls slowly at first, reflecting the discounted sale of nearly worthless products; expanding sales after six and twelve months allow further declines in inventories. Total assets decline sharply because the new plant is contributed to a joint-venture project with a foreign producer willing to supply new technologies. Production from the joint venture will be marketed by both companies. Note that profits and EBIT are reported on an annual basis.

On the liability side, Firm 1 appreciates that the bank's $300 million credit line is at its upper bound. Sue advised the team to repay the bank as soon as possible to demonstrate Sutcliffe Industries' recovery. This is nearly accomplished in the projections after the first twelve months. Vendor support expands slowly but then accelerates as a strengthening balance sheet and growing sales level reinforce promises made by Sue's team. Additional vendor credit partially replaces the bank loan. The common equity is assumed to give back the "announcement effect" and then climb gradually throughout the year. Sinking-fund obligations for the long-term debt are met.

If the targets are achieved, Sutcliffe Industries penetrates Altman's zone of ignorance after the first month and enters the unlikely-to-go-bankrupt range after the twelfth month. With the plan outlined and the team at work, Sue wrestles with the following doubts:

TABLE 3.11. Breakdown of Team Assignments in the Sutcliffe Industries Engagement

Problem	Assigned To	Goal
Excess inventories	Liquidation person	Divide products into three groups: saleable at full value, saleable at partial value, and obsolete
Excess accounts receivable and insufficient reserves for doubtful accounts	Accounting person	Conduct aging analysis, stop selling to slow-pay accounts, and increase discount offered to clients. Increase reserves
Insufficient accounts payables	Finance person	Discuss needs with sympathetic vendors and obtain increased time to pay. Use new funding to reduce bank debt
Insufficient sales	Marketing person	Develop plan to sell old inventory, stimulate new sales to old clients, and find new clients. Pay special attention to category-buster stores
Excess capacity	Liquidation, operations, and accounting persons	Review tax implications of plant closings, evaluate sale potential of both plants, and work with marketing team to avoid closing a plant that will be needed
Low worker morale	Operations person	Create incentive wage plan
Low productivity	Operations person	Reengineer the manufacturing process: focus on output, quality, and costs
Theft of materials	Accounting person	Establish control systems and prosecute violators to the full extent of the law
Lagging product development	Operations person	Seek joint venture with foreign producers given lack of R&D and cash shortage

1. What might go wrong?
2. Has she forgotten anything important?
3. Should she advise the team to take certain precautions?
4. Are there any valid warning signs to watch for?
5. What should she do if the plan flounders?

Break-Even Analysis

Break-even analysis is a crucial concept in corporate renewal that provides information on whether a distressed firm is salvageable. Corporate renewal, unlike traditional break-even analysis, derives several break-

TABLE 3.12. Targeting Corporate Recovery Using Altman's *Z*-Score

Variable	Coefficient	1996 Value	Target Value in 1 Month	Target Value in 6 Months	Target Value in 12 Months
Cash and securities		$32	$95	$170	$270
Accounts receivable		$172	$205	$230	$280
Inventory		$460	$450	$400	$350
Current assets		$664	$750	$800	$900
Accounts payable		$292	$300	$330	$400
Notes payable		$297	$247	$165	$18
Accruals		$26	$28	$30	$32
Current liabilities		$615	$575	$525	$450
Total assets		$1,649	$1,575	$1,500	$1,400
Retained earnings[a]		$523	$528	$548	$578
EBIT[a]		$69	$55	$90	$145
Market value equity		$220	$220	$230	$275
Book value of debt		$430	$430	$420	$400
Sales		$1,375	$1,560	$1,700	$2,000
Working capital/total assets	1.2	0.03	0.11	0.18	0.32
Retained earnings/total assets	1.4	0.32	0.34	0.37	0.41
EBIT/total assets	3.3	0.042	0.035	0.060	0.104
Market value of equity/book value of debt	0.6	0.51	0.51	0.55	0.69
Sales/total assets	1.0	0.83	0.99	1.13	1.43
Z-score		1.77	2.05	2.42	3.19

[a]Reported on an annualized basis.

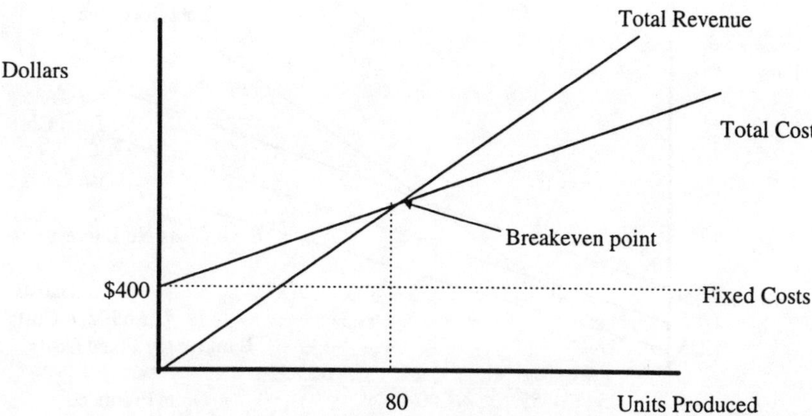

Fig. 3.1. Break-even analysis for XYZ, Inc.

even quantities for varying cost definitions. Figure 3.1 presents the information used in traditional break-even analysis.

Fixed costs at XYZ are $400 and include expenditures constant for all output quantities. Variable or direct costs are $5 per unit. The product sells for $10 per unit. Fixed costs include depreciation, amortization, rents, interest, salaries of certain personnel, and general office expenses. Variable costs include materials, sales commissions, and salaries of remaining personnel.[21] Traditional or profit break-even output is found using equation (1):

$$\begin{aligned}\text{Traditional breakeven} &= \text{Fixed costs}/(\text{Price} - \text{Variable cost}) \quad (1)\\ &= \$400/(\$10 - \$5)\\ &= 80 \text{ units}\end{aligned}$$

XYZ reaches breakeven if it sells eighty units where its total fixed plus variable costs equals its revenues. Profits are zero at breakeven. Selling less (more) than eighty units leaves XYZ with a loss (profit).

Crisis-based corporate renewal does not focus on achieving profit breakeven, as described in figure 3.1. In a crisis, noncash charges, such as depreciation and amortization, are ignored. This leads to a lower break-even output level, as shown in figure 3.2. XYZ has $125 of noncash fixed charges. Cash breakeven occurs at an output of fifty-five units. Cash flow is zero at cash breakeven if there are no irregularities regarding payments from customers or to suppliers.

In bankruptcy, the break-even target is operating income, since while the firm is under court protection interest payments are withheld

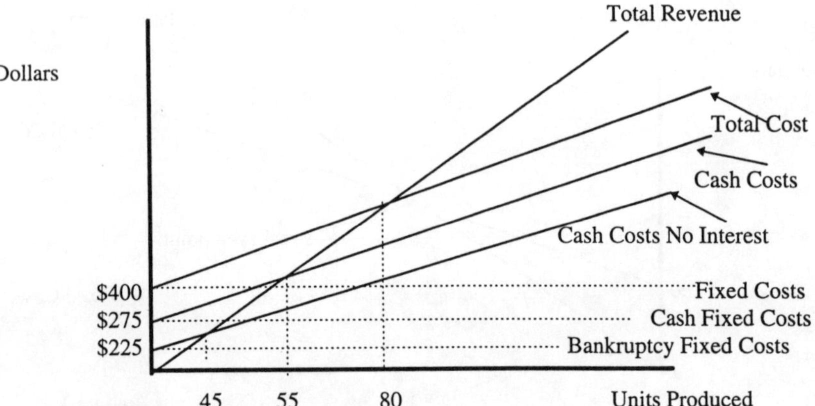

Fig. 3.2. Crisis and operating income break-even analysis for XYZ, Inc.

on unsecured obligations. Moreover, a firm that achieves EBIT or EBITDA breakeven can be reorganized instead of liquidated by creating a new capital structure that includes no debt, if necessary. XYZ's bankruptcy fixed costs are $225 and its EBITDA breakeven is forty-five units.

Profit, cash, and EBITDA breakeven provide three output goals to direct the corporate renewal process. If none of them are achievable, the firm cannot survive. A different set of break-even outputs is derived if the corporate renewal specialist reduces costs or raises product price.

Additional Funds Needed and Sustainable Growth

Management is responsible for forecasting a company's need for new funds. Additional funds support growth in sales. Even companies in financial distress experience growing sales due to inflation (which causes nominal increases) or industry factors leading to real increases in product demand. Generally, as sales increase, firms must invest more in their assets—inventories and accounts receivable and possibly fixed capital assets. Increased inventories enable the firm to deliver products ordered by customers, while additional receivables provide customers with credit.

Companies obtain new financing spontaneously as sales and output grow. Higher sales lead to increases in credit purchases from suppliers and accrued wages and taxes. These obligations are repaid in the ordinary course of business, but in the meantime they provide incremental financing. Net profits-after-dividend payments are an additional source of new funds.

Companies in financial distress may not be permitted spontaneous increases in liabilities. First, financial distress is usually associated with zero or negative profits. Second, suppliers to financially distressed companies may be unwilling to increase their credit exposure in the face of bankruptcy. These trade creditors may even seek to reduce the firm's draw by reducing the allowed payables amount or changing payment terms to induce or force the firm to repay its obligations. Regaining supplier confidence and obtaining incremental creditor financing are important functions of crisis management. Institutional lenders and banks may need mollification to persuade them to advance more money or at least not call in their loans. The turnaround manager must demonstrate to them that existing problems are recognized and corrective actions planned. If new financing is not found, the crisis manager might attempt to pay existing obligations at a significant discount, possibly as low as five or ten cents on the dollar. Intimating that bankruptcy is likely induces creditors to accept the offer. This strategy improves the balance sheet's appearance and may yield higher cash flow if interest-paying obligations are reduced. On the down side, it damages vendor relations. Creditors accepting these offers may face a preference charge later if the financially distressed company files a bankruptcy petition within ninety days.

Crisis managers also attempt to increase current asset utilization rates, particularly sales-to-inventory and sales-to-receivables ratios, while simultaneously raising the amount and the duration of trade credit. Fewer assets are required for the same level of sales if asset utilization ratios are successfully increased. If vendors grant expanded trade credit or lengthen the duration of credit, the firm has more funds.[22] Additional funds also are generated by liquidating superfluous capital assets. Of course, asset sales only provide a one-time boost in available cash. If the crisis manager is successful, new sales growth may not require any additional financing at all, and funds even may be generated for the company during the transition.

Deriving Additional Funds Needed

Assets and liabilities are subdivided into two categories: spontaneous and fixed. Spontaneous refers to assets or liabilities that increase directly with sales, while fixed assets and liabilities do not vary with sales. The two principal spontaneous assets are inventories and accounts receivable. Two major spontaneous liabilities are accounts payable and accrued liabilities.

Table 3.13 shows a balance sheet for Sandy Collar, Inc. In 1996, Sandy Collar produced at full capacity, with sales of $1 million. In 1996,

Sandy Collar earned $60,000 and paid $15,000 in dividends. Table 3.14 details those items in Sandy Collar's balance sheet expected to vary directly with sales, presenting them as a percentage of sales. The tables show that Sandy Collar's assets increase by fifty-three cents with each $1.00 increase in sales. Spontaneous liabilities—accounts payables and accruals—provide eleven cents of financing for each $1.00 of new sales. Note that the bank line is assumed to be exhausted, and the bank refuses requests for additional credit. The forty-two cent balance of spontaneous assets versus spontaneous liabilities is financed by internally generated

TABLE 3.13. Sandy Collar, Inc., Balance Sheet (December 31, 1996)

Assets	
Cash	$15,000
Receivables	115,000
Inventories	150,000
Fixed assets (net)	250,000
Total assets	$530,000
Liabilities	
Accounts payable	$70,000
Accrued taxes and wages	40,000
Bank debt (fully drawn)	100,000
Common stock	155,000
Retained earnings	165,000
Total liabilities and net worth	$530,000

TABLE 3.14. Sandy Collar, Inc., Balance Sheet Items Shown as a Percentage of Sales (December 31, 1996)

Assets		Liabilities	
Cash	1.5%	Accounts payable	7.0%
Receivables	11.5	Accrued taxes and wages	4.0
Inventories	15.0	Bank debt	NS[a]
Fixed assets (net)	25.0	Common stock	NS
		Retained earnings	NS
Total assets	53.0%	Total liabilities and net worth	11.0%

Spontaneous assets as a percent of sales	53%
Less spontaneous liabilities as a percent of sales	11%
Percent of each additional dollar of sales that must be financed	42%

[a]NS = not spontaneous

funds (i.e., retained earnings) or with external sources such as long-term debt.

Sandy Collar's sales are expected to grow by 20 percent to $1.2 million in 1997. If profit margin holds at 6 percent, profits will equal $72,000, while if the dividend payout rate remains at 25 percent, retained earnings will grow by $54,000. But Sandy Collar needs forty-two cents of new funds per dollar of new sales or 42 percent of the incremental $200,000—$84,000. Subtracting new retained earnings ($54,000) from needed new funds determines the money to be raised from new sources ($30,000) from a different bank or from new equity sales.

Less new money is needed if Sandy Collar has extra plant capacity, in which case it would be unnecessary to allocate twenty-five cents per dollar of new sales to acquiring new capital equipment. Net of spontaneous liabilities, Sandy Collar requires fewer funds:

[28% (New assets) − 11% (Spontaneous liabilities)] × New sales = $34,000

The company actually generates surplus money of $20,000, assuming $54,000 of new retained earnings.

A simple formula combines the information used above to calculate funds needed at Sandy Collar. The derivation determines additional funds needed or AFN.

$$\text{AFN} = (As/S)\,\Delta S + (Af/S)\,\Delta S - (Ls/S)\,\Delta S - M\,(1 - d)\,S^1 \qquad (1)$$

where

As/S = spontaneous assets as a percent of sales
Af/S = fixed assets that require new investment as a percent of sales
Ls/S = spontaneous liabilities as a percent of sales
ΔS = the change in sales
M = profit margin
$(1 - d)$ = the profit retention rate
S^1 = sales next period

Financial managers traditionally use the percentage-of-sales technique to forecast AFN. Percentage of sales starts with a known or assumed rate of increase in sales. Spontaneous assets and liabilities are assumed to have a constant percentage relationship to sales. Similarly, profit margin and the retention rate are assumed to be constant. AFN is than calculated as the simple product of the items in equation (1).

AFN is a critical tool for the turnaround manager, but the percent-of-sales assumption is imprecise and may even be hazardous. It is best to reexamine for accuracy:

- are sales really going to grow?
- does the firm want sales to expand?
- must spontaneous assets grow?
- can additions to fixed assets be avoided?
- can more credit be obtained from suppliers?
- can profit margin be enhanced?
- can dividends be decreased or terminated?

One description of corporate renewal is "teaching a company to make do with less." Regarding AFN, the task is to enable the firm to grow with less dependence on external funds.

Consider the effect on Sandy Collar's AFN (in the case where it needs additional capacity) if a turnaround manager makes the following changes:

1. the dividend, equal to 25 percent of net profits, is discontinued
2. suppliers extend additional credit, pushing accounts payable up to 10 percent of sales
3. cash, accounts receivable, and inventories are reduced from 28 percent of sales to 23 percent

The impact of this successful turnaround on AFN is seen in table 3.15, which breaks out the components of equation (1). Before the turnaround, Sandy Collar needed $30,000 of new money, almost 10 percent of current stockholders' equity, in order to obtain the assets essential for sales to rise by 20 percent. After the turnaround, only $8,000 is needed, just 2.5 percent of equity.

Sustainable Growth Rate

Some companies have limited access to outside funds. Financially distressed companies obviously are in this category, but startup companies

TABLE 3.15. Component Analysis of Additional Funds Needed

	Δ Sales	*As/S*	*Af/S*	−*Ls/S*	−*M*(1 − *d*)	AFN
Original	$200,000	0.28	0.25	0.11	(0.045) × S′	$30,000
Following a turnaround	$200,000	0.23	0.25	0.14	(0.06) × S′	$8,000

and privately held firms are often capital-constrained. Sustainable growth rate (SGR) determines how fast a company can grow without accessing any external funding sources. SGR is a handy tool for the corporate renewal specialist. Knowing SGR, a company without access to new money accepts new business provided that sales increase by less than SGR. Thereafter, the firm accepts new business only when an added sale is more profitable than an older sale to be declined given the capital shortage.

Two assumptions regarding corporate behavior underlie SGR.

1. the firm sells no new equity
2. the firm does not wish to change its capital structure

The first assumption reflects reality for firms in financial distress. The second assumption is more important. It implies that the firm's financial obligations grow to keep its debt/equity ratio unchanged. Given the first assumption, retained earnings are the only source of new equity. If the capital structure remains unchanged, the proportionate increase in equity is matched by an equal proportionate increase in total debt. This new debt is extended by trade creditors, drawn against existing bank credit lines, or arises from new indebtedness. In the Sandy Collar example, assume that the bank credit line can be increased.

Textbooks use several different formulas to present SGR. The simplest to work with (Higgins 1995) is

$$SGR = P \times R \times A \times \hat{T} \tag{2}$$

where

P = profit margin
R = profit retention rate
A = asset turnaround ratio
$\hat{T}$ = assets divided by equity (equity at the beginning of the period)

A good way to think about equation (2) is to note that if the firm's sales grow at any rate other than SGR, one of the four ratios on the right side of the equation must change. Two of the ratios, P and A, are operating ratios describing the firm's performance, the other two ratios, R and $\hat{T}$, describe the firm's financing choices. For example, should sales grow by more than SGR, the firm would have to either improve its operating performance or change one of its financing levers to obtain the assets required to achieve these sales. Several alternate profit margins may be used: normal profit margin, the net profit plus depreciation margin, or the cash flow to sales margin. The choice among the margins depends on the firm's need to replace existing capital goods and on its ability to use net profits.

Consider again Sandy Collar, Inc., which operates at full capacity.[23] Table 3.16 summarizes what is known about the firm.

Four ratios derived from table 3.16 calculate the firm's SGR.

P = Sandy Collar's after-tax profit margin = 6 percent
R = The retention rate = 75 percent
A = The asset turnover ratio = 1.887 (derived as \$1 million of sales divided by \$530,000 of assets)
$\hat{T}$ = The asset to equity ratio (using the beginning of the period equity value)
= 1.927 (\$530,000 divided by \$275,000).

Sandy Collar's SGR equals the product of these four ratios:

$$SGR_{\text{Sandy Collar}} = P\ R\ A\ \hat{T} = .06 \times .75 \times 1.887 \times 1.927 = 0.1636$$

That is, Sandy Collar can grow by 16.36 percent without needing new outside funding. If Sandy Collar grows at a rate less (more) than 16.36 percent, it generates (requires) new funds.

Assuming that Sandy Collar's 1996 growth rate equals its SGR (16.36 percent), its 1997 balance sheet is shown in the second column of table 3.17. Compared to 1996, current and total assets both grow at the same 16.36 percent. Similarly, current liabilities other than bank debt, bank debt, and stockholders' equity all grow at 16.36 percent. In

TABLE 3.16. Sandy Collar, Inc., 1996 Sales and Selected Balance Sheet Items

Current sales = \$1,000,000
Expected sales = \$1,200,000
Net profit = \$60,000
Dividends = \$15,000

Current assets	\$280,000	Current liabilities	\$110,000
Net fixed assets	\$250,000	Bank debt	\$100,000
		Shareholders' equity	\$320,000
Total assets	\$530,000	Total liabilities and net worth	\$530,000

Note: Beginning of period equity equals \$320,000 − [\$1,000,000 × .06 × .75] = \$275,000.

that case, the two SGR assumptions hold. First, no new equity is sold. Retained earnings lead to an increase in stockholders' equity. Second, the capital structure is unchanged:

$$\frac{\text{Debt}}{\text{Equity}_{\text{OLD}}} = \frac{(\$110{,}000 + \$100{,}000)}{\$320{,}000} = \frac{\text{Debt}}{\text{Equity}_{\text{NEW}}}$$
$$= \frac{(\$128{,}000 + \$116{,}360)}{\$372{,}350} = 0.656$$

Sustainable Growth Rate without Bank Capital

In case the bank does not want to increase its credit line beyond \$100,000, a bankless SGR, SGR_{BL}, is calculated. To find SGR_{BL} for Sandy Collar, begin with a less intuitively appealing version of the SGR equation (2), shown as equation (2′).

$$\text{SGR} = \frac{P \times R \times (1 + L)}{t - P \times R \times (1 + L)} \qquad (2')$$

where
L = the total debt/equity ratio
= 0.656 = (\$110,000 + \$100,000)/\$320,000
t = the asset/sales ratio
= 0.53 = (\$530,000/\$1,000,000)

TABLE 3.17. Sandy Collar, Inc., 1997 Balance Sheet Items under Different Growth Rates

Which SGR	SGR Sales Growth of 16.36%	SGR_{BL} Sales Growth of 12.88%	SGR_{APP} Sales Growth of 12.00%	SGR_{min} Sales Growth of 11.32%
Current assets	\$325,800	\$316,064	\$313,600	\$311,696
Net fixed assets	\$290,900	\$282,200	\$280,000	\$278,300
Total assets	\$616,700	\$598,264	\$593,600	\$589,996
Current liabilities other than bank debt	\$128,000	\$127,468	\$123,200	\$110,000
Bank debt	\$116,360	\$100,000	\$100,000	\$100,000
Shareholders' equity	\$372,350	\$370,796	\$370,400	\$380,000
Total liabilities and net worth	\$616,700	\$598,264	\$593,600	\$590,000

Plugging values from table 3.16 into equation (2′) yields the original SGR estimate:

$$\frac{.06 \times .75 \times (1 + .656)}{.53 - [.06 \times .75 \times (1 + .656)]} = 16.36\%$$

Now, if the bank will not extend more credit, the debt-to-equity ratio, L, is replaced with a nonbank debt-to-equity ratio, L'.

$$\begin{aligned} L' &= \text{nonbank debt to equity ratio} \\ &= 0.344\ (\$110{,}000/\$320{,}000). \end{aligned}$$

Using L' in place of L in equation (2′) yields SGR_{BL}, which describes how fast a company may grow when (a) the firm cannot sell additional equity, (b) the firm wants to maintain its capital structure, and (c) the bank has cut the firm off from additional credit. SGR_{BL} equals

$$\begin{aligned} SGR_{BL} &= [.06 \times .75 \times (1 + .344)]/[.53 - [.06 \times .75 \times (1 + .344)]] \\ &= 12.88\%. \end{aligned}$$

If Sandy Collar's sales increase by its SGR_{BL}, 12.88 percent, its 1997 balance sheet is that shown in the third column of table 3.17. Here current assets and net fixed assets both grow at 12.88 percent, the SGR_{BL}. Bank debt remains constant at \$100,000; shareholders' equity increases by \$50,796 (4.5 percent of the new sales level, \$1,128,800), 15.87 percent. Current liabilities other than bank debt increase by 15.88 percent. As required, the new nonbank debt-to-equity ratio is unchanged at 0.344 (\$127,468/\$370,796).

A concern about SGR_{BL} is how it assumes that current liabilities other than bank debt, mostly trade payables, increase at a faster rate (15.88 percent) than the rate of increase in sales (12.88 percent). Few trade creditors may be willing to provide such generous support to an account that cannot convince its banker to extend additional credit. If trade accounts are unwilling to replace the bank as the firm's lender, it will be impossible for the firm to achieve the sales level described by SGR_{BL}.

An SGR keeping accounts payable proportionate to sales, SGR_{APP}, is calculated with equation (2″)

$$SGR_{APP} = \frac{P \times R}{t - AP/S - P \times R} \tag{2″}$$

where *AP/S* is the assumed constant ratio of accounts payable to sales. For Sandy Collar, *AP/S* equals 0.11. Plugging this value into equation (2″) yields

$$SGR_{APP} = \frac{.06 \times .75}{.53 - .11 - .06 \times .75} = 12.00\%$$

If Sandy Collar's sales increase by its SGR_{APP}, 12.00 percent, its 1997 balance sheet is that shown in the third column of table 3.17. Current and net fixed assets both grow at 12 percent, the SGR_{APP}. Bank debt remains constant at $100,000; shareholders' equity increases by $50,400 (4.5 percent of the new sales level, $1,120,000), and current liabilities other than bank debt increase by 12 percent. Note that if the bank insists that the bank line be reduced, the firm must grow at a rate less than 12 percent.

The final version of the SGR relates to a firm that cannot raise either new debt (of any kind) or equity and that cuts its dividend to zero (Platt, Chen, and Platt 1995). This firm can grow at only a minimal rate, the SGR_{min}

$$SGR_{min} = \frac{P \times S'}{A} = \frac{.06 \times \$1{,}000{,}000}{\$530{,}000} = 11.32\% \qquad (2''')$$

where S' is prior year's sales and A is total assets. The last column in table 3.17 depicts the balance sheet in this case. Here the only new financing comes from $60,000 worth of retained earnings. Both current and net fixed assets grow at SGR_{min} and together consume the full $60,000 available.

Each of the SGRs listed in table 3.18 should be evaluated by the turnaround manager even though only one SGR applies in a particular situation. As the degree of distress increases, the SGR decreases. SGR has a twofold importance: avoiding growth that increases the need for funds and managing growth to insure that each client provides a sufficient profit.

TABLE 3.18. Alternate Sustainable Growth Rates

Type	Constraints	Size for Sandy Collar, Inc.
SGR	No new equity and constant capital structure	16.36%
SGR_{BL}	Same as above plus no new bank debt	12.88%
SGR_{APP}	Same as above plus proportionate increase in accounts payable	12.00%
SGR_{min}	No dividends or new debt	11.32%

The Alternative to Growth

Additional funds needed highlight the relationship between growth and the need for additional capital to support higher levels of inventories, accounts receivable, and new capital equipment for operations running at full capacity. There are two reasons why companies in crisis or undergoing turnaround management should not grow. First, new sources of finance are probably not available; in fact, companies in crisis face demands for immediate repayment from creditors. It would be best to devise a scheme to repay creditors and reestablish good credit standing. Second, growth covers up fundamental problems such as cost issues and other evidence of mismanagement; in this case, it allows the firm to chase expenses with revenues.[24]

Table 3.19 highlights profit and current asset levels for different growth and cost-containment alternatives. In the worst case, with growth the firm grows and ignores its cost structure. Losses grow to $55 while an additional $35 of new funding is required. In contrast, a negative growth strategy, seen in the fourth column, produces $35 of free cash that can repay existing debts. No growth with controlled costs yields $50 to be applied to past debts and eliminates the loss. Combining the last two cases would yield negative growth and cost control, the best result for a company in crisis.

Adopting a no-growth strategy does not mean refusing a new profitable order. Instead, a new profitable order is accepted, and an existing less profitable order is abandoned. Activity-based costing (covered in chapter 11), is a tool to help companies know which orders, customers, or products are profitable.

Probably the best strategy for distressed firms is to (a) reduce costs, (b) raise product prices, and (c) reduce sales levels. The first action

TABLE 3.19. Comparing Profits and Current Assets under Different Growth and Containment Strategies

	Original	With Growth	Negative Growth	Controlling Costs and Current Assets
Sales	$1,000	$1,100	$900	$1,000
Cost	$1,050	$1,155	$945	$1,000
Profit	($50)	($55)	($45)	$0
Accounts receivable	$200	$220	$180	$175
Inventories	$150	$165	$135	$125
Required new funds		$35	($35)	($50)

reduces losses, the second raises revenues while leaving costs unchanged, and the third frees up current assets.

Measuring Performance with EVA™[25]

How is corporate performance measured in corporate renewal? Several traditional profitability ratios—the profit margin, return on assets, and return on equity (ROE)—that evaluate the strategic and financial success of managerial decisions have been discussed. The recent emergence of a new standard provides a different perspective on company performance.

The new standard begins with "market value added" (MVA), which measures the difference between the equity market's perception of a company's future cash flows (total market value) and the amount of money invested in the firm (total capital usage).

$$\text{MVA} = \text{Total market value} - \text{Total capital}$$

Wall Street sees a company with a positive (negative) MVA as making desirable (undesirable) investments. MVA rises when a company makes investments with discounted future cash flows exceeding the investment's total cost.[26]

MVA projects a company's future. Another concept, economic value added (EVA), measures profitability in a single year. Starting with operating income, EVA is determined by removing both taxes and a charge for total capital usage.

$$\text{EVA} = \text{EBIT} - \text{Taxes} - (\text{Total capital used} \times \text{Weighted average cost capital})$$

Total capital used is a concept peculiar to EVA analysis, and it is not found on the balance sheet. In calculating total capital usage, capital items usually labeled as expenses (like R&D or employee development costs) are added to total balance-sheet assets. This broader definition of capital provides a more comprehensive measure of how much money is invested in a firm. Weighted average cost of capital multiplied by total capital used is derived from known after-tax cost of debt and one of two estimates of the cost of equity:

1. using the capital asset pricing model found in any modern financial management textbook
2. using the historic premium of equity earnings over debt (about 6 percent)

EVA also invents an extra expense—capital costs—that refines the measurement of profitability.

Traditional profitability measures are reported in percentage terms. For example, a firm might have an ROE of 12.5 percent, indicating that its net income equaled 12.5 percent of its invested equity. In contrast, EVA is reported in dollar terms. That same firm might have an EVA of $120 million, indicating that it earned $120 million after accounting for taxes and invested capital. This $120 million equals the net profits earned in that year on the firm's investments.

MVA and EVA are associated in that MVA equals the discounted sum of all future EVAs; that is, a company's stock price exceeds its supply of capital (MVA) by an amount equal to the net present values of all of its investments (many EVAs).

$$\text{MVA} = \sum_{t=1...N} EVA \Big/ (1+i)^t$$

EVA is not defined or explained in most finance textbooks, and few financial managers know their firm's EVA or use EVA to motivate workers. EVA is, in fact, an old concept first mentioned by Alfred Sloan, the financial pioneer at General Motors.[27] EVA is significant because it may be used as a single management tool to reconcile capital budgeting decisions, conduct performance appraisals, and calculate bonus payments. EVA is expressed in dollars and cents, making it the consummate

TABLE 3.20. 1994 EVAs and MVAs ($ in millions)

1994 Rank	1989 Rank	Company	MVA 1993	MVA 1988	EVA 1993	EVA 1988	Profitability Index[a]
1	3	General Electric	$55,586	$17,854	$418	−$163	1.1
2	7	Coca-Cola	$53,175	$12,585	$1,355	$504	2.5
3	5	Wal-Mart	$45,907	$14,341	$1,056	$530	1.8
4	2	Merck	$29,408	$18,503	$1,625	$663	2.6
5	6	Philip Morris	$28,790	$13,404	$1,887	$664	1.7
996	998	Ford	−$2,374	−$5,459	−$1,216	$1,938	0.3
997	84	Digital Equipment	−$5,975	$2,179	−$1,842	$580	0.2
998	1,000	General Motors	−$6,802	−$19,628	−$7,593	−$3,502	0.0
999	8	RJR Nabisco Holdings	−$9,395	$11,793	−$2,134	$461	0.5
1,000	1	IBM	−$16,606	$19,338	−$6,797	−$556	0.5

Source: "Stern Stewart Performance 1,000" (1995)

[a]The profitability index equals the five-year average rate of return on capital divided by the five-year average cost of capital.

management tool to choose investment projects and judge a manager's performance. Unlike competing profitability measures, EVA measures the economic return on total invested capital net of a cost of equity funds. In a study of 1,000 firms conducted by Stern Steward, Inc., EVA explained over 50 percent of the change in their MVAs.[28]

Which companies have good EVAs and MVAs? Moreover, are EVAs and MVAs merely surrogates for other profitability measures? Table 3.20 presents the top and bottom five EVA companies out of the 1,000 firms grouped by Stern Stewart. Both groups of companies include household names. General Electric, with its $55.5 billion MVA—the difference between its market value and the amount of capital invested—is the top-ranked company in 1994. IBM is ranked last and has a negative MVA; five years earlier, IBM was the top-ranked MVA company in the United States. Between 1989 and 1994, IBM's MVA declined by $36 billion as the worldwide demand for IBM's mainframe computers plunged and the company took write downs. The last column in table 3.20 contains a profitability index that compares returns and costs of capital. High ratio values indicate better returns on capital relative to its cost. Top-ranked EVA/MVA companies have significantly better profitability indexes than low-ranked companies.

Is the information in EVA/MVA exclusive or unique, or does it merely replicate facts already embodied in traditional profitability measures such as ROE, profit margin, or EPS? This issue is explored in table 3.21, where the ten companies in table 3.20 are compared using three

TABLE 3.21. ROE, Net Profit Margin, and EPS for the 5 Best and Worst EVA Companies in 1994

1994 EVA Rank	Company	1993 ROE	1988 ROE	1993 Net Profit Margin	1988 Net Profit Margin	1993 EPS	1988 EPS
1	General Electric	17.1	18.3	7.4	6.9	$2.59	$1.88
2	Coca-Cola	47.7	34.3	15.7	12.5	$1.68	$0.71
3	Wal-Mart	21.7	27.8	3.5	4.1	$1.02	$0.37
4	Merck	21.6	42.3	20.6	20.3	$1.87	$1.02
5	Philip Morris	30.7	26.9	7.0	8.0	$4.06	$2.22
996	Ford	16.2	24.6	2.3	5.7	$2.28	$5.48
997	Digital Equipment	−5.1	17.4	−1.7	11.4	−$1.93	$9.90
998	General Motors	44.1	13.1	1.8	3.8	$2.13	$6.82
999	RJR Nabisco Holdings	−0.1	24.5	−0.1	8.2	−$0.05	$5.92
1,000	IBM	−42.8	13.9	−12.7	9.2	−14.02	9.27

Source: Standard & Poors Compustat.™

additional profitability measures. The comparative results are stunning. EVA brings to light new information not displayed by ROE, net profit margin, or EPS. EPS, which combines net income and number of outstanding shares, is least similar to EVA, but ROE and profit margin also bear little resemblance to EVA (General Motors' ROE and Ford's profit margin rank them as top-performing companies, while their EVAs rank them among the lowest).

We cannot dismiss the older profitability measures. But EVA/MVA's analytical insights should be added to the turnaround manager's repertoire.

EVA/MVA and the Privately Held Firm

MVA cannot be calculated for privately held firms because they lack market values. However, EVA, which uses EBIT, tax, capital-usage, and capital-cost information, can and should be derived for privately held companies, and the information should be assessed in conjunction with other ratios.

Exercise

1. Obtain an annual report from a public company and calculate its
    - degree of operating leverage for each of the past five years
    - degree of financial leverage for each of the past five years
    - degree of total leverage for each of the past five years
    - Altman Z
    - Platt and Platt probability using Robert Morris and Associates' data on industry averages. If that data is unavailable, assume that each ratio is either 20 percent above or 20 percent below its industry average
    - additional funds needed
    - sustainable growth rate
2. Obtain the firm's MVA and EVA from the *Journal of Applied Corporate Finance* and compare them with that firm's other profitability measures.

CHAPTER 4

Ethical and Legal Considerations in Financial Distress

This chapter explores some ethical and legal issues pertaining to liability, responsibility, corporate organization, and fraud that affect distressed companies. Beyond bad luck, bad management, and bad economic conditions, some Chapter 11 petitions filed by companies and individuals are frauds. Their purpose is to misuse the Bankruptcy Code to relieve the debtor of legally binding financial obligations. The cost of these frauds is borne by society as a whole. This chapter examines a range of fraud and near-fraud activities, as well as other issues that elicit ethical and legal concerns when firms in financial distress file for bankruptcy.

Consumer Fraud

Consumer fraud typically involves the abuse of credit cards. Credit card fraud is relatively easy to perpetrate and is rarely prosecuted. Instead, creditors absorb their losses because the amount of damages to any single creditor are generally insufficient to warrant the investment of much time or effort in the bankruptcy court. Legal officials generally look the other way because it is difficult for them to distinguish between willful acts of fraud and poor financial judgment.

Individuals intent on defrauding credit card companies acquire multiple credit cards from different issuers. Goods are purchased with each card up to its maximum credit limit. Since the consumer is relatively asset-free and with limited income, he/she is unable to repay this debt and files for bankruptcy.[1] In some cases, the debtor sells the acquired goods and diverts the cash to other purposes. Credit card companies mail out unsolicited credit cards because the loss ratio from frauds is infinitesimally small compared with their ordinary profits.

An even more insidious fraud scheme uncovered recently on the West Coast goes one step further.[2] Before filing for Chapter 11, the person sends a bad check (i.e., from an account with an insufficient balance) to the credit card company as payment. Unaware that the check will bounce, the company dutifully records the payment in its computer system and clears the account for more transactions. By carefully timing these activities, the person purchases goods equaling twice his/her credit limit, which he/she sells at a discount for cash before filing in bankruptcy court.

A person who commits "simple" credit card fraud and who files a Chapter 11 petition is likely to be relieved of responsibility for those obligations by the bankruptcy court. Thousands of persons, overlooking those who got into credit trouble through ignorance or because their circumstances changed, have defrauded society of as much as $50,000 each in this manner. If the fraud is not prosecuted, the only penalty is that for a period of seven years it is virtually impossible for the individual to acquire new credit cards.[3]

A credit card company may file an involuntary Chapter 11 petition against an individual who defaults on payment obligations. If the individual is notified of impending bankruptcy court hearings and is told to attend and represent his/her own interest but does not show up, then his/her obligations to the credit card company are not relieved, though he/she is relieved of debts to other creditors.

Business Fraud

The commercial version of credit card fraud is called a bust-out (Schifrin 1994). In a bust-out, a person forms a corporation, builds goodwill with suppliers by ordering and punctually paying invoices, then recoups funds by selling the goods at a discount to other vendors or customers. After creating enough trust, the criminal places a massive order, disposes of the goods, and then declares bankruptcy or simply vanishes. Few assets remain, and creditors recover nothing.

Experts estimate that bust-out losses surpass $1 billion per year. Even the largest companies succumb to this fraud; for example, General Motors suffered a loss in excess of $100 million from a dealer who sold cars to the public but never paid for them. Competitive industries under pressure to accept new customers without adequate credit checking are the most susceptible to a bust-out. One defense is to avoid supplying relatively new customers with an unreasonable quantity of goods. Beyond that, firms are at the mercy of unscrupulous individuals.

Accounting Frauds and Near Frauds[4]

The name Ponzi scheme comes from the classic swindle perfected by Charles Ponzi during the 1920s. Ponzi raised money from investors by promising them astronomical returns virtually overnight. At first he delivered on his promises by funneling money from new investors to his original investors. Word-of-mouth endorsements generated still more business. But eventually Ponzi absconded with most of the new investment dollars.

Another classic fraud was perpetrated by Anthony De Angelis, who in 1963 sold Wall Street $175 million of fictitious salad oil. De Angelis's scheme was simple but effective: he borrowed money secured by what were allegedly storage vats of salad oil but were actually vats filled with water covered by a thin layer of oil. He was apprehended after an audit uncovered the fraud. Few companies are as dishonest or daring as Ponzi or De Angelis. Yet the corporate renewal specialist must remain vigilant against accounting tricks perpetrated by desperate or greedy companies.

Howard Schilit is the father of forensic accounting, a field that he ingeniously documents in his 1993 book, *Financial Shenanigans.*[5] According to Schilit, managers are motivated to perpetrate accounting tricks for three fundamental reasons:

1. they benefit personally
2. implementation is easy
3. apprehension and punishment are unlikely

Clearly, avarice is a key part of the equation, but Schilit also blames GAAP (generally accepted accounting principles) for issuing rules requiring managerial interpretation and reacting too slowly to correct deficiencies in financial reporting.

Frauds often target net income. Schilit describes "seven major shenanigans" that affect net income.

Increasing Current Income

1. Booking revenue early.
2. Inventing revenue from fictional customers.
3. Using nonrecurring transactions.
4. Delaying paying expenses.
5. Hiding liabilities.

Increasing Future Income

6. Reporting current revenues in a later period.
7. Accelerating expense payments.

The first five shenanigans increase current income, while the last two move current income to the future. None is ultrasophisticated, and any unethical executive is capable of exploiting them. Schilit's book is readable and entertaining and is strongly recommended to serious students. It documents twenty tricks to watch out for.

Can outsiders such as investors detect accounting frauds before they become public? Despite Schilit's coaching, few can breach this subterfuge. But a turnaround manager with access to internal information should, upon commencing an engagement, immediately investigate whether accounting frauds have occurred.

Recent examples of accounting tricks commonly used in the frauds are examined in the next section, with company names included. In most instances, new management was installed; in other cases, the fraud was perpetrated by individuals and was not a general corporate conspiracy. Interested students can find other examples of corporate accounting fraud in daily business newspapers.

Reporting Income from Fictional Customers

Cascade International, Inc., a high-flying stock in 1990 and 1991, purportedly operated 150 cosmetic counters leased from department stores, seventeen cosmetics stores, and seventy women's clothing stores. Cascade's fraud was similar to De Angelis's phantom salad oil swindle. Investigators learned that while Cascade did in fact have seventy clothing stores, it had no cosmetic counters and only one cosmetic store. A new team of auditors detected the fraud when they attempted to visit a cosmetic counter located in the middle of a desert.

As the scandal broke, Victor Incendy, Cascade's chairman and CEO, vanished. He was charged with "two counts of first-degree grand larceny, seven counts of making false filings to the SEC, and four counts of scheming to defraud" (Woo and Pearl 1992). The company was charged with filing exaggerated claims about the size and value of its operations. In December 1991 it filed for bankruptcy and was liquidated.

Cascade brazenly had presented "audited" financial statements to the Bank of Scotland several months prior to the scandal and received two $5 million loans. The deception purportedly extended within the firm as well. One executive reporting to Incendy said that he was unaware of the fraud because, he "trusted the company's audited financial statements . . . [and because] Mr. Incendy was always able to produce cash from [the cosmetics division] when the company's money-losing clothing stores needed an infusion" (Pearl 1992). Incendy raised this cash by selling unauthorized and worthless stock.

Reporting Income from Potential Customers

Kendall Square Research Corporation was a luminary in the world of supercomputing, combining some of the best names and money in the venture-capital and high-technology industries. The firm filed for bankruptcy protection in 1995. In 1993, it restated its 1992 and its preliminary 1993 results as seen in table 4.1 (Bulkeley 1993). Kendall's misjudgment was in disobeying the accounting rule that a sale takes place only when the buyer assumes all risks and benefits of ownership. In Kendall's case, "buyers" often did not pay for products, and some buyers had no funding to ever be able to pay.

The misrepresentation required 57 percent of reported nine-month 1993 revenues to be restated. This is an archetypal story of a company stretching the truth in order to survive. Accepted supercomputer industry accounting practices report sales to customers intending to pay using money from government and foundation grants. Trying to appear more successful than its twenty competitors in the nascent supercomputer business, Kendall "included shipments to universities that don't have funding, shipments to distributors that don't have customers, and shipments where payment is contingent on the customer getting upgraded machines in the future" (Bulkeley 1993).

Kendall is not alone. Other high-technology firms recently revealed that they too have been overly aggressive in reporting sales (Berton 1994). The practice extends to all businesses. Signs exist to help the turnaround manager uncover these frauds. For example, MiniScribe Corporation, a software vendor that went bankrupt in the late 1980s, booked 50 percent of its quarterly sales on the last day of the year.

TABLE 4.1. Kendall Square Research Corporation Original and Revised Sales and Income Figures ($ in millions)

	Net Sales		Net Income	
	Original	Revised	Original	Revised
1992	$20.5	$16.3	($12.7)	($17.2)
1993:1–1993:3	$24.7	$10.6	NR[a]	NR[a]

[a]Not reported

Similarly, Zachary Shipley, Kendall's new CFO, revealed that "orders tended to bunch at the end of certain quarters" (Berton 1994). More imaginative businesspeople might spread fictitious sales throughout the year, so observing the bookings rate is not enough. Another clue to overly aggressive sales reporting is to find cash flow falling while reported revenues grow.

Overstating Inventories

F&C International, Inc., a flavor and fragrance company, reported in April 1995 that its chairman, Jon Fries, had been fired after "inventory discrepancies" that allegedly occurred with his knowledge (Milbank 1993). In July 1994 Gibson Greetings reported that it had discovered overstated inventories resulting "from an allocation of overhead variances in a manner inconsistent with generally accepted accounting principles" (Narisetti 1994). Phantom inventories also helped bring down Phar-Mor, Inc., a budding health and beauty aid retailer.[6] In Phar-Mor's case, the fraud appears to have been willful and designed to finance pet projects of a company executive, including the World Basketball Conference.

Overstated inventories not only exaggerate a company's assets but also reduce its cost of goods sold and thereby increase its reported income. Because the effects of inventory fraud permeate every financial report, the turnaround manager is likely to find that a client overstating inventories has other problems more severe then originally anticipated. (See chapter 11 for more discussion on this topic.)

Report Whatever You Want

Sunrise Medical, Inc., reported in January 1996 that it had "found evidence of fraudulent financial reporting" at one of its subsidiaries (Rundle 1996). It stated that the "improper accounting was concealed" by at least four people, including a vice president of finance and three "lower-level employees who worked in the subsidiary's accounting and management information system department . . . through a series of improper accounting entries and falsified computer reports" (Rundle 1996). As a result, net income for 1994 and 1995 was overstated by 16 percent ($4 million) and 37 percent ($11 million) respectively. Income statements and balance sheets apparently were compiled without regard to reality to meet ambitious management goals. These individuals may have been motivated because they received bonuses when the company met its goals.

Off-Balance-Sheet Losses

Another trick, though not actual fraud, occurs when nonfinancial companies depend disproportionately on investment rather than operating income. This occurs most often in firms whose businesses have slowed and whose managers decide to speculate in equity or commodity futures. In 1997, Occidental Petroleum acknowledged speculating in oil futures to enlarge the firm's revenues. Net results, reported as investment income on the income statement, are the only indication of these investments. Nowhere is the size of the investment reported.

Pier 1 Imports, Inc., restated its net income in January 1996 for six quarters as a result of large "unauthorized" trades by its investment adviser. All told, losses amounted to about $20 million. In a more prominent case, Gibson Greetings reported nearly a $20 million loss from "unauthorized" trading in interest-rate swaps by its banker, Bankers Trust.[7] The accounting trick is not that these trades take place but that investors do not perceive the degree of risk assumed by the company.

Shine up the Future with Nonrecurring Current Charges

Another nonfraud accounting ruse is perpetrated by companies that repeatedly take extraordinary charges for the same item; for example, the effect of corporate renewal. The deception is compounded if ordinary expenses are included in the write-off. Theoretically, companies take extraordinary write-offs when unusual expenses occur, such as when a factory is closed, a product line is discontinued, or workers are laid off. The write-off collects nonrecurring charges and reports them in a single quarter, thereby letting future quarterly reports highlight the company's operations and not its past failures.

According to some of America's leading companies, a company can write off corporate renewal expenses every year: Citicorp reported these expenses for six consecutive years from 1988 to 1993, Eastman Kodak took five charges between 1989 and 1994, and Westinghouse Electric took seven charges in the period 1985–94 (Smith and Lipin 1996).[8]

Even more worrisome is how some companies include ordinary expenses in reported nonrecurring expenses. For example, Borden, Inc., included "package modernization [expenses] and a new advertising campaign" in its restructuring charge, while Kmart included "store openings, enlargements, relocation and refurbishment [expenses]" (Smith and Lipin 1996). Perhaps even more perfidious, the spice company McCormick took a restructuring credit, which it added to its net income to reduce a previous restructuring charge, "without mentioning it in its earnings announcement" (Smith and Lipin 1996). Similarly, Apple Computer's return to profitability in October 1996 partly resulted from having taken a too large restructuring charge earlier in the year (Smith and Lipin 1996).

The Securities and Exchange Commission now requires companies to disclose restructuring credits. Moreover, the Financial Accounting Standards Board requires companies taking corporate renewal write-offs (for business shutdowns and employee layoffs) to disclose when the expenses have occurred and to more fully describe them.

Director Liability and Responsibility in Financially Troubled Companies

Changing Responsibilities

Directors of corporations have a fiduciary responsibility to exercise care and loyalty to the company and its shareholders. Shareholders elect directors to control their companies, and when they are displeased with performance, shareholders sue company directors. Today these suits are a constant threat and influence directors' decisions. Directors generally have a contractual relationship, not a fiduciary duty, to creditors. (For more information, see *Current Issues Facing Massachusetts Based Companies in 1993* 1993.)

"Care" means that the director educates him- or herself about issues facing the corporation before reaching a decision. "Loyalty" means that the director acts in good faith and in the best interest of the corporation and its shareholders. The business judgment rule (BJR) evolved in the courts to protect directors against lawsuits alleging incompetence. Not every decision that a director makes is correct. Sometimes, despite best efforts, a director makes mistakes. Economic conditions change, global incidents arise, or consumer tastes change. For example, without the BJR, Coca-Cola shareholders might have sued its directors since New Coke™ was not a success.[9] The BJR says that directors are not liable for bad decisions if they

- had been informed
- acted in good faith
- believed their decision was in company shareholders' best interest

Without the BJR, reasonable persons might refrain from joining a board of directors for fear that some decision would be wrong and they would be sued.

As a firm's financial condition deteriorates, the director's duty to shareholders may become subordinated to the director's responsibilities to the company's creditors. This is especially important because creditor and shareholder interests may conflict. When directors acquire this responsibility to creditor interests, they are characterized by the courts as "trustees for the corporation's creditors." Trustees are expected to exercise the same care and skill that anyone of ordinary prudence would exercise in dealing with personal property. That is, they are expected to protect the creditors' assets.

The advent of bankruptcy profoundly changes the director's assignment because the best interest of everyone with claims on the corporation must be considered. However, shareholders continue to elect and/or remove directors. Some courts have said that the director's obligations to creditors arises before a company fails; they believe that a director's fiduciary duties to creditors begin once the company is insolvent. Recently the Delaware Chancery Court found that such duties arise when the company is operating "in the vicinity of insolvency."[10] The corporate law judge, Chancellor William Allen, wrote that "in the vicinity of insolvency, a board of directors . . . owes its duty . . . to the community of interest that sustained the corporation . . . to maximize the corporation's long-term wealth creating capacity." He notes that the economic interests of shareholders and creditors diverge. For example, instead of repaying creditors using the corporation's liquid assets, shareholders accept unlimited risk to keep the business operating. Judge Allen argues that accepting this risk is inequitable because creditors might lose everything in order to give shareholders a small probability of gain. Directors must reflect on the corporation's financial condition, especially before making decisions affecting the value of assets. This becomes more important as the firm's financial state worsens.

Courts use two insolvency tests:

1. bankruptcy test—when a company's debts exceed the fair value of its assets
2. equitable insolvency test—if a company is unable to pay its debts as they mature.

The first definition is hard to calculate in practice, since the fair value of assets is unknown and subject to large estimation risk. The second definition is impractical, since a company can usually liquidate assets at low prices to make a current payment.

Liabilities Arising from the Board Itself

Company directors are responsible to shareholders for monitoring management's performance and ethical behavior. That responsibility includes choosing a CEO who serves at the pleasure of the board. An adroit board of directors will remove an incapable or unethical company officer.

The board itself may impede discharging a malfeasant CEO and failure to do so may create a liability for the board. A board may fail to take action because[11]

- the CEO controls the board
- the board is ignorant of events
- the board is afraid to take action

CEOs dominate boards of directors by restricting the number of external nonaffiliated directors and by filling board seats with employees whose prospective employment depends on the CEO's acquiescence, and if outsiders on boards are the CEO's friends or family, they may not be independent.

Boards remain uninformed of events critical to the corporation if they permit the CEO to control the agenda for board meetings; thus, serious matters may never be discussed. Unprepared board members harm themselves and their companies if they use up meeting time asking educational questions when they should be probing for truths. Similarly, board members abdicate their responsibility if they panic and refuse to take positive actions.

Membership on a board of directors is a major obligation, and persons agreeing to serve should consider whether they can do the job to the level expected by shareholders.

Corporate Organizational Form: Introducing the Limited-Liability Company

The form of corporate organization chosen for a particular company is determined by a variety of factors, including tax considerations and liability issues. Clearly, there is a desire to minimize both. A new structure, limited-liability companies (LLCs) (*Black* 1994), recently has joined the list of organizational forms:

- sole proprietorships
- partnerships

- S corporations
- C corporations[12]

Some important differences among these structures are described in table 4.2.

The principal reason that businesses incorporate probably is to minimize tort or contract liabilities.[13] Continued reliance by professional service firms on the partnership form of organization is surprising after major accounting firms paid out hundreds of millions of dollars in liability settlements following the savings-and-loan scandals of the 1980s. LLCs provide liability shields similar to S and C corporations. This explains their burgeoning popularity since the Internal Revenue Service ruled in 1988 that LLCs would be taxed as partnerships.[14] Most states have now enacted LLC legislation.

The problem with incorporating is that if there are more than thirty-five stockholders and a C corporation is formed, income is doubly taxed. The first round of taxes is paid by the corporation. Dividends received by shareholders out of corporate earnings after tax are then taxed a second time. S corporations avoid double taxation, but they are restricted to thirty-five or fewer shareholders. The LLC structure, as seen in table 4.2, provides significant advantages: no double taxation and an unlimited number of participants.

TABLE 4.2. Differences among Organization Types

Structure	No. of Owners	Foreign Ownership Allowed	Limited Liability	Double Taxation	Multiple Forms of Stock[a]	Can It Be Owned by a Corporation?	Does Tax Basis Increase with Retained Earnings?[b]
Sole proprietorship	1	Yes and No	No	No	NR	No	Yes
Partnerships	>1	Yes	No[c]	No	NR	No	Yes
S corporation	<36	No	Yes	No	No	No	Yes
C corporation	1–∞	Yes	Yes	Yes	Yes	Yes	No
Limited-liability companies	>1–∞	Yes	Yes	No	Yes[d]	Yes	Yes

[a]No means that a single class of stock is issued. Yes means that various forms of stock are possible, including preferred stock and multiple classes of common stock.

[b]Relevant only at the time a business is sold, merged, or liquidated.

[c]In a limited partnership, limited partners have limited liability, but the general partners have no limits on their liability.

[d]And income, deductions, and losses need not be allocated proportionately.

NR = relevant.

Capital is more available to C corporations since they raise funds from both the public and private equity markets and the public and private debt markets. The restriction on the number of shareholders limits S corporations to the private equity market. Regardless of organizational form, lenders require small-business owners to personally guarantee loans; this requirement defeats limited-liability provisions and safeguards their principal. LLCs also suffer from this limitation.

Only privately held companies are eligible to become LLCs. Should the LLC later desire to go public, there are no tax consequences for converting to a C corporation.[15] LLCs are taxed like partnerships (i.e., a pass-through of income without taxation) as long as they possess no more than two of the four corporate characteristics listed in table 4.3. Limited liability probably is the one characteristic LLCs are reluctant to waive. An LLC can possess at most one other characteristic from the remaining three in table 4.3. The LLC often has a limited lifetime, with a termination date included in its charter.[16] Decentralized management is harder to achieve; one strategy is to have the LLC owned by a corporation so that the LLC itself exerts no management control. It is easy to restrict transferability of ownership; for example, sale of an LLC interest might only be allowed if positive earnings are achieved for two successive years.

Small-business owners should review the advantages of LLCs, possibly the perfect hybrid combining the versatility of a partnership with the limited liability of a corporation.

Pension Benefits in Distressed and Bankrupt Companies

Pension plans fund workers' retirement and supplement Social Security payments. Most pension plans historically were defined-benefit plans to which the employer contributed each pay period. More than forty-two

TABLE 4.3. Corporate Characteristics

Characteristic	Definition
Unlimited life	Bankruptcy, retirement, and similar changes do not affect the continuity of the enterprise
Centralized management	Decisions are reached by a subgroup of owners or their appointees, such as a board of directors
Limited liability	Owners' liability is limited to their invested capital
Transferability of ownership	Ownership can be sold to anyone at any time

million workers still belong to 65,000 defined-benefit plans (Beyer 1993). However, defined-benefit plans are anachronisms, and no new plans have been created in decades. Recently, self-directed retirement plans such as 401(k) plans are available to workers. An advantage of individually regulated plans is that workers may overemphasize their contributions during years of surplus income and reduce them later, when their expenses are higher.

In 1974, the Pension Benefits Guaranty Corporation (PBGC), a wholly owned U.S. government corporation, was established by the Employee Retirement Income Security Act (ERISA). The PBGC guarantees uninterrupted (though not necessarily full) pension benefits payments. It permits underfunded pension plans to be terminated only in cases of "severe financial hardship." Prior to ERISA, companies funded or did not fund pension plans at their own discretion; ERISA created a minimum funding contribution for ongoing pension plans. Companies that violate the minimum funding contribution are assessed an excise tax by the IRS. All single-employer defined-benefit pension plans pay annual insurance premiums of less than $100 per capita to the PBGC to help support the continued payment of pensions to retired persons whose pension plans have been terminated without sufficient assets.[17] PBGC guarantees monthly pension benefits of about $2,500.

The key to ERISA's vision of corporate responsibility for pension plan funding is the "control group," any collection of people or companies owning at least 80 percent of an underfunded company's equity. A control group is held to be jointly and severally responsible for maintaining a pension plan even if the group members never had any association with the plan. For example, Continental Airlines was viewed as part of Eastern Airlines' control group when Eastern went bankrupt with an underfunded pension. PBGC settled this case with Continental Airlines.

A defined-benefit pension plan may be terminated if it does not violate a collective bargaining agreement and if

- it has sufficient assets to pay all benefits or
- the plan sponsor and all members of its control group are in financial distress.

ERISA defines financial distress as Chapter 7 liquidation or Chapter 11 reorganization with the bankruptcy court deciding the plan must be terminated if there is an inability to remain in business unless the plan is terminated or if the company has a declining workforce for whom continued pension costs are oppressive.[18] The PBGC loses its authority over a corporation once it exits the control group. Hence, ERISA provides the

PBGC with the ability to terminate an underfunded plan if the control group is splitting up.

PBGC is not involved when a funded pension plan is terminated. Generally, the plan sponsor distributes the plan's assets by purchasing an annuity from an insurance company. At that point, the sponsor and the control group have no further pension liability. In contrast, terminating an underfunded plan creates a claim against the sponsor and its control group.

In bankruptcy proceedings, a PBGC claim frequently is the largest single claim. The claim is calculated as the difference between the plan's assets at the date of termination and the present value of vested accrued benefits at the date of termination. It is called an employer liability claim. The size of the employer liability claim depends heavily on the discount rate used in calculating present values. Judge Burton Lifland, chief bankruptcy judge for the Southern District of New York, ruled that the discount rate should be that rate earned by a reasonably prudent investor.

The most critical question related to employer liability claims is their priority status in bankruptcy proceedings. The debtor, other creditors, and the PBGC may not agree on the status of this claim. The status, at least in the eyes of the PBGC, depends on whether the termination date precedes or is subsequent to the bankruptcy filing, as demonstrated in table 4.4.

In each instance, the PBGC has staked out the high ground; that is, if it is awarded a priority status, its claim is relatively high versus that of other claimants. Administrative claims arise from services performed for the estate, and PBGC opponents argue that such claims arise from prepetition services conducted by employees and should be considered general unsecured claims.

This first part of the book has covered some of the basic issues in the field of corporate renewal. The next part, beginning with chapter 5, focuses on implementing crisis resolution and turnaround management.

TABLE 4.4. PBGC Claim Status (subject to court decisions)

Termination Date	Claim Perfected	Priority Status
Prepetition	Yes	Secured
Prepetition	No	Unsecured tax claim
Postpetition	Not Applicable	Administrative

Part 2
Implementation

CHAPTER 5

Turnaround Analysis

This chapter offers a detailed analysis of a number of methods and techniques affecting crisis resolution and turnaround management. These include approaches to management, organizational change, compensation, the role of a board of directors in turnaround, financing and production, and accounting as a management tool. The focus of this chapter is on implementing change.

Is a Turnaround Possible?

Distressed companies, like sick people, cannot all be cured. Knowing which companies are salvageable and which are beyond hope is a skill the turnaround manager needs. Companies in the latter category should be operated so as to maximize creditors' return following a liquidation or merger with a successful partner.[1] Postponing a closeout strategy greatly diminishes the enterprise's terminal value if customers abandon the firm and business relationships deteriorate. Hiring a corporate renewal specialist soon enough may avoid merger or liquidating the distressed firm at fire sale prices. And if the company is salvageable, the sooner the "company doctor" arrives, the sooner a palliative is applied.

Of companies that are not hopeless, only a portion will recover. Some turnarounds fail despite the best efforts of the turnaround manager. In an informal survey conducted during the 1996 national meeting of the Turnaround Management Association, I asked what proportion of their engagements achieved a corporate recovery. The results suggest that

- about 20 percent of all distressed companies recover
- at least 33 percent of all distressed companies are immediately classified as hopeless
- about 50 percent of companies originally classified as salvageable are saved

Managers of distressed companies should assume that their companies are in the top group and seek early professional help.

The best indication that a failing company has a reasonable chance for permanent recovery is the presence of three characteristic attributes.

1. a core business capable of generating cash flow, preferably showing a positive current EBIT and the ability to meet future challenges
2. a new source of finance, preferably long term
3. a management team capable of assuming operating control of the firm

A permanent core business is the quintessential ingredient of a successful turnaround. A core business has

- a proven product
- a pipeline of newer products
- loyal customers or a steady influx of new customers
- a reliable source of material supply
- sufficient stores of equipment to minimize near-term investment requirements
- a cooperative workforce

A core business either currently produces positive cash flow or can achieve cash breakeven after controlling costs or enhancing revenues. Operating income, EBIT, is the surest sign that a business is salvageable since interest expenses that turn EBIT into negative net income can be removed with reorganization.

Distressed businesses frequently contain a core business plus other possibly unrelated businesses added after the original business's initial success. Small business entrepreneurs and Fortune 500 companies alike commonly expand beyond their original core. Sometimes the expansion succeeds, and the new business dominates the original core. For example, Zenith, a radio manufacturer, now derives most of its revenues from the manufacture of televisions and cable control boxes. At other times, an expansionary strategy leads to failure, diluting the organization's resources or causing cash flow to dry up if the core business loses its competitive edge with management focused elsewhere.

Like a chef peeling a spoiled onion, the turnaround manager closes failed and failing businesses until the core business is revealed.[2] During the crisis resolution stage, the peeling process follows the triage philosophy, saving the relatively healthy at the expense of the mortally wounded, and jettisoning divisions, products, or people with negative cash flow. The turnaround or transformation stages require less aggressive tactics.

Who would want to lend money to a distressed business? Character and reputation are key factors considered in lending, and distress contributes to neither. The presence of a corporate renewal specialist may unlock capital sources especially if the current management team is perceived as unqualified, uncooperative, or the cause of the difficulties. The turnaround manager prepares a corporate renewal plan analogous in many ways to a business plan for a new business. The plan describes the company's troubles, how to remedy them, how to pay creditors, and how to avoid future problems. When a troubled company has a turnaround plan bankers may be lenient regarding loan covenants and repayment schedules, and may even allow additional lending.

The final attribute necessary to achieve a successful turnaround, good management, is the most problematic of the three, though it is not an issue when distress arises from external causes. The problem is to find, and persuade the board of directors to hire, a good permanent manager. Distressed businesses very often are small family-owned enterprises whose success came through a combination of hard work and careful control. Continued growth produces issues that the entrepreneur or his/her heirs may be unqualified to solve and unprepared to delegate to competent non-family managers. Public companies, too, are prone to "bad manager" problems when the board of directors is not independent and impartial. The corporate renewal specialist must deal with management ascension and replacement issues while simultaneously removing operating or financial obstacles.

Common Turnaround Managerial Styles

Turnaround managers embody a variety of individual styles, some are hard-nosed slash-and-burn experts, others are holistic healers or no-nonsense practical managers. Choosing the best turnaround manager for a particular situation is the critical first task of current management, the board of directors, or the U.S. trustee. While a number of important factors input that decision process, Table 5.1 surveys the types of engagements best suited to each type of turnaround manager. The slash-and-burn agent is best in a hurried downsizing, the holistic manager is best seeking solutions from all team member's inputs, and the practical manager is best at creating a structured and smoothly functioning organization.

In addition to stylistic differences, each turnaround manager exhibits different skills and attributes:

- good listener
- motivates people
- facile with numbers
- good negotiator
- involved in day-to-day business
- develops good control mechanism
- optimism

No individual possess all these traits at one time; for that reason, turnaround teams composed of several (i.e., three to six) persons are common.

The corporate renewal specialist learns what is wrong by being a good listener. How else could an individual with no industry background and no experience at a firm discover in several days how a good firm went bad? Interviews should start on the loading dock: shipping and receiving personnel know which products are hard to keep in stock, which are returned unopened, which have quality problems, and which suppliers ship late or ship defective parts. Other good listening spots are the factory floor, secretarial desks, and the lunchroom. Line and staff managers are vital parts of the fact-finding effort too, but self-interest may cloud their veracity.

An early task for the turnaround manager is restoring employee motivation. Bibeault (1982) recommends assuming that an individual's motivation parallels the company's current condition and carefully matches worker motivation and company turnaround cycles. Using my corporate renewal triad, company health and personal motivation are

TABLE 5.1. Choosing a Type of Turnaround Manager

Issue	Type of Turnaround Manager Chosen
Persistent negative cash flow	Slash and burn
Persistent negative EBIT	Slash and burn
Plunging sales	Slash and burn
Poor morale	Holistic
Low quality	Holistic
Slow design or innovation response	Holistic
Inadequate controls	Practical
Inadequate strategy	Practical
Inadequate accountability	Practical

matched, as shown in table 5.2. During the crisis-resolution phase, regenerating lost motivation is a difficult but critical task. First, trust must be reestablished. The corporate renewal specialist creates an honest environment in which accurate information is shared with workers. Then, linkages between the company's health and survival and the employees' own welfare are clarified. Restoring motivation is easier in the turnaround management phase of corporate renewal; during corporate transformation, motivational issues are addressed by changing the incentive system.

Financial analysis skills are needed to extract information from the distressed company's financial statements. The turnaround team usually contains a CPA or CMA. Of course, corporate renewal involves far more than managing by the numbers, but it cannot be done without numbers. Stephen Gray of the Recovery Group describes the three areas of specialization of financial analysts as balance sheet, profit and loss, and cash flow: the first is knowing how to reduce debts, the second is expertise at achieving breakeven, and the third is managing the cash. Andre Laus, Gray's partner, adds that the cash flow management gives the company time to allow the balance sheet and profit statement to be fixed.

Corporate renewal usually involves asking someone to give up something important to them, like wages or benefits. Negotiating skills are essential. A good negotiator understands how to listen, judge emotions, and compromise. Remember the fairy tale in which the sun and the wind tried to get a man to remove his jacket.[3] The man was willing; what was needed was a winning strategy. Similar planning is required to induce a person to work for a lower wage or fewer benefits, a landlord to lower the rent or shorten a lease, a supplier to reduce the unit price, a customer to pay bills more quickly, or a creditor to discount a payable. Some concessions come smoothly, others follow pitched battles. Without negotiation skills, corporate renewal is infeasible.

It may appear odd to include taking charge and "getting one's hands dirty" as essential turnaround skills. But an effective turnaround requires

TABLE 5.2. Company and Personal Motivational Conditions

Company Condition	Motivation
Corporate transformation	Strong but unstable
Turnaround management	Torn but renewable
Crisis resolution	Crushed

intimate knowledge. Nothing substitutes for what is learned by talking one on one with employees, vendors, creditors, and customers. Albert Dunlop, a most successful turnaround manager, talks with constituents and immerses himself in the business most of the day.[4] Peter Alcock argues that this knowledge facilitates strategic change, which he feels is where corporate renewal adds value.

Accounting controls reveal surprises before they erupt (see the accounting section in this chapter). Accounting control systems establish measures to evaluate the operating process. Using these measures, upper management can hold operating managers responsible and motivate them with an incentive system. Systems should monitor inventories, receivables, capital expenditures, payables, and cash.

Optimism is intrinsic to corporate renewal. It is an essential perspective while ordering layoffs, reducing wages and benefits for active and retired workers, and negotiating with creditors. An optimist is someone who perceives these activities as not firing fifty workers but saving the jobs of the remaining one hundred.

Turnaround Philosophies

Two turnaround styles, slash and burn and holism, are manifestations of underlying philosophies. Slash and burn is better known, owing to the media's acerbic portrayal of the recovery process wherein people are fired wholesale without regard to their length of service, age, or welfare. A more accurate portrayal of what transpires in a slash-and-burn turnaround is that every aspect of the business—people, plants, products, and processes—is evaluated, and only those making a sufficient positive contribution are retained. The slash-and-burn philosophy assumes that after a period of success, businesses grow sloppy and lazy. Fixing them entails removing superfluous resources and divisions. When a slash-and-burn turnaround is conducted during a crisis, evaluation and dismissal happen so fast that the impression is that human suffering is disregarded. But the goal is to save a business. Slash and burn is probably the best philosophy in a crisis.

The second philosophy, holism, regards poor communications, low morale, and lack of cooperation as responsible for distress. Holistic turnarounds seek employee support and work to imbue them with team spirit. In the words of one turnaround manager, "I gather all the employees together in one room and ask them to hold hands and pull together to help me find a way to save the company and all their jobs." Holism refutes the notion that the company is unhealthy; instead, it views the situation as resulting from the various resources failing to work together.

This approach saves jobs by fixing problems rather than downsizing the jobs away. Holistic turnarounds are best suited for companies in the turnaround management or corporate transformation mode.

Promoting Organizational Change

Proper corporate renewal is a daily ritual, carried out by constantly asking two fundamental questions:

- what are we doing wrong?
- what could we do better?

Corporate renewal's dual objectives are to override complacency and self-satisfaction and to seek constant improvement. In this environment, change is both welcome and frequent. The standard operating procedure found in rigid companies is replaced by an evolutionary structure. Few companies go through these exercises because most lack the required courage and vitality. Instead, signs of distress are overlooked until the underlying disease is so advanced that quick action is essential—i.e., a crisis arrives. In a crisis, there is no time to survey the company systematically and recommend a program of gradual change; instead, the crisis manager is forced to be an agent of rapid change.

All change, whether deliberate or hurried, threatens entrenched individuals and groups who fear the loss of advantage. Rapid change is especially worrisome, since it comes all at once and it allows insufficient time to rationalize the transition. Experienced employees are useful allies in a change situation. The turnaround manager must assuage their fears and induce their cooperation in the change process. Allowing their concerns to widen into explicit opposition jeopardizes the entire operation.

Change encompasses everything from minor modifications of discrete activities like how buyers select fashions or the frequency of emptying lockboxes to companywide reengineering, restructuring, or total quality management efforts. Human nature is such that resistance to change increases

- the less often it is accomplished
- the more startling the change
- the older the participants
- the less cogent the description of what is to come
- the more varied its effects among participants

A change effort is more likely to succeed if common sense and understanding are used, if its ramifications are outlined in comprehensible terms, and if injured parties are treated well. Simply instituting a change policy is insufficient; gaining the cooperation and support of employees is essential.

Wyatt Company (*Best Practices in Corporate Renewal* 1993) surveyed executives at companies that engaged in corporate renewal in both the 1980s and 1990s. Their study determined that 74 percent of companies responding to the survey downsized their operations (got smaller), while 69 percent reorganized (fit things together differently). The motivation for change was overwhelmingly to reduce costs and expenses (90 percent of respondents) and to improve profitability (85 percent). Sixteen other goals were cited, ranging from increasing a competitive advantage (64 percent) to reducing vulnerability to takeovers (5 percent).

Change is characterized as either repetitive or radical. Repetitive change has a track record; its outcome is expected. For example, a multidivisional company pleased with the results of an early retirement program offered in one division extends the offer to other divisions. Divisional responses vary, but the range is determinate. Change is repetitive whether the knowledge source is oneself or the shared experiences of others. By contrast, radical change applies to totally new ideas whose outcomes are unknown. Uncertainty makes radical change more costly and risky than repetitive change. Radical change becomes repetitive change when insights are gained from similar companies' experiences. Direct competitors may withhold confidential information, but consultants' memories serve the same end.[5]

Change targets may be the whole company, a division, a department within a division, or particular individuals, such as engineers. The choice of change targets depends on exigencies confronting the company as well as available resources and time. The more comprehensive the target, the more costly, complex, and uncertain the results. Companywide change, even on a single issue, faces a wide range of values, cultures, and experiences, which raises the stakes. In contrast, change at the bottom, like changing how engineers are compensated, confronts fewer idiosyncrasies.

The Change Agent

The person leading the change effort is the change agent who may be an internal employee or a consultant hired to lead the exercise. Choosing between internal and external agents depends on the change target, the scope of the change, and its repetitive or radical nature. If costs are unimportant, introducing an external professional is probably a good idea. The change agent's responsibilities are to

- communicate corporate goals
- work with a team to identify problems and solutions
- understand and pacify fears and hostilities of affected parties
- inspire affected persons to join the change
- complete the change
- impart the change mentality to others

The change agent is the designer and cheerleader. Both responsibilities are important because valuable advice that is ignored is wasted.

A good strategy helps the change agent gain acceptance of his/her ideas. Chances for success are improved when the company adopts these four precepts.[6]

1. The order to produce change must emanate from the CEO or the board of directors.[7] Power breeds acceptance and support.
   a. The change agent needs sufficient power to complete the task.
   b. The directive must be unambiguous and its general principles widely disseminated to avert resistance.
2. The change program should be based on a clearly articulated vision or agenda delineating an outline for the future.
   a. A team of internals should design, direct, and defend the plan.
      i. Too large a group is ineffectual; too small a group lacks sufficient knowledge and may not present all views.
   b. Ideas contributed by affected individuals and groups should be included, though the change agent must control the agenda by adding missing elements and removing self-serving suggestions.
3. Forces that derail changes must be neutralized.
   a. Intractable employees must be discharged.
   b. Processes that impede change must be modified.
   c. Support is gained by communicating early successes.
4. The change concept must be mainstreamed to make it self-perpetuating.
   a. Systems and incentive structures should be reproducible.
   b. The message must be spread to other units.

Companies doing corporate renewal every day have institutionalized the process by following the four precepts of authority, vision, buy-in, and extension. Change must always be purposeful, and its disruptions and pains balanced by positive results.

The success of a change program also is influenced by how and where it is initiated. The next section discusses the best ways to introduce change.

Introducing Change: Leavitt's Four Approaches

Getting people to accept change is never easy. They understand intellectually the necessity for change, but emotionally they prefer that someone else do it. Resistance to change arises when the proposal is undiplomatic.[8] Finding a tactful approach simplifies the entire process. Harold Leavitt (1987) described four ways to introduce change. These are shown in table 5.3.

Suppose that an airline's profits and market share are down. Pricing and route structure issues are rejected as culprits because of the industry's oligopolistic market structure and healthy overall performance. A survey reports low customer satisfaction and loyalty. An internal investigation of employee attitudes toward customers reveals a systematic pattern of insolent and disrespectful behavior. A change is imperative. The least diplomatic approach presents employees with evidence and demands that they change their behavior. Resistance is inevitable. Each of Leavitt's four approaches offers a more diplomatic approach to attain change.

The structural approach modifies corporate policies. Corporate policies circumscribe employee behavior and maintain procedures and policies to guide employees in every situation. However, deficient guidelines yield contrary results. The airline may have focused too intensely on cost control and too little on customer management. Relaxing existing rules may greatly improve customer satisfaction. For example, the rule stipulating a $5.75 maximum expenditure per passenger on meals can be relaxed on flights of duration of three hours or more, or daily newspapers can be distributed on morning flights.

The second approach, the technological, is more dynamic. It re-

TABLE 5.3. Ways to Introduce Change

The Approach	Example Procedure
Structural	Implement new rules and policies
Technological	Reengineer the company
Task-based	Move to a total-quality-management orientation
People-based	Provide incentives to induce participation

Source: Leavitt 1965

shapes the entire process of building and delivering a product. Reengineering institutes change technologically. Greater improvement is possible with technologically based change programs, but these risk alienating employees and destroying the product.[9] The outcome of a reengineering exercise might be that business and other full-fare travelers are catered to with their own check-in counter, waiting room, early boarding privileges, and better meals.

Task-based approaches to change look to the individual. For example, the airline can empower employees who have continual customer contact to be more accommodating. Rules and regulations are rewritten to allow

- frequent travelers to be upgraded into first class on a space-available basis
- large groups to prebook seating arrangements
- tickets to be cashed in and reticketed for a small fee
- employees to use their discretion to relieve disagreeable circumstances

These revisions appeal to both employees and customers; consequently, they are likely to succeed. The approach is indirect since the employee is not disciplined over his/her past behavior that led to the problem, but the cultural change it promotes minimizes future problems.

The last approach to change, the people-based one, is more direct. It achieves change by improving the employee's skills and attitudes. The employee is educated in both what and what not to do, cautioned to avoid detrimental behavior, and taught better manners. This approach may halt further injury to the airline's reputation, but it will not reverse previous damage.

Which of Leavitt's approaches is most appropriate depends on the problem at hand, the company, its corporate renewal protocol, and its employees. Personality interactions determine which strategy is most successful. Moreover, Leavitt's four approaches are interrelated; changes in any one lead to changes in the other three.

Lewin's Model of Change

One of the first social psychologists, Kurt Lewin, developed a model of organizational change (1951) that explains how companies should filter change through their organizations. Lewin perceived three distinct phases of change: motivation, demonstration, and inauguration. During the motivational phase, the current system is scrutinized and exposed as unsatisfactory. The employee learns that change is necessary. During the demonstration phase, a new approach is shown to employees and its benefits are noted. During the inauguration phase, the new system replaces the old. Lewin's model humanizes the change process by recognizing that the employee's needs and fears must be taken into account. He encourages the change agent to positively reinforce employee gains.

Success and Failure of Change Efforts

Change faces a variety of impediments. Most change efforts are less successful than anticipated. The Wyatt study found that the principal deterrents to organizational change are employee resistance and a dysfunctional corporate culture.[10] Resistance arises if communications break down. Management's responsibilities are to dispel anxieties and foster a climate that unifies the needs of the company and its employees.

For nine out of ten restructuring objectives, Wyatt found that fewer than half of all companies met their organizational change goals; the exception, reducing costs and expenses, was achieved by 61 percent of companies (Stewart 1994). Not only did most change efforts fail to produce the desired results, but many introduced deleterious consequences: 62 percent created workload problems, 56 percent adversely impacted morale, and 52 percent lowered the workers' commitment to the company. The lesson is that companies must approach change with caution and rely on expert help whenever it is available.

Questions

1. How would you select members of the change team? Is choosing one person per group in the organization preferred to selecting the best individuals? Will the composition of the change group affect the final change program?
2. Describe a situation in which each of Levitt's four approaches to change is best suited.
3. As a change agent, how could you increase employee receptivity to your ideas? Are there other steps that decrease the resistance to your ideas?
4. Describe anticipated employee resistance to a change and then prepare a company response to it.

Compensation Systems

Redesigning incentive systems to reward and punish behaviors plays an important role in corporate renewal efforts by focusing attention on ways to motivate employees. A study by Buck Consultants (Buchholz 1996) reported that at Fortune 1000 companies the proportion of total bonus compensation paid to hourly workers grew from 4.5 percent in 1993 to 7.8 percent in 1997, while the proportion of Fortune 1000 companies using bonuses grew from 26 percent to 37 percent during the same period. Incentive pay is even more important for managerial workers. Middle manager bonuses averaged 10 to 17 percent of base salary in 1996, while those paid to executives often exceeded 100 percent (Buchholz 1996). The next section examines the objectives and designs of alternate compensation systems.

The Objective of Compensation Systems

Compensation systems establish a framework for wage and benefit packages paid to various types of workers employed by a firm. Formal compensation systems may not be used in smaller or newly organized firms; their informal systems either may reward all workers about equally or may provide a different package for each worker. As companies mature, they are forced to adopt formal compensation plans.

Three ideas underlie compensation plans: the psychology of motivation, contracts, and our system of ethics. Motivational theory evolved from the original Freudian notion of *instinct theory* (i.e., behavior depends on inherited instincts, not rational decision making) into frameworks such as *reinforcement* or *cognitive theory.* Reinforcement theory argues that behavior is governed by learning and is based on memories of rewards and punishments bestowed on prior activities. In contrast, cognitive theory argues that behavior corresponds to one's view of the future and is goal oriented. The two dominant compensation paradigms, the Hay compensation system and the principle of pay for performance, are rooted in these contrasting theories. Hay systems display a sequence of compensation matrices as motivational devices to induce employees to work hard and gain advancement, while pay-for-performance systems apply a "carrot-and-stick" approach.

Contracts define the work relationship between employer and employee. They may be verbal (implicit) or written (explicit). Acs and Gerlowski (1996) define four characteristics common to all labor contracts:

1. they describe voluntary exchanges
2. they identify motivations and rewards
3. they can be modified
4. they are relational and incomplete, i.e., they do not account for every possible eventuality

It is especially important that contracts be relational since neither party possesses complete information.[11] For example, neither knows the other's current health or future plans. High transactions costs are incurred if either party wants to acquire additional information, for example, by requiring and paying for physical examinations each year. Sampson (1995) argues that contracting costs, including transaction costs, are reduced when trust becomes an essential part of the labor relationship. Kim and Mauborgne (1995) reason that managers create trust by guaranteeing that decisions are fair, subordinates are included in decision making, and an appeals system exists.

Ethical standards vary among people, cultural groups, and nations. Hence, it is wrong to characterize someone's behavior as unethical simply because it is unlike the conduct one finds typical. However, it is clear that ethical business behavior promotes and does not impair future business transactions. That notion is pivotal to the creation of an ethical compensation system. After consummating the compensation system, both parties should feel that they want to continue the relationship. The employer needs to be fair and reasonable if it wants to protect its reputation as a provider of good jobs.

Compensation systems

- motivate workers to achieve attainable incentives and corporate performance goals
- help workers define career goals and paths
- rationalize pay differences between employees in the same job classification
- assign (though do not rationalize) pay differences between job classifications
- guide managers in promoting individuals
- provide a framework for collective bargaining negotiations

Most companies apply either a highly structured and impersonal Hay system (discussed in the next section) or a more individualized merit-based pay system. Hay systems show up in unionized operations and in companies unable or unwilling to respond to each individual's needs.[12] By contrast, pay-for-performance systems are indispensable tools for companies that expect every employee to perform at 100 percent; companies that repair historic problems through corporate renewal are likely candidates for pay-for-performance programs.

Each compensation system is best suited for specific circumstances, not equipped for every contingency. Costly compensation system mistakes arise when the system in place becomes inappropriate for the circumstances; for example, after an influx of new competitors or following a successful unionization vote. Ill-suited compensation systems materialize when companies expand, shrink, or face changing needs. Soon after beginning an engagement, the turnaround manager examines a company's compensation policy to verify that employees are receiving the right signals.

A fascinating example of how material harm befalls a company with the introduction of the wrong compensation system is seen in the rapid decline of a once high flyer after its acquisition by an older well-established firm. The culture at Data Resources, Inc. (DRI), the pioneering economic consulting firm in Lexington, Massachusetts, sanctioned the payment of unusually high salaries to its cadre of talented young professionals as a reward for their extraordinary achievements and dedication. The firm's growth was explosive. In 1980, McGraw-Hill, the large publishing empire, acquired DRI for $103 million. McGraw-Hill objected to thirty-year-old managers at DRI earning more than editors with twenty years of experience at its mainstay *Business Week* magazine and imposed a new pay system on DRI that backed away from the concept of pay for performance. Not long afterwards, DRI's growth rate faltered, and McGraw Hill's management questioned why it had been lured into purchasing DRI.

For managers, especially the turnaround manager, the incentive component of pay systems is most critical since

- underperforming employees may be partially responsible for the business' condition
- the underperformance problem might be cured by modifying the compensation system

During periods of financial distress, original wage and work rules are often recontracted to reshape the firm's cost structure and possibly imbue a new work culture. Gilson and Vetsuypens (1993) even found recontracting among executives of distressed enterprises: more than half of their sample of CEOs of financially distressed firms experienced nearly 50 percent reductions in their cash compensation *each year* during a period of financial reorganization. Nonexecutive compensation also decreases during such periods, though by smaller percentages. Recontracting occurs even at healthy firms when new incentive systems are required; for example, United Airlines' pilots agreed to productivity and compensation modifications to permit the carrier to combat low-cost rivals. As a result of the compromise, the ranks of unionized pilots increased.

The Hay Compensation System

The prevalent wage policy in corporate America, the Hay system, is named after its developer, Edward Hay, who worked at General Foods nearly fifty years ago. Under a Hay pay system, each job carries a specific wage, and employees are promoted to higher-paying jobs as rewards. Most companies separate their list of occupations into numerous job classifications. Each classification has its own Hay schedule. The Hay compensation schedule is comprised of many tiers, each of which may have a number of steps. Under a Hay pay system, each employee is placed in a specific wage tier and step, and worthy employees are rewarded with promotions to better-paying jobs. The compensation program pay ranges are fixed for each tier and step. Consider the pay grades used for butchers at a large national supermarket chain in table 5.4. Grades delineate responsibility or training, while steps describe on-the-job experience levels. Base salaries are beginning pay rates for each experience level.

A Hay compensation schedule lets managers reward productive employees and establishes incentives to stimulate their development. A manager may promote better employees multiple steps within a grade while upgrading average workers by a single step. Multiple steps also allow wages within a grade to rise steeply.

Steps may overlap grades; for example, grade 3, step 3 receives more remuneration than grade 4, base wage. Overlapping steps and grades are more likely in job classifications where productivity is related to both experience and training. For example, a grammar school teacher with a B.A. degree and ten years of experience may be better qualified and higher paid than a new graduate with an M.A. degree.[13] Grades allow higher entry for better-qualified employees, while steps allow more experienced workers to be fairly compensated. One advantage of an overlapping system for Grocery Land, Inc., is that it can hire butchers from competitors at prevailing market wages without upsetting the union or current employees.

TABLE 5.4. Grocery Land, Inc., Pay Grades for Butchers

Grade	Base	Step 1	Step 2	Step 3
1	$17,500	$17,900	$18,100	$18,300
2	19,000	19,200	19,400	19,600
3	20,000	20,500	21,000	21,500
4	21,300	22,500	23,900	25,000
5	24,500	27,000	29,500	32,500

How do employees react to a Hay pay system? In theory, a Hay system motivates employees to acquire firm-specific human capital (Acs and Gerlowski 1996).[14] Human capital is the adroitness on the job and interpersonal skills that allow an employee to remain with the firm long enough to rise to a high pay grade or step. Under the pay-for-performance plan, the employee makes a human-capital investment only when it leads, with certainty, to an instantaneous increase in productivity and compensation. Moreover, Hay pay systems may signal to employees their importance to the company and its future. In addition, the Hay system's seemingly complex wage-scale algorithm that defines the relative importance of various workers at different levels may help employees focus on the enterprise's long-term mission.

On the negative side, Hay systems may discourage workers who view the tangle of job classifications, steps, and grades as an artificial barrier confining them to a lifetime of low pay and limited prestige. Union shops in particular find their upper Hay system tiers inhabited by older workers, some of whom may be less productive or energetic than their younger counterparts; this may demoralize younger workers.

In addition, job classifications systems may, in due time, haunt companies. Unionized and quasi-unionized companies (i.e., large non-unionized firms that purchase labor peace (Jensen 1993) allow their employee ranks to swell by permitting multiple job-classification systems. For example, a major negotiation issue at Raytheon, Inc., during 1996 is reduction in the number of job classifications. The union insists that each job be filled by a person classified in that job classification. With declining workloads, some workers are paid for eight hours for less than a full day's work. Trimming the number of classifications allows four six-hour-per-day jobs to be refashioned into three eight-hour jobs.

Pay for Performance

The antithesis of a Hay compensation plan is a pay-for-performance or merit-based pay system. A pay-for-performance system notifies the worker how productivity is measured (e.g., in tons of steel produced, number of return customer visits, or on-time performance), and as milestones are reached, compensation increases. Merit-based pay systems are traditional for taxi drivers, professional golfers, waiters, street musicians, and real estate brokers, among others; they are common, though not universal, for other workers, including stock brokers, sales clerks, and even college professors; and they are being introduced in countless other professions.

An outstanding example of a merit-based pay system is Continental

Airlines' development of an incentive plan to improve the airline's ranking in the on-time performance derby. Greg Brennerman, Continental's chief operating officer, said "If employees don't want an on-time airline, we will not be an on-time airline" (McCartney 1995). Continental announced that it would pay a bonus of $65 per employee each month that the airline ranked in the top half of the Department of Transportation on-time rankings. Within one year, the airline had catapulted from ninth in a ten-airline race to third. A well-designed pay-for-performance program enlivens the corporate culture, stimulating workers to discover additional productivity-improving actions. In addition to improved on-time rankings, Continental's plan yielded fewer delays so that more flights are scheduled every day, fewer dollars are spent rerouting delayed passengers, injuries are down, and morale is up.

Another example of how a merit-based pay system yields desirable results concerns executive compensation. Jensen and Murphy (1990) found little association between the wealth of the average CEO and the increase in the value of his/her firm's common stock; there was about a $3 increase in personal wealth per $1,000 increase in corporate stock value. In other words, the average CEO's compensation is not tied to the firm's performance. A study by Gilson and Vetsuypens (1993) of seventy-seven firms that either filed for bankruptcy or sought to restructure their debts found that after bankruptcy or restructuring these firms rearranged managerial incentives to link managerial wealth to corporate performance. Afterwards, the wealth/stock value relationship exceeded that reported by Jensen and Murphy by several times. Moreover, in the Gilson and Vetsuypens study, new CEOs received little of their compensation as direct wages, and most came as stock options or restricted stock. The message is clear: distressed companies in need of substantial improvement in corporate performance rely on pay for performance and abandon the traditional fixed-wage system.

One problem, at least for some external observers, is that merit-based pay plans targeted at executives can be too successful. These executives' compensations grow when the firm prospers. But when their firms achieve extraordinary success, some journalists question the morality of pay-for-performance contracts.

Consider these examples: in 1988 Michael Milken earned $550 million at the investment bank Drexel Burnham Lambert; in 1992 and 1993, Michael Eisner, the president of Disney, earned over $200 million. In both cases, these men had pay-for-performance contracts. Milken's contract was simple: he received one-third of the firm's profits from trading in high-yield securities. Eisner's contract provided an annual bonus and stock options based on Disney's net income and ROE.

Were these contracts immoral? The Milken situation is clear cut. This man, by himself, created the market for junk bonds. Before that innovation, Drexel was an insignificant player in the world of high finance. After Milken's breakthrough, Drexel became one of the most profitable firms in the securities industry. Without Milken, Drexel was nothing. With him and his pay-for-performance contract, both the firm and the man prospered. Was anybody harmed by this contractual arrangement? There appear to be no victims. More importantly, the arrangement yielded many winners, including the stockholders of Drexel Burnham, Milken's coworkers, and Milken himself. Eisner's situation is similar. Before he ascended to the Disney helm, the firm was the object of an aborted takeover and had paid greenmail to corporate raiders pursuing underperforming assets. Under Eisner's leadership, Disney became an entertainment industry giant and is now the takeover agent, not the victim.

Other analysts view pay for performance as counterproductive. For example, Acs and Gerlowski (1996) argue that since work contracts are relational and incomplete (i.e., not every eventuality is clarified in the contract) a merit-based pay system might persuade workers to pressure employers for an incentive structure favoring one group or one skill over another (Gilson and Vetsuypens 1993). Of course, capable managers are not easily co-opted by employees. Others reject merit pay systems because they encourage workers to concentrate on themselves without regard to the company's needs. But this argument misses the point entirely: a well-conceived pay-for-performance scheme stimulates both the company's and the workers' best interests.

Compensation Plans in a Turnaround

The turnaround manager is not always free to adopt a new compensation system. Unions and senior employees comfortable with familiar plans and procedures resist the transition. During a crisis, the turnaround manager gains latitude; however, the severity of the emergency generally is not common knowledge. The problem is exacerbated in privately owned companies, especially family-owned businesses, that maintain strict confidentiality in their business affairs. Communication skills are essential at this stage. Worker forums and candid labor-management discussions educate the workforce about the current state of affairs. The key is to be honest, open, and direct. Credibility is essential: never promise anything that cannot be delivered, and never make an idle threat.

Occasionally, political or economic forces conspire to make an established Hay system untouchable. For example, Air France, after losing in excess of a billion dollars in 1994, attempted to reduce labor costs by changing wage scales and work rules, only to be forced to back down after raucous demonstrations shut Orly Airport in Paris for a week. In similar situations, an effective way to occasion change is to create a hybrid compensation system that tacks a pay-for-performance bonus component onto the existing fixed-compensation system. While the hybrid compensation system does not reduce costs, it does promulgate financial signals that encourage productivity gains and attacks the existing corporate culture.[15] Another possibility is to adopt a two-tiered wage system in which older workers remain in the original Hay system while newer employees are hired under an incentive plan system. If the two-tiered system is well constructed, older employees perceive the benefits of the new system and ask to join the group.

A period of corporate renewal offers an excellent opportunity to design and implement a new merit-based compensation system.[16] Workers not covered by union or employment contracts have little recourse. Well-informed employees may be prepared to do something radical to revitalize the enterprise. A merit-based pay system, as seen in table 5.5, is crafted by

- reducing or even eliminating the hourly or monthly component of the wage package
- adding a variable wage component related to some target achievement

The first action lowers fixed costs and shocks employees into the new reality. The second action focuses employees on management's goal and provides financial incentive.[17] In version 1 of table 5.5, the original wage package is equaled if workers achieve the target. Below the target, compensation falls, while above the target, compensation rises. Version 2 is a more extreme example of the merit-based pay system. It eliminates the straight wage component altogether and adopts an accelerated rate of increase for the variable component (see *New York Times* 1996b). At the target, total wages increase beyond their original level while past the target a healthy wage increase is paid. Below the target wages fall dramatically.

An effective merit-based pay system lowers the average cost of production either by reducing worker compensation or by raising productivity. A target or lever defining the incentive system and explaining what management wants and what workers will get in exchange must be found and communicated to workers. Generally, the lever is output related, such as the number of units produced during a factory shift or the revenues received at the cosmetics counter during a sales shift. Incentive levers also may be input related (broken picture tubes at a TV assembly plant or gold dust lost at a jewelry factory) or associated with customer satisfaction (number of complaints or compliments).

Clyde Hamstreet, the winner of the Turnaround Management Association's turnaround manager of the year award in 1995, presents pay-for-performance paradigms to employees graphically to relate the message that change is not a pay cut but instead is a way to tie compensation to a target (Hamstreet 1995). For example, he might distribute the chart in figure 5.1 to illustrate the impact of a new pay system. The wage to be paid, as a function of the number of units produced, is found along the dotted line in the figure. A graphical representation clearly illustrates that wages depend reaching a target.

Wesco Distribution, Inc., is a perfect example of the impact incentive-compensation systems can have on underperforming assets (see O'Brien 1997). In 1993, Wesco was an unprofitable multi-billion-dollar subsidiary of Westinghouse Electric. Turnover was high, and employee confidence was moribund. After attaining independence from Westinghouse via a leveraged buyout, Wesco adopted a remuneration plan that tied compensation to performance. The results were stunning: a small profit was earned in 1994, followed by $25 million and $33 million of profits earned in 1995 and 1996, respectively. The key to this

TABLE 5.5. Revising a Pay Package to Include a Merit-Based Component

	Original	Revised Version 1	Revised Version 2
		Straight Wage	
	$14.00/hour	$6.00/hour	$0.00/hour
		Variable Wage Component	
At 25% of target		$2.00/hour	$1.00/hour
At 50% of target		$4.00/hour	$6.00/hour
At 75% of target		$6.00/hour	$11.00/hour
At 100% of target		$8.00/hour	$16.00/hour
At 125% of target		$10.00/hour	$21.00/hour
		Total Wage	
At 25% of target	$14.00/hour	$8.00/hour	$1.00/hour
At 50% of target	$14.00/hour	$10.00/hour	$6.00/hour
At 75% of target	$14.00/hour	$12.00/hour	$11.00/hour
At 100% of target	$14.00/hour	$14.00/hour	$16.00/hour
At 125% of target	$14.00/hour	$16.00/hour	$21.00/hour

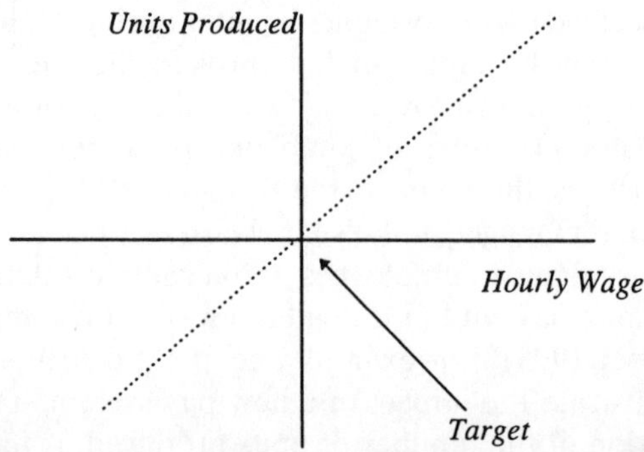

Fig. 5.1. Demonstration of a pay-for-performance plan

turnaround was the liberation of the employee compensation system from a fixed rate model. The compensation of top salespeople has jumped from $70,000 in 1993 to over $140,000 in 1996. Similarly, the compensation of top branch managers has increased from $100,000 to $160,000 during the same period. And employee turnover has fallen by more than 50 percent.

Sources of Finance for a Distressed Business

Original Sources

Companies decline for many reasons, but the major reason why businesses fail is that they run out of funds. A company that reports negative profits or negative cash flows over an extended period can survive as long as it continues to pay its bills. Most businesses require creditor support and obtain it from sources such as

- suppliers who extend credit for new purchases
- factors who buy accounts payable from suppliers unable to wait for payment
- factors who buy accounts receivable held by the debtor
- banks that provide lines of credit
- asset-based lenders
- leasing companies
- landlords

The creditor-debtor relationship is cordial as long as both parties thrive. The relationship sours if the debtor's financial condition weakens and the creditor notes that predicament. Creditors abandon clients in a severe financial crisis and for other less obvious reasons, including

- reaction to persistent late payments
- receipt of worrisome credit report
- detecting sloppy management practices
- industry in decline
- neighborhood in decline
- suffering from their own distress

Banks must exercise caution when ending a lending relationship. They must document the reasons for their concern and provide the customer with adequate warning and lead time to locate a new banking source; otherwise, the bank risks a lender's liability lawsuit.[18] Replacing a lost financing source is not trivial even for a healthy company and may be impossible for a troubled company. A bank worried about lender liability must avoid

- acting capriciously
- unreasonably withholding credit
- behaving inconsistently and irregularly

An equally damaging event for a company is losing the support of its factors, institutions that buy the paper it issues to suppliers in exchange for fresh inventories.[19] Factors play a vital role in the daily operations of many businesses. Many smaller vendors are financially incapable of retaining promissory notes until their customers or clients have sufficient liquidity to convert the notes into dollars. For example, Bradlees, Inc., an East Coast retailer, filed for Chapter 11 after factors grew cautious over the company's outlook. Bradlees, like all retailers, buys inventories and issues promises to pay for goods later. Factors buy that paper at a discount ranging between 4 and 10 percent and wait to be repaid in the normal thirty or sixty days. Bradlees's officials spent "more than a month of [futile] discussions . . . [with] factors in New York that control shipments of goods from a number of suppliers" (Pereira 1995). When these discussions failed, the company filed. Most retail failures follow similar catastrophic decisions by factors.

Creditors, such as factors, generally abandon distressed companies knowing that in bankruptcy court, should the creditor resort to a Chapter 11 filing, full repayment of their obligation is unlikely.[20] Finance companies gather intelligence about their commercial accounts from trade newspapers and credit bureaus and from the insights of sales personnel.[21] Cost considerations may limit these informational searches to only the largest active accounts. Seeking still more information, certain large companies and some factors employ early warning models (see "Applying EWS Models in a Turnaround," chapter 3) that aid in the early detection of financial distress. The low marginal cost of putting an extra account into a credit-scoring model makes that technology cost effective for companies with many smaller customers.

When a negative report is obtained on a customer, some suppliers respond by canceling all shipments; others adopt a strategy wherein they retain title to their shipment until payment is received; still others reduce the size but increase the frequency of shipments to reduce their average exposure to losses. Companies that habitually encounter distressed credits have perfected more astute strategies designed to maximize their profits before the account fails, for example

a) demanding that the troubled account also take shipment on slow-selling (out-of-date) merchandise
b) raising prices charged to this account to reflect its heightened risk

If the customer remits the balance for a shipment containing both ordinary and out-of-date merchandise, the vendor wins big, while in the event of a bankruptcy before repayment, the vendor's bankruptcy claim is increased by the value of out-of-date merchandise shipped. A claim on a product that might not otherwise have been sold is as valid in bankruptcy as a claim on a highly marketable product.

The logic underlying the strategy of raising the price charged to a distressed account is that it is impossible to predict accurately exactly when the account will fail even though its failure in the future is highly likely. With doubts about the timing of the firm's demise, the plan is to ship and be paid for enough units before the bankruptcy to not only cover costs in the bankruptcy but also earn a profit on all shipments from the date of the negative report on the customer.[22] Consider the analysis

TABLE 5.6. Strategic Analysis of Pricing to a Distressed Account (per unit)

	Original Price	New Price
Price	$18.00	$20.00
Cost per unit	$15.00	$15.00
Profit per unit	$3.00	$5.00
Shipments to cover cost	5	3

prepared in table 5.6 for an electronic goods supplier contemplating selling additional merchandise to a retailer whose payment delays (against a 2/10 net thirty-day invoice) have increased from thirty-five days last year to forty-five days three months ago to fifty days today. Assuming that the retailer continues to pay in fifty days, at the original price ($18.00) per unit, the firm must survive 250 days (5 × 50) before the electronics goods supplier covers its costs. By raising its price to $20, it reduces its break-even number of days to 150 days (3 × 50), or only three shipments. Should the retailer refuse to accept the price increase, the supplier may decide to cancel future shipments since a 250-day survival period may be too risky.

New Sources for a Stabilized Business

New sources of finance are difficult to find even for formerly distressed businesses that have been stabilized. Vendors, banks, and suppliers who lost money during the period of distress are reluctant to reinstate the relationship. The revived firm's unfavorable reputation may endure for several years. However, a recovered distressed business may obtain new financing from either straight bank loans or asset-based loans established based on fact and not on reputation. These loans are compared in table 5.7. Bank lines are relatively inexpensive, highly flexible, and indicative of a high degree of creditworthiness, which may invite other creditors to revisit the debtor. However, a bank line is unattainable until the formerly distressed business rectifies all of its past difficulties. Asset-based loans

TABLE 5.7. Sources of New Financing

Type of Financing	Minimum Standards Demanded	Costs	Repayment Terms
Bank loan	1. 12 months of positive earnings 2. Positive cash flow 3. Various financial-ratio tests	1. Prime rate plus 1–2% 2. Closing costs of 1% 3. May require corresponding deposits	One year renewable
Asset-based loan	1. Evidence that the crisis is past 2. Unencumbered inventories and accounts receivable	1. Prime rates plus up to 4–10% 2. Closing costs of 1% 3. May require corresponding deposits 4. May ask owner/CEO for a personal guarantee	Repay as inventories or receivables are liquidated; otherwise one year

are fully collateralized using inventories, accounts receivable, or fixed plant as security. The asset-based lender may require a 1.5:1 or even a 2:1 ratio of asset value to loan.

The commercial finance industry, asset-based lending, arose in 1906 when two encyclopedia door-to-door salesmen pioneered an installment payment plan. Commercial Credit Company was formed in 1912, and Walter E. Heller & Co. (now Heller International, a subsidiary of Fuji Bank) was formed in 1916 (Rutberg 1994). Asset-based lending has expanded greatly since 1980.[23] Asset-based loans are now even sold on Wall Street, where consumer accounts receivable are packaged and sold like mortgage-backed securities (Rutberg 1994). From the lender's perspective, a good asset-based loan is relatively risk-free since it is secured by real property and is lucrative, earning the lender three hundred or more basis points over the prime rate.[24] From the debtor's perspective, an asset-based loan provides access to money at a time when more traditional lenders are cautious.

Another source of financing is to sell off or liquidate part of the business. Liquidations conducted while the company is in the throes of distress likely will be unsuccessful as bidders perceive the seller's limited options. In contrast, liquidations or business sales conducted after the resolution of distress are unhurried and should be more successful. Yet few entrepreneurs favor this option since

- they have built the business themselves
- they view it as an acknowledgment of their own failure

In reality it is just the opposite. Good management principles endorse selling off a low-profit, low-growth business to raise money to support a high-profit, high-growth business. Businesses must invest their scarce resources where they are likely to earn the high reward.

An unusual cash-raising method employed by companies in bankruptcy is referred to in the Code as a 363(f) sale. Under Section 363 a company sells off assets free and clear of all liens and encumbrances. This strategy is followed when no other source of capital exists. In the Braniff Airways case, the company tried to sell all of its assets under section 363 but was told this was out of the ordinary course of business and required a liquidating plan. However, the airline was permitted to sell off several planes to raise cash.[25]

A final source of funds is to find new investors either by selling new stocks or bonds or by merging with another business that has free cash. This strategy is more suitable for larger companies, which have the advantage of being listed on a stock exchange or are better known to possible merger partners. Either option may be problematic for small businesses and impractical during and after the onset of financial problems. However, a small business may be able to sell new stock shares to its employees or exchange stock for salary concessions. In either case, the usual corporate control issues arise, and an additional concern arises from having minority shareholders employed at the firm. The bond market, even the junk bond market, is inhospitable to small business. However, employees may be willing to forgo salary in exchange for bonds that convert into common stock. Finally, a recovered small business seeking to locate a merger partner has the dual problem of small revenues and a tarnished reputation. Merger brokers and other professionals need to overcome these obstacles.

Asset-Based Loans[26]

From a banker's perspective, companies fall into three categories, which are compared in table 5.8. Both noninvestment-grade and middle-market companies are candidates for asset-based loans if they have sufficient collateral. The difference between collateral and assets is described pithily in Sidney Rutberg's (1994) quote from Walter Heller, a founder of the asset-based lending industry, "I don't lend against assets. I lend against collateral." Heller viewed assets as mere numbers that someone puts on the balance sheet; in contrast, collateral is the liquidation value of the security. Interest rates are set to compensate the bank for risk and are higher for middle-market companies than for non-investment-grade companies. Today, asset-based loans are based on asset values according to

TABLE 5.8. Decomposition of Company Types by Bankers

Type of Company	Investment Grade	Noninvestment Grade	Other: Middle Market
Cash flow	Impressive cash flow	Good cash flow	May be sporadic
Commercial paper user?	Yes	No	No
Relationship with banks	No longer borrows from banks	Borrows from banks, but bank does not take a collateral position	Borrows from banks, but bank takes position against assets
Debt characteristics	Uses short-term debt only. No long-term debt	May have significant debts	Highly leveraged, privately held, and pays high dividends to owners
Riskiness	Very low	Medium	High

the general principles described in table 5.9. The lender must know its collateral, and people are put on site to perform appraisals and open boxes and drawers.

The asset-based lender is repaid from funds the debtor collects in cash or on its receivables. This leaves the creditor with no free cash. This allows the bank to monitor the firm's sales and facilitates repayment. In the event of a bankruptcy, the DIP generally requests a cash order allowing it to withhold funds from the bank and use them in the ordinary course of business. The judge may grant an order for sixty days and may possibly extend it for up to 180 days. The cash order allows the firm to use cash as it is generated out of receivables instead of having this money go to the bank. At that point, the firm needs DIP financing, and the lender is concerned that its collateral will be drained away. A cash order puts great pressure on the lending bank to become the DIP financier. A typical DIP lending facility agreement sheet is presented in table 5.10.

TABLE 5.9. Asset Categories and Lending Amounts

Asset	Lending %	Depends On
Receivables less than 90 days old	Up to 85%	Collection history
Inventory	5%–80%	Finished goods, wholesale, manufactured, commodity, or energy
Machinery/equipment	50%–100% of book or 50–60% of appraised value	Appraisal

TABLE 5.10. Fragrances for Your Nose, Inc.'s, DIP Lending Agreement

Agent	Big Bank, Inc.
Facility amount	$100 million ($75 sub limit for letters of credit)
Term	Expires December 31, 1998, with consummation of plan of reorganization
Underwriting status	Underwritten by Big Bank, which has syndicated it to 7 banks
Security/collateral	Secured by superpriority administrative claim
Interest rate	Prime plus 0.5%
Letter of credit fees	1.5% per annum for trade and standby letters of credit
Commitment fee	0.5% of unused portion of funds
Cleanup requirement	None
Borrowing base	55% of cost value of inventory
Capital spending limitation	$12 million per annum
EBITDA covenant	Must exceed $7.5 million per quarter
Minimum inventory levels	May not fall below $32 million

The GPA Example:
A quintessential example of a relatively healthy but financially constrained company using asset-based lending to secure new financing is GPA Group of Ireland, the world's dominant aircraft lessor (*Wall Street Journal* 1996b). GPA buys billions of dollars worth of airplanes from Boeing, McDonnell Douglas, and Airbus Industries and then leases them to airlines.[27] Leasing appeals to airlines, whose ability to borrow funds is constrained by their highly leveraged balance sheets, irregular cash flows, and uncertainty regarding the number of planes needed. Beginning in 1992, concerns about liquidity at GPA arose following the failure of its $1 billion initial public offering of common stock. Eventually its bank transferred GPA's loan into the workout category until General Electric Company (GE) provided interim financing (which also gave GE the option to buy 90 percent of the company).

GPA resolved this situation by issuing $4 billion in asset-backed securities. The asset in this case was revenue anticipated from existing leases on 229 aircraft held by eighty-three airlines. Using these funds, the bank line was mostly repaid, relieving the critical concern, and residual funds bolstered the company's balance sheet. The most remarkable aspect of this transaction was summed up by a corporate bond analyst who said, "These are the same planes and the same cash flows. All you've done is redirect them to another company" (*Wall Street Journal* 1996b). GPA was not insolvent or lacking a core business. Its predicament was that its net worth was tied up in hard assets (leases). The financial reengineering effected by asset-based lending transformed fixed assets into liquid funds.

The Role of the Board of Directors during Corporate Renewal[28]

"Corporate control and governance" describes the relationship among the board of directors, shareholders, and individuals making decisions for the firm (see Berle and Means 1932).[29] During ordinary times, management is charged with the responsibility of making decisions for the firm; during a crisis, however, creditors may supplant management or at least share this capacity. Shareholders increasingly are represented by agents.[30] Members of the board of directors are not employees or agents of the corporation but fiduciaries[31] for the shareholders.

The question considered in corporate control and governance is: Who is in charge of the company? State laws, the fiduciary duties statutes, unequivocally respond that it is the company's board of directors.

Case law, adjudicated principally in Delaware because of its large number of major corporations, vests additional authority in the board.

What are the duties of a board of directors? Most states' fiduciary duties statutes charge directors with ensuring that management acts in the best interest of the corporation. To carry out that charge, the board selects management (typically just the CEO, who then hires the corporation's other officers); at other times, the board terminates existing management. An implied additional duty of the board of directors is to debate, investigate, and vote on corporate strategy. The board is not expected to develop strategy. During a crisis, the two duties converge; the board must consider whether it has confidence in a person and in his/her strategy. If management is a disappointment and fails to articulate a plausible turnaround plan, the board removes and replaces it. Neglecting its duties may put the board at risk from lawsuits, negatively impact the performance of company equity, and jeopardize the future of the enterprise.

Recently, a number of major firms shuffled CEOs after their boards of directors concluded that the incumbents were failing. General Motors removed its president and CEO at a pivotal moment in the history of the automobile company and replaced him with a GM director, John Smale, former CEO of Proctor and Gamble. Similarly, Warren Buffett, a major shareholder and director of Solomon Brothers, became CEO after the board lost confidence in the current management. Apple Computer's board, in well-publicized incidents, discharged first Steven Jobs (an original founder) and then John Scully (who had been hired away from Pepsi) in disputes over strategy and its implementation.

A checklist of topics to be pursued by a board of directors during a crisis is detailed in table 5.11. The tasks are assigned to board subcommittees or task forces, which hire consultants such as turnaround managers to conduct the investigation. A board's overriding mission is to judge whether a firm is salvageable in terms of the necessary ingredients for a successful turnaround:

- capable management
- a new source of financing
- a continuing profitable business

The board examines the leader's honesty and capability as well as compensation and company strategy. CEOs are on boards of directors, and as such it is inappropriate to appoint an executive to a task force investigating his/her own competence in crisis management. He/she should abstain from voting on the subcommittee's findings.

The board of directors itself may be an obstacle undermining the company's recovery. Theoretically, the board of directors is independent and dynamic and is capable of decisiveness in a crisis. However, some corporate boards are unable to discharge their duties. This occurs when the board

- is not independent of the CEO
- is not comprised of a majority of external directors
- is not sufficiently aggressive
- is unable to build a consensus
- is unskilled in crisis management

TABLE 5.11. Issues Confronting a Board of Directors of a Troubled Company

Topic		Issues and Actions
Evaluate leadership	1	Define what is the problem
	2	Decide what skills are needed to solve the problem
	3	Evaluate the CEO's strengths and weaknesses
	4	Retain CEO or hire a new CEO
	5	Set milestones to evaluate performance independent of excuses and circumstances
	6	Fire incompetents
Review strategy	1	Determine what business the company is really in
	2	Evaluate the competition and its competitive strengths versus the company's
	3	Determine what additional investment is required
	4	Review pro formas
	5	Decide whether to invest or exit
	6	If exit, by sale, merger, or liquidation
Assess status	1	Decide what resources are needed to overcome difficulties
	2	If resources exist and leadership is in place, decide time frame within which to expect recovery
	3	If resources are lacking or leadership problems are intractable, decide among merger, liquidation, and bankruptcy
Search for fraud	1	Examine transactions for signs of self-dealing
	2	Bring in accountants to audit books
	3	If evidence is found, is there insurance or bonding?
	4	Report findings to regulatory and police authorities
Provide management with the proper incentives	1	Determine management's indispensability to problem solving
	2	Develop an incentive program using stock options or restricted stock that ties management compensation to corporate performance

Ineffectual boards of directors are often captives of the CEO and unable to exercise free thought or action. A board is ensnared when packed with friends, family members, or close business associates of the CEO. The filial bond is cemented when lucrative consulting contracts are awarded by the corporation to board members. A board is similarly compliant to the CEO's ambitions when officers of the corporation make up the majority of its members. Corporate executives are not independent of the CEO; in fact, they are subordinates whose careers and remuneration depend on remaining in the CEO's good graces. Other than CEO succession, there generally is no satisfactory rationalization for appointing corporate officers other than the CEO to serve on the board of directors.[32]

The composition of the board of directors affects its ability to function and lead in a crisis. A qualified board is a mosaic of expertise, aptitudes, and personalities useful in both current and future situations. Members are chosen for their valuable legal, financial, marketing, manufacturing, or international skills. It is difficult to replace an entire board during a crisis, but individual members may resign out of fear of lawsuits or having their names besmirched. Unless the board is designed originally with consensus building and aggressiveness as objectives, it is likely to be stymied in a crisis. Few companies anticipate failure. Failure is anathema to the spirit of entrepreneurship, so few companies put corporate renewal specialists on their boards. This is satisfactory, provided that suitable counsel and guidance are engaged at times of crisis.

Negotiations[33]

Very little of what people do happens without negotiating. We negotiate work responsibilities, where to live, political decisions, rules for various games, and who is on what side. Successful people are usually able negotiators. Some people are better negotiators than others; some people enjoy negotiating, while others abhor it; but there is no getting around the fact that all people negotiate all the time.

The road to corporate renewal is often unmarked, and the journey is likely to produce traumatic changes affecting management, creditors, and employees. Inaction provides an illusion of safety, but a stalemate is calamitous and may accelerate the onset of a crisis. The corporate renewal specialist needs to apply negotiating skills to bridge disparate opinions and induce workers and employers to embrace and to adopt radical change.

The best negotiators seem to possess innate talents, but everyone becomes a better negotiator by learning the fundamentals of the negotiating process. Only a basic overview of a very complex topic is presented below, highlighting key features and identifying how outcomes are influenced.[34]

The Essence of Negotiations

Negotiations seek to resolve well-defined problems. These are the material ingredients of a negotiation. Material issues are clearly articulated, rational, and systematic; in salary negotiations, for example, they concern the hourly rate of pay, the definition and treatment of overtime, and benefit arrangements. But human agents may also bargain from an emotional level.[35] Emotional issues are unconscious and unspoken; they include cultural, ethnic, socioeconomic, and other distinctions among negotiators.

Negotiations concern material issues, but they may fail if emotional issues intervene. To minimize this risk, trained negotiators identify relevant emotional issues affecting themselves and their opponents. They may lay these issues on the table to alert both parties to these unseen pitfalls. Despite such candor, emotional conflict may lurk behind contrived material disagreement and be hard to detect. Intransigent negotiating positions are a sign of mislaid emotional antagonism, though they may also indicate material obstacles.

Alternate Outcomes

Negotiations are either distributive or integrative, as shown in table 5.12. Distributive bargains are zero-sum situations with a winner and a loser. One party's gains are the other party's losses. Wage negotiations are distributive; the more the employer pays (loses), the more the worker receives (wins). Integrative bargains are win-win: both parties accrue net benefits. For example, negotiating to change work rules to increase profits and thereby increase employee profit sharing is integrative; both the employer and the employee are better off. Integrative bargains are easier to resolve than distributive ones. A more favorable negotiating atmosphere is created by turning a zero-sum negotiation into a win-win one, although that is not always possible.

TABLE 5.12. Types of Bargains

Types of Bargains	Outcomes
Distributive	Zero sum
Integrative	Win-win

Dispositions

A negotiator's disposition (i.e., style or psychology) is established by

- how important the issue is to him/her
- how much he/she cares about the opponent
- the opponent's disposition

A negotiator's style ranges between competitive and compromising, as seen in table 5.13. A good negotiator can adjust to an opponent's psychology and behavior. When I care a great deal about an issue, for instance, during wage negotiations, I am either competitive or collaborative. When I seek to maximize my own gains as in a zero-sum bargain, I am competitive. In contrast, I act collaboratively when I value the opponent's needs, understand that the bargain is win-win, and attempt to maximize the combined gain of both parties. I compromise when I am moderately interested in the issue and in the opponent's needs.

When the issue is unimportant to me, my disposition may be either helpful or withdrawn. Consider the irrelevant issue of the color of uniform worn by my delivery drivers. If I want to foster a long-term relationship with these drivers, my negotiating stance can help. I acquiesce to their request and may even pay for the new uniforms. By contrast, if I feel no attachment to my drivers or am inclined to hire new drivers, I withdraw and ignore the issue. Of course, dispositions are fluid and adjust to fit the bargaining pattern. For example, if the opponent ignores a collaborative negotiator's cues, a skilled negotiator may switch to a competitive mode.

Every negotiation concerns at least two parties. How important the

TABLE 5.13. Negotiation Styles

Styles	How Important the Issue Is to Me	How Much I Care about the Opponent's Needs
Competitive	High	Low
Collaborative	High	High
Helpful	Low	High
Withdrawn	Low	Low
Compromising	Medium	Medium

issue is to each and how much each cares about the other's needs determines what each brings to the negotiations. The attitudes of the two sides interact and shape to what extent negotiations will be agreeable, easy, and successful. The matrix in table 5.14 compares the temperaments of a hypothetical employer and employee as they begin a negotiation.

The cells in the matrix describe the outcome expected from every combination of employer and employee disposition. The matrix leaves out other determinants of negotiation outcomes such as subject (i.e., critical or perfunctory), relationship between parties, and outcome of previous negotiations. Anomalous outcomes are more likely with smaller stakes, amicable parties, and exceptional preceding outcomes. The important lesson shown by the matrix is that benefits accrue if you can move your negotiating counterpart into a collaborative mode.

Along the diagonal (shown in italics), where similar temperaments meet, results are unambiguous; that is, two competitive negotiators conflict or two compromising negotiators agree. Many off-diagonal outcome cells are also unambiguous: pairing a competitive and a helpful team produces agreement since the competitive party's demands are accommodated by the helpful party. Fifteen of twenty-five cases result in agreements; in five other cases there is no outcome, which is indicated as a rejected bargain. Four outcomes are uncertain, with results depending on the relative strength of each party. For example, pairing competitive and withdrawn negotiators produces either conflict or rejection. There is uncertainty because neither party feels any responsibility for the other, but the competitive one seeks an agreement on its terms while the other is indifferent and willing to abandon the process. The bargain is rejected if the withdrawn side walks away, and a conflict results if the competitive side refuses to quit and insists on negotiations.

TABLE 5.14. The Interaction of Negotiating Dispositions: The Employer and the Employee

	Employee				
Employer	Competitive	Collaborative	Helpful	Withdrawn	Compromise
Competitive	*Conflict*	Agreement	Agreement	Conflict/ rejected	Agreement
Collaborative	Agreement	*Agreement*	Agreement	Rejected/ agreement	Agreement
Helpful	Agreement	Agreement	*Agreement*	Rejected	Agreement
Withdrawn	Conflict/ rejected	Rejected/ agreement	Rejected	*Rejected*	Rejected
Compromising	Agreement	Agreement	Agreement	Rejected	*Agreement*

Involvement

Parties to a negotiation may be very concerned, partially concerned, or unconcerned about a particular topic. Concern no doubt relates to the perceived consequences of the negotiation. Level of concern is also related to a person's negotiating disposition.[36] It is possible to judge a party's concern about an issue from recent circumstances or past behavior. This information is useful to a clever negotiator who can interpret an opponent's disposition, negotiating psychology, and strategy.

What is vital to one group is immaterial to another. A number of factors determine the importance of an issue:

- present and future financial impacts
- number and attractiveness of alternatives
- duration of agreement
- how outcome affects future negotiations
- whether outcome is widely disseminated or confidential
- how long the issue may be of concern

Disposition is altered as circumstances change and overtures are received from an adversary. In a crisis, everything reverts back to the negotiating table. Negotiators pursue givebacks by offering something in exchange: lower wages or modified work rules for saved jobs, lower input prices and longer repayment schedules for new orders being placed, or deferred rental payments for no Chapter 11 filing. No contract is ever final: to rewrite an agreement, the negotiator must communicate the degree of crisis, and the opponent must listen. Government tax collectors are the least flexible bargainers, although the Internal Revenue Service now accepts partial payments on back taxes (Rowland 1995).

Factors Influencing Negotiation Outcomes

Nothing guarantees negotiating success: not a successful prior negotiation, not a crisis atmosphere, and certainly not personal friendship. On the other hand, nearly all negotiations can be successful. Certain strategies promote success. The most important, but undoubtedly the most difficult, is to turn zero-sum bargains into win-win bargains. Consider a wage negotiation: at the simplest level, it is distributive because the more I pay you, the less I keep myself. The bargain is integrative, however, if you convince me that your higher productivity resulting from the wage increase more than compensates for my higher costs. The way to foster this transformation is to create a healthy exchange of ideas that leads to trust. Wertheim (1995) suggests that the following procedures help make this transformation:

Company

1. Evaluate proposals against objective criteria, such as expected profits, and be sure to combine ideas from both parties.
2. Partition large issues into small pieces, simplifying the calculation of costs and benefits.

Personal

3. Find the common enemy, such as waste or inefficiency. First arrange to ameliorate the problem, and then fashion how to distribute the gains.
4. Figure out the opponent's needs. For example, if job security is as important as a higher wage, then neither party may really want an excessive wage rate.
5. Do not rely on verbal communication. Put ideas onto blackboards, charts, etc., and document points of similarity.
6. Make small concessions as a show of good faith, especially when what is given away has limited value to you.

If it is not possible to turn a zero-sum bargain into an integrative transaction, the next best alternative is to convert a competitive opponent into a compromiser.

A second strategy for achieving negotiating success is to recognize in advance what each party needs from the bargain and what each will do to achieve it. You should have a sense, before beginning, of where you must be at the end. The worst time to figure out a strategy is during the negotiation itself. Several questions that promote self knowledge are

1. What is the most you would offer and the least you would take? Know where your "walk away" point is.
2. What is the least your opponent would take and the most he/she would offer? Know your opponent's "walk away" point.
3. What are your options should the bargain break down?
4. What are your opponent's options should the bargain break down?

It is imperative that you know the real issue in a crisis. Otherwise, an insignificant secondary issue may assume a greater importance than it warrants. If lesser problems become a diversion, actual problems are neglected; resentment grows as participants watch time and the company's chances erode. The elevation of a minor problem to the negotiating table occurs when (a) parties prefer to discuss the most palatable issues and not the most important, or (b) because the real problem goes undetected. For example, the owner/CEO of a small business may be the real problem, and the solution may be to induce him/her to retire voluntarily. If the turnaround manager fails to unravel the true issue from the surrounding flotsam, valuable time, energy, and resources are drained while negotiating over distracting issues like executive remuneration levels or the number of salespeople to fire. The turnaround manager unearths the truth quicker by seeing the world through the eyes of each participant, not just according to his/her own perspective.

A third strategy establishes a success-oriented working agenda that positions resolvable issues up front and moves discordant topics to subsequent sessions or assigns them to special working groups. This agenda is as valid as one based on alphabet, history, or dollar ranking. Issues should be sorted according to whether or not they can be untangled. The agenda should look forward and not dwell on past failings. Even with the agenda under control, it is prudent to withhold information about your own position. Initially, demand more than you expect in order to gauge the opponent's response; later, communicate your real needs. Revealing your needs too early puts you at a subsequent disadvantage.

A fourth strategy eliminates obstacles that impede the bargaining process. The important thing is getting the two sides to agree: everything else is gratuitous. Among the actions that contribute to completing a bargain are

- when parties are separated by divergent predictions, make the bargain contingent, e.g., wages increase if a specified event occurs
- if the two parties disagree about the current value of future cash payments (i.e., they have different discount rates), the offer should exploit differences in the time value of money
- if the two parties disagree about inherent riskiness (i.e., they have different risk-adjusted discount rates), the offer should exploit differences in risk aversion
- avoid personalizing the negotiations; nothing is achieved by casting blame at someone, especially if he/she is sitting at the negotiating table
- do not trivialize any problem, but treat each as a fact and find its solution
- get parties accustomed to saying yes; start by making costless proposals they can accept

Trivial matters that interfere with the process must be removed, allowing participants to focus on the target.

Finally, be circumspect in how language is used: avoid making statements that might be inflammatory, respond to unreasonableness with silence, and ask questions. Language skills and factual communication reduce tension, improve the negotiating atmosphere, and unearth harmonizing issues. Carefully chosen words forge a community of interests that goes beyond the hardened positions of rhetoric. For example, focus on how to save jobs or become more competitive rather than on how many dollars should be paid to hourly workers.

Perhaps the most important point to remember is that "the only agreement that works is one in which all parties walk away happy."[37] Both parties must feel that the outcome merits their acceptance and support, otherwise it will break down. Winning a Pyrrhic victory at the bargaining table but losing the war because worker morale is destroyed and loyalty evaporates is no good.

Questions

1. How would you define a good negotiator?
2. Comment on this statement: "A good negotiator gets people to do what they do not want to do."
3. Salary negotiations are normally distributive. How would you transform salary negotiations into integrative bargaining?
4. In a crisis, negotiations are more competitive because the opponent's future cooperation may not be needed. How much should workers concede to convert a competitive negotiation into a collaborative one? What additional factors does your answer depend on?
5. Since a negotiator's concern about an issue diminishes as the person's future involvement declines, what sort of person is best suited to be the negotiator for a company or for its union?

Procurement Options and Transfer Pricing

Lowering the cost of purchasing materials and other inputs is a major goal of turnaround management. Many distressed companies are unaware of the three procurement options, and this causes their costs to be higher than necessary and contributes to their distress. Raw materials, partially finished goods, and even finished goods may be acquired by

1. establishing production in house
2. purchasing on the spot market
3. purchasing under long-term contract

Each choice has special advantages and disadvantages, as seen in table 5.15.

Internal production is not an option for every firm. A certain size, sophistication, and financial well-being are necessary if a firm is to integrate vertically and not suffer injurious effects. Producing both inputs and outputs is rewarding, but the incremental return must compensate for the associated internal conflicts and risks and the bureaucratic and opportunity costs that arise.[38] Transfer prices are a key ingredient when both inputs and outputs are produced and establish charges paid by the output division for inputs. Transfer prices allow the input-producing division and its manager to be evaluated and rewarded.[39] Transfer-price mechanisms look to the economic structure of the input-good industry and consider the availability of external input supplies (see the following section).[40]

There also are advantages to remaining a specialized producer and purchasing inputs from suppliers. A higher degree of sophistication in the legal and operations areas is required to purchase inputs under contract rather than on the spot market: this expertise guides the preparation of legal documents specifying cost and performance details. Another problem with contract purchases is that small companies are compelled by their limited order size to sole-source requirements from a single manufacturer. Delivery delays are catastrophic without a backup supplier. For example, in 1997 Toyota Motors had to shut production for several days after a fire in its brake-supply factory. Larger firms gain a pricing advantage from intrasupplier competition.

Spot purchases are simple transactions in which money and goods are exchanged. Spot-market prices are usually less than contract prices; however, during shortages, spot buyers are shut out of the market or are

TABLE 5.15. Procurement Choice Matrix

Choice	Advantages	Disadvantages
Internal production	• On time delivery • Possibly lower cost • Can order overtime shifts as needed	• Workers and machines are idle at times • Quality may be lower • Less R&D spending than competitors
Spot-market purchases	• Purchase precisely what is needed • No inventory	• Cost may be higher • No relationship with supplier
Contract purchases	• Long-term supply is guaranteed • Establishes supplier relationship that minimizes related concerns	• Cost may be higher • Supplier may take advantage as time goes by

charged multiples of the contract price. If producers do not supply the contract market, buyers are compelled to buy in the spot market.

Making the wrong procurement choice leads many companies into distress. For small businesses this is dangerous territory; some tasks, such as internal production or contract purchasing, are too sophisticated for them to control. The turnaround manager engaged by a small business may need to terminate an internal production unit, to establish market discipline internally with transfer prices, or to abrogate a purchase contract, possibly by threatening bankruptcy. In larger companies, union contracts and seniority provisions complicate the task of closing down internal production units. Similarly, large firms may face resistance when they try to nullify purchase contracts.

The Impact of Incentives on Procurement

Managers are hired to acquire essential inputs that mesh with the company's goals and resources.

- at the lowest possible cost
- in ample number
- in sufficient quality
- in a timely manner

These objectives are mutually incompatible. How the manager chooses among these goals is shaped by corporate incentives instituted to steer his/her judgment. For example, a manager rewarded for on-time delivery is likely to prefer in-house production, a manager rewarded for acquiring materials at a low cost might choose spot-market purchases, and a third manager rewarded for meeting high material-quality standards might choose a contract-purchase option. Are these choices right for the company? Perhaps, but unless the board of directors or the turnaround manager establishes long-term incentives that reward the manager as the company as a whole prospers, the choices may be wrong.

OEMs and Outsourcing

Outsourcing occurs when companies shift production to external suppliers. The main reason to outsource is to lower the cost of acquiring inputs, though sometimes companies outsource to overcome a capital constraint or a factory space shortage, to improve delivery times, or because the external supplier offers a superior product. In addition, outsourcing is a common tactic to

- move production from a union to a nonunion shop
- sever complacency fostered by insouciant management
- settle a rift between two internal divisions
- avoid environmental regulations
- break a bureaucratic bottleneck

When should companies outsource production? The decision calculus to choose between internal and external production is based on a price comparison adjusted for differences such as delivery times or quality. Companies should outsource when they can save money. However, outsourcing may forge ill feelings within the plant, the company, or the community, especially following layoffs. If the potential for ill will is worrisome, a company may avoid outsourcing unless it achieves a substantial cost savings.

Original equipment manufacturer (OEM) relationships arise once a company outsources. The dominant role of OEMs in the automotive and high-technology industries clearly demonstrates the advantage of specialization by final product producers. OEMs supply components integrated into other products. For example, Gateway 2000 buys hard disks from Seagate Technology and monitors from Sony because that way Gateway gets a lower cost and a better product than if it tried to make those items itself. Similarly, General Motors buys tires from Goodyear and steel from Bethlehem Steel.

Midsized businesses are probably the biggest culprits in terms of underutilizing outsourcing. The principles of outsourcing apply to every business, large and small. A crisis manager should identify which OEMs are supplying a client and inquire why others are not employed; the manager should request clear and cxplicit evidence before permitting a distressed company to proceed with or begin internal production. Outsourcing is covered in greater depth in the next section of this chapter.

Transfer Pricing

What is the price of an internally produced component? The answer to this question is similar to the old joke about where a 700-pound gorilla sleeps: anywhere he wants. Transfer prices (interdivisional prices) are not legislated or controlled except when the final purchaser is the federal government.[41] They can be set anywhere. This freedom gives managers the opportunity to circumvent an outsourcing decision analysis by artificially setting internal transfer prices too low. To avoid this predicament, the board of directors or the corporate renewal specialist should consider having external consultants who use accepted methodologies to

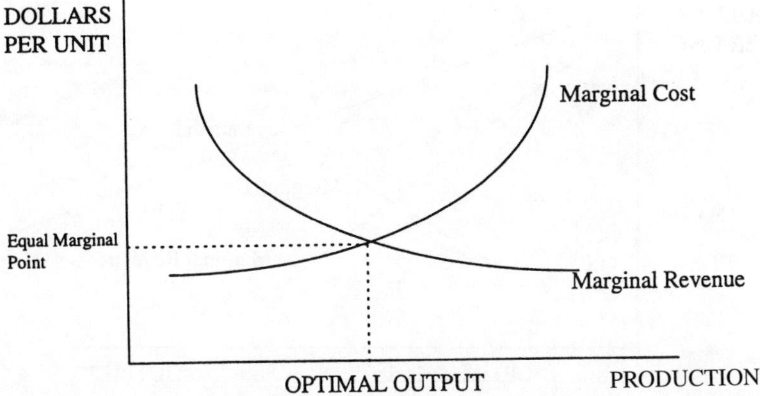

Fig. 5.2. Optimal production point

determine transfer prices. The rational approach to transfer-price setting, the economic model, requires the internal production division to set prices at its profit-maximizing level. Well-designed incentives for manager and workers insure that the economic model is followed.

Transfer pricing delves deeply into the realm of economics.[42] Basic economic price-setting and output determination rules state that a firm should produce until

Marginal revenue = MR = MC = Marginal cost

MR equals the incremental dollars the firm receives from the sale of one extra unit of product; MC is the dollar cost to the firm of producing one incremental unit of output. As shown in figure 5.2, MR falls as more units are sold because price must decline to induce more consumers to buy the product; MC rises as more units are produced because of diminishing returns. The equal marginal point defines the one spot where the two curves intersect. By setting prices such that MR and MC are equal, the firm identifies its optimal output: the point where it maximizes profits. Optimal price, labeled $P_{optimal}$, is found on the product-demand curve at the point above the intersection of the MC and the MR curves, as seen in figure 5.3.

There are three basic transfer-pricing examples:

1. no external market, i.e., the product must be produced internally
2. product is sold externally by many producers in a competitive market
3. product is sold by an external monopolist

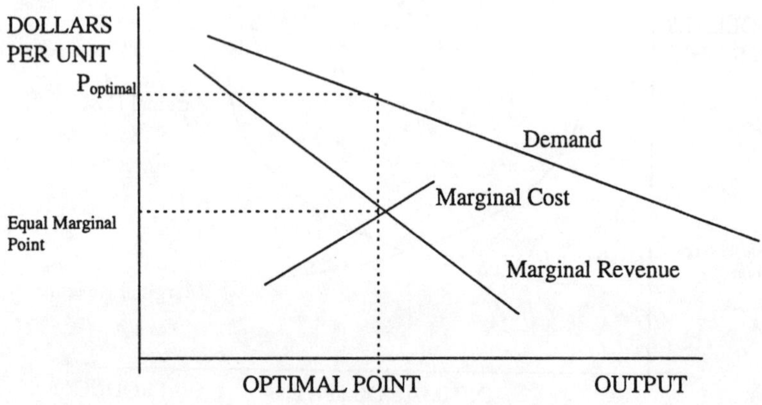

Fig. 5.3. Optimal price

We explore only the first case in this book, though the other two are essentially similar. Case one includes the most real-world situations, either because the internal product is singular or because the firm asserts the impossibility of buying exactly what it needs from another vendor.[43] Figure 5.4 diagrams the transfer-pricing solution for Ajax Coffees. Ajax sells premium coffees in gourmet shops. The product is blended internally by one group of employees and then marketed internationally by another group of employees.

Figure 5.4 is distinctive because there are now separate MC curves for each company activity ($MC_{blending}$ for the cost of preparing the coffees internally and $MC_{marketing}$ for the cost of selling the product) and one combined curve, MC, for the company as a whole (the vertical sum of the other two). The optimal output point is found as bcfore, where MC equals MR. This point also defines the optimal market price, P_{market}.

How many bags of coffee should the internal group produce? Plainly, the answer is the same number as the number of bags optimally sold (otherwise orders will go unfilled or extra bags will be produced). What price should the internal group set for these bags? The answer is that the price should equal their marginal cost, $MC_{blending}$, which is seen in figure 5.3 as $P_{internal}$. Charging a price equal to marginal cost does not mean that the blending group earns no profit; it earns zero profit only on the last unit sold. The profit equals the difference between their total costs and their total revenues ($P_{internal}$ times the number of bags sold). With $P_{internal}$ the firm has a signal to decide whether to buy a similar blend of coffees premixed or whether to continue blending its own coffee. Also, the manager of the blending activities is rewarded for controlling costs if the unit's profit contribution rises.[44] Actual prices, $P_{internal}$ and P_{market}, are easily determined.

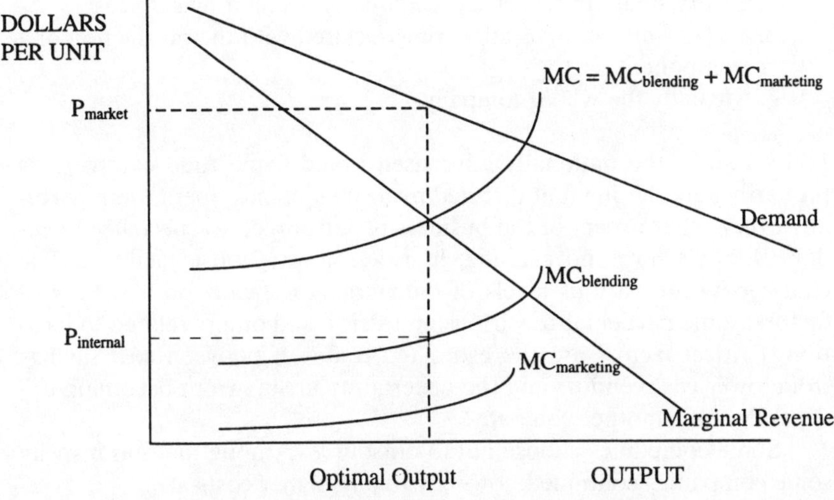

Fig. 5.4. Transfer pricing with no external market

There are two conditions under which internal production should cease.

- $P_{internal}$ exceeds the external price
- the internal division is losing money and replacement products can be purchased, resulting in a smaller loss

On the other hand, quality arguments may justify internal production.

Outsourcing and Insourcing

Virtually unknown as recently as the late 1980s, outsourcing is today a common business practice.[45] Insourcing, the opposite strategy, is being rapidly adopted by innovative firms with excess capacity. Outsourcing occurs when a firm replaces some or all of its workforce with a contract to obtain products or services from another vendor. Insourcing happens when a firm agrees to perform work for another company, even a direct competitor. Both sourcing strategies are risky, but both can heighten a firm's profitability by allowing it to focus on its core expertise.

Outsourcing

Outsourcing work to another firm usually takes the form of a fee-for-service arrangement wherein a fixed payment is made in exchange for the guaranteed delivery of a product or service. The contract may involve

1. a very small unit, such as custodial or accounting services
2. larger units, such as all work associated with the production of a component part
3. virtually the whole company

Libby Foods, the nationally advertised brand-name food company, is primarily a marketing unit directed by a small management team; virtually every other aspect of the business is outsourced to specialized vendors. Libby's owns no canning, logistic, or warehouse facilities. The choice between various levels of outsourcing depends on a variety of factors, some particular to various industries, and others related to location. Critical factors are the estimated trade-off between cost savings from lower cost vendors and the uncertainty arising from becoming too dependent on another company.

Some companies choose not to outsource. Among the reasons why some companies continue knowingly to pay higher costs are

- greater reliability of input supply
- advanced warning of product shortages and quality difficulties
- expectation that future production costs will fall
- difficulty of innovation with off-site production

The only unacceptable rationalization for not outsourcing is the statement "We don't do it that way."

Outsourcing also offers certain advantages. It can achieve seven objectives:

1. lowering the average and incremental costs of production
2. making price-led costing a reality
3. transitioning from unpredictable to fixed-cost environment
4. reversing egalitarian-based benefits allocation
5. motivating remaining workers to be more productive
6. freeing up production space, research and development, and managerial time for higher-value-added activities
7. opening new markets

Despite the media's insistence that achieving lower costs is the principal objective of outsourcing, each of the six other objectives is a worthy goal. In fact, a company may agree to compensate a supplier at a higher rate than it paid internally if the external company can deliver a higher-quality product, a shortened product cycle, reduced repair services, or a diminution of internal conflicts.

Once the decision is made to outsource, the firm puts the contract to replace certain activities out to bid. Creating a forum where suppliers can compete is an essential component of outsourcing. A single bid or a wired contract is unlikely to provide the benefits listed above. The request for proposal must clearly describe such things as work content and timing so that each bidder offers a comparable service. Competition forces external purveyors to submit proposals offering the lowest possible price and the best possible service. Moreover, unlike the normal situation, where workers anticipate wage increases every year, an outsourced contract is likely to remain flat provided that the purchaser has the right to put the contract out for bids again.

According to Peter Drucker (1993), cost-led pricing, where supplier costs are accepted and prices are set as a markup over costs, is a major business sin. He proposes price-led costing instead. With price-led costing, the firm informs its supplier of its pricing plan for next year, perhaps reducing prices by 4 percent; to retain the contract, the supplier must reduce its own prices to the firm by 4 percent. Price-led costing allows Japanese companies to bring their product to market at the right price point. For example, Infiniti motors recently announced a $5,000 permanent price cut on its luxury model, the Q45, to better position the car against its competition. Part of this reduction is explained by supplier price cuts to Infiniti. American companies need to become price-led costers. Outsourcing creates an opportunity to use this cost-controlling strategy.

Another advantage to outsourcing is that the supplier guarantees a fixed price to the buyer.[46] In contrast, with work performed internally, any number of events may result in costs exceeding their original estimate. An ordinary problem like the delayed arrival of a key input may, for example, push work into the overtime pay period and lead to an increase in costs. After outsourcing, this and other risks are absorbed by the supplier. However, if contract terms are negotiated too rigidly with too little profit for the supplier, any mistake may so financially cripple them that bankruptcy results. General Motors (GM) is very involved in keeping its suppliers healthy; it retains one of the largest turnaround management firms in the United States to work with its weakest suppliers.

Benefits generally are not provided to workers proportionate to their value to the company but are instead offered across the board to all workers.[47] In some cases, Federal legislation mandates egalitarianism, as with 401(k) and 403(k) pension plans. But in other cases, such as health benefits, vacation time, or sick days, companies voluntarily provide benefits equally to all full-time employees. As long as these benefits are relatively inexpensive, companies extend them to all workers, in part so that they appear to be treating their workers well. Such largesse seriously raises the cost of labor when benefit costs escalate. Total labor costs for low-value-added workers can get too high, pricing them out of the market. Job retention requires either that unions sanction the return of excessive salary or benefits or that they promote productivity-increasing work rule changes or investments to keep their members competitive with nonunion workers. However, many unions resist any suggestion of givebacks. The corporate response is to outsource the lowest-value-added jobs to escape burdensome benefits costs.

Consider the automobile industry, where over the years the United Auto Workers (UAW) has negotiated rich contracts for its members. Table 5.16 compares the hourly salary and benefits paid by UAW and nonunion employers, both of which supply automobile companies with brake parts. Unionized workers earn 87 percent more, benefits included, than their nonunion counterparts. Their benefits are fully 260 percent more than nonunion benefits. Not surprisingly, GM, Ford, and Chrysler are attempting to outsource more of their work to nonunion providers, and the union is resisting. GM's purchasing department already spends in excess of $70 billion per year, and that figure will surely rise. GM is now trying to concentrate its orders on fewer suppliers to give them greater economies of scale, which should allow them to offer GM lower prices (Blumenstein and Stern 1996).

Outsourcing also energizes and refocuses workers surviving the realignment. Eliminating a nonperforming or overpaid group of workers improves the firm's health and motivates workers penalized by the sloth or overpayment of their dismissed brethren. Outsourcing combined with an incentive-based compensation system that rewards hard work and dedication works especially well.

Additional motivation comes from partially outsourcing work so that workers learn the true market value of their labors. The per-unit cost paid to external sources creates a benchmark against which to compare internal costs and productivity. In 1990, PacifiCorp, an electric

TABLE 5.16. Salary and Benefits Comparison: Union vs. Nonunion

Item	Union	Nonunion	Union Premium
Salary	$27.00	$18.00	50%
Benefits	$18.00	$5.00	260%
Total	$43.00	$23.00	87%
Benefits as a percent of the total	42%	22%	

Source: Wall Street Journal (1996d)

utility holding company that owns coal mining subsidiaries, announced that it would start to purchase coal from the least expensive source even if doing so meant outsourcing jobs from its own mines. Competition became reality the next year when the company trucked in 300,000 tons of coal. Market forces cannot be ignored. The union saw that either wages and benefits must fall or productivity had to rise. "The following year productivity soared" (Holden 1996). Similarly, in Indianapolis, where some trash-collection jobs are outsourced, remaining workers' productivity rose 40 percent (Zachary 1996).

Outsourcing frees up resources for more profitable uses. It allows companies to manage assets consistent with their opportunity costs. Consider Excel Communications, a large long-distance telephone supplier. The long-distance telecommunications market is highly competitive, which makes capital a relatively scarce resource. How did Excel obtain sufficient funds to build a network? The company's strategy is to resell telephone services by buying access to long lines, at steep discounts, from other suppliers such as AT&T, MCI, and Sprint and then rebundling and reselling the service. That is, Excel outsources the production side of its business, which increases capital available for acquisitions. Outsourcing frees up scarce resources.

Finally, outsourcing can open up new markets. Eastman Kodak Company sold the sales, marketing, and equipment-service operations of its copier business to an English company, Danka Business Systems PLC, but retains the manufacturing end of the business (Nelson 1996). The more profitable divisions of the copier business were sold. The agreement requires Danka to sell Kodak copiers for ten years. Kodak hopes that Danka will sell its copiers worldwide, thereby expanding its business. In fact, Kodak projects that in one year the division's annual net income will become positive after suffering losses of $40 million per year.

Problems with Outsourcing

Outsourcing is not trouble-free. It must start with a fair and equitable contract that clearly articulates the supplier's responsibilities and the penalties incurred if contract terms are violated. Next, the relationship with the supplier must be carefully supervised to insure that the company receives everything required by the contract. Finally, management must prepare a backup plan in case the supplier must be relieved.

A clear metric of outsourcing failure is that productivity falls after a task is reassigned. An example of outsourcing failure is the outsourcing of some accounts-payable work. Vendors entice accounting departments with promises of substantial cost savings from computer automation and customized software (Berton 1996). However, some companies discover that the savings are illusory; costs rise as some bills are paid repeatedly and others are not paid at all. Computers are less adaptable than outsourced humans.

Difficulties also surface if what the company outsources becomes a chief source of strategic advantage in its market. For example, some companies, such as Black and Decker Home Products, differentiate themselves and make their products more identifiable through careful application of industrial design. But industrial-design departments are expensive and often are outsourced early. Once outsourced, product design loses its overall corporate focus.[48]

Another danger is that the supplier may someday steal the purchaser's customers (*Economist* 1996). Etrade, a large internet stockbrokerage firm that went public in the summer of 1996, was established in 1982 as a software firm developing products for financial companies. After observing the profits earned by its customers, Etrade entered the brokerage business itself several years later.

Perhaps the greatest outsourcing risk is that unions may shut down companies that either begin or attempt to increase outsourcing. In early 1996, the UAW imposed a seventeen-day strike on GM that ultimately idled twenty-nine assembly plants because of a shortage of parts. The strike reduced the automaker's profits by $900 million (Blumenstein and Christian 1996). Both sides declared victory after the strike ended. Strikes against outsourcing practices are certain to proliferate.

Outsourcing alone is not sufficient to produce a rebound in corporate profits. The company simultaneously must shed overhead costs as it reduces its workforce. The Libby Foods example is in many ways the archetype; the corporation is nearly virtual, existing only on paper. Necessary consolidations include selling or leasing superfluous buildings and real property and must include revising executive and managerial positions to maintain the proper resource balance.

Outsourcing decisions that prove to be injurious, e.g., quality is found to suffer, should be immediately canceled. A well-designed contract allows an outsourcing firm to terminate the relationship under certain contingencies defined and agreed to by both parties.

Insourcing

Insourcing firms are paid to perform work assignments for other companies. The idea is neither exotic nor novel. Consider these examples:

- thoroughbred horse farms board animals for independent trainers
- french fries are mass produced and sold to restaurants

- tenants sublease excess office space
- companies haul cargo for others in their own trucks to avoid traveling empty on return trips

More than 30 percent of name-brand manufacturers sell knockoff brand products to their competitors. This is insourcing. The recent change is that insourcing is becoming common.

The five major motivations for insourcing include a desire to

1. profit from a high-value-added activity
2. profit from an activity having special entry requirements, such as capital equipment or government certification
3. employ rather than lay off spare workers
4. develop an impenetrable reputation as the provider of a certain service to all market participants
5. acquire information about competitors' prospective product designs

Aircraft maintenance is high-value-added activity. AMR Corporation, the parent of American Airlines, agreed to maintain aircraft owned by America West Airlines, an upstart airline competitor, despite the price pressures these new lines put on the larger carriers like American (*Wall Street Journal* 1996a). AMR knew that if it refused, other carriers would take on the assignment and AMR then would lose these extra profits.[49] In a similar vein, several electric utilities with nuclear expertise and clearance from the Nuclear Regulatory Commission established consulting firms to do business with other utilities.

Wearguard Corporation, a manufacturer and retailer of uniforms, became an insourcer to offset the seasonality of its order inflow (Petzinger 1996). During the summer months, uniform orders decline. To manage this slowdown, Wearguard's workforce mixes 1,200 full-time employees with four hundred temporaries who are let go in the summer. However, Wearguard observed that temporaries have high training costs and lower quality. It considered outsourcing jobs but contractors failed to match internal efficiency and consistency. The solution was insourcing with a partner: Cross Country Motor Club, a firm that handles distressed-motorist calls for automobile clubs and manufacturers. Cross Country's business expands during the summer months, exactly as Wearguard's business slows. The fit between the companies was perfect. Wearguard agreed to assign its surplus workers to Cross Country during summer months; during the rest of the year, Cross Country's workers are delegated to work for Wearguard.

Companies also insource work in order to foster a market perception of the preeminent quality of their own product. Video camera producers follow this strategy. Many companies sell video cameras, but only two companies make them. The salesperson's assertion, "It's made by Sony," not only extends the quality label to the product being sold by another vendor but also elevates Sony in the eyes of the consumer.

Insourcing companies seeking information about competitors' products have crossed the ethical boundary. Arguments that this behavior and the common practice of hiring people who formerly worked for the competition are identical ignores the fact that the individual can be prosecuted if he/she violates a proprietary agreement and the insourcer does not disclose its intentions or purpose when the contractual arrangements are being drafted. Nonetheless, the practice exists.

Auctions

The disposal of superfluous corporate assets seeks to obtain the highest possible return. One method is to sell assets in an auction. The three primary types of auctions are compared in table 5.17.

With English auctions, all bidders know the current bid of other participants. Art galleries like Christie's or Sotheby's employ this type of auction. They yield excellent prices when there are many knowledgeable buyers. If there are few bidders or if bidders lack information about the true value of the item on the block, an English auction may yield unacceptably low prices.

In contrast, in both sealed-bid and Dutch auctions the bidder is unaware of the current bids of the other participants. Recent government sales of cellular telephone frequencies and oil leases employed sealed bids. Dutch auctions are operated in the flower markets of Holland. Both of these structures work best when there are few bidders.

TABLE 5.17. Comparison of Types of Auctions

Type	Action	Winner
English	An auctioneer solicits higher and higher bids	Highest bidder
Sealed-bid	Participants submit sealed bids	Highest bidder; in one variant the winner pays the second-highest bid price
Dutch	Auctioneer states a high price and lowers it gradually	Person willing to agree to the highest price

Since the number of bidders in liquidations is limited, it is probably advisable to avoid English auctions.

William Vickrey received the 1996 Nobel Prize in economics, in part for his work on sealed-bid auctions (Phillips 1996). A variant of sealed-bid auctions, known as Vickrey auctions, occurs when the highest bidder wins but he/she pays the second-highest bid price. The idea is to get people to bid their true values since they only pay the true-value estimate of the person who has the next highest valuation.

Accounting as a Management Tool

Imagine the chaos if all employees in a business spoke different languages. Accounting sweeps away this anarchy. Although the statement sounds trite, it is true that accounting is the language of business. The turnaround manager frequently finds a Tower of Babel in distressed businesses that lack a common vision. In these businesses, the marketing people preach unit sales, research and development teams emphasize new products, and operations personnel stress defects per thousand units. Accounting is the adhesive that can bond functional areas together. The measures used in each department translate into impact on the firm's financial position. One of the first tasks in corporate renewal is to convince all parties, internal and external, to embrace the accounting description of the company and its financial condition.

Accounting data provide vivid testimony about a company's recent and historical performance. It contributes a virtually unlimited catalogue of informational statistics or ratios that documents an enterprise's strengths and weaknesses.

Ratios also create meaningful corporate targets readily communicated throughout the organization and to creditors and lenders whose continued support is essential to the enterprise. Targets are the foundation of any good incentive plan that judges, rewards, and encourages employees. Accounting provides a route away from distress.

The crisis manager establishes turnaround targets to achieve explicit goals: profit or cash breakeven, inventory or receivables reduction, or lengthening of the payables period. Articulating goals as quantitative targets helps assess incremental progress and creates a platform from which goals can be revised.

Exactitude is not the same thing as truthfulness. Accounting information may mislead or even lie; unethical managers may manipulate or purposely distort accounting information to provide false impressions to creditors, investors, or employees.

Principal Financial Statements

The three principal financial statements—balance sheet, income statement, and statement of cash flows—are the nouns and verbs of the accounting language. The balance sheet compares a firm's assets to its liabilities and shareholders' equity at a moment in time. The company's resources with earnings potential are balanced against the claims of creditors and shareholders. In contrast to the snapshot quality of the balance sheet, the income statement presents the firm's earnings over a time interval, typically a quarter or year. Like the income statement, the statement of cash flows also reflects a specific time interval and presents a firm's net cash inflow and outflows.

Valuation of monetary and nonmonetary items plays an important role in the preparation of financial statements. Financial statements are especially valuable because they can be compared among companies. Standardization of valuation methods and definitions is essential, otherwise the information content of financial statements is sacrificed. Generally accepted accounting principles (GAAP) is the standardized set of rules for the preparation of financial statements. GAAP regulations are promulgated by the Financial Accounting Standards Board (FASB), a nonpublic organization.[50] Its proclamations are indexed with names like "FASB Statement No. 1."

Assets on the balance sheet are owned resources likely to provide the firm with future cash flows. Monetary assets (cash, marketable securities, and accounts receivable) due within one year are valued at the level of cash the firm is likely to receive; those due after one year are valued at the present value of future cash flows. Nonmonetary assets (inventories and plant and equipment) are valued at historical costs. Liabilities are obligations to pay for benefits already received. Liabilities for services not yet received, such as labor contracts, are not valued on the balance sheet.[51] Liabilities due within a year are valued at the amount of cash necessary to discharge the obligation; those due after a year are valued at the present value of future cash outflows. Warranty expenses are valued at the expected cost of providing the service.

The income statement compares revenues and expenses. A sole proprietorship or a small partnership is likely to employ a cash accounting system. Cash accounting recognizes revenues when cash is received and recognizes expenses when cash is paid out. A cash accounting system, however, fails adequately to mate revenue and expense flows. GAAP mandates accrual accounting. This is revenue recognition after the firm's duties are concluded and it has received cash or a reliable receivable and expenses are matched against revenues. Expenses not plainly associated with the sale of a particular unit are recognized as they are paid.

Statement of Cash Flows

The statement of cash flows summarizes net cash flows, aggregating total cash flow from component cash flows: operations, investment, and financing activities. Operating cash flows are derived from the sale of the product or service, investment cash flows from the purchase or sale of noncurrent assets to run the business or funds invested in other businesses, and financing cash flows from the acquisition or repayment of capital. The statement of cash flows' importance was acknowledged after the bankruptcy of profitable firms that inadequately planned their cash needs.[52] Cash flow generally does not equal income flow:

- cash receipts do not equal recognized revenue
- cash expenditures do not synchronize with revenues
- investing and financing activities produce additional cash inflows or outflows

In the statement of cash flows, cash flow is derived separately for each category, and then the parts are combined into a total net change in cash position, as seen in table 5.18.[53] A statement of cash flows for Jersey Foods, Inc., in 1996 and 1997 is presented in table 5.19.

Jersey Foods experienced a dramatic negative turnaround in 1997 as its healthy annual profits plunged and became a loss following trouble with contaminated products. What about Jersey Foods' cash flow? The most elementary measure of cash flow combines net income and any noncash charges against income, such as depreciation, depletion, or amortization. On that simple basis, Jersey Foods' cash flow is positive: negative $74,000 plus $103,000. The formal analysis in the statement of cash flows refers to this sum as working capital from operations. Balance-sheet activity also affects cash flow. Jersey Foods had large changes in its accounts receivables, inventories, and accounts payable. Uses of funds to increase current assets decreases cash flow. Similarly,

TABLE 5.18. Schematic for the Statement of Cash Flows

Activity	Inflow from Sale Of	Outflow from Purchase Of	Cash Flow
Operations	Products or services	Goods or services	Cash flow from operations
Investing	Investments, property, or equipment	Investments, property, or equipment	Cash flow from investing
Financing	New equity or debt	Existing equity or debt from cash dividends	Cash flow from financing
			Total

sources of funds that expand current liabilities increase cash flow. Cash flow from operations equals the sum of working capital provided by operations and balance sheet activities affecting cash flow.

Investing and financing activities are additional sources of cash flow. Cash flows from investment are derived from the purchase or sale of noncurrent assets, like machines or factories, and from business ventures. Jersey Foods experienced a steady cash drain from its purchase of fixed assets. Its other investment activities produced cash flow in some years and cash drains in other years. Financing cash flow during 1997 shifted radically as the financial markets responded to its changing fortunes. Short-term loans dried up; new long-term debt and equity offerings replaced this source of cash flow. The cessation of dividend payments conserved cash in 1997. Overall, following a healthy $375,000 increase in cash in 1996, Jersey Foods' cash position deteriorated by $35,000 in 1997.

The simplistic notion of cash flow—net income plus noncash charges—overestimates the real cash-flow picture at Jersey Foods. As a

TABLE 5.19. Statement of Cash Flows for Jersey Foods, Inc. ($ in thousands)

	1996	1997
Operations		
Net income	$483	$−74
Depreciation	101	103
Working capital from operations	$584	$29
Δ in receivables (increase)	−19	−21
Δ in inventories (increase)	−145	−159
Δ in accounts payable (decrease)	129	156
Cash flow from operations	$549	$5
Investing		
Fixed assets purchased	$−201	$−194
Other investments	45	−29
Cash flow from investing	$−156	$−223
Financing		
Δ in short-term loans (decrease)	$21	$0
Δ in long-term loans (decrease)	0	134
Δ in common stock (decrease)	−17	49
Dividends	−22	0
Cash flow from financing	$−18	$183
Change in cash	$375	$−35

first approximation, the simple measure is more accurate than net income alone, but it clearly is less satisfactory than the statement of cash flows.

Jersey Foods' statement of cash flows provides the turnaround manager with penetrating insights. First, operations were approximately cash-flow neutral in 1997. While a prosperous firm would not be satisfied with cash-flow neutrality, in a crisis it indicates that a distressed firm will be able to pay its bills, provided it maintains vendor support. Second, the purchase of new fixed assets depleted Jersey Foods' cash. If these assets are essential, a crisis looms, though leasing is an alternative. Third, sources of financial cash flows were stretched thin; the bank stopped extending new credit, the new equity and debt markets were not unlimited, and the dividend was curtailed.

Areas of Managerial Discretion

Companies are somewhat like apples at the grocery store, all red on the outside but some with worms or bruises on the inside. Company differences arise from real sources, such as stronger technology or newer factories, and from artificial sources such as accounting choices. Corporate renewal targets real problems; it should not be distracted by accounting issues. The next section describes managerial accounting choices that affect how companies look in financial statements.

Inventories

Managers choose between first in, first out (FIFO) or last in, first out (LIFO) accounting assumption.[54] This is a "flow of costs" assumption and refers to the order in which items are sold out of inventory. The assumption is important because the cost of purchasing merchandise varies over time. FIFO assigns the cost of the first item acquired to the first item sold and assumes that the cost of remaining inventory is from the most recent purchases. In contrast, LIFO assigns the cost of the last items acquired to the first items sold and assumes that the cost of remaining inventory is from the beginning purchases. Table 5.20 itemizes these

TABLE 5.20. FIFO and LIFO Accounting Comparison

	Cost of Goods Sold	Effect on Net Income	Inventories	Effect on Inventory
FIFO	Old goods	Higher	New goods	Higher
LIFO	New goods	Lower	Old goods	Lower

assumptions. How input costs are assigned to units sold affects the cost of goods sold, reported on the income statement, and the value of inventories shown on the balance sheet. Table 5.21 shows that for a company selling three units in the first year and producing four units, both production and sales increase by one unit in each successive year. Production costs increase by $1 each year. Note that the company must adopt one of the two accounting methods. Table 5.21 illustrates that under FIFO accounting, costs in inventory are basically new, while cost of goods sold may include some older, less expensive, costs. In contrast, with LIFO accounting, costs in inventory are new, old and very old, while goods sold are generally new and more expensive. Because FIFO

TABLE 5.21. FIFO and LIFO Operations

Unit	Year Produced	Year Sold	FIFO Cost of Goods Sold (Black), Inventory (Gray)				LIFO Cost of Goods Sold (Black), Inventory (Gray)			
			Year				Year			
			1	2	3	4	1	2	3	4
1	1	1								
2	1	1								
3	1	1								
4	1	2								
5	2	2								
6	2	2								
7	2	2								
8	2	3								
9	2	3								
10	3	3								
11	3	3								
12	3	3								
13	3	4								
14	3	4								
15	3	4								
16	4	4								
17	4	4								
18	4	4								
19	4	5								
20	4	5								
21	4	5								
22	4	5								

companies use a somewhat lower estimate of cost of goods sold than LIFO companies (assuming that costs rise over time), they tend to report higher incomes.[55] In addition, FIFO companies show higher inventory levels than LIFO companies.[56] A turnaround manager knows that a company can look more profitable and appear to have more inventory by switching from LIFO to FIFO accounting.

Depreciation

Purchases consumed within a year are expensed in the current period. Purchases with a useful life exceeding a year are capitalized and depreciated over their useful life. Depreciation is a noncash charge against revenues. Annual depreciation expense is determined by the interaction of an item's historic costs, its useful life, its residual value, and its annual depreciation factor.

$$\text{Depreciation expense} = \delta\,(\text{Historical cost, Useful life, Residual value, Depreciation method})$$

Historical cost appears on the asset's invoice; the Internal Revenue Service provides a range of useful lives for various asset categories; residual value is estimated from experience; and the annual depreciation factor depends on the choice of depreciation methods.

GAAP permits both straight-line and accelerated depreciation. With the former, depreciable cost is written off in equal installments over an item's useful life; with the latter, early depreciation charges are larger than subsequent expenses. Both techniques result in the same total depreciation over an item's useful life. Straight-line depreciation is used in preparing financial statements at most companies, though they generally use accelerated depreciation for tax reporting. Depreciation differences between financial and tax reports contribute to a firm's deferred tax liability on its balance sheet.[57]

Leases

Operating leases are not reported on the balance sheet, though the income statement includes the associated expense, but capital leases are shown on the balance sheet. A capital lease increases both the firm's reported assets (equipment under capital lease) and its liabilities (obligations under capital lease). The income statement includes depreciation against the asset and an interest expense charge derived from the total leased payment.

Operating leases present managers opportunities for off-balance-sheet financing, where no trace of assets acquired for use appears on the balance sheet. A turnaround manager investigates the level of operating leases at the commencement of an engagement.

Pensions and Health Care

Pension plans are either defined-benefit or defined-contribution plans. Under the former, the company's total obligation depends on employee retirement and death. As retirement age falls and death rates decline, corporate defined-benefit liabilities rise. Under the latter, the employer is required to make a current contribution to a fund, and how much a person receives in retirement depends on the amount of money accumulated in the fund.

Obligations under defined-benefit plans are reported, according to FASB Statement No. 87, in the notes to the financial statements. The notes reveal the size of the unfunded pension liability. FASB Statement No. 106 extends the reporting requirement to defined health-benefit plans. Unlike pensions, however, unfunded health-care liabilities are not fully reported until the worker reaches retirement.

Internal Accounting Controls

Employee and external fraud are resource drains that deplete a firm's cash flow. Internal accounting controls, if properly instituted and strictly enforced, limit the impact and occurrence of these cash drains.

Where does employee theft occur? Anywhere that employees en-

TABLE 5.22. Employee Frauds and Errors and Avoidance Techniques

Loss Area	Examples	Avoidance
Purchasing	Paying the same invoice twice	Only pay from original invoice; cancel purchase orders after receipt
Purchasing	Buying for personal use	Different employees should request purchases, authorize payment, and cut checks
Purchasing	Overpaying	Check arithmetic
Inventory	Slippage, obsolescence	Minimize inventories and find a supplier who will ship quickly
Accounting	Paying phantom employees	Have managers verify status
Accounting	Paying bogus invoices	Require two signatures on large checks and insist that original invoices accompany all requests
Accounting	Slippage from petty cash	Authorize a single person to withdraw from the petty-cash drawer
Accounting	General fraud	Spread power among several employees to increase anxiety over detection; for example, have another employee receconcile bank statements

counter money or company property; in other words, everywhere (*Wall Street Journal* 1995c). Table 5.22 lists various actions that cause needless corporate expenditures and ways to avoid them. Most renewal engagements uncover lax accounting controls. If employee theft is suspected, changes should be instituted immediately to minimize honest employee anxiety and maximize dishonest employee behavioral changes. Employees should be notified of the new policy at an open meeting or via a detailed letter. Creating public discussion of what needs to be accomplished and how it benefits the company and protects jobs is essential. Employees should never be dismissed or punished without legal advice, and all evidence of wrongdoing or misappropriation of funds should be retained.

Probably the best protection against internal fraud is to have different people auditing or reconciling accounts than those responsible for authorizing or cutting checks. Costs are higher this way, but it saves money in the long run. Small businesses are more susceptible and less prepared to stymie employee fraud or oversight than are larger businesses. The entrepreneur or owner/manager can establish the right atmosphere by regularly examining the books and bank records. Fear of detection is the best protection.

Losses due to fraud or error on the part of suppliers, consultants, or financial institutions go undetected if internal accounting controls are weak. Companies are generally more vigilant against external deception than internal fraud. The simple but effective avoidance techniques listed in table 5.23 minimize damages resulting from external errors or frauds. When a situation arises with external parties, discuss misgivings with

TABLE 5.23. External Frauds and Errors and Avoidance Techniques

Perpetrator	Examples	Avoidance
Supplier	Bidding a low price and billing a higher price	Only pay from original invoice
Supplier	Overcharging for freight, taxes, or handling	Demand net-pricing terms up front
Supplier	Shipping fewer units than were purchased	Confirm every small order and spot-check larger shipments
Consultants	Excessive hourly billing	• Demand 15-minute time verification sheets • Institute a piece-rate contract
Consultants	Excessive expense charges	Institute a piece-rate contract
Consultants	Unauthorized use of company credit cards, vehicles, etc.	Contract should describe consultants' perquisites, if any
Financial institution	Payments credited to wrong account number	Reconcile bank statements regularly

their corporate supervisors before accusing the company or its employees of misdeeds. Perhaps the problem is an error and not a deception. Retain all evidence, however, until the matter is settled.

The task of detecting cases of external fraud or error is simplified if internal nonaccounting staff employees help out. Employee apathy and a willingness to look the other way invite external parties to steal. It may be necessary to institute financial incentives to motivate employee cooperation. Employees should be told that they wouldn't let a stranger balance their personal checkbooks, but here they are letting one overcharge the company and put their jobs at risk. The trouble with establishing financial incentives is that vigilance tasks really are part of everyone's job. On the other hand, a truck driver is not a detective. In the right setting, a simple honesty policy may be as effective as financial incentives. Peter Alcock, who renewed Winchester Gun, remarked that he always looks for underweight or low-quality shipments from suppliers seeking to recover something from an account that is past due.

CHAPTER 6

Employee Downsizing

This chapter examines the choices, methods, and ramifications associated with downsizing people, plants, products, or processes during corporate renewal. Must a company with too many employees downsize?[1] Anyone with experience in the workforce knows that the answer to this question is unequivocally NO! At various times each day, every company, even those actively recruiting new personnel, experiences periods of slack time when certain workers are nonproductive or even idle; in some companies, slack periods are more protracted, extending into days, weeks, or even months before a strategy to reduce the workforce is implemented. To grasp why procrastination is not necessarily irrational requires that we integrate microeconomics, labor and inventory theories, and just-in-time production. These models provide the theoretical framework to understand layoffs. A short overview of the models and their conclusions is provided for the general reader in the first part of this chapter. In the chapter's later sections, the subject is considered from a practical perspective.

Economic Considerations

Microeconomic theory assumes that consumers maximize their utility (i.e., satisfaction) and that businesses maximize their profits. Both maximizations are constrained by the income available to the consumer or the level of consumer demand for the firm's product. Let us turn our attention to the producer alone, since our immediate interest is to explain why some producers lay off excess workers and others retain them.

There are two basic types of industries: competitive and oligopolistic.[2] In the former, there are numerous firms, each of which sells basically the same product, while in the latter, firms face little or no competition. The competitive firm in a competitive industry must accept the industry's normal price as its own since no consumer would pay more than that price for its goods. Thus, the competitive firm sells as many units of its product as it wants to at the industry price. In contrast, an oligopolistic firm chooses the price at which to sell its product and thus influences its product-demand level. Both firms seek to maximize their profits. The competitive firm does so by minimizing its cost of production and selling products until no further profits are available. The oligopolistic firm maximizes profits by finding the optimal price level and then minimizing its cost of production for the demand level associated with that price.

Microeconomic theory describes cost minimization as a trade-off between the unit cost of inputs (i.e., resources) and their marginal productivity. Unit resource costs are usually held constant. Feasible resource combinations (such as mixtures of machines, skilled and unskilled workers, and materials) come from the firm's production function (i.e., a mathematical relationship that describes output changes resulting from incremental changes in resource usage).[3] The least-cost input mix capable of producing the desired output is the optimal resource combination.

There are two general types of production functions: fixed proportions and neoclassical functions. The first type, developed by Wassily Leontief, a Nobel Prize–winning economist, assumes that factors of production (i.e., inputs) must be used in fixed proportion. The other type assumes that resources are infinitely variable in the production process. The producer's task, to minimize costs for a fixed level of output, is to discover the least-cost mix of resources given his/her production function.

Leontief Production Function

When a company's technology, or production function, is characterized as fixed proportions, it must use proportionately more (less) workers as its output increases (decreases). This relationship is illustrated in figure 6.1 using the traditional microeconomic concepts of an isoquant (i.e., a curve describing the various input combinations that can produce a given output) and an isocost curve (i.e., a curve showing the amount of inputs—individually or combined—that can be purchased for a fixed amount of money). The optimal input mix is found at the point where the isoquant and isocost are tangent (i.e., just touching).

The firm depicted in figure 6.1, uses five machines and three workers to produce one unit of output; two units of output require ten machines and six workers, and so on. The firm expands its output along the expansion ray. If, however, a fourth worker is added when five machines are already owned, no extra output results. Similarly, adding a sixth machine when three workers are already employed adds no incremental

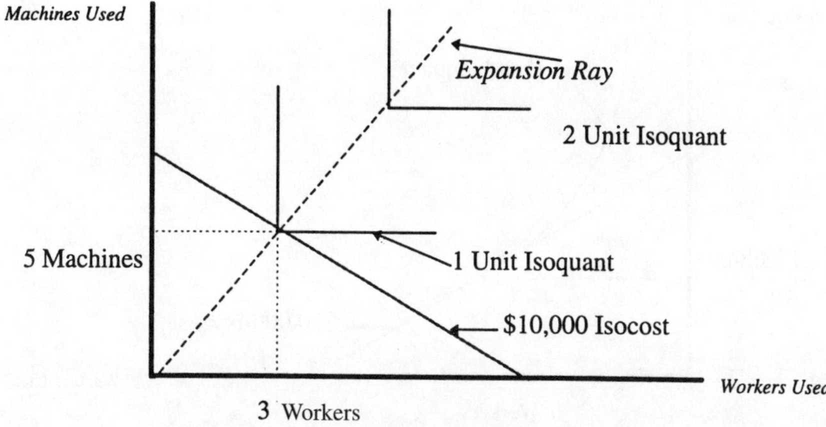

Fig. 6.1. Finding the least-cost mix of machines and workers with a Leontief production function

output. With this peculiarly rigid production function, the choice of inputs is independent of either the wage rate or the interest rate. Few companies are straddled with such inflexible technologies.[4] As the demand for its product grows, this firm hires more workers. If output decreases after workers are hired, then the firm has surplus workers.

Neoclassical Production Function

Most firms can substitute workers for machines or machines for workers in production. That is, if wages rise, the firm can buy more machines and use fewer workers. An isoquant representing one output unit from this type of production function is depicted in figure 6.2 where, again, it is compared with a $10,000 isocost. The optimal, least-cost input mix found at the tangent point combines one machine and six workers. Should wages rise (fall), the new tangent point would occur at an optimal input combination with more (fewer) machines and fewer (more) workers. When this firm expands its production beyond one unit, it may or may not maintain the 1:6 ratio of machines to workers, but it definitely will hire the input combination that minimizes its production costs.

With the neoclassical production function, underutilization of the workforce is possible if there are unanticipated contractions in desired output that move the firm to a lower isoquant (similar to the Leontief case above) or if a shift in relative wages means that workers are more costly than other inputs. Microeconomic theory says little about the

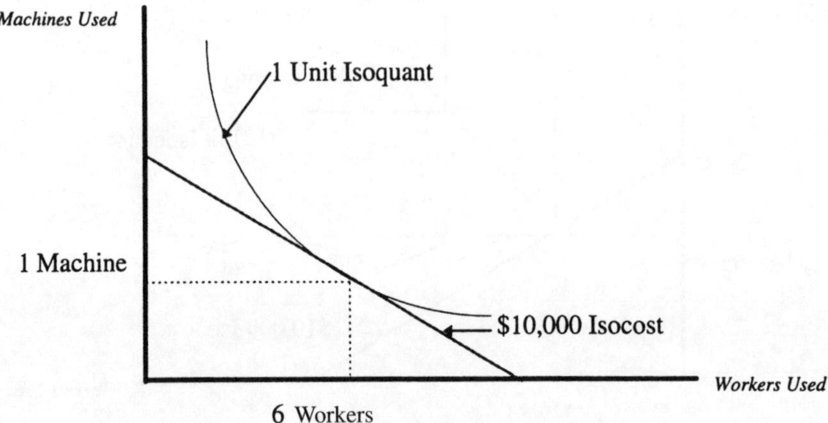

Fig. 6.2. Finding the least-cost mix of machines and workers with a neoclassical production function

adjustment process following an output or wage shock. In practice, the firm's manager may immediately lay off surplus workers or may delay a layoff until the future is certain. The layoff decision compares the trade-off between assured savings on the one hand and indefinite costs on the other. Savings are readily computed as the sum of curtailed wages and benefits for laid off workers.[5]

Costs associated with layoffs are more difficult to calculate with certainty. There are two types of layoff costs: direct and indirect. Direct costs are reasonably well defined and estimable, while indirect costs are more problematic and harder to estimate. Direct layoff costs include

- higher unemployment insurance payments
- severance payments
- continued benefits payments
- counseling or outplacement expenses

These expenses are foreseeable based on the firm's own experiences and the dictates of corporate policy.

Indirect layoff costs include

- lost business following negative word-of-mouth and press reports, depressed morale of continuing workers leading to declining productivity, and quality-control problems
- rehire costs should wage or product-demand conditions recover
- higher labor costs if the firm develops a negative reputation

Estimation of indirect costs from the experience of other firms in the industry is possible, but this is a wild card.

Putting the costs and benefits of layoffs into a single algebraic equation, as in equation (1), clarifies why some firms hesitate to order layoffs.

$$\text{Gains} <=> \text{Costs}$$

$$\text{Wages and benefits savings} <=> \text{Direct costs} + \textit{Unknown indirect costs} \quad (1)$$

Procrastination is a sound policy if the differential between gains and direct costs is minuscule since there then is greater likelihood that, with indirect costs included, total costs exceed gains. Using the same reasoning, more afflicted firms in an industry are expected to conduct layoffs if one firm in the industry manages a successful layoff.

Other Employment Models

The EOQ-Type Model

One of the most widely adapted economic models is Baumol's (1952) cost-minimization paradigm for determining the optimal level of inventories. Baumol's own work focused on the demand for money; other researchers used Baumol's framework to describe how a company minimizes its physical inventory costs, and I use this framework to describe how a company decides how many extra, not-currently-productive employees to hire.

The intellectual underpinning of the Baumol model is that total inventory costs rise along with the stock of goods in inventory (due to higher carrying costs) and fall as inventories are ordered less frequently but in larger volume. These two costs move in opposite directions, since a reduction in ordering frequency saves money consumed in the administrative function but then increases the average volume of inventories, which raises interest and other carrying costs. The trade-off between ordering and carrying costs is shown in figure 6.3. The total cost curve in the figure combines the two ingredients of inventory costs. For a company that knows its annual inventory needs with certainty, optimal order size is found at the point where the total-cost curve reaches its minimum point. Assuming that new inventories are delivered instantaneously, these inventories are worked down to zero, at which point the company reorders. The model is referred to as the economic ordering quantity, or EOQ, model since it yields the economic or least-cost ordering quantity.[6]

With minor adaptation, the EOQ framework demonstrates both

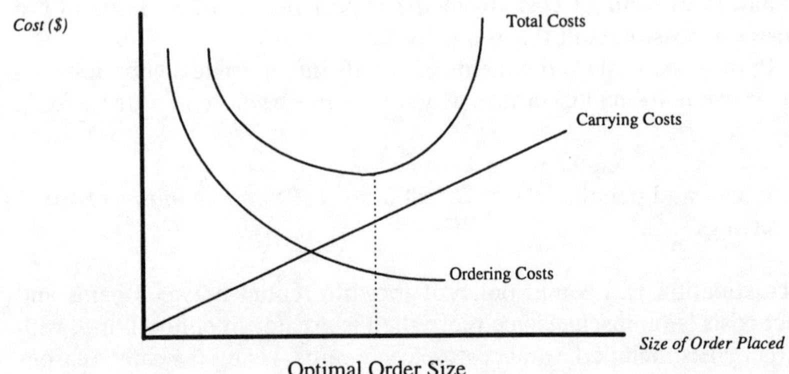

Fig. 6.3. Baumol's inventory model

how companies determine the number of not-currently-productive workers to hire at one time and how they decide how many of these workers to lay off when circumstances change. First consider the question "Would a company want to have inactive or extra workers?"[7] The answer to this question may be either yes or no. The answer is no if the environment is stable and the existing workforce is unlikely to retire or quit or if hiring new workers is free and instantaneous. With those conditions, a surplus stock of workers is unnecessary. The answer is yes if the employee turnover rate is nonzero or if hiring is costly or delayed. In those instances, companies need extra employees to smoothly and economically fill future employment needs.

How many inactive workers are needed? The number of inactive workers desired by the company is a fraction of the active workforce, α, which accounts for future turnover and growth, as seen in equation (2).

$$\text{Inactive workers}_t = \alpha_t \text{ Active workers}_t \tag{2}$$

where α is the factor describing the number of desired idle workers and t denotes year. The total number of employees equals the sum of active (productive) and inactive (nonproductive) workers. Assuming that active workers retire or quit steadily throughout the year, the firm constantly must hire new workers if it hires only one inactive worker at a time. Alternatively, when a batch of inactive workers is hired at one time, they are recruited and trained as a group and transferred individually into the active workforce as turnover occurs. Similarly, new workers hired to fill employment needs resulting from output growth are hired individually or in a group.

The maximum number of desired inactive workers is constant over time when no growth is expected in the active workforce and the turnover rate is steady. In that case, α_t equals α_{t-1}, and there is no change in the number of desired inactive workers, as in equation (3).

$$\Delta \text{ Inactive workers} = \alpha_t \text{ Active workers}_t - \alpha_{t-1} \text{ Active workers}_{t-1} = 0 \quad (3)$$

In that case, the number of new inactive workers hired during a year equals the number of workers who retire or quit, $\alpha_t \times$ (active workers).

It is necessary to increase the proportion of total employment that is inactive workers, α, as the expected growth in sales and hence the need for active workers increases and as the turnover rate of existing workers increases. When growth is anticipated, a larger number of new inactive workers is hired during a year. Then α_t does not equal α_{t-1}, and using equation (3), the number hired equals

$$\text{New hires} = \alpha_{t-1} \times (\text{Active workers}) + \alpha_t \times (\Delta \text{ Active workers})$$

When the turnover rate increases, the number of inactive workers hired increases as α itself shifts upward.

New inactive employees can be hired all at once (one time per year), one at a time (as many times per year as workers retire or quit or new positions open up), or some number in between. Fixed costs associated with the hiring process are significant, especially for several of its components:

- design and placement of advertisements
- screening of the applicant pool
- training of new hires
- adjustment period during which new hires learn their jobs

As a consequence, there are distinct economies of scale to hiring and training that should encourage multiple hirings as a way of lowering costs. Moreover, postponements in filling job vacancies caused by hiring too few inactive workers soon enough results in lost production, declining sales, and lower profits. The total cost of hiring includes the direct hiring costs listed above and the indirect cost of lost profits. Hiring a larger group of employees at one time lowers hiring costs by reducing

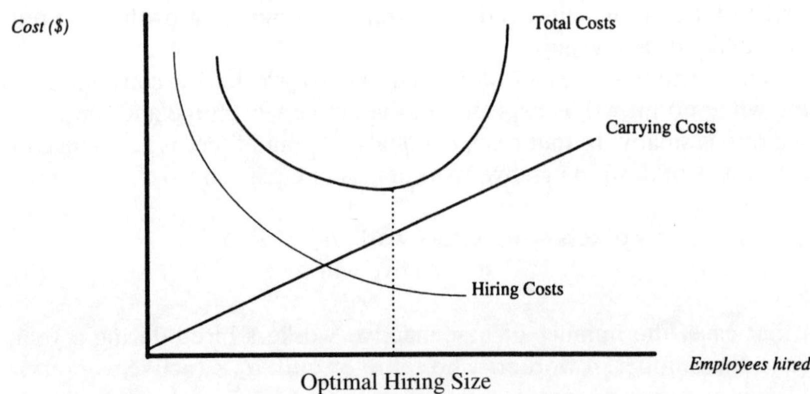

Fig. 6.4. An inventory theoretic employment model

lost profits due to a worker shortage and fixed hiring costs, but it increases the inventory of inactive workers, which imposes other costs.

A company's decision about the number of workers to hire at one time as not yet working but already trained or in training personnel depends on two factors, the cost of holding an inventory of extra workers (wages and benefits) and the cost of hiring new workers. The optimal number hired at one time increases as carrying costs decrease or hiring costs increase. But since these move in opposite directions, the optimal number hired at one time is found by trading off the two costs, as shown in figure 6.4.

Most firms maintain a supply of extra workers. The number of these employees grows as wages and benefits decline, as hiring costs decline, and as the company expects more growth in product output. Layoffs result when any factor determining the maximum size of the pool of inactive workers moves in the opposite direction; that is, layoffs increase when

- wages and benefits increase
- hiring costs (either direct or indirect) decrease
- expected future output is lower than anticipated

According to the neoclassical model, wage and benefit increases also imply layoffs.

Just-in-Time Hiring

Since the early 1980s the just-in-time (JIT) concept has revolutionized manufacturing. Before JIT, companies held large stocks of inventories—

raw materials, work in progress, and other inputs—to protect against shortages. With JIT, a close working relationship between producer and supplier replaces a pool of inventory. In addition, JIT eliminates the recurring periods of waiting and not working that are typical in normal production, allowing each worker to be productive more of the time. Many reengineering efforts include aspects of JIT. For example, ordering and shipping delays are reduced by linking a supplier's warehouse with information technology to a customer's retail outlets, which allows the retailer to operate with less inventory (see reengineering details in chap. 8).

JIT theory applied to the hiring and firing process suggests that fewer workers are required if the firm has alternate labor suppliers available. For example, the supply of not yet productive but employed workers is reducible

- by outsourcing unanticipated work to a dependable producer
- by developing working relationships with temporary agencies
- by nurturing a symbiotic relationship with high schools, vocational schools, community colleges, or universities to channel student interns and graduates to the firm

In theory, with JIT employment a firm requires no surplus workers. Moving to JIT induces layoffs as the inventory of inactive workers is eliminated.

Practical Downsizing Issues

For many companies, the objective is not downsizing per se but reducing the total wage bill, the money paid to workers in salaries and benefits. This objective is satisfied either by laying off extra workers or by reducing compensation packages. A number of considerations affect the choice between a reduction in the number of workers and a reduction in wages and benefits as described in table 6.1. Wage and benefit cuts are less effective than layoffs in producing substantial wage bill savings, and there are few examples of companies reducing compensation by 30 percent or more.[8] This is a result of the morale, worker productivity, and public relations consequences of either policy.[9] Unions are a key player in these deliberations; their willingness to compromise defines how management behaves. Another key factor is the company's position in the corporate renewal classification scheme. For instance, during a corporate transformation exercise, layoffs are unlikely, though cutting future increases in wages and even reducing benefits is quite permissible; at the other extreme, in crisis management both layoffs and wage/benefit cuts are executed.

Survey analysis performed by *Fortune* magazine (Faltermayer 1992) indicates that companies resort to a variety of techniques to reduce employment or their total wage bill. Covering responses from 909 major companies, the survey, summarized in table 6.2, indicates a general disinclination among downsizing employers to impose destructive shocks on their workers. There is not even a layoff or dismissal category in the table. Note, however, that the *Fortune* sample contains larger, more financially secure companies that probably are engaged in corporate transformation rather than either turnaround or crisis management. Smaller companies and those with greater financial exigencies are more likely to rely on layoffs than on the techniques listed in table 6.2. Moreover, a more recent survey might reveal greater reliance on layoffs by even the largest companies.

TABLE 6.1. Factors Influencing the Choice between Layoffs and Wage/Benefit Cuts

Factor	Layoffs Are More Appropriate If	Wage/Benefit Cuts Are More Appropriate If
Amount of savings required	• A major cost reduction is required immediately	• Costs are excessive but the business is reasonably healthy
Morale and productivity issues	• The workforce is impermanent • The workforce is unwilling to embrace change • There is little output difference between workers	• Productivity is related to experience • Spouses of many workers have similar benefits available through their employers
Ability to hire workers when times improve	• Many qualified unemployed workers	• The pool of unemployed dries up during periods of prosperity
Union rules	• The least-qualified workers, regardless of seniority, can be laid off	• Recontracting is permitted • Nonunion firms offer fewer wages or benefits
Cost of unemployment-compensation insurance	• The firm has an unsullied historical layoff record	• Excessive layoffs in the past have resulted in penalty insurance rates
Compensation or benefits are above the industry average	• The union is unwilling to renegotiate	• The layoff threat is believed by employees

Empirical Evidence on Downsizing

While many companies resort to downsizing or employee layoffs, many do not achieve anticipated results. A Census Bureau report prepared by Martin Baily, Eric Bartelsman, and John Haltiwanger classified only 65 percent of downsizing companies as successful (Noble 1994). The study examined 140,000 companies over the decade 1977–87. Downsizing companies, those whose employment levels fell during the decade, comprised 55,527 firms out of the larger sample. Of these firms, 36,238 experienced growth in labor productivity and profits during the decade; for the remaining 19,289 downsizing companies, both productivity and profits declined. That is, fully one-third of firms laying off employees became even more inefficient and less profitable. It is worth noting that the average productivity gain attained over the decade by successful downsizing firms, about 9 percent, was nearly matched by the 7 percent growth in productivity by the successful upsizing (growing employment) firms. These intriguing results suggest that serious care and thought are

TABLE 6.2. How Companies Downsize (based on 909 companies)

Method	Description	Percentage of Firms Using
Hiring freeze	No department is allowed to hire new or replacement workers; selective hiring freezes permit hirings in special situations	70%
Cut overtime	Reduce proportion of total work time in the overtime category	45%
Retrain/redeploy	Select high-quality but superfluous workers and train them for positions in other divisions	44%
Reduce to part time	Instead of laying off workers, reduce their work hours. A critical issue is whether hours are cut below the benefits-eligible level	22%
Job sharing	Permit two workers to share one job	14%
Fire and rehire as consultants	Lay off workers and then rehire them as consultants at rates of pay that may exceed their total wage and benefit levels. However, they are fired at a moment's notice	11%
Unpaid vacations	Force workers to take time off without pay	9%
Fewer hours worked per week	Reduce normal workload from perhaps 40 hours to 37.5 hours per week	9%
Reduce hourly or monthly pay	Reduce pay scales or incentive payments	6%

Source: Faltermayer (1992: 72)

mandatory in any downsizing campaign, and unfocused downsizing not anchored to a larger corporate renewal strategy is likely to fail.

The Downsizing Message

Layoffs produce immediate cost savings. They also deliver three serious messages, two of which are transmitted to employees and one to external stakeholders. The first message is that all jobs at this company are at risk. Capable workers react by considering job opportunities elsewhere; incompetent workers search for places to hide. An all-too-common occurrence when companies commence a layoff is that their best workers leave the firm within three months anyway. The renewal manager must be prepared to dispel exaggerated employee fears with extensive and accurate communication.

The second message is aimed at employees expected to stay with the company: future employment depends on the company becoming more efficient and productive. If this message is managed well, the company can achieve an even greater cost reduction than is predicted from the layoff alone. The third layoff message, that the firm's future is at risk, is received by nonemployees and generates harmful consequences. Sending a message of weakness may cause customers to retreat, competitors to besiege the market, and financial markets to reassess the firm.[10] The turnaround manager must be prepared to overcome these threats.

Not only do downsizing companies regularly misconstrue how employees and other stakeholders will interpret these messages, but they frequently misjudge how the press will characterize the company's actions. There are few predicaments, such as an oil spill or a political scandal, in which a company receives the vitriolic press coverage accompanying a major layoff announcement (see the AT&T discussion later in this chapter). Journalists pounce on human-interest aspects of the story: the number of employees released, the contagious layoff effect in the community's service sector, an expected decline in local real estate values, and the plight of current pensioners. Rarely does an article explain how a layoff preserves the jobs of continuing workers. Passions overheat when corporate executives receive million-dollar compensation packages while workers are being laid off.[11] Among other tasks, the renewal manager must combat the affects of negative publicity.

The new science of corporate renewal creates a business reality in which change is the sole permanent feature and behaviors are molded by carefully planned incentive schemes. Surprisingly, the transition to this new world is generally embraced by labor unions and employees, corpo-

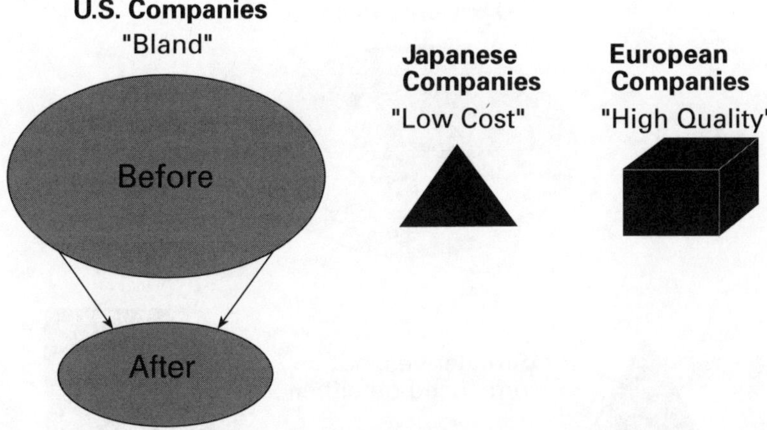

Fig. 6.5. Downsizing the wrong way

rate managers and investors, politicians and the press. The progressive globalization of business transactions, resulting from lasting reductions in barriers to trade and the advent of exchange on the Internet, fosters acceptance of the new order. High-cost businesses and those lacking a quality or technological niche are unlikely to survive and continue to employ workers in the emerging free and competitive marketplace. A team consciousness is spreading, fed by the knowledge that all must contribute if success is to be achieved.

The Emergence of Downsizing

The concept of downsizing arose during the 1970s when American automobile companies first encountered stiff resistance from European and Japanese manufacturers. As the share of vehicles produced in the United States declined and automakers' profits eroded, the big three (GM, Ford, and Chrysler) independently resolved to downsize their operations. Working in haste, they were only partially successful: the companies became smaller but no better. Without a strategic plan, downsizing targets company size or number of employees but does not correct fundamental problems.[12]

The situation confronting the automobile companies is illustrated in figures 6.5 and 6.6, where triangles represent manufacturers paying close attention to costs and prices, cubes represent companies occupying the quality niche, and ovals represent companies producing bland (neither inexpensive nor high performance) vehicles. The size of the geometric

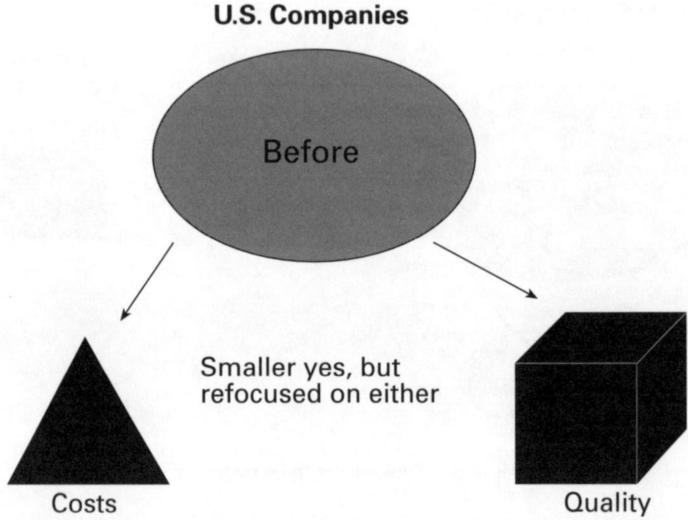

Fig. 6.6. Downsizing the right way

shapes represents the relative size of the three national competitors. In figure 6.5, the American companies downsized from large to small, but their products remained unchanged.[13] Prior to downsizing, foreign competitors surpassed American products with low prices and high quality; after downsizing, smaller American companies were trounced by the same competitors for the same reasons. Market share erosion in the domestic automobile market was not stemmed until the late 1980s, when companies strategically downsized and refocused on issues of concern to consumers: price and quality (fig. 6.6).

Nonstrategic Downsizing

Nonstrategic downsizing produces size reductions. If there are five factories, then several are shut; if there are 10,000 workers, then several thousand are fired. Attention is not given to determining the company's optimal size, which employees it should retain, or its appropriate market niche. Instead, the objective is to reach the break-even level for a given output by reducing expenses everywhere. However, if sales decline, then additional layoffs are necessary to maintain financial breakeven. Serial downsizings, when several rounds of layoffs occur in a relatively short period of time, demoralizes the workforce but can occur because the fundamental problem remains unresolved.

Nonstrategic downsizing is recommended only during a crisis, when expenses must be slashed immediately. There is an unfortunate risk of essential services, key employees, or budding enterprises being discontinued in an effort to break even. Soliciting input from line managers on who to lay off and what to eliminate helps minimize this risk. Sometimes filtering the list of layoffs through a committee uncovers errors before they are implemented, but committees jeopardize the entire downsizing effort and should be used sparingly.

In some cases, nonstrategic downsizing is designed to impress Wall Street analysts, not to solve real problems. A prominent Fortune 50 company revealed the emptiness of its plans when it responded to the question of why was it downsizing by saying, "We're doing it because everyone else is." Not a good answer, and its stock declined after an initial upward movement. Or consider the emptiness of Eastman Kodak's plan: the *Wall Street Journal* (1996c) accused it of dumbsizing when it fired a $15/hour plus benefits worker in a downsizing effort only to rehire her immediately at $65/hour (the employee received $20/hour without benefits from a temporary agency).

Strategic Downsizing

With strategic downsizing, as represented by figure 6.6, the objectives are to reduce expenses while refocusing the company's strategy. Cutbacks, as performed in nonstrategic downsizing, occur if they reduce expenses or strengthen the company's competitiveness. Three company characteristics are reviewed in strategic downsizing:

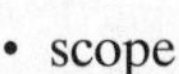
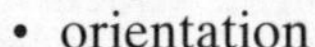

- scope
- orientation
- scale

Their first letters spell out "SOS," the international symbol of distress. Scope is the number of separate businesses in which a company participates through direct ownership, partnerships, or joint ventures. As they mature, most businesses expand their scope by capitalizing on new opportunities and markets or leveraging their strengths (i.e., people, technologies, and plants). Ordinarily these expansions are into related fields (e.g., a plumbing-supply company offers ceramic tiles for shower stalls) but some reach into unexpected areas (e.g., Virgin Records creates an international airline, Virgin Atlantic). Despite top managers' preference for overseeing larger, more complex organizations,[14] increased scope may be detrimental.[15] Managerial responsibilities are confused in a multilayered business. Moreover, managers may not calculate, or may ignore, each separate business's or product's profitability and may continue unprofitable segments.[16] During a downsizing effort, excessive scope is detrimental unless it contributes to the firm's cash flow and value.

Orientation refers to a business's strategy in both a perceptual and factual sense. Orientation begins with how consumers view the company's products on a number of dimensions, such as cost versus quality, convenience versus selection, services provided, and reputation. Orientation also includes real decisions: to outsource manufacturing or perform it internally, to rely on JIT inventories or stockpile supplies, or to provide credit to customers or only accept cash. Some choices provide little value to the firm; others are remnants of failed attempts to attract new business. Strategic downsizing reviews and resets all orientation decisions.

Scale describes size, location, and markets. Companies and their products are small, medium, or large, have plants or operations in one or many locations and in one or many countries, and sell products or services in various countries or continents or on the Internet. Activity-based-costing methodology, the subject of chapter 11, provides a framework by which to calculate each product's, plant's, and market's profitability. Over the long run losses are intolerable, and the unit responsible for them must be excised. During a strategic downsizing review, each scale decision is reexamined and its contribution to the firm's cash flow and value reassessed.

Clearly, one reason for the preponderance of nonstrategic downsizing is the enormous effort required for the alternative, concurrently reviewing and reevaluating literally hundreds of historic decisions. Rightsizing (discussed in the next section) is a compromise approach to downsizing and arose from a need to simplify the process.

Another concern is how companies may be misdirected by the person leading the strategic downsizing effort. Personal agendas, related to business ties or personal biases and relationships, may contradict the corporate agenda. This problem is especially pernicious, since it may sabotage an otherwise well-conceived and executed downsizing exercise. Allowing external experts to guide downsizing reduces the incidence and severity of this risk.

Rightsizing

Rightsizing is a commonly employed downsizing methodology. It omits aspects of the strategic review of scope, orientation, and scale. Rightsizing, though incomplete, is superior to nonstrategic downsizing during periods of corporate transformation or turnaround management.

Rightsizing investigates whether the firm's historic growth and expansion contributed to its permanent welfare. The goal is to reconfigure the firm's components to exclude noncontributing parts, which are sold off or liquidated.[17] Three basic questions are asked during rightsizing:

1. What businesses should we be in?
2. Which job positions are indispensable?
3. Which workers should fill the jobs?

The first question reviews current businesses for possible continuation or elimination. Each business's present and future contributions are assessed and compared against a benchmark. Contributions include positive elements such as cash flow and reputation and negative conditions such as future investment needs. Businesses are judged according to their direct and indirect contributions to the whole firm; synergies between businesses are identified and specific losing operations are perpetuated to safeguard joint profits with other units, but other losing businesses are discontinued.

The second rightsizing question seeks to reengineer the human resource. The objective is to minimize the cost and maximize the efficiency of operating the remaining businesses. The final rightsizing question determines which workers should fill the positions in the reshaped surviving units. The alternatives are to choose only from current workers or to open up positions to all workers, including those not currently employed.

Rightsizing a Business

Consider the rightsizing efforts of a not-for-profit business: a university. The university opened as a college of liberal arts; professional schools were added as markets developed and faculty interests expanded. This university is in the midst of a budget crisis in which revenues are insufficient, given the current level of costs.[18] Continuing deficits threaten the university's solvency, so its trustees decree that cost be reduced to the level of expected revenues while disrupting as little as possible the university's overall quality. The present form of the university and its five colleges (business, engineering, law, liberal arts, and nursing) is depicted in

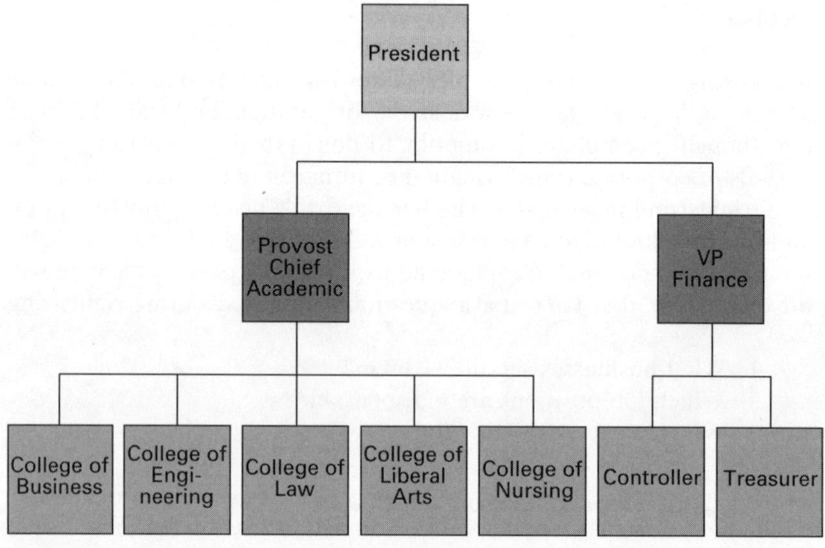

Fig. 6.7. Rightsizing

figure 6.7. The university has a decentralized structure wherein its top three administrators articulate targets for enrollment, revenue, cost, and quality that are met by managers (deans) in each of its business units. The top-level structure, with a president to perform fund-raising, a provost to manage the academic side, and a vice president of finance to handle money matters, is probably appropriate. But the number, size, and position of the university's colleges are subject to question.

Rightsizing begins by reviewing the university's college structure, that is, its stand-alone business units. Matters concerning the university include a college's cash flow, reputation, alumni support, and future investment needs. This information on all the colleges is distilled and helps define which colleges are kept and which are terminated. Information about each college is compared in table 6.3. Additional information is valued by decision makers and is possibly gathered, but at some point a decision is made. The facts in table 6.3 lead to the following conclusions:

- the engineering college causes the budget problem
- nursing may create a future deficit
- liberal arts may be a short-run cash cow but is hurting the university's image and fund-raising in the long run
- business and law currently are winning units

Rightsizing is not a scientific process; consequently, many alternative solutions may be suggested by a single set of facts. The alternatives are compared according to their benefits and costs, as seen in table 6.4. The first solution, keeping all the colleges open, is included because it alienates the fewest employees and must be considered, but it is not a true solution because it ignores the trustees' mandate.[19] It might appeal to a powerless board of trustees or an ineffectual president. Dropping the engineering college seems to be a good idea on first blush, but if future donations decline it may be a very costly idea. Ending the nursing program has few immediate drawbacks and does address a future budget problem, though it does not improve the current budget picture. Dropping both engineering and nursing would confront both immediate and long-run budget problems but could jeopardize the remaining college's solvency if sufficient overhead is not removed, causing other colleges to fall below their break-even points.[20]

The solution may not be to drop any colleges but to reduce current or future expenditures to the level of anticipated revenues. For example, the request by the nursing school to affiliate with a major hospital or medical school or the engineers' request for a new building can be denied.[21] In this mode, troubled businesses may be run as cash cows with excess cash drained off and no further investments made. Keeping all the colleges open and balancing the budget with cutbacks could result in a decline in both employee morale and educational quality and may lead to a spiral of decline.

Another way to reduce the number of businesses without cutting out colleges is to combine various colleges. In both examples shown in figure 6.8, the university rightsizes from five down to three colleges. The choice of which colleges to combine depends both on natural fit and on

TABLE 6.3. Choosing Which Businesses to Be In

College Quality	Business	Engineering	Law	Liberal Arts	Nursing
Cash flow	Strongly positive	Strongly negative	Strongly positive	Positive	Breakeven
Reputation	Moderate	Moderate	Excellent	Poor	Moderate
Alumni support	Average	Above average	Average	Below average	None
Investment needs	Little	Requires a new building	More chaired professors	Little	Requires affiliation with a major hospital or medical school

budgetary considerations. The dollar savings from joining units is less dramatic then when a unit is dropped.[22] However, the reduced cost savings are balanced against a smaller revenue decline if all five types of students continue to enroll (albeit in smaller numbers) in the three megacolleges.[23] This practice is common in the business world. GM is considering combining its GMC small truck division with its Pontiac division. Similarly, Federated Department Store has combined its Macy's and Jordan Marsh subsidiaries. Average costs are reduced if economies of scale increase, as is the case for most industries.

The second rightsizing issue concerns which job positions are to be filled in the continuing businesses. This step must begin with a clean piece of paper so that the job selection rationalization is based on need and not on history. The old management idea of zero-based budgeting is incorporated here. No jobs are sacrosanct; everything must be rejustified. Each continuing business develops an organizational chart that specifies a hierarchy of functional responsibilities.

TABLE 6.4. Rightsizing Alternatives

Choices	Advantages	Disadvantages
Keep all colleges	• Creates fewest enemies	• Major cost reduction not achieved • Ignores future capital-investment problems
Drop engineering	• Balances budget • Deals with future capital-investment problem	• Alienates strong alumni group
Drop nursing	• Deals with future capital-investment problem • Requires no layoffs	• Does not improve short-run budget problem • Removes school from a market that may grow
Treat nursing as a cash cow	• Deals with future capital-investment problem • Keeps school in a market that may grow	• May hurt reputation if quality suffers
Drop engineering and nursing	• Balances budget • Deals with future capital-investment problem	• May unbalance budget in remaining schools when overhead is reallocated
Drop engineering and treat nursing as a cash cow	• Balances budget • Deals with future capital-investment problem • Minimizes overhead increase in other schools	• Alienates strong alumni group

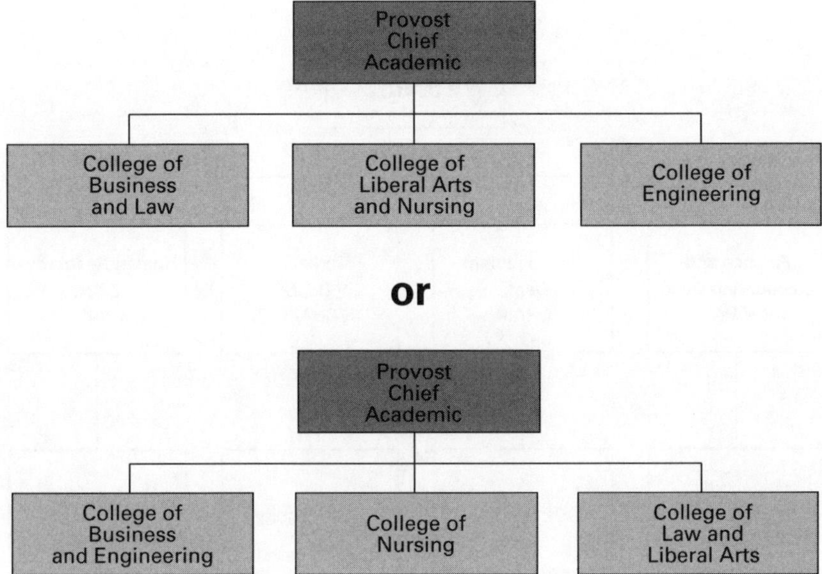

Fig. 6.8. Two alternative configurations

For each functional area, the minimum number of persons to be hired in each category is specified, and their expected educational, emotional, and experiential characteristics outlined. The objective is to determine the minimum number of employee positions necessary to carry out efficiently the mission of the business.[24] During the drafting process, names of particular current employees are not associated with specific jobs. Rather, jobs are described in general. During the third and final rightsizing phase, individuals are selected for the positions defined in step two.

At this point, in the first phase of rightsizing, a structure has been defined for the university. Assuming that a college of business is to be kept, figure 6.9 illustrates the second phase of rightsizing for that college. Here the college defines its own optimal structure. Originally, the college had six departments, six departmental chairmen, and thirty faculty, five in each department. Rightsizing condenses the business college's structure to four departments. Savings arise from two sources: first, by shrinking to four departments, fewer chairmen and related support personnel are required; second, eight faculty positions are terminated because the new structure reduces the number of undersized classes taught and facilitates the combination of several partially staffed

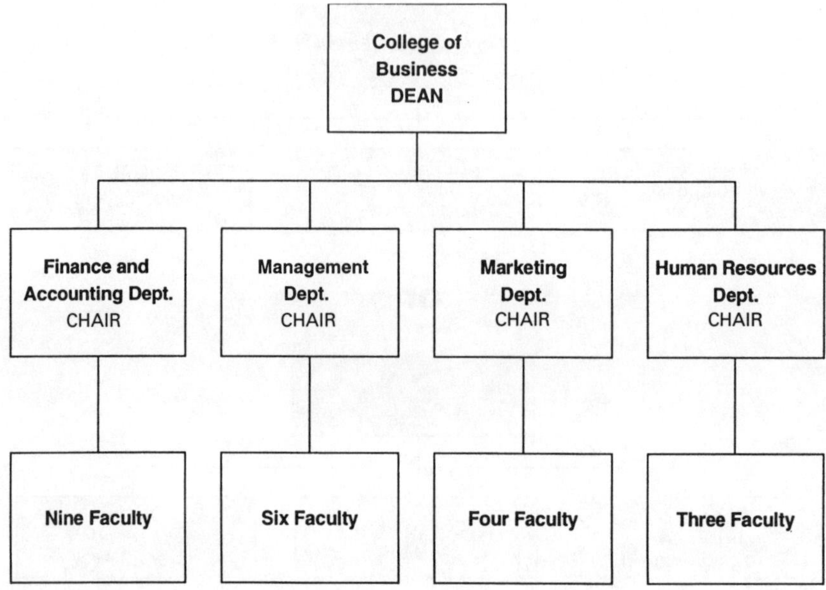

Fig. 6.9. Defining the college of business

but fully paid jobs into one fully staffed position. Although advice about restructuring should be solicited from informed persons in the affected areas, rightsizing decisions should come from the outside.

The third phase of rightsizing, depicted in table 6.5, is when the company decides who should staff jobs outlined in the prior phase. There are likely to be more workers than jobs, which is why employees perceive this phase as creating unemployment. There is a greater negative impact on current employees if the search for the best workers is expanded beyond current workers to include all available qualified persons. Table 6.5 shows that forty workers apply to fill the twenty-two available slots: the thirty original faculty and ten new persons (in italics). The critical aspect of this exercise is to create a single rank ordering in terms of quality of available workers, both experienced and inexperienced. Annual performance appraisals and interviews with managers help rank current employees. New applicants are evaluated and graded according to some objective criteria and positioned among the current employees' rankings. Hiring decisions should conform to the rank ordering. For example, in table 6.5, the finance and accounting department hires nine workers, eight workers already employed by the university and one new worker. One existing worker is not rehired. Altogether, four new workers and eighteen original workers are slotted into the jobs devised in the second phase of rightsizing. Twelve workers are laid off. Unionized companies or universities with a tenure system might be compelled to rehire all existing employees before any new workers are hired. One strategy to overcome this barrier to efficiency is to induce retirements or separations by offering severance packages targeting unionized employees. The Harvard Business School is so concerned about an aging workforce that it is buying back tenure from some employees.

Comparing Rightsizing and Downsizing

Strategic downsizing includes changes in scope, orientation, and scale, separately, in tandem, or altogether. Rightsizing, in contrast, is a limited version of strategic downsizing. It considers only scope issues directly; scale issues arise indirectly. The larger strategic downsizing inquiry for the university we have been examining is described in table 6.6 and has seven cantilevered plans. To allow these ideas to be presented in one moderate-sized table it is assumed that the number of colleges is the only scope issue, that expense versus quality is the only orientation issue, and that sheer size is the only scale issue that matters in this case. In fact, many other dimensions are reviewed in a strategic downsizing. Each plan yields estimable cost savings and an associated diminution in quality. Before choosing how to proceed, it is necessary to consider how the budget may further be disrupted if disappointed consumers switch to alternate vendors (i.e., another university). The university's trustees select a plan to implement.

TABLE 6.5. Finding the Best Person for Each Job

Finance/ Acct.	Hired	Management	Hired	Marketing	Hired	Human Res.	Hired
Person 1	X	Person 1	X	*Person 1*	X	Person 1	X
Person 2	X	Person 2	X	Person 2	X	*Person 2*	X
Person 3	X	Person 3	X	Person 3	X	*Person 3*	X
Person 4	X	Person 4	X	Person 4	X	Person 4	
Person 5	X	Person 5	X	Person 5		Person 5	
Person 6	X	Person 6	X	*Person 6*		Person 6	
Person 7	X	Person 7		Person 7		Person 7	
Person 8	X	Person 8		*Person 8*		Person 8	
Person 9	X	*Person 9*		Person 9		*Person 9*	
Person 10		*Person 10*		Person 10		Person 10	

Note: New Employees in italic

The university wants to balance its budget and maintain an acceptable quality level. Each plan in table 6.6 pursues those goals but with intrinsically different targets in mind:

- changes in scope reduce the number of market segments the firm/college pursues
- changes in orientation modify the firm's appearance and operations
- changes in scale diminish the proportions of specific units

Obviously, the best approach to downsizing in a given situation depends upon a host of special conditions peculiar to that situation:

- labor relations
- global factors
- environmental issues
- market competitiveness
- technology

The plans in table 6.6 begin by separately affecting scope, orientation, or scale; then they attack these factors in pairs; in the final plan, everything changes. Downsizing pairs of attributes (e.g., orientation and scale) or all three characteristics requires considerable coordination, planning, and cooperation. Management's commitment must be total and unwavering.

Management Structure and Task-Based Layoffs

The complement of personnel required to run a business is affected by a decision to follow either a centralized or a decentralized organization structure. During the second phase of rightsizing, that decision is recon-

TABLE 6.6. Strategic Downsizing of a University

Scope	Orientation	Scale
Fewer colleges	No change	No change for survivors
No change	Reduce expenses even if quality declines	No change
No change	No change	Reduce size of certain colleges
Fewer colleges	Reduce expenses even if quality declines	No change for survivors
No change	Reduce expenses even if quality declines	Reduce size of certain colleges
Fewer colleges	No change	Reduce size of certain colleges
Fewer colleges	Reduce expenses even if quality declines	Reduce size of certain colleges

sidered. Unnecessary layers of employment and associated costs resulting from organization structure issues may be uncovered in this review. The gains realized from expense reductions are only one input to be considered in this decision; however, since the centralized/decentralized dichotomy is the cornerstone of the incentive program that motivates employee performance, changes are made with great care.

Continuing with the university example, consider the description of tasks performed by the five current deans in the chart at the top of table 6.7. This array of tasks is consistent with the university's decision to operate decentrally, with each dean given the liberty to achieve in his/her own way the targets defined by the president. Liberty carries with it responsibility: a dean must manage his/her college's human resource function (i.e., hiring and firing of faculty and tenure decisions), strategy and its implementation (i.e., mission statement, degrees offered, and measures of excellence), community involvement (e.g., public speaking and offering scholarships), and budgeting. The current five-dean structure partially is a by-product of the university's five-college business structure, but it also arises from a decision to decentralize.

In the bottom half of table 6.7, a revised set of mandatory activities for the deans is defined for a centrally organized university. This structure moves budgeting and hiring and firing decisions into the provost's office. Deans are then only responsible for strategy and community outreach. The question to ask is, "How many deans are needed?" This

TABLE 6.7 Task-Based Rightsizing. What Activities Must a Dean Perform?

	Human Resource	Strategy and Implementation	Community Involvement	Budgets
A. Decentralized Organization Structure				
Business	X	X	X	X
Engineering	X	X	X	X
Law	X	X	X	X
Liberal Arts	X	X	X	X
Nursing	X	X	X	X
B. Centralized Organization Structure				
Business		X	X	
Engineering		X	X	
Law		X	X	
Liberal Arts		X	X	
Nursing		X	X	

exercise is called task-based rightsizing. With the colleges differing so greatly in size and with fewer functions performed in the dean's offices, as seen in table 6.8, at least one and perhaps two dean positions are unnecessary in a centralized structure. Centralization allows staff positions to be reduced in colleges keeping their deans, since some staff now serve all colleges in the provost's office.

Colleges losing their deans might be administered by committee or a senior faculty member. Strategy development might falter and eventually lead the college to be absorbed elsewhere in the university. A real concern is how to keep the faculty and staff focused and efficient without the incentives and disincentives created by the presence of a dean.

The same recommendation applies when companies are centrally organized; they should consider whether a move to a decentralized process might be cost-effective. The key to downsizing and rightsizing is to test everything and keep the parts that work.

Choosing the Layoff Target

People, Plants, Products, or Processes (the Four Ps*)*

Early in an engagement, the corporate renewal specialist seeks to bring the firm to break-even output. Break-even output has been explained in chapter 3; simply put, it is that production level at which the corporation's revenues equal its costs. There are several types of break-even output—profit, cash, and EBITDA breakeven—that progressively exclude more types of costs. EBITDA excludes interest, taxes, depreciation, and amortization; cash excludes only depreciation and amortization; profit breakeven includes all types of costs. EBITDA breakeven covers variable costs (crudely defined); cash breakeven stems the outflow of precious cash; and profit breakeven enhances the accounting statement and may encourage the restoration of lender and vendor support. Generally, cash breakeven is the target early in a crisis, while profit breakeven is the goal at the end of the crisis.

TABLE 6.8. Which Colleges Need a Dean?

	Number of Students	Decentralized: Need a Dean?	Centralized: Need a Dean?
Business	2,593	Yes	Yes
Engineering	859	Yes	Depends
Law	3,730	Yes	Yes
Liberal arts	394	Yes	No
Nursing	1,291	Yes	Yes

Corporate renewal reduces total revenues for two reasons. First, companies in crisis are short of cash. Growth demands new capital to support higher levels of inventories and accounts receivable. By shrinking sales, surplus money actually is generated (refer to chap. 3). Second, corporate renewal curtails one of a corporation's prime resources—people, plants, products, or processes (the four *P*s) in the movement toward breakeven and then profitability. Processes include how raw materials are ordered, how new products are chosen, how checks are issued, and many other mundane and special tasks. Sales revenues decline after layoffs. This section reviews the layoff factor in the downsizing decision.

Clearly, the four *P*s are interconnected, and reducing one diminishes the others. Yet the linkage is imperfect because a plant may produce many products, products require different combinations of plants and people, and people migrate between both plants and products.

Naive downsizing is confused by the connectivity between the four *P*s and cuts everything in equal percentage. This strategy results in "the baby being thrown out with the bathwater." Consider these reductions:

- People—each team, functional area, or division lays off 10 percent of its employees
- Plants—each plant reduces total expenditures (research and development, promotion, etc.) by 10 percent
- Products—each product group reduces its number of products by 10 percent

The inadequacy of this naive strategy is patently obvious, yet many executives untrained to manage a crisis embrace it. Its only advantage is that it requires no reasoning or complex decision making. It leads companies to terminate both productive and unproductive people, retain both efficient and inefficient plants, and constrain both successful and unsuccessful product groups. Peter Drucker (1993) has a marvelous description for this sort of behavior: "starving your successes in order to feed your failures." When resources are diverted from good to bad activities, companies put their good activities at risk. Equal-percentage layoffs are justified only if every worker is equally adept, every plant is equally productive, and every product is equally profitable. A better idea is to target resources individually for layoff.

In developing a layoff strategy the key questions are which resources to lay off, how much to reduce them, and when to lay them off. There are two basic systems that can be followed:

- attack the four *P*s simultaneously
- concentrate the cuts on one prime resource.

Both approaches provide unique benefits but also have specific costs, as seen in table 6.9. The renewal manager weighs the balance between costs and benefits for each engagement.

When a decision is made to fix the four *P*s all at once, a hierarchical listing is created ranking the corporation's problems from worst to best, using information provided in interviews with management, employees, customers, and others.

The renewal team is working against a deadline, using finite human and financial resources. The team compares its strength and depth with the problem list before attacking problems identified in the hierarchy. Treating the worst problem often is deferred because of insufficient resources. The manager in charge must constantly assess whether using the simultaneous layoff process squanders layoff resources.

If instead the layoff process concentrates on one of the four *P*s, the initial decision concerns which resource to fix. Fixing diverse resources yields benefits in varying amounts that accrue over different time periods. The timing of benefits is described in table 6.10, while table 6.11 shows the amount of benefits expected from layoffs of each prime resource.

A natural inclination is to address the people resource first, because

- the human-resource department provides a well-defined list of employees
- progress reports are understood easily
- benefits accrue immediately

Whichever resource becomes the target, opportunities to reduce other prime resources appear after the first-round layoff. Reductions in one resource create slack in others.[25] For example, shutting a plant makes

TABLE 6.9. Benefits and Costs of Concentrating or Not Concentrating Layoff Activities

Layoff Method	Benefit	Cost
Reduce all resources simultaneously	The worst part of each prime resource is fixed as soon as possible	The fix to each resource may be too small to accomplish much good
Concentrate on one resource	One resource's troubles are resolved to the fullest extent possible	Problems with the other prime resources are not corrected until later

some workers superfluous, while firing workers results in unnecessary plants.

Plant layoffs involve more issues than people, product, or process layoffs. Factors affecting plant closings include

- Is its output essential?
- Is the plant fully depreciated?
- Can its equipment be retooled?
- Is the plant unionized, and what extra benefits does the union demand?
- Does the plant have a relatively low wage structure?
- Have binding promises been made to local or state governments in exchange for tax reductions, etc.?

Plant layoffs are less prevalent because of (a) the complexity of issues involved in the decision-making process, (b) the lower immediate impact on costs or profits, and (c) the poor public-relations impact such a decision creates. On the positive side, plant layoffs generate greater cost reductions than either people or product layoffs.[26]

Product layoffs are especially tricky since they demand a sophisticated strategic analysis of the firm's position now and in the future. The

TABLE 6.10. Timing of Benefits from Layoffs of People, Plants, and Products

Impact On	People	Plants	Products	Process
Financial costs	Immediate	Long run	Immediate, intermediate, and long run	Immediate
Profits	Immediate	Long run	Immediate, intermediate, and long run	Immediate
Creditor's opinion	Immediate	Immediate	Intermediate or long run	Never
Equity's opinion	Immediate	Immediate	Immediate	Never

TABLE 6.11. Amount of Benefits from Layoffs of People, Plants, and Products

Impact On	People	Plants	Products	Process
Profits	Depends on severance pay, continued health benefits, etc.	Depends on plant disposition costs and whether plant is sold or mothballed	Depends on product stage of development	Possibly substantial
Worker morale	Least improvement	Moderate improvement	Moderate improvement	Positive
Company notoriety	Substantial	Substantial	Least	None

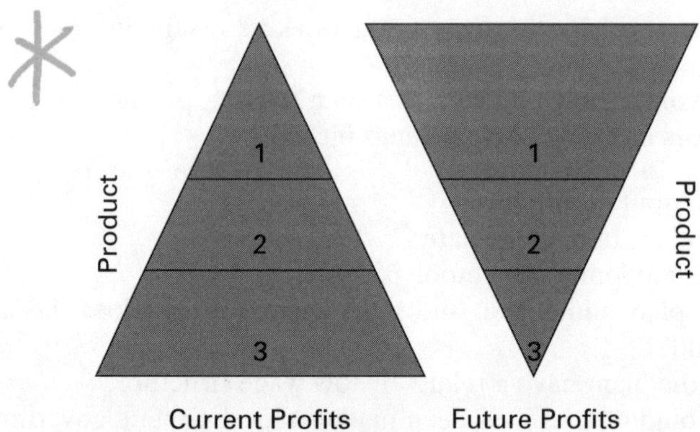

Fig. 6.10. Profitability of products, now and in the future

illustration in figure 6.10 depicts the strategic choices available to a firm with three products. The first product is assumed to be under development, the second product is assumed to have been recently introduced, and the third product is the mainstay of the company. In a crisis necessitating a product layoff, which product should be cut? Using Intel's products as an illustration, since they are well known, product 1 is the P6 chip, product 2 is the Pentium chip, and product 3 is the 486 chip. One key question is, when does the future arrive?

Product 1 has the lowest profits this year; in fact, the product may be unprofitable, as shown in table 6.12. Product 3, in contrast, generates the most profits. The situation is reversed in the future. Getting to the future requires a major investment in product 1, some investment in product 2, and no investment in product 3. Dropping product 1 saves development costs but leaves the company with no future; laying off product 3 saves the fewest current dollars but protects the future. The decision depends on the company's desperation. A desperation index is an imprecise measure of the number of days remaining until creditors file an involuntary bankruptcy petition. If the desperation index is less than 100 days, the situation is most desperate; i.e., a crisis. If the index

TABLE 6.12. Strategic Factors in a Product Layoff

Product	Current Profits	Product Development Costs	Future Profits
1	Lowest	Highest	Highest
2	Medium	Very low	Medium
3	Highest	None	Lowest

exceeds approximately 365 days, the situation is less desperate. The corporate renewal specialist should estimate and constantly update a desperation index for every engagement. Table 6.13 combines the desperation index with a strategic decision chart for the firm with three products.

If the firm is most desperate, with fewer than 100 days left before its assets are seized, product 1, the hope and future of the company, must go. Depending on where in the development process the product is, it may either be sold or shut down. A moderately desperate firm, with 100 to 365 days until it enters Chapter 11, may have sufficient time to nurture product 1 until it is sold or brought to market. Time is gained for product 1 by laying off product 2. This decision is risky since certain near-term profits are lost in exchange for possible future gains. A less desperate firm, with more than 365 days on the desperation index, would accelerate the obsolescence of product 3, treating it like a cash cow by maximizing its cash contribution and minimizing its cash expense.

Process changes usually cost less and may yield major gains. They are helpful in all varieties of corporate renewal but are especially important in corporate transformation. Process changes move the firm toward the right way of conducting business. Examples include a dinner theater adding an extra bartender to relieve congestion during a short intermission, to Saturn cars being value priced so that the consumer need not bargain with a salesperson. Ideas for process changes come from observation (i.e., walking the floor) and example (i.e., imitating the policies of more successful competitors).

A Corporate Example

Apple Computer, Inc., had a terrible 1995. First, early in the year it underestimated the demand for its high-end product offerings; as a result, it lost many potential sales to the competing Windows platform.

TABLE 6.13. Product Layoff Decisions and the Desperation Index

Desperation Index	Strategic Choice	Explanation
Most desperate	Lay off product 1	Has the highest expenses and the lowest current profits
Moderately desperate	Lay off product 2	Reduces more expenses than product 3 but yields more future profits than laying off product 1
Least desperate	Lay off product 3 but as slowly as possible	Reduces future profits the least

Second, it overestimated Christmas seasonal demand for its low-priced Macintosh Performa model and was forced to cut prices by as much as 25 percent to get inventories out of the factory and off retailers' shelves. Third, its strongest market, Japan, experienced a dramatic computer price war that caused Apple's gross margin to plunge from 29 percent in 1994 to just 15 percent in 1995 (Carlton 1996b). Japan was the first market in which Apple took a vigorous stand against low-priced IBM clones. Finally, its executive suite became a revolving door, as one executive after another left to join rival firms.

What should Apple do? Some analyst argued that its primary problem, not allowing competitors to clone its products, had to be corrected after a decade of neglect. Others said that Michael Spindler, the chairman and CEO of Apple, failed to provide corporate leadership in the fast-changing personal computer world and should be replaced. Management held a third view, that the cash outflow and reported net losses that suddenly hit Apple's financial reports had to be excised. For the first fiscal quarter ending December 29, 1995, Apple reported a $69 million loss.

Rather than take the usual approach of just laying off people, Apple chose to lay off products. It reported that the intention of the layoffs was to "fundamentally change our business model." According to the *Wall Street Journal,* Apple "will . . . de-emphasize various low-end products and concentrate on the higher end of the education, home and business markets (Carlton 1996b). Layoffs would follow the change in focus, with about one-quarter of the current workforce expected eventually to leave the firm as product sales shifted to the higher-margin sector.

Layoff Legal Restrictions: WARN and COBRA

WARN: Worker Adjustment and Retraining Notification Act of 1988

Business interests and worker concerns are incompatible on the issue of what to do with redundant employees. The business view is that superfluous workers should be immediately discharged. After all, workers are a variable production input. Employees, on the other hand, reason that theirs is a long-term commitment to the company and in exchange the company should

- refrain from laying them off (treat them like a fixed cost)
- give ample advanced warning of layoffs (a year or more)

In the 1996 automobile labor negotiations, GM (which accounts for 1 percent of the nation's economic output) wanted the freedom to fire workers and outsource, while the United Auto Workers wanted to maintain employment (Bradshaw 1996). The settlement gave workers a modest wage increase and allowed GM to shut several unprofitable parts plants, resulting in 30,000 layoffs over a three-year period. In exchange, GM agreed to maintain employment at 95 percent of current levels.

Few companies today, even in Japan, the land where once jobs were for life, consider employees to be permanent. Today, layoffs occur with regularity. Policy makers have decided that employees gain immeasurably if imminent layoffs are signaled in advance. Advance warnings let them avoid making large financial commitments, begin job searches, and generally replan their future.

Before the enactment of the Worker Adjustment and Retraining Notification Act of 1988 (WARN), federal law did not proscribe any aspect of the layoff process. The law mandates that workers be given sixty days' notice of an impending layoff if

- the company has more than 100 employees
- at least one-third of the workforce at a particular location is to be laid off

Companies are exempt from the law, however, if they are distressed. The logic behind this exemption is that a distressed company seeking fresh capital or a new investor might create unnecessary panic if it publicly announced an impending layoff.

Prior to WARN, large, well-endowed companies generally avoided layoffs, but when they were necessary linked them to generous severance benefits packages. Smaller concerns simply dismissed their workers. In the six-year period preceding passage of WARN, only 8.6 percent of workers received at least one month's notice prior to being laid off (Addison and McKinley 1993). Because of exemptions, during the period 1988–1991, only 8.2% of employees received at least a month's notice of a layoff (*New York Times* 1993a).

COBRA: Consolidated Omnibus Budget Reconciliation Act of 1985

COBRA mandates that a company offer laid-off employees the right to buy health coverage from the corporation's health provider for a period of eighteen months following the individual's separation. The fee charged for this coverage need not include any subsidy or partial payment from the corporation. Many employees drop this coverage as soon as they find economical insurance through other vendors. Prior to the legislation, some employees, especially those with preexisting medical problems, could not find any replacement insurance after being laid off.

Layoffs: The Logic and Limitations of Severance Agreements

Companies with too many employees choose to downsize either passively or aggressively. Passive downsizing utilizes a hiring freeze and natural attrition. Companies with relatively young workforces with few workers nearing retirement need to spark the attrition process by making jobs elsewhere more attractive: no salary increases, reducing wages where possible, downgrading health plan coverage, and shrinking contributions to the pension plan. The risk of a passive downsizing policy is that the best employees leave, while workers unemployable elsewhere remain. Passive downsizing is best suited when individual workers' capabilities are less important: in low-skill occupations, where teams perform work collectively, or where individuals are closely supervised.

Aggressive downsizing, the alternate tactic, persuades employees to voluntarily separate from the company or else be discharged. Voluntary separations are better for company morale and productivity then firings. Severance packages induce workers to quit or retire. They contain a variety of individual components. Table 6.14 describes standard severance package items and their benefits and costs. Cost is the obvious

TABLE 6.14. Benefits and Costs of Severance Plan Packages

Plan Component	Benefit	Cost
A number of days' pay granted for every year of employment	• Appeals to older, more expensive workers • Boosts morale of continuing employees	• Substantial total costs • May drive out the best workers and leave behind workers who cannot get another job
Unused sick leave and vacation days paid in cash	• Days may have had to be paid anyway • No loss of production	• Is more expensive than carrying forward these days
A fixed cash bounty paid to a specified number of employees	• Caps the program's total cost • Appeals to lowest paid	• May not attract enough volunteers
Earlier eligibility in the retirement plan	• Appeals to older, more expensive workers • May be inexpensive	• May create unrealizable expectations for continuing workers
Provide outplacement service and continued office space	• Low cost • Good for morale	• May not attract enough participants
Continued health plan coverage until retirement age	• Appeals to older, more expensive workers	• May create a cost of uncertain dimension

disadvantage of severance packages. Healthy corporations downsizing to reshape their divisional structure or control costs can afford severance programs. Distressed companies downsizing to stop cash outflows may not be able to afford inducements.

The Age Discrimination in Employment Act of 1967 protects workers older than forty against layoffs that result in their being replaced by younger workers.[27] Healthy firms avert this obstacle by not firing anyone older than forty except in cases of egregious behavior or misconduct. The problem is moot for distressed companies that fire and do not rehire. Companies not firing any older workers may be overstaffed with senior managers, foremen, and experienced workers at all grades. The architect of a severance program may find this a propitious time to induce older workers to leave voluntarily. Several plan components in table 6.14 are especially attractive to older workers.

Cost/Benefit Calculations

When the cost of severance programs is immaterial, any job-reduction goal can be met. More typically, downsizing efforts face tight budgets and strict cost constraints, and senior managers should be required to articulate the return on investment (ROI) expected from each severance dollar spent.[28] The required ROI is established in the context of the company's total investment possibility frontier. All companies observe a variety of positive cash-flow investment opportunities. The allocation of scarce corporate resources to downsizing is part of the overall corporate investment plan. An investment in the severance plan must earn an ROI at least as great as the project displaced by the severance package.[29]

The expected ROI of each component of a severance package is compared against the company's hurdle ROI.[30] Severance plan components with ROIs in excess of the company's hurdle rate are good investments provided that the company can acquire sufficient funds; components with ROIs below the hurdle rate are abandoned. Consider the example in table 6.15.

The company offers to buy out long-term employees (with twenty or more years of service) with a severance payment equal to one week of pay per year of employment. For simplicity, all workers are assumed

- to earn the same $52,000 per year
- to have been hired at twenty years of age
- to be idle 25 percent of the time.

The company has a 20 percent ROI hurdle. A larger proportion of older workers are expected to accept the buyout offer, with the percentage rising to 100 percent at age sixty. With the anticipated plan acceptance rate, the total cost is $325,000. These costs are compared with

1. the present value of savings accumulated over the employee's remaining working life
2. the cash flow effect in year one

If fewer than 25 percent of workers accept the offer, savings equal the total wage bill of retiring workers; if more than 25 percent of workers retire, however, new workers are hired to maintain output and there are no incremental savings for workers beyond the 25 percent level.[31]

Savings are valued over the remaining working life of employees who are assumed to be 25 percent idle, without the buyout, until they voluntarily retire. If business improves, future idleness may decline; the break point, currently 25 percent, where savings cease would need to be adjusted.

The column in table 6.15 labeled "Present Value of Savings/Person" calculates the discounted value of annual savings until retirement, using the hurdle ROI as the discount rate. Net benefits from the severance plan equal the "Present Value of Savings/Person" less the "Cost of Plan/Person." Net benefits are positive in every case in table 6.15. A risk in offering severance is that older workers might have voluntarily retired or even died. Companies might prefer to exclude older workers from the offer since their net benefits, see table 6.15, are smaller than those of younger workers. However, legal requirements may forestall this option. Total net benefits to the corporation are found by multiplying the number of workers accepting the severance offer times the difference between the present value and the cost of the plan. Provided that net discounted benefits exceed zero, the severance plan serves the company.

TABLE 6.15. Cost/Benefit Calculation for a Severance Package Plan Component

Plan Component: 1 week pay per year of employment for any 20-year or more employee who retires (assume all workers earn $52,000, hiring age of 20, retirement age of 65, 25% idle time, and 20% discount rate)

Years Worked	Number of Employees	Percentage Retiring	Cost of Plan/Person	Present Value of Savings/Person	Cash Flow in Year One
20 years	10	20%	$20,000	$257,275	$32,000 × 2
25 years	8	25%	$25,000	$253,218	$27,000 × 2
30 years	6	50%	$30,000	$243,125	$22,000 × 3
35 years	4	75%	$35,000	$218,009	$17,000 × 3
40 years	1	100%	$40,000	$155,511	$12,000 × 1

The first-year cash-flow impact of a severance plan is diminished by the up-front severance payment. In table 6.15, year one cash flow is $12,000 for the oldest workers and $32,000 for those with twenty years' experience.[32] Cash is dear to the firm in crisis. The $40,000 cash settlement to the oldest workers may be prohibitively expensive given the expected cash flow of $1,000 per week. On the other hand, a $20,000 up-front payment to a younger worker may be justified. The corporate renewal specialist must prepare a selective severance package targeted to those divisions and intracompany groups with the most profitable demographic characteristics.

There are two unknowns in the analysis in table 6.15: the percentage of workers likely to accept a buyout offer and the proportion of idle time for the average worker and its duration. Uncertainty is reduced by simulating various possible outcomes. Informal surveys suggest the appropriate range around which to begin the simulations.

$$\text{PVSavings} = \sum_{t=0}^{\text{Retirement}} [(\text{Salary until retirement})] \Big/ (1 + \text{Discount rate})^t$$

and

$$\begin{aligned}\text{Cash Flow Year 1} &= \text{Cost reduction} - \text{Cost of plan}\\ &= (\text{Salary} - \text{Cost of plan})\end{aligned}$$

Severance Plan Ethics

Workers are laid off when companies are in distress. Many have desperation indexes in the near-bankruptcy range. Depression and anger may overpower the ethics of employers and employees. This is a mistake. Ethics are critical at such times; otherwise cash flow or cost containment gains may be lost.

TWA's collapse exemplifies how ruinous disharmony arises after an ethical lapse. Carl Icahn acquired TWA in a high-priced, leveraged takeover. One motivation was his belief that TWA's excessive wage scale could be reduced. After the takeover, wages were unilaterally reduced, workers responded by walking off the job, and a situation of permanent antagonism developed. This culminated in a bankruptcy and the eventual ownership of the airline by its workers. Had Icahn a different ethical perspective, a superior outcome may have ensued. Similar antagonisms arose from cost-containment efforts at Caterpillar Tractor, Inc., Food Lion, Inc., and numerous mining companies.

The following questions help define a manager's ethical framework: Is it ethical to layoff workers in order to

- reduce the number of excessive workers?
- hire nonunion workers?
- hire less expensive workers?
- hire younger workers?
- hire foreign workers?

There are no universally correct answers to these questions. The answer may depend on the firm's desperation index. But in the deepest crisis, is any action ethical? A moral imperative is to ask yourself silently the companion question, "What if you were the person to be laid off?"[33] The focus in corporate renewal is saving the company, but managers wrestle with these moral issues. Try filling in the blank spaces in table 6.16 to see where you fall on this question.

What is the purpose of a severance package? In one view, severance plans penalize failing companies' incompetence. In an opposite view, severance plans provide assistance to help tide workers over until they find new jobs. Some workers accepting severance plans may face an ethical dilemma if they quickly find a new job: should they return the severance package to their old employer? In part, the answer to this question depends on the benefits received. Table 6.17 lists some typical severance benefits and asks the reader to decide if they should be returned.

Few workers would return a lump-sum cash payment, but most would tell an old employer to drop their health coverage when a new

TABLE 6.16. Ethic Choices: Employers

Is a Firm Unethical If It Discharges Workers in Order To:	If Its Desperation Index[a] Equals 100	If Its Desperation Index[a] Equals 365
Fire excessive workers		
Hire nonunion workers		
Hire less expensive workers		
Hire younger workers		
Hire foreign workers		

[a]The desperation index measures the number of days until a company files for bankruptcy.

TABLE 6.17. Ethic Choices: Employees

Should a Worker Return:	Yes	No
Continued health coverage?		
Cash for earned but not taken sick days and vacation?		
A lump-sum cash payment?		

employer's plan picks them up. Those not informing their old employer seek to punish them for the sin of laying them off. As with most ethical issues, the question is not what is legal but what is right.[34]

There are no correct answers to these questions. Every person searches for his/her own comfort point. Some of the burden rests on the employer. If the employer expects workers to take certain actions once they find new jobs, the employer must let them know what is expected of them in return for severance benefits. Contracts encourage a well-defined understanding.

Firing Executives

Firing someone is not pleasant, and firing another executive is even more unpleasant if people share a long work history or their association extends outside the workplace. During a crisis, executive dismissals are essential for several reasons:

- executives are better paid, have more benefits, and cause more SGA (selling, general, and administrative) expenses than other workers
- the number of executives is swollen by new office technologies, cronyism, and a historical unwillingness of executives to fire other executives
- corporate morale suffers if layoffs are confined to nonexecutives
- top management may be incapable of devising a turnaround

A careful and deliberate strategy is needed so that executive dismissals are in the corporate good and so that personal relationships do not interfere with them.

Either an external or an internal renewal manager is assigned the task of deciding which executives are to be retained. In either case, the assignment is to reduce the size of the corporate office and the ranks of its line managers. This charge is broadly communicated, thereby empowering the decision maker and directing employee hostility away from other managers. The advantage to keeping the job in house is that an internal knows the company, its operations, and many of its employees and can quickly attack the problem. The disadvantage is that the internal manager is unskilled in corporate renewal and must learn on the job. Moreover, internals may be too lenient because of concerns about their future relationship with continuing employees or their career paths.

Firing a single or small number of executives presents a special class of problems ranging from violence in the workplace to stigmatized workers and morale problems, unfair firing, age discrimination, and breach-of-contract lawsuits. Ironically, more finesse is required to fire a single worker than to terminate a large group. The simplest and possibly the best strategy is to confront the individual in his/her office, document the problem, and outline an exit strategy. The targeted executive is probably aware that his/her work is unacceptable or that the firm faces a reduced demand for executives. If the news is anticipated, actually receiving it may be anticlimactic and a source of relief, especially if a generous basket of severance benefits is provided:

- continued salary and health insurance coverage for a time
- use of an office and a secretary
- outplacement assistance

No one wants to be the bearer of the bad news. In most companies, the assignment is handled by one individual, who becomes known as the hatchet person.

Sometimes a direct firing strategy is unnecessary, and with subtle pressures executives may voluntarily quit. Theoretically, a voluntary exit decision is reached when more employee needs, such as those represented by Maslow's hierarchy, are satisfied elsewhere. Companies can motivate voluntary departures by leaving a worker's needs unsatisfied.

Maslow defines five stages of needs that are fulfilled by a job. Table 6.18 ranks these needs in descending order and shows how an executive's job provides for their attainment. Voluntary separations are increasingly likely when a job fails to satisfy these needs.

Five strategies to encourage individual executives to quit, borrowed from the Washington bureaucracy, are discussed below.[35] While some may find these strategies unethical, they are successful.

1. Put Them in Blue Jeans in a Pinstripe World

Shake things up. Give the worker a new job that obviously is not a promotion. Get the executive out of his/her old office, change his/her

TABLE 6.18. Maslow's Need Hierarchy

Needs	Fulfillment Factor
Achievement	Challenge in the workplace
Ego	Title, compensation, number of subordinates
Group	Executive office dynamics
Safety	Health insurance and job security
Physiological	Minimum salary to live the desired lifestyle

responsibilities, and cut him/her off from the regular group of coworkers. The less pleasing the new assignment the better: it may be in a different city or a different branch of the company, and it may demand different skills. External opportunities shine brighter when compared to an ignoble future with a current employer.

Japanese firms are masters at this. Their never-fire-anyone system of management produces many dysfunctional executives who officially have a job for life. Because firms do not want to mix productive and unproductive workers and want to "put these workers into blue jeans," failed Japanese executives are transferred to distant locations with windowless offices and spend the entire day with nothing to do.

2. Tell'm I'm Not In

Independent thinking, at least up to a point, is an executive privilege. Forcing a formerly independent executive to secure approval for every decision signals the firm's low opinion of that person. If the senior executive whose approval is needed never returns phone calls or responds to memos, the situation may become intolerable.

3. Have Them Dot Every i *and Cross Every* t

Successful executives learn how to cut through channels to minimize bureaucratic duties and to maximize productive time. Their proposals obtain speedy approval and funding, their budgets are reviewed and authorized, and their requisitions are submitted and satisfied.

To make a pleasant job unpleasant, end this simplicity. Force the executive to become a bureaucrat, endlessly shuffling papers between offices.

4. Send Them to Siberia

Within a company, executives are treated similarly. They have similar offices and secretarial support, they receive bonuses and salary increases at about the same time and in the same proportion, and they have commensurate access to clubs and special perquisites.[36]

Not treating one executive in the customary fashion may speed that person's departure. An exceptionally effective idea is to reassign his/her secretary/administrative assistant; many executives are helpless without support. If that maneuver fails to produce the desired result, hitting pocketbook issues like promotions, bonuses, and salary increases registers more clearly.

5. Have Them Find the Holy Grail

Every company has its Holy Grail (i.e., some unreachable objective). The Holy Grail might be to land the Wal-Mart account or maybe to get the Eastern division to achieve breakeven. Assigning that impossible mission to executives and informing them that their futures depend on its successful completion sends the signal that it is time to move on.

Questions

1. Are these strategies ethical?
2. How do these strategies contradict Maslow's needs?
3. Define other strategies to get executives to voluntarily leave. Are your choices ethical?
4. If workers will not quit, is it more ethical to fire them?
5. Are there less objectionable ways to get executives to voluntarily leave?
6. Would you want to be the person who fires others in your firm?

Pension Plan Changes That Induce Retirement

There are two principal types of pension plans, defined-benefit plans (DBP) and defined-contribution plans (DCP). Several important differences between them are seen in table 6.19. DBPs automatically treat all employees as plan participants. Presumably, employees regard a DBP as part of their total remuneration package since their cash wage is lower than it would be without the plan and they do not contribute directly to the plan. Employers providing DBPs are not required to pay the pension's full value into the plan immediately. As a result, many pension plans are underfunded.[37]

Employees must contribute to a DCP plan, usually with regular deductions out of each paycheck from their pretax gross income. If the

TABLE 6.19. Differences between Defined-Benefit and Defined-Contribution Pension Plans

	Defined Benefit	Defined Contribution
Who is included in the plan?	All employees	Voluntary participation
Does the employee make a direct financial contribution?	No	Yes
Does the employer contribute?	Yes	Only if the employee participates and makes a contribution
Does the employer's current contribution equal the present value of the pension?	No	Yes

employee stops contributing, so does the employer. Participation in a DCP is entirely voluntary. Transitory labor market employees, workers expecting to change jobs, and those unable to afford the mandatory employee contribution may never volunteer to join the plan, making DCPs much less expensive than DBPs. Both the employer and the employee contribute the full value of their portion of the pension as it comes due, so that the pension is always fully funded.

Historically, DBP plans were the only game in town; as of 1995, at least 80 percent of companies with 1,000 or more employees had one (Damato 1995). More recently, DCPs are the pension plan of choice because they offer more investment flexibility to the employee and because they do not shackle the employer with future pension costs. Not a single DBP has been created since the mid-1980s.

DBPs remit a defined annual payment determined by the retired employee's age, years of service, and ending pay level. Congress created an agency of the federal government, the Pension Benefits Guarantee Corporation (PBGC), to guarantee DBP payments to retired employees. The PBGC seizes dramatically underfunded pension plans and then manages their retirement portfolios and pays retirement benefits to subscribers. It also takes an active role in bankruptcies to protect retirees' rights and regularly (with a two-year delay) publishes a list of the largest underfunded pension plans, which is reproduced in table 6.20.

DCPs, such as 401(k) savings plans or 403(b) plans, are popular with employers because their obligation does not begin until the employee joins the plan, carries no future liability of an undetermined size, and is basically unregulated. The DCP pension drawn by a retired employee is determined by the size of his or her personal retirement pool. Single employees and married employees without children may choose

TABLE 6.20. Ten Largest Underfunded Pension Plans in 1994 ($ in millions)

Company Name	Pension Liability	Percent Unfunded
1. Ravenswood Aluminum Corp.	$144	71%
2. Bridgestone-Firestone, Inc.	$575	45%
3. LTV Corp.	$3,550	46%
4. Keystone Consolidated Inds.	$196	43%
5. Starfire Holding Corp.	$1,253	46%
6. Laclede Steel Co.	$182	41%
7. Chiquita Brands International	$203	39%
8. Uniroyal Goodrich Tire	$960	38%
9. Westinghouse Electric Co.	$5,525	36%
10. Mack Trucks	$474	35%

to contribute more than employees with children. Those with children may increase their contributions after their dependents finish school. The employer's contribution is usually a fixed percentage of salary, usually between 5 percent and 20 percent, contingent on the employee making a minimum contribution (as low as 1 percent and as much as 5 percent of salary). Employees self-direct their DCPs into stocks, bonds, or money-market investments managed by a professional investment firm like Fidelity or Vanguard. Their investment mix can shift as they approach retirement age.

Pension benefits in a DBP increase nonlinearly with years of service and employee age to reward employee loyalty and retain experienced workers. Benefits also grow if the worker's salary increases. By exploiting nonlinearity, employers use DBP as a tool to induce employees to accept an early retirement buyout. The buyout offer might grant employees a pension calculated as if they had served five extra years and as if they were five years older. In some offers, companies agree to increase the employee's basic wage used in determining the pension to factor in wage increases anticipated over the next year or two. Buyout offers of this variety are especially attractive to older workers with many years of service who anticipate retiring within the next five years. Moreover, they are favored by employers since they require no immediate out-of-pocket expenditures and may cost less if the pension fund is overfunded. In the worst case, the employer's cash flow is not affected until some time in the future.

Consider the annual retirement benefits per $1,000 of salary granted by the DBP plan outlined in table 6.21. A sixty-year-old employee with thirty years of experience earning $50,000 per year would have an annual retirement benefit of $20,000 ($400 × 50). In five years, with thirty-five years of experience and the same $50,000 salary, the pension rises to $32,500 per year. If a 10 percent wage increase is factored in, the pension becomes $35,750. The sixty-year-old employee might be reluctant to retire with a $20,000 pension and no social security. However, with five extra years of service and age assumed and a 10 percent wage increase added on, the worker very well may agree to retire on $35,750 per year, especially since social security becomes available at age sixty-two.

New Developments in Pensions

The Internal Revenue Service in February 1996 issued tax rules for a new variety of pension plan, the cash balance pension (CBP). The new plans are a hybrid of features of both DBPs and DCPs. Like DCPs, the new plan allows employees to carry an existing pension plan with them when they change employers. Like DBPs, the return on CBPs is guaranteed by the employer (Johnston 1996).

An employer with a CBP pension plan contributes a fixed percentage of each employee's income to the plan each year. The employer decides how the accumulated funds are to be invested and guarantees an investment return.[38] If the plan earns a return in excess of the promised return, the employer is permitted to discontinue making annual payments. The employee has three options upon leaving a job:

1. roll the CBP into an individual retirement account
2. leave the accumulated funds with the existing employer
3. invest the funds in the new employer's CBP

Layoffs: Rehiring Fired Workers

Recently, a *Wall Street Journal* article headlined that Kmart had advertised job openings but had restricted recently laid-off Kmart employees

TABLE 6.21. Annual Retirement Benefits per Thousand Dollars of Ending-Year Salary

Years of Service	Retirement Age	Annual Benefit/$1,000
20	50	$50.00
	55	$52.00
	60	$55.00
	65	$60.00
25	50	$190.00
	55	$200.00
	60	$220.00
	65	$240.00
30	50	$350.00
	55	$375.00
	60	$400.00
	65	$425.00
35	50	$560.00
	55	$590.00
	60	$620.00
	65	$650.00
40	50	$830.00
	55	$870.00
	60	$910.00
	65	$950.00

from applying for those jobs. (*Wall Street Journal* 1995d) Laid-off workers had been required to sign an agreement providing them with severance benefits, such as continued health-care benefits for a specified time period or a lump-sum cash payment, in exchange for agreeing not to seek reemployment at Kmart. The practice of not rehiring laid-off workers is widespread.

The principal reason companies refuse to open future employment opportunities to laid-off workers is morale. A worker whose life is disrupted by an unexpected layoff conceivably harbors ill will toward the company, his/her former supervisors, and fellow workers who escaped the layoff. Sabotage, trouble making, and even spying for a competitor are the feared outcome of rehiring workers. No evidence has ever been collected to support these fears, but their mere possibility seems sufficient to keep companies from reversing this policy.

Rehiring your own has several advantages. First, a former internal knows how the system works. The learning curve is flattened. Second, if the severance contract is well written, unused benefits are repaid to the employer and, in this case, the employer knows when the individual takes another job.

Layoffs at AT&T: A Long History

Few companies have been as battered by radical technological change and deregulation as has AT&T since the mid 1980s. During the decade ending in 1996, AT&T laid off over 125,000 workers in six stages, taking special charges against income of $28.77 billion ($22.31 per share) (Keller 1996b). The most recent layoff, in January 1996, is subjected to closer scrutiny because

- it is the largest AT&T layoff, involving 40,000 workers and a $4 billion charge against earnings[39]
- AT&T presumably is an expert in personnel reduction after five previous layoffs

AT&T's plan is not perfect. It does, however, exemplify a management approach combining generosity and authority that should be considered by other companies planning layoffs.

Despite its immense size, $79.61 billion in 1995 revenues, AT&T has performed poorly since 1983 following divestiture of its local operating companies (NYNEX, Bell Atlantic, etc.). In the twelve years after divestiture, net income was negative twice, 1988 and 1993, and operating income dramatically declined four times. In 1996, AT&T took the offensive, splitting itself into

- a long distance, wireless, credit card, and systems-integration company
- a computer business (formerly NCR)
- a manufacturer of telecommunications equipment (formerly Western Electric)

AT&T's original shareholders receive shares in the two new businesses proportionate to their original ownership position, and an initial public offering of the telecommunications equipment company is expected to raise $4 billion for AT&T.

AT&T's unbundling strategy allows independent managers in the new businesses to confront increasingly competitive markets. For example, AT&T's dominance of the long-distance market has declined to such an extent that in late 1995 the Federal Communications Commission, in recognition of the changed market structure, relaxed its restrictions on AT&T, thereby allowing it to respond quickly and aggressively to competitors' pricing behavior. Without the layoffs and the corporate breakup, AT&T's cost structure could have kept it from being profitable at the new price levels.[40] Robert E. Allen, chairman of AT&T, summed this up:

> To the extent we can get in trim, we'll produce better margins, more flexibility and more cash flow to invest in other opportunities. We've radically changed the focus and cost structure of the new AT&T . . . to defend our markets and attack others. (Keller 1996b)

Moreover, AT&T hopes to return to the local telephone markets from which it has been absent since 1983. In one element of that strategy, AT&T is now the largest cellular telephone company in the world (Keller 1996a). Its cellular revenues grew at 26 percent in 1995, compared to a 4.8 percent growth rate in traditional long-distance revenues.

After the January 1996 layoff, AT&T employed 110,000 workers and had revenues of about $50 billion. The telecommunications equipment manufacturer employed another 108,000 workers and had revenues of about $20 billion. The computer business, with revenues of $8.16 billion in 1995, previously announced its own layoff of 8,500 workers.

The actual downsizing followed a two-step process: a voluntary buyout and then an involuntary layoff. AT&T's objective was to ascertain which employees might voluntarily separate so that the fewest possible individuals would be disrupted. Nearly 6,500 of the 72,000 managers offered the buyout in November 1995 accepted it (almost 15 percent of the total needed) (Hanley 1996a). The layoff and buyout severance packages do not materially differ;[41] by announcing a richer buyout than severance package, AT&T could have achieved a higher voluntary acceptance rate (Hanley 1996b). Instead, AT&T equalized the offers to avoid upsetting employees, who already suffered from severe morale problems after five prior layoffs. Mending worker morale is essential if the strategy of attacking new markets is to prevail. Fairly treating departing coworkers is one route to that restoration. Another approach was to have every person informed of his/her layoff in person by his/her immediate supervisor.

AT&T did not reveal its method of selecting workers to be laid off, though a rightsizing approach is probable. A manager doing rightsizing is given a target number of subordinates and the latitude to select the best-qualified workers. AT&T is partially unionized, so its layoff pattern must not conflict with union rules, but buyouts overcame layoff rules.

AT&T granted liberal severance benefits to laid-off employees, as detailed in table 6.22.[42] Employee unions and management negotiated the final package. Clerical employees preferred to receive more of their benefits up front and in cash, while managers elected to extend severance over time and to favor workers nearing retirement. The formula deriving the lump-sum payment for managers is based on both age and years of service, while the formula for clerical workers is based on seniority.

Questions

1. Was AT&T obligated to pay any severance benefits?
2. Why did AT&T pay severance benefits?
3. Would AT&T need to pay similar severance benefits in a future layoff?
4. Which workers are likely to have accepted the buyout?
5. How would you have revised the buyout offer to raise the rate of acceptance?
6. Must a buyout be offered to all workers, or can it be targeted at a defined group, such as older workers, managers in the credit card division, etc.?
7. Based on the design of the severance package, what would you guess were the job prospects of clerical workers?
8. Do workers have an ethical responsibility to return their severance package if they immediately find a better job?

A Corporate Renewal Engagement[43]

Global Foods, Inc., (Global) is a midsize manufacturer that specializes in the production of imitation (i.e., store-brand or in-house-brand) food items sold to large supermarket chains. Global specializes in look-alike products that stores position next to national brands. Store-brand items sell at an average 20 percent discount from national brands but return a 25 percent gross margin, nearly double what grocers earn on national brand sales.

Otis Young, a twenty-four-year-old graduate of Northeastern University, founded Global in 1974. During five years of cooperative-education work assignments arranged by the university, Young worked for Market Shoppers, Inc., the largest local supermarket chain, where he eventually became an assistant store manager. Upon graduation, the firm offered him a full-time job managing its original store. Store-brand items accounted for approximately 3 percent of sales, and generic goods represented another 2 percent of sales. Generic brands, sold in plain white packages with crudely stenciled labels and inferior-quality products inside, were a short-lived idea that came into vogue during the economy's adjustment to higher energy prices following the oil embargo crisis. As a store manager, Young knew that his store's bottom line and his personal bonus improved with sales of off-brand items. Consumer brand loyalty, reinforced by coupons and advertising, limited sales of off-brand items.

Three years of working full time (sixty-plus hours per week) for someone else fired Young's entrepreneurial spirit. Working at night, he developed a business plan for Global, and with the help of his parents and two college roommates raised $250,000 of startup capital. Before quitting his job, Young arranged to sell the first knockoff product, mouthwash, to Market Shoppers. Young's plan was simple. He imported the English strategy, developed by Sainsbury, Inc., of matching or even surpassing the quality of national brands with his knockoffs. He kept

TABLE 6.22. AT&T's Severance Package

Employee Type	Lump-Sum Payment	Health Benefit Continuation	Retraining and Relocation	Early Pension Eligibility
Manager	6–42 Weeks	1 Year	$10,000	If within 2 years of normal age
Clerical	1–104 Weeks	None	None	None

Source: Derived from Hanley (1996b)

Note: Workers accepting the buyout received an additional eight-week payment; laid-off workers received this benefit as continued employment for eight weeks.

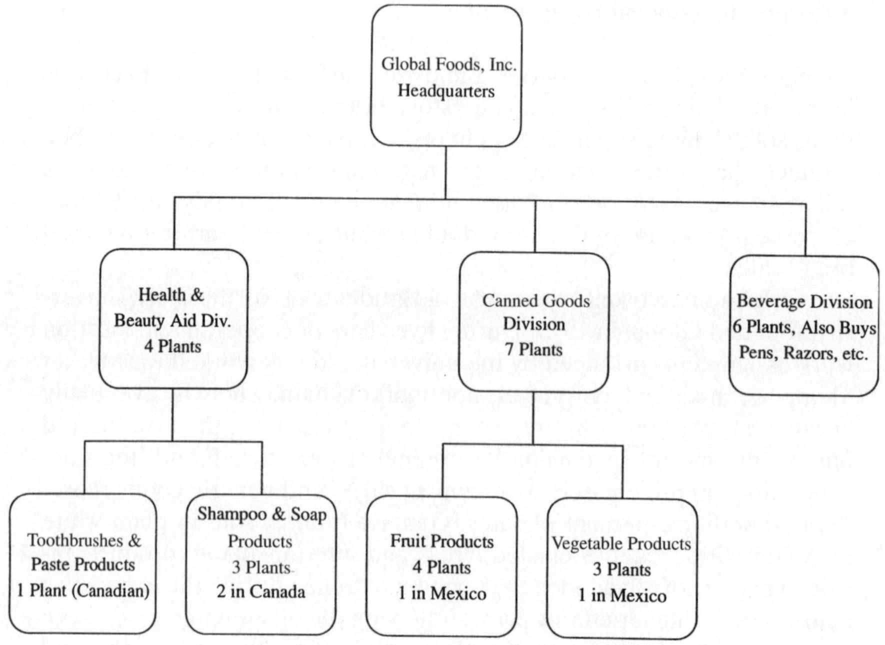

Fig. 6.11. Global Foods: divisional chart

costs and prices low and easily attracted new customers. The company expanded in two ways: new accounts and new products.

Profitability began in year one. Sales grew astronomically: 104 percent annually from 1974 to 1980 and 36 percent annually from 1980 to 1990. Soon Global became a national player in the imitation-brand business (see fig. 6.11). Table 6.23 summarizes Global's income statement. Global expanded from one product in 1974 to four hundred SKUs in 1996.[44] Global manufactures most of the products itself at seventeen manufacturing sites in the United States, Canada, and Mexico.[45] A small percentage of items, including pens, cigarette lighters, and razors, are purchased from other manufacturers. Beside most manufacturing sites is a companion distribution center. Global remains headquartered in Chelsea, Massachusetts.

Worker loyalty at Global is steadfast, based partly on an affinity for Young but also on a perception that its compensation plan is fair. In fact, wage levels lag the industry by approximately 5–7 percent. Almost 25 percent of employees are part-timers, earning 20 percent less than full-time workers and ineligible for most benefits. Full-time employees receive 80 percent medical coverage at their choice of HMO, a $500 annual dental allowance, ten vacation days after the first year, rising to twenty after ten years of employment, seven holidays off, and a DCP matching employees' contributions up to 5 percent. The pension plan's principal investment is Global stock; it now owns approximately 21 percent of the company.

Global's balance sheet and sources and uses of funds are presented in tables 6.24 and 6.25 in slightly abbreviated form. Global's crisis began at the end of 1995. Trade creditors demanded that Global reduce its days payable. Young exhorted them to relent and bought some time by reminding them of prior business dealings and future business possibilities. Table 6.26 shows Global's largest creditors. Only the first creditor is secured, by inventory and receivables. Dividends to shareholders were ended as of the fourth quarter of 1996.

Global's relationships with its bank and long-term creditors also are in peril. A sinking-fund obligation of $32.5 million per year for ten years on the pre-1996 debt load commences in 1997. The $50 million bank credit line is converted into a one-year term loan if, among other things, notes payable hit the $50 million limit or stockholders' equity falls below $100 million. At the end of 1996, the bank syndicate delivered two cautionary letters to Global documenting indenture-agreement violations by its inventory turnover and debt-equity ratios. The letters stated that Global needed to submit a plan to ameliorate the violations.

Young and his two college roommates owned 76 percent of Global's equity and served as its president and CEO, COO, and CFO, respectively. In 1990, investment bankers proposed an initial public offering indicating a value in excess of $1.5 billion. The three friends rejected the proposal, preferring to retain control and maintain their investment in Global. However, much of this value had evaporated along with Global's net income. Cash flow in 1996 was negative; there were $45.34 million in losses, dividends of $39.41 million, and depreciation of $42.6 million.

Global's difficulties started in 1990 with two unanticipated events:

1. Sainsbury and other non-U.S. grocery behemoths began to buy up U.S. grocery chains and demand price concessions from suppliers like Global or else substituted some of their own goods for U.S. supplies.
2. Branded-goods producers whose sales had felt the impact of imitations responded by sharply cutting prices. The two leaders in this movement were Kellogg's in the cereal arena and Philip Morris in the tobacco and cookie businesses.

TABLE 6.23. Global Foods' Income Statement

	1974	1975	1976	1977	1978	1979	1980
Sales	$ 0.41	$ 1.01	$ 2.23	$ 3.14	$ 8.20	$ 15.82	$ 29.58
Cost of goods	$ 0.20	$ 0.47	$ 1.03	$ 1.48	$ 3.77	$ 6.96	$ 13.67
Gross margin	$ 0.21	$ 0.54	$ 1.20	$ 1.66	$ 4.43	$ 8.86	$ 15.91
Total G&A	$ 0.10	$ 0.21	$ 0.53	$ 0.63	$ 2.39	$ 4.08	$ 7.40
Depreciation	$ 0.04	$ 0.06	$ 0.10	$ 0.12	$ 0.30	$ 0.60	$ 1.10
EBIT	$ 0.07	$ 0.27	$ 0.58	$ 0.91	$ 1.74	$ 4.18	$ 7.42
Interest	$ 0.05	$ 0.08	$ 0.12	$ 0.15	$ 0.40	$ 0.85	$ 1.55
Taxes	$ 0.01	$ 0.10	$ 0.23	$ 0.38	$ 0.67	$ 1.67	$ 2.93
Net income	$ 0.01	$ 0.10	$ 0.23	$ 0.38	$ 0.67	$ 1.67	$ 2.93
Dividends	$ —	$ —	$ —	$ —	$ —	$ —	$ —

	1988	1989	1990	1991	1992	1993	1994
Sales	$ 397.14	$ 523.62	$ 639.25	$ 672.80	$ 731.64	$ 727.57	$ 709.36
Worker salaries							
Plant managers' salaries							
Fixed plant & warehouse costs							
Raw materials & packaging							
Cost of goods	$ 198.57	$ 264.81	$ 326.02	$ 349.86	$ 391.43	$ 381.97	$ 365.32
Gross margin	$ 198.57	$ 258.81	$ 313.23	$ 322.94	$ 340.21	$ 345.60	$ 344.04
	50%	50%	49%	48%	46%	47%	48%
Distribution							
Employee salaries							
Shipping							
Maintenance, rent, and other FC							
Total distribution							
Corporate							
Corporate staff							
Corporate management							
Total corporate							
Total G&A	$ 95.30	$ 115.24	$ 140.28	$ 154.70	$ 175.60	$ 196.51	$ 191.48
	24%	22%	22%	23%	24%	27%	27%
Depreciation	$ 13.33	$ 15.88	$ 19.77	$ 22.48	$ 25.88	$ 28.73	$ 31.29
EBIT	$ 89.95	$ 130.70	$ 153.19	$ 145.76	$ 138.73	$ 120.36	$ 121.27
Interest	$ 17.90	$ 19.40	$ 23.25	$ 26.25	$ 27.75	$ 27.75	$ 27.75
Taxes	$ 36.02	$ 55.65	$ 64.97	$ 59.76	$ 55.49	$ 46.30	$ 46.76
Net income	$ 36.02	$ 55.65	$ 64.97	$ 59.76	$ 55.49	$ 46.30	$ 46.76
Dividends	$ 9.01	$ 13.91	$ 39.41	$ 39.41	$ 39.41	$ 39.41	$ 39.41

1981	1982	1983	1984	1985	1986	1987
$ 47.74	$ 71.43	$ 104.15	$ 141.83	$ 152.14	$ 180.14	$ 234.12
$ 22.44	$ 32.86	$ 44.78	$ 62.41	$ 64.07	$ 81.06	$ 110.04
$ 25.30	$ 38.57	$ 59.37	$ 79.42	$ 88.07	$ 99.08	$ 124.08
$ 12.82	$ 18.54	$ 30.18	$ 39.74	$ 42.89	$ 48.65	$ 60.90
$ 1.80	$ 2.70	$ 4.25	$ 6.00	$ 6.50	$ 8.10	$ 10.28
$ 10.69	$ 17.33	$ 24.93	$ 33.68	$ 38.68	$ 42.32	$ 52.91
$ 2.40	$ 3.65	$ 6.05	$ 8.55	$ 8.90	$ 10.40	$ 13.40
$ 4.14	$ 6.84	$ 9.44	$ 12.57	$ 14.89	$ 15.96	$ 19.75
$ 4.14	$ 6.84	$ 9.44	$ 12.57	$ 14.89	$ 15.96	$ 19.75
$ —	$ 1.71	$ 1.71	$ 3.14	$ 3.14	$ 3.99	$ 3.99

1995	Health	Foods	Bev	1996	Health	Foods	Bev
$ 702.62	$ 333.55	$ 185.42	$ 183.65	$ 694.39	$ 396.79	$ 188.48	$ 109.12
$ 207.87	$ 102.19	$ 35.35	$ 70.33	$ 255.69	$ 153.94	$ 67.94	$ 33.80
$ 10.78	$ 4.65	$ 2.98	$ 3.15	$ 13.07	$ 5.80	$ 3.81	$ 3.46
$ 71.36	$ 20.54	$ 19.99	$ 30.83	$ 93.45	$ 30.67	$ 25.36	$ 37.42
$ 64.81	$ 39.62	$ 18.76	$ 6.43	$ 97.20	$ 62.21	$ 27.25	$ 7.73
$ 354.82	$ 167.00	$ 77.08	$ 110.74	$ 459.40	$ 252.62	$ 124.37	$ 82.42
$ 347.80	$ 166.55	$ 108.34	$ 72.91	$ 234.99	$ 144.18	$ 64.11	$ 26.70
49%				34%			
$ 29.18	$ 10.98	$ 8.34	$ 9.86	$ 25.79	$ 11.26	$ 8.81	$ 5.72
$ 71.17	$ 33.97	$ 13.49	$ 23.71	$ 67.90	$ 37.24	$ 14.69	$ 15.98
$ 24.77	$ 5.31	$ 9.34	$ 10.12	$ 26.38	$ 6.44	$ 9.73	$ 10.22
$ 125.12	$ 50.26	$ 31.17	$ 43.69	$ 120.07	$ 54.93	$ 33.22	$ 31.92
$ 25.67	$ 12.30	$ 7.12	$ 6.25	$ 24.27	$ 12.39	$ 7.55	$ 4.33
$ 46.09	$ 25.07	$ 9.63	$ 11.39	$ 46.40	$ 25.78	$ 9.88	$ 10.75
$ 71.76	$ 37.37	$ 16.75	$ 17.64	$ 70.67	$ 38.16	$ 17.43	$ 15.08
$ 196.88	$ 87.63	$ 47.92	$ 61.33	$ 190.75	$ 93.09	$ 50.65	$ 47.00
28%				27%			
$ 37.91	$ 8.67	$ 13.89	$ 15.35	$ 42.58	$ 10.43	$ 16.52	$ 15.64
$ 113.01	$ 70.25	$ 46.53	$ (3.77)	$ 1.66	$ 40.65	$ (3.06)	$ (35.93)
$ 34.00	$ 8.43	$ 14.69	$ 10.88	$ 47.00	$ 11.66	$ 20.30	$ 15.04
$ 39.51	$ —	$ —	$ —	$ —			
$ 39.51	$ 61.82	$ 31.84	$ (14.65)	$ (45.34)	$ 28.99	$ (23.36)	$ (50.97)
$ 39.41				$ 39.41			

TABLE 6.24. Global Foods' Balance Sheet

	1974	1975	1976	1977	1978	1979
Assets						
Current assets						
Inventory	$ 0.01	$ 0.03	$ 0.07	$ 0.10	$ 0.26	$ 0.53
Acc rec	$ 0.05	$ 0.12	$ 0.28	$ 0.38	$ 1.03	$ 2.08
Cash and other assets	$ 0.23	$ 0.41	$ 0.44	$ 0.73	$ 0.94	$ 1.84
Total current assets	$ 0.29	$ 0.56	$ 0.79	$ 1.21	$ 2.23	$ 4.45
Fixed assets	$ 0.80	$ 1.10	$ 1.90	$ 2.40	$ 5.90	$ 11.90
Accumulated depreciation	$ 0.04	$ 0.10	$ 0.19	$ 0.31	$ 0.61	$ 1.20
Net fixed assets	$ 0.76	$ 1.01	$ 1.71	$ 2.09	$ 5.30	$ 10.70
Total assets	$ 1.05	$ 1.56	$ 2.50	$ 3.30	$ 7.53	$ 15.15
Liabilities						
Notes payable	$ 0.20	$ 0.25	$ 0.50	$ 0.75	$ 1.50	$ 3.00
Accounts payable	$ 0.08	$ 0.21	$ 0.46	$ 0.63	$ 1.64	$ 3.09
Current liabilities	$ 0.28	$ 0.46	$ 0.96	$ 1.38	$ 3.14	$ 6.09
Long-term debt	$ 0.25	$ 0.50	$ 0.70	$ 0.70	$ 2.50	$ 5.50
Stockholder equity	$ 0.52	$ 0.62	$ 0.84	$ 1.22	$ 1.89	$ 3.56
Total	$ 1.05	$ 1.56	$ 2.50	$ 3.30	$ 7.53	$ 15.15

	1987	1988	1989	1990	1991	1992
Assets						
Current assets						
Inventory	$ 8.32	$ 15.02	$ 20.73	$ 25.63	$ 28.56	$ 33.03
Acc rec	$ 35.86	$ 62.89	$ 83.35	$ 102.10	$ 106.54	$ 116.66
Cash and other assets	$ 38.57	$ 53.37	$ 71.08	$ 72.13	$ 87.52	$ 75.26
Total current assets	$ 82.74	$ 131.27	$ 175.16	$ 199.87	$ 222.62	$ 224.95
Fixed assets	$ 205.50	$ 266.50	$ 317.50	$ 395.30	$ 449.60	$ 517.60
Accumluated depreciation	$ 41.92	$ 55.24	$ 71.12	$ 90.88	$ 113.36	$ 139.24
Net fixed assts	$ 163.59	$ 211.26	$ 246.39	$ 304.42	$ 336.24	$ 378.36
Total assets	$ 246.33	$ 342.53	$ 421.54	$ 504.29	$ 558.86	$ 603.31
Liabilities						
Notes payable	$ 4.03	$ 4.03	$ 4.03	$ 12.50	$ 12.50	$ 12.50
Accounts payable	$ 39.90	$ 64.09	$ 86.36	$ 105.08	$ 109.31	$ 122.67
Current liabilities	$ 43.93	$ 68.12	$ 90.39	$ 117.58	$ 121.81	$ 135.17
Long-term debt	$ 130.00	$ 175.00	$ 190.00	$ 220.00	$ 250.00	$ 265.00
Stockholder equity	$ 72.41	$ 99.41	$ 141.15	$ 166.71	$ 187.05	$ 203.14
Total	$ 246.33	$ 342.53	$ 421.54	$ 504.29	$ 558.86	$ 603.31

1980	1981	1982	1983	1984	1985	1986
$ 1.06	$ 1.50	$ 2.00	$ 2.87	$ 4.21	$ 4.41	$ 5.82
$ 3.87	$ 6.07	$ 9.32	$ 14.04	$ 19.58	$ 20.92	$ 26.75
$ 3.05	$ 4.20	$ 7.28	$ 12.16	$ 17.05	$ 28.58	$ 29.92
$ 7.98	$ 11.77	$ 18.60	$ 29.07	$ 40.84	$ 53.91	$ 62.49
$ 21.90	$ 35.90	$ 54.00	$ 85.00	$ 120.00	$ 130.00	$ 162.00
$ 2.30	$ 4.09	$ 6.79	$ 11.04	$ 17.04	$ 23.54	$ 31.64
$ 19.61	$ 31.81	$ 47.21	$ 73.96	$ 102.96	$ 106.46	$ 130.36
$ 27.58	$ 43.58	$ 65.81	$ 103.03	$ 143.80	$ 160.37	$ 192.85
$ 5.50	$ 5.50	$ 5.50	$ 5.50	$ 5.50	$ 4.03	$ 4.03
$ 5.59	$ 8.95	$ 13.54	$ 19.03	$ 25.37	$ 26.68	$ 32.18
$ 11.09	$ 14.45	$ 19.04	$ 24.53	$ 30.87	$ 30.71	$ 36.21
$ 10.00	$ 18.50	$ 31.00	$ 55.00	$ 80.00	$ 85.00	$ 100.00
$ 6.49	$ 10.63	$ 15.76	$ 23.49	$ 32.93	$ 44.67	$ 56.65
$ 27.58	$ 43.58	$ 65.81	$ 103.03	$ 143.80	$ 160.37	$ 192.85

1993	1994	1995	1996			
			Total	Health	Foods	Bev
$ 32.65	$ 31.53	$ 32.18	$ 44.05	$ 19.25	$ 12.44	$ 12.36
$ 116.41	$ 114.86	$ 113.96	$ 114.15	$ 47.39	$ 47.12	$ 19.64
$ 56.22	$ 44.95	$ 14.43	$ 3.94	$ 2.25	$ 1.07	$ 0.62
$ 205.29	$ 191.34	$ 160.57	$ 162.14	$ 68.89	$ 60.63	$ 32.62
$ 574.60	$ 626.60	$ 759.20	$ 853.50	$ 210.50	$ 330.30	$ 312.70
$ 167.97	$ 199.26	$ 237.17	$ 279.75	$ 68.15	$ 82.46	$ 129.14
$ 406.63	$ 427.34	$ 522.04	$ 573.76	$ 142.35	$ 247.85	$ 183.56
$ 611.92	$ 618.68	$ 682.60	$ 735.90	$ 211.24	$ 308.47	$ 216.18
$ 12.50	$ 12.50	$ 15.00	$ 45.00			
$ 124.38	$ 123.80	$ 125.12	$ 133.17			
$ 136.88	$ 136.30	$ 140.12	$ 178.17			
$ 265.00	$ 265.00	$ 325.00	$ 425.00			
$ 210.04	$ 217.39	$ 217.47	$ 132.73			
$ 611.92	$ 618.68	$ 682.60	$ 735.90			

TABLE 6.25. Global Foods' Sources and Uses of Funds

	1974	1975	1976	1977	1978	1979
Cash	$ 0.50	$ 0.23	$ 0.41	$ 0.44	$ 0.73	$ 0.94
EBIT	$ 0.07	$ 0.27	$ 0.58	$ 0.91	$ 1.74	$ 4.18
Interest	$ (0.05)	$ (0.08)	$ (0.12)	$ (0.15)	$ (0.40)	$ (0.85)
Taxes	$ (0.01)	$ (0.10)	$ (0.23)	$ (0.38)	$ (0.67)	$ (1.67)
Dividends	$ —	$ —	$ —	$ —	$ —	$ —
Depreciation	$ 0.04	$ 0.06	$ 0.10	$ 0.12	$ 0.30	$ 0.60
Change in NP & LT Debt	$ 0.45	$ 0.30	$ 0.45	$ 0.25	$ 2.55	$ 4.50
Change in AP	$ 0.08	$ 0.12	$ 0.25	$ 0.17	$ 1.01	$ 1.45
Change in inv	$ (0.01)	$ (0.02)	$ (0.04)	$ (0.03)	$ (0.17)	$ (0.26)
Change in AR	$ (0.05)	$ (0.07)	$ (0.16)	$ (0.10)	$ (0.64)	$ (1.06)
Capital expenditures	$ (0.80)	$ (0.30)	$ (0.80)	$ (0.50)	$ (3.50)	$ (6.00)
Ending cash balance	$ 0.23	$ 0.41	$ 0.44	$ 0.73	$ 0.94	$ 1.84
Days payable	74.8	74.2	75.3	73.1	72.8	71.3
Receivable days	45.1	44.2	46.1	44.7	45.7	48.1
Inventory days	20.1	22	23.4	24.5	25.6	27.6
Outstanding loans	$ 0.45	$ 0.75	$ 1.20	$ 1.45	$ 4.00	$ 8.50
Interest rate	10%	10%	10%	10%	10%	10%
Interest paid	$ 0.05	$ 0.08	$ 0.12	$ 0.15	$ 0.40	$ 0.85
Tax rate	50%	50%	50%	50%	50%	50%

	1986	1987	1988	1989	1990	1991
Cash	$ 28.58	$ 29.92	$ 38.57	$ 53.37	$ 71.08	$ 72.13
EBIT	$ 42.32	$ 52.91	$ 89.95	$ 130.70	$ 153.19	$ 145.76
Interest	$ (10.40)	$ (13.40)	$ (17.90)	$ (19.40)	$ (23.25)	$ (26.25)
Taxes	$ (15.96)	$ (19.75)	$ (36.02)	$ (55.65)	$ (64.97)	$ (59.76)
Dividends	$ (3.99)	$ (3.99)	$ (9.01)	$ (13.91)	$ (39.41)	$ (39.41)
Depreciation	$ 8.10	$ 10.28	$ 13.33	$ 15.88	$ 19.77	$ 22.48
Change in NP & LT Debt	$ 15.00	$ 30.00	$ 45.00	$ 15.00	$ 38.47	$ 30.00
Change in AP	$ 5.50	$ 7.72	$ 24.19	$ 22.28	$ 18.72	$ 4.22
Change in inv	$ (1.41)	$ (2.50)	$ (6.69)	$ (5.71)	$ (4.91)	$ (2.93)
Change in AR	$ (5.83)	$ (9.11)	$ (27.03)	$ (20.46)	$ (18.76)	$ (4.44)
Capital expenditures	$ (32.00)	$ (43.50)	$ (61.00)	$ (51.00)	$ (77.80)	$ (54.30)
Ending cash balance	$ 29.92	$ 38.57	$ 53.37	$ 71.08	$ 72.13	$ 87.52
Days payable	65.2	62.2	58.9	60.2	60	59.3
Receivable days	54.2	55.9	57.8	58.1	58.3	57.8
Inventory days	26.2	27.6	27.6	28.9	28.7	29.8
Outstanding loans	$ 104.03	$ 134.03	$ 179.03	$ 194.03	$ 232.50	$ 262.50
Interest rate	10%	10%	10%	10%	10%	10%
Interest paid	$ 10.40	$ 13.40	$ 17.90	$ 19.40	$ 23.25	$ 26.25
Tax rate	50%	50%	50%	50%	50%	50%

1980	1981	1982	1983	1984	1985
$ 1.84	$ 3.05	$ 4.20	$ 7.28	$ 12.16	$ 17.05
$ 7.42	$ 10.69	$ 17.33	$ 24.93	$ 33.68	$ 38.68
$ (1.55)	$ (2.40)	$ (3.65)	$ (6.05)	$ (8.55)	$ (8.90)
$ (2.93)	$ (4.14)	$ (6.84)	$ (9.44)	$ (12.57)	$ (14.89)
$ —	$ —	$ (1.71)	$ (1.71)	$ (3.14)	$ (3.14)
$ 1.10	$ 1.80	$ 2.70	$ 4.25	$ 6.00	$ 6.50
$ 7.00	$ 8.50	$ 12.50	$ 24.00	$ 25.00	$ 3.53
$ 2.50	$ 3.35	$ 4.60	$ 5.49	$ 6.34	$ 1.30
$ (0.53)	$ (0.44)	$ (0.50)	$ (0.87)	$ (1.33)	$ (0.20)
$ (1.79)	$ (2.20)	$ (3.25)	$ (4.72)	$ (5.55)	$ (1.34)
$ (10.00)	$ (14.00)	$ (18.10)	$ (31.00)	$ (35.00)	$ (10.00)
$ 3.05	$ 4.20	$ 7.28	$ 12.16	$ 17.05	$ 28.58
69	68.4	69.2	66.7	65.3	64
47.8	46.4	47.6	49.2	50.4	50.2
28.2	24.4	22.2	23.4	24.6	25.1
$ 15.50	$ 24.00	$ 36.50	$ 60.50	$ 85.50	$ 89.03
10%	10%	10%	10%	10%	10%
$ 1.55	$ 2.40	$ 3.65	$ 6.05	$ 8.55	$ 8.90
50%	50%	50%	50%	50%	50%

1992	1993	1994	1995	1996
$ 87.52	$ 75.26	$ 56.22	$ 44.95	$ 14.43
$ 138.73	$ 120.36	$ 121.27	$ 113.01	$ 1.66
$ (27.75)	$ (27.75)	$ (27.75)	$ (34.00)	$ (47.00)
$ (55.49)	$ (46.30)	$ (46.76)	$ (39.51)	$ —
$ (39.41)	$ (39.41)	$ (39.41)	$ (39.41)	$ (39.41)
$ 25.88	$ 28.73	$ 31.29	$ 37.91	$ 42.58
$ 15.00	$ —	$ —	$ 62.50	$ 130.00
$ 13.37	$ 1.71	$ (0.59)	$ 1.33	$ 8.05
$ (4.47)	$ 0.38	$ 1.12	$ (0.65)	$ (11.88)
$ (10.12)	$ 0.25	$ 1.55	$ 0.90	$ (0.19)
$ (68.00)	$ (57.00)	$ (52.00)	$ (132.60)	$ (94.30)
$ 72.26	$ 56.22	$ 44.95	$ 14.43	$ 3.94
61.2	62.4	63.7	65	70
58.2	58.4	59.1	59.2	60
30.8	31.2	31.5	33.1	35
$ 277.50	$ 277.50	$ 277.50	$ 340.00	$ 470.00
10%	10%	10%	10%	10%
$ 27.75	$ 27.75	$ 27.75	$ 34.00	$ 47.00
50%	50%	50%	50%	50%

Global responded by cutting its margins and introducing still more products. The latter strategy derived from Young's belief that Global could always profit by introducing new look-alike products until the name-brand manufacturer felt the competition and cut its price. The race to introduce new products and maintain profits began in 1991, when Global had 135 products, mainly canned goods, health and beauty aids, and beverages.

Finally one night in November 1996 at the pre–board meeting dinner, Young's mother, a board member, asked, "How come we're making more products and less money?" No one answered her. Young knew the company needed to be restructured.

Young had always been a hands-on manager, doing almost everything himself, from choosing new plant locations to setting prices to testing new products in development. Not being familiar with corporate renewal, he read a number of books. He learned that entrepreneurs have difficulty dismantling what they have assembled, so the corporate renewal task should be assigned to an outsider.

Global's accountants knew Young intended to restructure and suggested he talk with the corporate recovery team in the consulting arm of their firm. Following a meeting in which the consultants catalogued their accomplishments, the board agreed to hire the team to prepare a restructuring plan. The management team would remain in charge of daily operations and business decisions. Information gathered by the team is presented in tables 6.27–6.31 and figures 6.12 and 6.13.

TABLE 6.26. Global Foods' Major Creditors (excluding long-term debt)

Creditor	Amount Owed
Bank of Shawmut	$45,000,000
Consolidated Dairies, Inc.	$15,528,000
Orange Growers Co-op, Inc.	$11,793,000
Stairs Container Corp.	$9,135,000
Interstate Truckers Ltd.	$9,068,000
Guaranteed Trucking, Inc.	$8,195,000
Quail Pharmaceuticals Co.	$7,899,000
Health and Beauty, Inc.	$7,453,000
Ready Glow Products Co.	$7,854,000
Verity Meats Poultry and Dairy, Inc.	$6,368,000

Student Assignment

1. How should personnel, financial, product, and other targets be set in a restructuring?
2. Who should be laid off?
3. Should any products be discontinued? Which ones?
4. What incentives should be given to induce employees to leave. Be specific about blue- and white-collar employees.
5. How can Global insure that the best workers remain and the least qualified leave?
6. Does Global have an age discrimination problem to contend with? Gender discrimination? The company does not maintain gender data.
7. Which plants should Global shut?
8. Which processes should Global change?
9. How and when should Global inform its customers of these changes? When should the changes occur?
10. Do ethical concerns arise in restructurings? What about at Global?
11. Are there good alternatives to a restructuring?
12. What information do you need to prepare a reengineering report?
13. What other guidance would you give the board?
14. What other questions need to be asked?

TABLE 6.27. Global Foods' Plant Information ($ in millions)

#	Location	Year Built	Fixed Costs[a]	Plant Capacity[b]	Utilization in 1996	Total Employed[c]	Book Value	Original Cost
				Health & Beauty				
1	Mass.	1974	5.1	0.91	90%	1,292	$ 2.18	14.5
10	Texas	1987	3.0	0.86	49%	346	$ 39.35	52.0
11	Canada	1987	5.5	1.34	83%	1,092	$ 33.00	55.0
16	Mexico	1995	7.0	2.95	99%	1,658	$ 53.65	58.0
			20.6	6.06		4,388	$ 128.18	179.5
				Food Division				
5	California	1983	4.0	0.70	85%	562	$ 9.37	18.8
6	Georgia	1984	1.3	0.34	0%	–	$ 9.50	14.0
7	Georgia	1986	2.4	0.64	73%	316	$ 14.50	20.0
9	Alabama	1987	1.4	0.39	0%	–	$ 31.05	37.0
14	Texas	1989	2.3	0.62	82%	336	$ 30.78	37.5
15	Florida	1990	3.8	0.93	58%	377	$ 41.60	52.0
17	Mexico	1995	4.8	1.78	24%	208	$ 48.10	52.0
			20.0	5.40		1,799	$ 184.90	231.3
				Beverage Division				
2	Mass.	1978	4.8	0.75	76%	215	$ 4.35	22.0
3	California	1981	4.6	0.73	93%	228	$ 9.75	33.0
4	Mass.	1982	3.2	0.58	81%	153	$ 7.80	21.0
8	Alabama	1986	4.9	1.20	87%	229	$ 37.80	63.0
12	Florida	1988	6.9	1.44	54%	191	$ 42.00	60.0
13	Florida	1989	6.4	1.24	98%	288	$ 45.00	60.0
			30.8	5.94		1,304	$ 146.70	256.0
Total companywide			71.4			7,492	$ 459.78	

[a]Fixed costs include maintenance, rent, and fixed overhead.

[b]Plant capacity combines fixed investment dollars with plant/age, giving relative capacity across all plants.

[c]Includes plant workers and managers.

TABLE 6.28. Global Foods' Distribution Centers ($ in millions)

Location	Year Built	Fixed Costs[a]	Plant Capacity[b]	Utilization in 1996	Workers Employed[c]	Book Value
			Health & Beauty			
Mass.	1974	2.0	1.11	92%	112	2.4
Texas	1987	1.6	1.50	95%	97	6.3
Canada	1987	1.7	1.30	91%	96	5.5
		5.3	3.91		305	14.2
			Food Division			
California	1983	2.4	1.57	92%	77	4.6
Mass.	1983	2.4	1.29	62%	46	4.2
Missouri	1984	1.8	0.95	65%	38	7.2
Georgia	1986	0.9	0.39	94%	26	6.1
Texas	1989	0.8	0.70	87%	22	15.4
Canada	1992	1.0	0.50	36%	11	25.6
		9.3	5.40		220	63.1
			Beverage Division			
Mass.	1978	2.7	1.42	86%	71	1.4
California	1981	2.1	1.15	72%	46	5.1
Missouri	1984	1.9	0.95	83%	48	6.4
Alabama	1986	1.5	1.21	31%	14	7.4
Florida	1988	1.1	0.82	24%	8	8.0
Canada	1989	0.9	0.68	47%	13	8.5
		10.2	6.23		200	36.8
Total companywide		24.8			725	114.1

[a]Fixed costs include maintenance, rent, and fixed overhead.

[b]Plant capacity combines fixed investment dollars with plant/age, giving relative capacity across all plants.

[c]Includes workers and managers.

TABLE 6.29. Global Foods' Product Summary

Product Summary										
	Year Introduced	Plants Producing	Market Share[a]	Retail Price	Wholesale Price	Margin 1995	Margin 1996	Units (millions) Sold '96	Sales Revenue '96	Gross Margin '96
Health & Beauty										
Bleach	1975	1,10,11,16	38%	$ 1.15	$ 0.86	58%	28%	60.56	52.23	14.62
Dental floss	1981	1,10,11,16	24%	$ 1.35	$ 1.01	65%	33%	25.24	25.60	8.45
Deodorant	1991	1,10,11,16	5%	$ 1.60	$ 1.20	65%	40%	15.94	19.12	7.65
Ear cleaners	1985	1,10,11,16	13%	$ 1.20	$ 0.90	49%	32%	8.29	7.46	2.39
Fabric softener	1995	1,10,11,16	2%	$ 3.99	$ 2.99	50%	24%	9.56	28.61	6.87
Hair conditioner	1988	1,10,11,16	1%	$ 1.35	$ 1.01	65%	48%	3.19	3.23	1.55
Hair spray	1995	1,10,11,16	2%	$ 2.69	$ 2.02	62%	30%	9.56	19.29	5.79
Laundry detergent	1987	1,10,11,16	17%	$ 2.69	$ 2.02	69%	40%	81.28	163.98	65.59
Mouthwash	1974	1,10,11,16	13%	$ 2.69	$ 2.02	65%	48%	10.36	20.90	10.03
Nail polish remover	1989	1,10,11,16	7%	$ 0.99	$ 0.74	55%	41%	22.31	16.57	6.79
Shampoo	1981	1,10,11,16	4%	$ 1.11	$ 0.83	53%	43%	12.75	10.63	4.57
Shaving cream	1984	1,10,11,16	2%	$ 1.11	$ 0.83	62%	36%	9.56	7.97	2.87
Soap	1993	1,10,11,16	1%	$ 0.99	$ 0.74	28%	21%	9.56	7.10	1.49
Spray starch	1994	1,10,11,16	0.5%	$ 2.79	$ 2.09	25%	18%	0.80	1.67	0.30
Tampons	1995	1,10,11,16	0.5%	$ 2.80	$ 2.10	63%	45%	1.59	3.35	1.51
Toothbrushes	1977	1,10,11,16	3%	$ 2.20	$ 1.65	65%	44%	4.78	7.89	3.47
Other (average)	various	1,10,11,16	3.5%	$ 1.43	$ 1.07	35%	20%	1.12	1.20	0.24
									396.80	144.18

Food										
Applesauce	1985	5,7,15,17	18%	$ 0.99	$ 0.74	48%	31%	21.21	15.75	4.88
Frosted cereal	1990	5,7,15,17	11%	$ 2.09	$ 1.57	61%	33%	17.28	27.09	8.94
Frozen broccoli	1982	5,7,15,17	5%	$ 0.69	$ 0.52	35%	23%	7.86	4.07	0.93
Frozen corn	1982	5,7,15,17	17%	$ 0.59	$ 0.44	37%	23%	40.06	17.73	4.08
Frozen peas	1982	5,7,15,17	16%	$ 0.59	$ 0.44	35%	23%	31.42	13.90	3.20
Oatmeal	1988	5,7,15,17	28%	$ 1.69	$ 1.27	49%	45%	11.00	13.94	6.27
Popcorn	1982	5,7,15,17	23%	$ 1.09	$ 0.82	56%	33%	18.07	14.77	4.87
Pretzels	1980	5,7,15,17	38%	$ 1.09	$ 0.82	55%	39%	44.78	36.60	14.28
Salt	1979	5,14	68%	$ 0.79	$ 0.59	56%	34%	8.90	5.27	1.79
Sugar	1978	5,14	35%	$ 1.99	$ 1.49	67%	43%	13.75	20.52	8.82
Whole wheat	1985	5,7,15,17	9%	$ 1.09	$ 0.82	36%	36%	17.67	14.45	5.20
Other (average)	various	5,7,15,17	5%	$ 1.49	$ 1.12	34%	19%	3.93	4.39	0.83
									174.54	64.09
Beverage										
Beer	1992	2,12	1%	$ 3.00	$ 2.25	38%	26%	0.80	1.79	0.47
Cola	1983	2,3	18%	$ 0.79	$ 0.59	35%	19%	14.31	8.48	1.61
Ginger ale	1984	2,3	38%	$ 0.79	$ 0.59	36%	22%	15.11	8.95	1.97
Milk[b]	1981	3,4,8	49%	$ 1.39	$ 1.04	53%	24%	48.71	50.78	12.19
Orange juice	1982	3,4,8,13	28%	$ 1.49	$ 1.12	55%	27%	27.83	31.10	8.40
Root beer	1983	2,3	38%	$ 0.79	$ 0.59	48%	25%	7.56	4.48	1.12
Seltzer water	1984	2,3	58%	$ 0.59	$ 0.44	48%	26%	5.77	2.55	0.66
Tomato juice	1988	2,3,8	3%	$ 0.99	$ 0.74	45%	38%	0.30	0.22	0.08
Wine	1993	2,12	0.5%	$ 3.00	$ 2.25	48%	40%	0.20	0.45	0.18
Other (average)	various	2,3,12	5%	$ 0.84	$ 0.63	25%	8%	0.50	0.31	0.03
									102.13	26.71

[a]In stores where products are sold.

[b]Some markets.

Note: Thanks to Geraldo Lamounier for help in developing this table.

TABLE 6.30. Global Foods' Age, Salary, Managerial Compensation, and Worker Salaries

	Age Distribution by Division								
	Age Distribution			People			People Years		
	Health	Food	Beverage	Health	Food	Beverage	Health	Food	Beverage
Age									
60+	4%	23%	6%	210	529	106	13,238	33,298	6,691
50–59	10%	36%	9%	525	827	159	28,892	45,500	8,762
40–49	35%	28%	33%	1,839	643	584	82,735	28,955	26,285
30–39	31%	10%	35%	1,628	230	620	56,995	8,043	21,683
20–29	20%	3%	17%	1,051	69	302	26,265	1,724	7,523
	100%	100%	100%	5,253	2,298	1,771	208,125	117,520	70,944
				Average Age by Division			39.6	51.1	40.1
	Salary Distribution by Division (without benefits)								
	Breakdown			People			Salaries		
	Health	Food	Beverage	Health	Food	Beverage	Health	Food	Beverage
Salary									
$100K+	1%	1%	1%	53	23	18	6,566	2,873	2,213
80–99K	1.5%	2%	1.5%	79	46	27	7,092	4,136	2,390
60–79K	2.5%	2%	5.5%	131	46	97	9,193	3,217	6,815
40–59K	14%	19%	5%	735	437	89	36,771	21,831	4,425
20–39K	24%	31%	13%	1,261	712	230	37,822	21,371	6,903
<20K	57%	45%	74%	2,994	1,034	1,310	50,902	17,580	22,267
	100%	100%	100%	5,253	2,298	1,771	$ 149,156	$ 71,008	$ 45,013
				Average Salary by Divison			$ 28.24	$ 30.90	$ 25.43

Managerial Compensation (1996) (without benefits)

	Distribution			Number of Managers			Total Salaries ($ in thousands)		
	Health	Food	Beverage	Health	Food	Beverage	Health	Food	Beverage
Average salary									
$ 125K	1%	1%	1%	53	23	18	$ 6,566	$ 2,873	$ 2,213
$ 90K	1.5%	2%	1.5%	79	46	27	$ 7,092	$ 4,136	$ 2,390
$ 70K	2.5%	2%	5.5%	131	46	97	$ 9,193	3,217	6,815
$ 50K	0%	0%	0%	—	—	—	—	—	—
$ 30K	0%	0%	0%	—	—	—	—	—	—
$ 17K	0%	0%	0%	—	—	—	—	—	—
Total	5%	5%	8%	263[a]	115[b]	142[c]	$ 22,851	$ 10,226	$ 11,418
Average Manager's Salary by Division							$ 87,000	$ 89,000	$ 80,625

Worker Salaries (without benefits)

	Distribution			Number of Workers			Total Salaries ($ in thousands)		
	Health	Food	Beverage	Health	Food	Beverage	Health	Food	Beverage
Average salary									
$ 125K	0%	0%	0%	—	—	—	—	—	—
$ 90K	0%	0%	0%	—	—	—	—	—	—
$ 70K	0%	0%	0%	—	—	—	—	—	—
$ 50K	14%	19%	5%	735	437	89	$36,771	$21,831	$4,425
$ 30K	24%	31%	13%	1,261	712	230	$37,822	$21,371	$6,903
$ 17K	57%	45%	74%	2,994	1,034	1,310	$50,902	$17,580	$22,267
	95%	95%	92%	4,990	2,183	1,629	$125,495	$ 60,782	$ 33,595
Average Worker's Salary by Division							$ 25,147	$ 27,842	$ 20,630

[a]210 work at corporate headquarters, 48 in plants, and 5 at distribution centers.
[b]80 work at corporate headquarters, 33 in plants, and 3 at distribution centers.
[c]103 work at corporate headquarters, 35 in plants, and 5 at distribution centers.

TABLE 6.31. Global Foods' Employee Distribution

	Health and Beauty	Food	Beverage	Total
Worker breakdown				
Corporate	349	196	164	708
Plants	4,342	1,768	1,270	7,380
Distribution	299	218	195	712
Management breakdown				
Corporate	210	80	103	393
Plants	48	33	34	116
Distribution	5	3	5	13

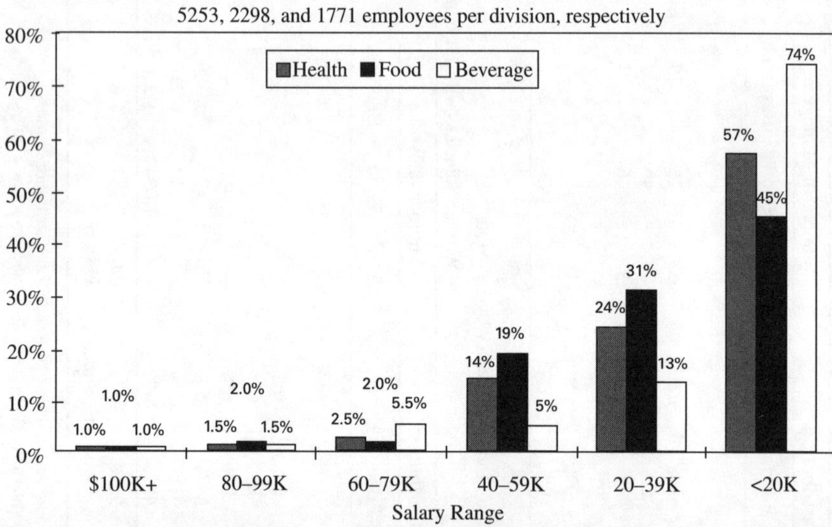

Fig. 6.12. Nonmanagerial salary breakdown

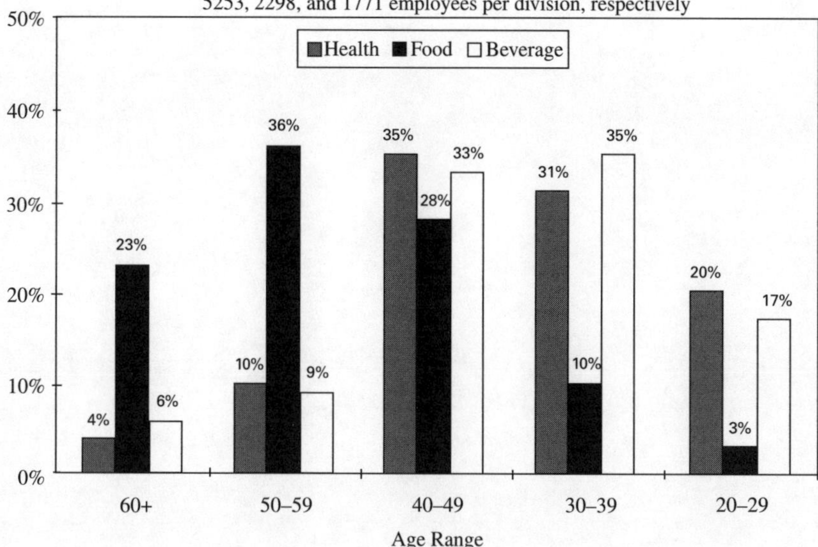

Fig. 6.13. Age distribution

Part 3
Advanced Issues

CHAPTER 7

Crafting a Plan of Reorganization

The primary documents submitted to the courts in a bankruptcy case are a disclosure statement and a plan of reorganization (POR);[1] the combined document is henceforth referred to as the POR. PORs are massive, highly technical documents, sometimes reaching upwards of 1,000 pages.[2] The essence of the plan, how to reorganize the company, is actually fairly simple and is likely to consume only a few pages; the other pages conform to legal or contractual requirements or contain boilerplate material. Corporate renewal specialists knowledgeable in investment banking should be the architects of the plan; lawyers should prepare the legal documents.

This section concerns the financial reengineering that underlies the POR. Just as process reengineering (see chap. 8) starts with a blank sheet of paper and concludes with a new way to do an old job, financial reengineering abandons the company's existing financial mosaic in favor of a workable redesign. Two nonlegal tasks are involved in developing a POR

1. correcting flaws in the corporate strategy
2. determining how to satisfy prebankruptcy obligations

Strategic change is highly idiosyncratic depending on case-specific factors such as the quality of management, the availability of new credit, the presence of competitors, the age of the capital stock, and the growth potential of the market. Thus, it is surveyed fleetingly here. The second task is the main subject of this chapter.

Strategic Changes

Bankruptcy is not the ideal time to change a company's strategy, but it is not the worst time either. One advantage is that in bankruptcy the debtor can reject leases and other executory contracts.[3] As a result, leases (e.g., on retail outlets, factories, airplanes, etc.), employment agreements (with executives or labor unions), or supply arrangements (with vendors or partners) can be abrogated. The ability to renege on prior agreements without incurring out-of-pocket expenses[4] facilitates abrupt strategic change.

Examples of companies making radical changes include Merry-Go-Round Enterprises, a retailer that entered bankruptcy in January 1994 and announced in November 1995 that it would close 375 stores and phase out its Chess King store outlets (*Wall Street Journal* 1995f). The motive was strategic: to focus on thriving store chains and close unprofitable chains. Probably the best-known strategic change out of bankruptcy occurred when Interstate Stores, a general-merchandise retailer, perceived the growth potential in the toy market and changed into Toys-R-Us, later the dominant purveyor of toys in the world.

Strategic shifts out of bankruptcy are not always successful. For example, Continental Airlines created Continental Lite to imitate the success of Southwest Airlines. The strategy failed and almost returned Continental Airlines to bankruptcy. One explanation for why strategic changes fail is the debilitating effect on employees of being bankrupt. By the time a company files for bankruptcy, the best employees are gone or will be soon. This explains some of the high salaries paid in bankruptcy to key employees able to redefine their strategic positions with the consent of judges and creditors.[5]

Determining the Treatment of Obligations

There are five steps in the procedure for resolving how best to settle bankruptcy claims.

1. create pro forma income statements
2. determine cash flow
3. calculate the present value (PV) of cash flows
4. choose a capital structure
5. determine the level of excess cash

The overall objective of these steps is to determine the company's value. Value then is split into new debt and equity securities, awarded along with excess cash to satisfy claims in the case.[6] Original debt and equity holders receive new securities according to both the absolute priority rule (APR) and their perceived power rankings. The APR establishes a specific repayment order, but violations of the APR occur frequently, with senior creditors receiving less than they deserve and junior creditors receiving more than their fair share (Franks and Torous 1993). Frequently, a class of claims that indicates capability and willingness to impede the proceedings is overcompensated. These squeaky wheels pursue such tactics as asking for unnecessary court hearings, demanding tedious asset verifications, and pursuing doubtful legal theories.

The capital structure decision—the choice between debt and equity—is dictated by the needs of the institutions in the bankruptcy and by the debtor's cash flow. Certain creditors such as banks prefer cash or debt securities, while vulture investors prefer equity. Regardless of the amount of debt desired, if the company's operating income is insufficient to pay the requisite interest, new equity is created.

Certain creditors inordinately favor cash over any security of a company emerging from bankruptcy. Some bankruptcy plans take advantage of this inhibition and offer creditors a choice between cash (e.g., ten cents per dollar of claim) and new debt or equity worth perhaps fifty cents per dollar of claim. Provided this choice is presented to the entire class of claims, the Bankruptcy Code allows these elections.

An Example

This simple example clarifies formulating a scheme to treat prior obligations. AB Company previously owed $1,900 to two classes of claims, $700 in a secured bank line and $1,200 in an unsecured note. A post-bankruptcy debtor in possession (DIP) credit line for $250 was established to facilitate new inventory purchases. The new line has an interest rate of 11 percent per annum. There had been 3,000 shares of stock in AB. Ignoring both inflation and growth in future sales, AB's pro forma income statement is presented in table 7.1.[7] Note that two versions are shown: with and without interest. In the first case, only equity is created in the bankruptcy; in the second case, equity and bonds requiring $200 of annual interest are constructed. To simplify the presentation, assume that cash flow and net income are identical.

TABLE 7.1. AB Company's pro Forma Income Statement

	Case with No Interest Paid	Case with Interest Paid
Net sales	$1,500	$1,500
Cost of goods and selling	1,200	1,200
EBIT	300	300
Interest	0	200
Net income	$300	$100

What is AB Company worth if the year described in table 7.1 recurs forever? In that case, net income is a consul (the same amount each year) and PV is derived using the formula:

$$PV = \frac{\text{Net income}}{\text{Cost of funds}}$$

PV equals the total value of future discounted earnings. PV also equals the market value of AB's equity and debt.

For a nonbankrupt company, cost of capital is calculated as the weighted average cost of debt[8] and equity funds.[9] The standard formula for cost of funds creates confusion for a bankrupt company without an existing capital structure since the present value of the firm rises along with the debt-equity ratio. This gives the false impression that the financial architect creates corporate value on paper and that the debt problem is resolved by creating more debt. What is needed in bankruptcy is a single cost-of-capital estimate that approximates the cost of funds within a reasonable range. I call it the bankruptcy cost of capital.

There are a number of satisfactory ad hoc procedures to estimate a single interest cost for companies in bankruptcy, including using

- a competitor's average cost of funds
- the firm's prebankruptcy average debt and equity cost
- the weighted average cost of debt plus the cost of equity derived using a 9 percent (150 percent of the historic debt-equity premium difference) premium over the cost of debt

The first and second solutions are easily implemented, but neither uses current company data. The third choice is based on current company data, but the 150 percent factor is arbitrary. The third choice generally produces the highest cost-of-funds estimate and is the most conservative technique.

There are good reasons for adopting conservative standards when valuing a bankrupt company. For one thing, the cost of overoptimism exceeds the cost of undue pessimism: a future bankruptcy versus an underestimated value. AB's bankruptcy cost of capital is estimated by summing the cost of the DIP financing, 11 percent, and then adding a 9 percent equity premium. This estimated bankruptcy cost of capital approximates the cost for a debt-free company. The present value of AB's cash flow is calculated from table 7.1's net income as

$$PV = \frac{\$300}{(.11+.09)} = \$1{,}500$$

How does this value translate into new securities? The architect of the plan or reorganization has complete discretion to create securities fitting the company's needs and purposes. The only limitation is that the sum of new debt and presumed value of new equity must be equal to or less than the value of the firm. The plan architect can create a debt-free company that issues only equity or a company with one share of stock and the rest of the value in debt. Normally, companies issuing stock must submit to scrutiny from the SEC. Bankrupt companies issuing stock face fewer regulations; these cases are called 12g reorganizations.

The column marked "Case with Interest Paid" in table 7.1 reports net income when $1,000 of debt securities is created. The interest paid, $200, is calculated using the same cost of funds (20 percent) used to estimate PV. With that amount of debt, net income equals $100. The PV of $100 using a 20 percent discount rate is $500. In that case, the total value of AB is

$$\text{Value of AB} = \$1{,}000 \text{ (Value of debt)} + \$500 \text{ (Value of equity)} = \$1{,}500$$

which is the same as when no debt is created. Unless the interest rate used to derive PV is identical to the interest rate assumed to be paid on the debt, the two columns in table 7.1 yield different PV estimates.

Finding Excess Cash

Before filing for bankruptcy protection, companies accumulate cash to avoid a shortage during the initial bankruptcy period. Once in bankruptcy, they request a cash collateral order from the judge to hold cash generated by operations rather than let it return to the lending institution. Subsequently, a DIP line of credit is sought from a bank specializing in troubled debts. During the course of a bankruptcy, inventories and accounts receivable may grow relative to a shrinking asset base. Consequently, a company emerging from bankruptcy may be too liquid. Superfluous dollars, measured by inspecting current assets, are available to augment the distribution of new securities to creditors. Alternately, the extra dollars squeezed out of current assets are retained by the corporation to reduce the size of the new credit line. DIP financing is exchanged for a new credit line with a lender solicited before plan confirmation to replace the DIP financing.

Crafting the Plan

AB Company is assumed to extract $100 from its current assets. Table 7.2 compares what is available for distribution and what is owed. AB's resources are insufficient for it to repay all its creditors. In some cases, resources exceed claims, all creditors are repaid, and new common stock is allocated to original shareholders.[10]

The resources detailed in table 7.2 can be combined in a variety of ways in preparing a POR to compensate creditors. Two divergent examples of PORs are illustrated in tables 7.3A and 7.3B. In both cases, the market and book values of debt securities are assumed to be equal.[11] The assumed value for a percentage point of AB Company's equity is calculated with the formula in equation (1)

$$\text{Value 1\% of Equity} = \frac{\$1{,}500 - \text{Debt}}{100} \tag{1}$$

where debt equals the amount of debt created in the POR. In table 7.3A's plan, each percentage point of equity is worth $5, while in table 7.3B's plan it is worth $10 because fewer dollars of debt are created. The value recovered by secured and unsecured creditors in each plan is similar; however, the first plan puts twice as much debt on the reorganized company, resulting in a lower equity value.

Equity receives 5 percent of the new company in the first plan. Sometimes in contested cases a minimal distribution is awarded to old equity holders to avoid delaying plan approval. The plan might state that unless the equity class approves the plan during the voting process, the next plan will cram down the equity class to nothing. In the second plan, equity receives nothing from the start, partly because in that plan unsecured creditors receive only equity. They are unwilling to placate the equity class by sharing the new stock with them and insist on receiving all remaining shares after the secured class's allocation. If the equity class has sufficient power, it might be offered warrants to buy the new stock at a certain price at some time in the future.

TABLE 7.2. AB Company's Claims and Resources

Resources to Give Away		Claims to Pay	
Present value	$1,500	DIP financing	$250
Excess cash	100	Secured bank line	700
		Unsecured note	1,200
		Common shares	3,000 shares

Secured lenders in the second plan receive more than they are owed. This outcome is not infrequent and results from uncertainty about the new equity's value. Part of the uncertainty is due to the time passing between developing the pro forma income statement and crafting a final POR. In some cases where vulture investors acquire senior claims and accept only new equity in exchange, their returns have substantially exceeded the original claim amounts.

Valuation Issues

What is an asset worth? That query underlies many modern business topics, from trading on the stock and bond markets to the ambiguity of what creditors recover in a bankruptcy. Perhaps the best answer to the question is what someone else is willing to pay. But that definition is insufficient for assets not for sale or valuable only to the current owner. A myriad of value definitions exists. Usually one is appropriate for each situation. Several value definitions are listed in table 7.4 in decreasing order of their likely dollar amount:[12]

TABLE 7.3A. Alternate Reorganization Plan for AB Company

	Allocation				
Claims to Pay	Reinstated	Cash	Debt	Equity Ownership	Recovery
DIP financing	$250				$250
Secured bank line		$100	$600		$700
Unsecured note			$400	95%	$875
Common shares				5%	$25
Total	$250	$100	$1,000	100%	

TABLE 7.3B. Alternate Reorganization Plan for AB Company

	Allocation				
Claims to Pay	Reinstated	Cash	Debt	Equity Ownership	Recovery
DIP financing	$300[a]				$250
Secured bank line		$150	$500	10%	$750
Unsecured note				90%	$900[b]
Common shares				0%	$0
Total	$300	$150	$500	100%	

[a]By replacing more than was owed to the DIP lender, AB Company generates new cash.
[b]90% of the equity is worth more than 95% in Plan A since this plan uses less debt.

Consider the value of United Airlines. Market value equals the sum of its equity and debt values, as seen in equation (2)

$$\begin{aligned}\text{Market value} &= [\text{Equity value}] + [\text{Value of debt}] \\ &= [\text{Number of shares} \times \text{Stock market price}] \\ &\quad + [\text{Market value debt}]\end{aligned} \tag{2}$$

Why is the value of debt included? After all, an acquisition occurs when all of United's equity, not its debt, is bought.[13] But market value measures not acquisition cost but the market's perception of a company's total worth. If the debt is valueless, so is the equity.

United's replacement value equals the cost of buying all the planes, spare parts, trucks, uniforms, passenger goodwill, and other assets owned by the airline. Replacement value is nearly impossible to ascertain with precision; for example, the used airplane market currently has no ten-year-old 747 aircraft with Pratt and Whitney engines available. Professional appraisers are available to estimate unknown values.

Insurance value equals the sum recoupable by United from insurance companies if all of its assets are lost or destroyed. Insurance policies are designed to protect assets at either book or replacement value. For rapidly depreciating assets, such as aircraft, the choice of protection plans exerts a considerable impact on insurance value. Many companies self-insure their assets to reduce insurance premiums; in that case, insurance value is zero.

Book value of total assets appears on the balance sheet as the net value of total assets. By contrast, liquidation value is an unknown, though professional appraisers can estimate orderly or distressed liquidation proceeds. Distressed liquidations waste little time promoting the sale or attracting knowledgeable buyers. This allows firms to be shuttered and employees discharged immediately.[14] Distressed liquidations

TABLE 7.4. Measures of Value

Valuation Method	Definition
Market value	Value in a publicly traded market (e.g., the New York Stock Exchange) or established via a public auction
Replacement value	The cost of purchasing replacement items
Insurance value	Proceeds from owned insurance policies
Book value	Net value after deducting depreciation from purchase price
Orderly liquidation value	Proceeds from a carefully orchestrated sale of all assets conducted without dispatch or duress
Liquidation value	Proceeds from a fire sale of assets

collect on average about ten or fifteen cents per dollar of book value. Orderly liquidations may require six months to a year's time to create interest in the liquidation but may generate as much as sixty or seventy cents per dollar of assets. However, an orderly liquidation requires continued expenditures to maintain the business until the liquidation occurs.

Valuation in Bankruptcy

The liabilities of companies in bankruptcy are known and fixed in dollar amount,[15] but asset values are uncertain. Valuation is a critical element in the bankruptcy process. There are three parts to this issue:

1. Is the firm a going concern? In a going concern, the present value of future cash flows is positive and greater than liquidation value. If yes, the business should reorganize; if no, the business should liquidate.
2. What is a reasonable estimate of the firm's going-concern value? This is the value that creditors and shareholders fight over as alternate plans of reorganization are proposed.
3. What is the value of a firm that is not a going concern? In that case, insolvency or reorganization accounting supersedes GAAP accounting. With insolvency accounting, valuation of assets is determined by net realizable values, nonsalable assets such as goodwill are abandoned, and off-balance-sheet assets such as royalty overrides count as assets.

Bankruptcy resolution depends critically on valuations. Hired professional appraisers provide independent and unbiased value assessments. Data obtained from appraisers help resolve issues such as

- Is the value of real property sufficient to cover all of a secured obligation (residual amounts are classified as unsecured claims)?
- Is a bankruptcy POR feasible, and does it pass the best-interest-of-creditors test?
- Was sufficient value exchanged, or was a prebankruptcy transaction a fraudulent conveyance?
- Has the debtor provided adequate protection?[16]

As with all estimation processes, there is great uncertainty. Values should be estimated in a range and not as a point estimate, assumptions influencing valuation should be described, and discount-rate assumptions should be clearly stated.

Valuing Holding-Company Debts

Holding-company debt is particularly troublesome to value. As its name implies, a holding-company holds common stock in its subsidiaries. The enigma arises when the subsidiary owning physical assets raises money secured by its assets. If the subsidiary collapses, its creditors seize its assets, leaving little for holding-company creditors to take if they acquire control of the holding company. What then are the holding company's debts worth?

Consider the shell holding company, Marvel Holdings, which issued $550 million in junk bonds. Marvel Holdings' sole asset is about 80 percent of the common stock in Marvel Entertainment, a comic book and sports card company. Marvel Entertainment stock traded in late 1995 at nearly $15 per share, while Marvel Holding's bonds traded near par. Marvel Entertainment raised $650 million of secured bank debt on its own. After overpaying in an acquisition, Marvel Entertainment's stock plunged to about $5 per share in October 1996, and the bonds fell to seventy-two cents on the dollar. Following the announcement of intricate financial maneuvers to get new equity into Marvel Entertainment, the bonds dipped to seventeen cents on the dollar, since their call on 80 percent of Marvel Entertainment's equity would dip to a 16 percent share. Moreover, the secured bank debt would strip out most of the assets. Junk-bond holders anticipated an exchange offer forcing them to convert into equity (Sandler 1996). In this case at least, the answer to the valuation questions is "not very much."

Using the Threat of Bankruptcy

An old Norwegian saying declares, "Wood warms you twice: once when you cut it and once in the fire." Like wood, bankruptcy protects companies in two ways: before they file a court petition, the threat of bankruptcy is a potent weapon of survival; after they file, bankruptcy keeps creditors at bay and provides for an orderly resolution of prior obligations. In order for the threat of bankruptcy to be an effective weapon, the corporate renewal specialist must be knowledgeable about bankruptcy law and its practical implications.[17]

The major consequences on creditors of a company going bankrupt are

- the automatic-stay provision keeps creditors from seizing assets even when their debts are secured and payments are past due
- the repayment to creditors is determined in a plan of reorganiza-

tion that must be approved by all creditors; approval may come from a cramdown if creditors cannot agree
- the APR defines a strict repayment scheme
- bankruptcies take twenty-four months on average to complete
- during bankruptcy, interest on most debts is not paid or accrued
- leases can be rejected
- approximately 10 percent of corporate assets are consumed by professional fees and other expenses during a bankruptcy

The net result is that creditors lose when debtors file for bankruptcy protection. This loss legitimizes the debtor's threat of going bankrupt.

Bankruptcy is also costly to the debtor, since after a filing

- the debtor becomes a DIP with expanded legal responsibilities
- management decisions, other than in the ordinary course of business, are submitted to the court and creditors and are contingent on court approval
- business is lost as clients transfer to solvent competitors; government contracts may require nonbankrupt status
- management's time devoted to resolving the bankruptcy is siphoned away from doing business
- administrative expenses are paid out of shareholders' equity

Thus, creditors know that companies avoid going bankrupt if possible, and the stage is set for a stalemate. Negotiation skills are critical to achieving a successful outcome; brinkmanship can create an impasse that precipitates a bankruptcy filing.

Continental Airlines and the Denver International Airport

The city of Denver replaced its aging Stapleton Airport with a behemoth for the twenty-first century, the Denver International Airport (DIA), at a cost of $3.4 billion. Before authorizing construction, the city council required planners to get airlines to lease most of the planned gates at the new airport. In the 1980s, Continental Airlines agreed to lease twenty gates for an annual fee of $59 million (*Wall Street Journal* 1995b). But that was before Continental's disastrous Continental Lite venture. Furthermore, Continental determined that Denver was not a profitable hub for it because of United Airlines' dominance of the airport and the DIA's higher operating costs.

Continental requested a discharge from its long-term obligation to lease unused gates at DIA. Denver's city councilors were reluctant to accede but faced Continental's threat to file bankruptcy. The airline had emerged from a previous bankruptcy in 1990. City councilors knew about Continental's troubles and realized that a compromise was necessary. In bankruptcy, Continental would reject all the leases, stop lease payments, and classify the leases as unsecured creditors. The city and Continental agreed to reduce the lease to just ten gates and cut the annual fee to $27 million.

Before the agreement, the airport expected to earn $27 million. Losing $22 million from the Continental lease reduces profitability to just $5 million, though interest and principal on the city's airport bonds is paid. Continental's insistence on trimming its lease obligation creates a stalemate, since at the new level the airport debt is at risk.

Reforming the Bankruptcy Laws

In 1995 President Clinton formed a commission to review existing bankruptcy laws and recommend improvements. The stimulus for this commission was collective dissatisfaction with the overall effect of the 1979 amendment to the Bankruptcy Code. Among the most frequently articulated concerns about the law are

- companies linger unduly long in bankruptcy (average 24 months)
- fees paid to professionals such as lawyers and accountants consume too great a share of the bankruptcy estate
- the Code is prodebtor and prompts too many companies and individuals to file
- management and boards of directors are unnecessarily protected, continue to receive unreasonable compensation, and have for a time the exclusive right to file a POR

The commission was scheduled to submit its recommendations within two years.

The commission's suggestions may be influenced by academic proposals on how bankruptcy laws should be changed; they are summarized below. The first paper specifies desirable characteristics for a bankruptcy law, and the second paper describes how a bankruptcy law would function to realize those characteristics. The final idea seeks to keep companies out of bankruptcy and to keep those that do enter bankruptcy from wasting resources.

Whitman and Garstka

Martin J. Whitman and Stanley J. Garstka (1992) contend that an ideal bankruptcy system would guarantee

- swift case resolution
- low cost
- harsh penalties for bad investments
- fairness and equity
- a feasibility test of long-term survival
- reallocating corporate assets to their optimal use

Whitman and Garstka's goal is to maximize social welfare. Social welfare is an academic, nonquantifiable concept representing the aggregate benefit accruing to all individuals in a society. A bankruptcy code that encourages or permits wasteful expenditures on nonproductive activities is not welfare-maximizing.[18] Allowing debtors to remain in bankruptcy virtually forever obviously is not welfare-maximizing. They leave to others how these objectives are to be achieved.

McCrory Corporation is an example of a company that stayed in bankruptcy too long and consumed precious corporate assets. As of early 1996, the court had already prolonged seven times management's exclusive period in which to file a POR. Over that span, total assets declined, while management continued to earn substantial wages and benefits. Initially, management proposed that all creditors quickly receive a full repayment on their claims, then reduced the offer to fifty cents on the dollar for senior creditors; a third prospective plan is expected to offer considerably less (Lowenstein 1996; Platt 1991).

The bankruptcy case of Eastern Airlines also exemplifies the abuses that rankle Whitman and Garstka. When the airline entered Chapter 11, its $3.7 billion of assets exceeded its total liabilities by more than $300 million (Franks and Torous 1993). Creditors should have exited that case nearly whole. Instead, the bankruptcy judge authorized the airline to continue flying despite its inability to cover its operating costs. Management asked for and received numerous extensions to its exclusive period. When the airline eventually was liquidated, secured creditors received just $340 million (Franks and Torous 1993).[19] Its remaining assets were dissipated while Eastern continued to fly. The judge apparently viewed his responsibilities to the local community as more important than those to creditors.

Lucian Bebchuk

Bebchuk proposed a simple yet elegant mechanism that achieves most of Whitman and Garstka's objectives for an optimal bankruptcy law (*New York Times* 1993b). His plan is based fundamentally on the APR. A key idea underlying the Bebchuk plan is that the company's exact value is unknown. Valuation issues consume a major share of bankruptcy resources. The Bebchuk plan allows the market to establish company value by assigning the company to senior creditors but allowing junior creditors to repurchase the company by fully repaying senior creditors.

Consider the list of claims in table 7.5. In a reorganization adhering to the APR, the senior secured class is fully repaid before the junior bondholders or the equity class receive anything; similarly, the junior class is fully repaid before the equity class receives any allocation. Bebchuk's proposal starts with an initial allocation to claim holders that replicates the APR: the senior class is given the company (i.e., all of its shares), but then the junior class receives warrants to buy the company from the senior class, and the equity class receives warrants to buy the company from the junior creditors.

The attractive feature of Bebchuk's plan is that it imposes the valuation decision on each successive class of creditors. If they believe the company is more valuable than $200, in the case of the junior creditors in table 7.5, then they will exercise their warrants and repurchase the firm.[20] If they believe the value of the firm is less then $200, however, the junior bondholders will allow their warrants to expire. If they place a high value on the firm but either do not want or are not permitted to own equity, they can sell their warrants to other investors. Equity holders can purchase the company from junior creditors for $500: $300 to repay their claim and $200 to repay what they paid to senior creditors.

TABLE 7.5. Bebchuk's Reorganization Scheme

Creditor	Amount of Claim	Allocation in Bankruptcy
Senior secured	$200	100% of equity in the reorganization firm
Junior bond	$300	100% of A warrants[a]
Equity	100% ownership	100% of B warrants[b]

[a]The A warrants can purchase 100% of the company's equity from the senior creditors for $200.
[b]The B warrants can purchase 100% of the company's equity from the junior creditors for $500.

Platt

I advocate creating a Chapter 10 bankruptcy category in the Bankruptcy Code. In Chapter 10, as currently in Chapter 11, a company is protected for 120 days from its creditors, but officially it remains in bankruptcy limbo. During this grace period, the company is required to hire an external corporate renewal agent whose tasks are

- to manage the firm, though current management is retained as consultants
- to uncover the source and possible solution to its problems

Following the 120-day period, the company may be discharged from bankruptcy if it has arranged an out-of-court restructuring with its creditors, or it can convert the case to a regular Chapter 7 or 11.

The premise is to give companies and their creditors one last opportunity to work out a settlement, which is in the best interest of both parties. The role of the turnaround agent in Chapter 10 combines features of the existing trustee and examiner positions. The agent both runs the firm and investigates and discloses facts pertinent to a settlement.

Questions

1. Define the right objectives for a future bankruptcy law.
2. Is it right that the DIP continues to operate the firm and is responsible for the development of the POR?
3. Should the interests of workers and the community be allowed to supersede those of creditors?
4. Is it fair that a relatively senior creditor can vote against a plan and stop its implementation?
5. Does society have an interest in the resolution of bankruptcy?
6. Should the Security and Exchange Commission take an active role, as it once did, to represent the interest of equity holders?
7. Is it right that claims are traded in bankruptcy, allowing groups to achieve a veto capacity?
8. Comment on the practicality of the Bebchuk plan.
9. What happens to vulture investors in the Bebchuk plan?
10. Comment on the practicality of the Platt plan.

Exercise: Developing a Plan of Reorganization: Seaman Furniture Company

Julius Seaman founded the Seaman furniture store chain in 1933. He opened the first store in Brooklyn, New York, and subsequently opened thirty-six additional stores. His strategy catered to price-sensitive consumers in the market for stylish and accessible household furnishings. The company's concept of reasonably priced quality goods eclipsed the competition in the tristate New York, New Jersey, and Connecticut area, and it prospered.

Leveraged buyouts (LBOs) were in vogue in the late 1980s. Seaman Furniture Company (Seaman's), with its dominant position in an economically fertile region of the country, was regarded as an excellent LBO candidate. Seaman's prebuyout financial statements are contained in table 7.6. In the three years preceding the 1987 buyout, sales grew by 121 percent, and net income increased by 34 percent. The number of stores opened increased from twenty-two to twenty-five. Assets grew by a staggering 191 percent, paid for by an equities offering and sizable increases in accounts payables, long-term debt, and capitalized leases.

In December 1987, SFC Holdings Corp. (Holdings), a company formed by Kohlberg Kravis Roberts and Company (KKR), purchased via a tender offer 10.5 million shares of Seaman's publicly traded common stock at $26 per share, or $273 million.[21] The stock had traded in a range of 11 3/4–30 3/4 in 1987 and 25–46 1/2 in 1986. In February 1988, Holdings merged with and into Seaman's and became a privately held concern. The remaining common stock was converted into the right to receive Seaman's 15 percent junior subordinated payment-in-kind debentures due 1999 (the "Old Debentures"). A total of $73.7 million in Old Debentures were issued. The total purchase price was $359,341,000.

Senior lenders (banks) led by Chemical Bank advanced $265 million to Holdings to finance the tender offer and the merger. The banks were secured by pledges of Seaman's stock. Seaman's balance sheet in April 1988 after the buyout is shown in table 7.7. Two items emerge: over $250 million of goodwill is recorded as an asset, and long-term debt is now $327 million. Goodwill equals the surplus of the purchase price over the book value of assets. Seaman's had become a highly leveraged company whose success depended on continued growth and profitability.

Circumstances did not favor Seaman's. The combination of a regional recession and high interest payments pummeled the company. Income summaries are presented in table 7.8. From the start, like many late-1980s LBOs, Seaman's lost money, but its operating income was positive. The cash drain was moderated by the sizable noncash charge on the income statement to amortize goodwill. Positive operating income but a net loss due to interest payments were common to most late-1980s LBOs, indicating that the buyouts had been financed mostly by debt. To survive, such companies must sell off assets to reduce debts. This route to survival was inaccessible to Seaman's: its primary asset was goodwill. It owned only one of its store sites and leased the others. To

TABLE 7.6. Seaman Furniture Company Financial Statements ($ in thousands)

Income Statement				
	1984	1985	1986	1987
Total sales	$104,247	$139,730	$171,916	$230,034
Cost of sales	64,961	87,245	106,670	141,528
Selling expenses	27,039	34,239	41,785	56,926
Income taxes	837	1,168	10,698	16,400
Loss discontinued operations	54	8	0	0
Net income	11,356	17,070	12,763	15,180

Balance Sheet Assets				
Cash and equivalents	$11,712	$8,322	$8,266	$12,188
Accounts receivable	3,225	4,234	15,206	13,080
Inventory	9,314	11,578	10,513	22,806
Prepayments	790	508	994	1,223
Total current	25,041	24,642	34,979	49,297
Net property	4,731	4,266	9,250	27,638
Other assets (leased)	5,360	5,107	5,199	11,707
Total	35,132	34,015	49,428	88,642

Liabilities				
Accounts payable	$5,363	$6,621	$9,163	$16,050
Income taxes	414	588	5,559	3,475
Accruals	5,942	5,315	4,354	7,679
Other (deposits)	5,716	6,793	9,629	12,242
Total current	17,435	19,317	28,705	39,446
Long-term debt	4,507	4,549	0	7,127
Mortgages (capitalized leases)	407	0	4,597	11,637
Deferrals	233	233	1,312	614
Common stock	63	63	66	136
Paid in capital	259	259	5,722	12,687
Retained earnings[a]	12,229	9,595	15,181	30,361
Total	35,133	34,016	55,583	102,008

[a]Seaman's reincorporated in 1985 from a Subchapter S corporation to a C corporation. Distributions to the subchapter keep the retained earnings below their expected levels.

survive, Seaman's would have to grow materially and immediately (Platt and Platt 1997).

The recession in 1988 and 1989 caused Seaman's sales to stagnate, resulting in a $27.5 million loss before taxes in fiscal 1989. The company's inability to make $3.1 million in cash interest and principal payments to its bankers in August 1989 and $10 million in payments in October 1989 put it into default. Seaman's and the banks agreed to resolve the default with a restructuring. Outstanding indebtedness of $280 million was written down to $150 million (the "New Senior Indebtedness") maturing in November 1992.[22] In exchange, the senior lenders received 18.5 million shares of common stock, making them equal partners with KKR. Moreover, the debt was secured by pledges of stock on Seaman's subsidiaries.

TABLE 7.7. Seaman Furniture Company Balance Sheet ($ in thousands)

Balance Sheet Assets	
	1988
Cash and equivalents	$18,494
Accounts receivable	31,999
Inventory	29,846
Prepayments	5,011
Total current	85,350
Net property	27,481
Other assets (leased)	31,443
Goodwill	257,418
Total	401,692
Liabilities	
Accounts payable	$11,455
Income taxes	0
Accruals	19,001
Other (deposits)	13,000
Debt due	20,177
Total current	63,633
Long-term debt	327,510
Common stock	1
Paid in capital	16,594
Retained earnings	(6,046)
Total	401,692

Needing new capital, Seaman's then

- sold $28 million in Series A 12 percent payment-in-kind senior subordinated notes due in October 1998 to a KKR-controlled partnership
- sold $7 million in Series C 12 percent payment-in-kind senior subordinated notes due in October 1998
- sold $7 million in Series D 12 percent payment-in-kind senior subordinated notes due in October 1998 to the Seaman family
- and gave $25 million in Series B 12 percent payment-in-kind senior subordinated notes due in October 1998 to the senior lenders as partial consideration for agreeing to the 1989 restructuring

Further negotiations resulted in exchanging $73 million[23] in outstanding Old Debentures for $18.5 million in new 12 percent junior subordinated notes due in May 1999 (the "New Debentures") and 2.93 million shares, or 7.3 percent, of the common stock.

Following the exchange offer, the ranking of securities for right of payment in the event of a bankruptcy is described in table 7.9. Non-compromising Old Debenture holders retain a higher dollar amount of indebtedness but sacrifice a little in the ranking. To retain key personnel, 3.1 million shares of stock were sold at $0.01 per share, in exchange for worthless options.

TABLE 7.8. Seaman Furniture Company Income Summaries ($ in thousands, year ending April)

Income Statement					
	4 Months in 1988 Ending April 30	1989	1990	1991	1992
Total sales	$81,307	$279,348	$266,865	$264,280	$227,178
Cost of sales	56,177	176,802	171,779	174,557	159,078
Selling expense	22,497	79,542	84,313	87,654	80,974
Operating income	2,633	23,004	10,773	2,069	(12,874)
Interest	13,939	44,034	32,048	13,449	11,203
Amortizing and writing down of goodwill	2,421	6,511	204,175	1,416	51,842
Income taxes	(4,707)	(4,809)	(8,390)	(20)	0
Extraordinary credit	0	0	32,395	0	0
Net income	(9,020)	(22,732)	(184,665)	(12,776)	(75,922)

Seaman's overall debt was reduced by $159 million in the 1989 restructuring. Most of this "haircut" was taken by senior lenders. In exchange they received 40.1 percent of Seaman's equity. The Seamans restructuring hit KKR with its first financial loss, tarnishing its stellar reputation. One inducement extended to get KKR's agreement was that Seamans released KKR and its partnerships from any future fraudulent-conveyance claims.

The economic climate in the Northeast failed to brighten in the years following the 1989 restructuring. A soft new housing market, coupled with weakened consumer confidence, resulted in a 15 percent decline in Seaman's sales from May 1, 1990, to April 30, 1992. Most of the new funds raised after the 1989 restructuring serviced the existing debt rather than expanded sales. By December 1991, vendors saw the end approaching and halted further credit extension. Efforts to get the banks to restructure the New Senior Indebtedness were ineffectual.

On December 31, 1991, Seaman's filed for bankruptcy protection in the U.S. Bankruptcy Court, Southern District of New York. The bankruptcy court allowed a $25 million DIP line of credit from General Electric Capital Corporation to enable Seaman's to remain in business. Obligations under the DIP line are secured by a first-priority security interest in and lien on any and all of the property and assets of the debtor, Seaman's. The debtor closed fifteen of thirty-seven stores and reduced its workforce by 28 percent. Real property leases on those stores either were rejected following Section 365 of the Bankruptcy Code or were assumed and assigned to third parties. The new business plan focused Seaman's business on the New York metropolitan area. A $15 million line of credit was anticipated following emergence from bankruptcy, some of which would be used to pay off General Electric Capital Corporation, which was owed $10.5 million.

TABLE 7.9. Seaman Furniture Company Seniority Ranking of Debt Securities in 1989

Right of Payment Ranking
New senior indebtedness
Series A notes
Series B notes
Series C notes and series D notes are pari passu
New debentures
Old debentures

Student Assignment

The following pages summarize material contained in Seaman's bankruptcy disclosure statement and plan of reorganization. Included in this material is the actual arrangement proposed in the POR to satisfy all bankruptcy claims. Your first task is to work through the information and to fathom the details of the plan of reorganization. Then develop a better plan of reorganization based on your own assessments, projections, and sense of what would constitute a reasonable capital structure for Seaman's after emerging from bankruptcy.

The process of crafting a POR is subjective and influenced by compromises and exertions of power. It involves more than simply plugging values into a formula. There is no reason to believe that the Seaman's plan presented in the following pages is either legitimate or unrivaled; it is merely the plan that mustered sufficient support from its classes of claims to receive approval. There is no need to accept the pro forma income statement or the liquidation valuations as accurate; all you know about them is that the proponents of the plan were able to get the parties to agree to use them.

UNITED STATES BANKRUPTCY COURT
SOUTHERN DISTRICT OF NEW YORK

In re SEAMAN FURNITURE COMPANY OF UNION SQUARE, INC., SEAMAN FURNITURE COMPANY, INC., THE LEATHERWORKS AT SEAMANS, INC., BARGAINS UNLIMITED, INC., SEAMAN CREDIT CORP. AND PARALAX DEVELOPMENT INDUSTRIES, INC., *Debtors.*	Chapter 11 Reorganization Case Nos. 92 B 40011 through 40016 (FGC) Jointly Administered

First Amended Disclosure Statement
First Amended Joint Plan
of Reorganization
and
Related Documents

July 22, 1992

Shearman & Sterling
599 Lexington Avenue
New York, NY 10022
(212) 848-4000
Counsel for the Debtors

UNITED STATES BANKRUPTCY COURT
SOUTHERN DISTRICT OF NEW YORK

In re SEAMAN FURNITURE COMPANY OF UNION SQUARE, INC., SEAMAN FURNITURE COMPANY, INC., THE LEATHERWORKS AT SEAMANS, INC., BARGAINS UNLIMITED, INC., SEAMAN CREDIT CORP. AND PARALAX DEVELOPMENT INDUSTRIES, INC., *Debtors.*	Chapter 11 Reorganization Case Nos. 92 B 40011 through 40016 (FGC) Jointly Administered

FIRST AMENDED DISCLOSURE STATEMENT PURSUANT TO SECTION 1125 OF THE UNITED STATES BANKRUPTCY CODE FOR SOLICITATION OF ACCEPTANCES OR REJECTION OF PROPOSED PLAN OF REORGANIZATION AS SUBMITTED BY THE DEBTORS AND DEBTORS IN POSSESSION

July 22, 1992

Shearman & Sterling
599 Lexington Avenue
New York, NY 10022
(212) 848–4000
Counsel for the Debtors

INTRODUCTION AND REPRESENTATIONS

Introduction

Pursuant to Section 1125 of the United States Bankruptcy Code (the "Bankruptcy Code"), 11 U.S.C. §1125, Seaman Furniture Company, Inc. ("Seaman Furniture"), Seaman Furniture Company of Union Square, Inc., The Leatherworks at Seamans, Inc., Bargains Unlimited., Seaman Credit Corp., and Paralax Development Industries, Inc., debtors and debtors in possession in the above-referenced jointly administered Chapter 11 cases (collectively, the "Debtors"), submit this Disclosure Statement for their First Amended Plan of Reorganization (the "Plan"). A copy of the Plan accompanies this Disclosure Statement as Exhibit A. This Disclosure Statement has been prepared by the Debtors and delivered to all known parties entitled to vote on the Plan for the purpose of disclosing information that will allow such parties to make an informed decision when exercising their rights to vote to accept or reject the Plan.

This Disclosure Statement and the Plan should be read and studied in their entirety prior to voting on the Plan. You are urged to consult your legal counsel about the Plan and its effect on your legal rights before voting.

IN THE OPINION OF THE DEBTORS, THE TREATMENT OF CREDITORS UNDER THE PLAN CONTEMPLATES A GREATER RECOVERY THAN THAT WHICH IS LIKELY TO BE ACHIEVED UNDER OTHER ALTERNATIVES FOR THE REORGANIZATION OR THE LIQUIDATION OF THE DEBTORS. ACCORDINGLY, THE DEBTORS BELIEVE THAT CONFIRMATION OF THE PLAN IS IN THE BEST INTERESTS OF THE CREDITORS AND INTEREST HOLDERS AND RECOMMEND THAT YOU VOTE TO ACCEPT THE PLAN.

On July 22, 1992, after notice and a hearing, the United States Bankruptcy Court for the Southern District of New York (the "Court") entered an order approving this Disclosure Statement in its entirety.

All capitalized terms used and not otherwise defined herein have the meanings assigned to them in Article I of the Plan.

Representations

No person is authorized by any of the Debtors in connection with the Plan or the solicitation of votes for the Plan to give any information or to make any representation other than as contained in this Disclosure Statement and the exhibits annexed hereto or incorporated by reference or referred to herein, and if given or made, such information or representation may not be relied upon as having been authorized by any of the Debtors.

NO REPRESENTATIONS CONCERNING THE DEBTORS OR THE PLAN ARE AUTHORIZED OTHER THAN AS SET FORTH HEREIN. ANY REPRESENTA-

TIONS OR INDUCEMENTS TO SECURE YOUR ACCEPTANCE OF THE PLAN OTHER THAN AS CONTAINED HEREIN SHOULD NOT BE RELIED UPON BY YOU.

THE INFORMATION CONTAINED HEREIN HAS BEEN PREPARED BY THE DEBTORS IN GOOD FAITH, BASED UPON INFORMATION AVAILABLE TO THE DEBTORS AS OF THE DATE HEREOF. THE DEBTORS ARE UNABLE TO WARRANT OR REPRESENT THAT THE INFORMATION CONTAINED HEREIN IS WITHOUT ANY INACCURACY ALTHOUGH THE DEBTORS HAVE USED THEIR BEST EFFORTS TO ENSURE THAT SUCH INFORMATION IS ACCURATE. NOT ALL OF THE INFORMATION HEREIN CONCERNING THE PLAN HAS BEEN SUBJECT TO A VERIFIED AUDIT. ALL FINANCIAL INFORMATION HAS BEEN COMPILED FROM THE RECORDS OF THE DEBTORS. THE DEBTORS BELIEVE THAT THIS DISCLOSURE STATEMENT COMPLIES WITH THE REQUIREMENTS OF THE BANKRUPTCY CODE.

THE STATEMENTS CONTAINED IN THIS DISCLOSURE STATEMENT ARE MADE AS OF THE DATE HEREIN, UNLESS ANOTHER TIME IS SPECIFIED HEREIN, AND DELIVERY OF THIS DISCLOSURE STATEMENT SHALL NOT CREATE ANY IMPLICATION THAT THERE HAS BEEN NO CHANGE IN THE FACTS SET FORTH HEREIN SINCE THE DATE OF THIS DISCLOSURE STATEMENT AND THE DATE THE MATERIALS RELIED UPON IN PREPARATION OF THIS DISCLOSURE STATEMENT WERE COMPILED.

THIS DISCLOSURE STATEMENT MAY NOT BE RELIED ON FOR ANY PURPOSE OTHER THAN TO DETERMINE HOW TO VOTE ON THE PLAN, AND NOTHING CONTAINED HEREIN SHALL CONSTITUTE AN ADMISSION OF ANY FACT OR LIABILITY BY ANY PARTY, OR BE ADMISSIBLE IN ANY PROCEEDING INVOLVING ANY DEBTOR OR ANY OTHER PARTY, OR BE DEEMED CONCLUSIVE ADVICE ON THE TAX OR OTHER LEGAL EFFECTS OF THE REORGANIZATION ON HOLDERS OF CLAIMS AGAINST OR INTERESTS IN ANY OF THE DEBTORS.

THE DESCRIPTION OF THE PLAN CONTAINED IN THIS DISCLOSURE STATEMENT IS INTENDED AS A SUMMARY ONLY AND IS QUALIFIED IN ITS ENTIRETY BY REFERENCE TO THE PLAN ITSELF, WHICH IS INCLUDED AS AN EXHIBIT HERETO. EACH CREDITOR AND INTEREST HOLDER IS ENCOURAGED TO READ, CONSIDER AND CAREFULLY ANALYZE THE TERMS AND PROVISIONS OF THE PLAN.

THIS DISCLOSURE STATEMENT HAS BEEN APPROVED BY ORDER OF THE COURT, DATED JULY 22, 1992, AS CONTAINING INFORMATION OF A KIND AND IN SUFFICIENT DETAIL TO ENABLE A HYPOTHETICAL REASONABLE INVESTOR TYPICAL OF HOLDERS OF CLAIMS OR INTERESTS OF RELEVANT CLASSES TO MAKE AN INFORMED JUDGMENT CONCERNING

WHETHER TO VOTE FOR OR AGAINST THE PLAN. THE COURT HAS NOT VERIFIED THE ACCURACY OR COMPLETENESS OF THE INFORMATION CONTAINED HEREIN, AND THE COURT'S APPROVAL OF THIS DISCLOSURE STATEMENT DOES NOT IMPLY THAT THE COURT ENDORSES OR APPROVES THE PLAN.

A BALLOT MAY ACCOMPANY THIS DISCLOSURE STATEMENT FOR USE IN VOTING ON THE PLAN.

THE COURT HAS SCHEDULED A HEARING ON CONFIRMATION OF THE PLAN TO COMMENCE ON OCTOBER 1, 1992, AT 9:30 A.M. THAT HEARING WILL BE HELD BEFORE JUDGE FRANCIS G. CORNED AT THE BANKRUPTCY COURT, ALEXANDER HAMILTON CUSTOMS HOUSE, ONE BOWLING GREEN, NEW YORK, NEW YORK 10004. THE HEARING ON CONFIRMATION MAY BE ADJOURNED FROM TIME TO TIME BY THE COURT WITHOUT FURTHER NOTICE, EXCEPT FOR AN ANNOUNCEMENT MADE AT THE HEARING OR ANY ADJOURNMENT THEREOF.

Classes of Claims

The disclosure statement established the following classification of claims against the debtor. Several small (e.g., less than $10,000) or inconsequential classes of claims have been deleted from the classification scheme.

Administrative Claims

These claims described in Section 503(b) of the Bankruptcy Code include wages, salaries, and commissions for services in the bankruptcy case. The debtor estimates a total of $2,075,080.62 in allowed administrative claims, of which $1.315 million are professional fees, $383,000 are reclamation expenses, and $376,000 are postpetition rents on rejected leases. Section 507(a)(1) gives all of these claims priority. This class is paid in cash in full.

Priority Tax Claims

Priority tax claims receive priority from Section 507(a)(7) of the Bankruptcy Code. The debtor estimates $224,560.19 in allowed tax claims other than sales tax claims (property taxes), and $1,464,502.40 in allowed sales tax claims. Tax authorities will accept repayment over six years, but they will not accept partial payment. This class is paid off entirely in equal parts over six years.

Unimpaired Classes of Claims

Class 1 IRB Claims
This industrial revenue bond claim originally financed the development of Seaman's warehouse. Provided that claimants agree to waive past defaults, this claim is reinstated.

Impaired Classes of Claims

Class 2 Bank Group Claims[24]
These claims arise under the credit agreement (except for the Series B senior subordinated notes, which appear elsewhere). The allowed bank claim amounts to $153,025,229.12.[25]

Class 3 General Unsecured Claims
General unsecured claims are unsecured claims against the estate except for those listed elsewhere. This claim aggregates to $26,700,000.

Class 4 Series A Senior Subordinated Note Claims
Series A senior subordinated note claims arise from the Series A 12 percent payment-in-kind senior subordinated notes due 1998. These claims amount to $35,864,338.

Class 5 Series B Senior Subordinated Note Claims
Series B senior subordinated note claims arise from the Series B 12 percent payment-in-kind senior subordinated notes due 1998. These claims amount to $31,613,395.

Class 6 Series C Senior Subordinated Note Claims and Series D Senior Subordinated Note Claims
Series C and Series D senior subordinated note claims arise from the Series C and D 12 percent payment-in-kind senior subordinated notes due 1998. These claims amount to $17,932,172.

Class 7 12 Percent Junior Subordinated Note Claims
These claims arise from the 12 percent junior subordinated notes due 1999. These claims amount to $24,252,803.

Class 8 15 Percent Junior Subordinated Note Claims
These claims arise from the 15 percent junior subordinated notes due 1999. These claims amount to $22,378,031.

Impaired Class of Interest

Class 9 Old Common Stock Interests
These claims arise from the old common stock of Seaman's.

The plan's proponent is the DIP. In the liquidation analysis seen in table 7.5, a higher percentage of claims are recovered via reorganization than liquidation. It is mandatory that this best-interest-of-creditors test be passed before a company can reorganize. The self-interest of a plan's proponents may influence the test's outcome. It is worth noting how the $402 million asset value at the time of the LBO in 1988 evaporated to just $45 million in gross proceeds expected from a liquidation. The plan distributes five million shares of stock with an additional ten million shares held in the corporate treasury. Prior to bankruptcy, management owned 6.1 percent of the common stock. The plan of reorganization wipes out all old shares and does not immediately provide any new shares to management.

The debtor envisions a smaller company concentrated in the New York City metropolitan area. Same-store sales are expected to grow dramatically in the years following emergence from the bankruptcy court. However, the pro forma income statement reports unstable net income flows, though operating income is steady (table 7.6). Cash flows are projected in table 7.7. If the pro forma underestimates (overestimates) future net income and cash flows, the assumed value of the new common stock is deflated (inflated). In the first instance, junior creditors far down on the repayment hierarchy are given too little, if anything at all; in the second instance, the best-of-interest-of-creditors test distorts the best solution.

The balance sheet in table 7.8 shows steadily rising equity value. The plan of reorganization swaps new equity which it values at $8–$10 per share for most of the old debt (see table 7.9).

Questions

1. Does the plan follow the APR?
2. What is Seaman's tax loss carryforward, and what is it worth?
3. Why does the pro forma balance sheet not include bank debt and yet the income statement includes interest payments?
4. What is the firm's value?
5. Is this stock worth about $9 per share?
6. Would the company be better off if it issued more debt and less equity?
7. If sales grow by more than 25 percent over the 1994–97 period, why does net income barely increase?

TABLE 7.10. Seaman Furniture Company Liquidation Analysis

Exhibit to the Disclosure Statement
Liquidation Analysis
(Millions of Dollars)

Asset	Projected Balance at 10/1/92	At Liquidation Recoveries Of	Liquidation Value Low	Liquidation Value High
Cash	$ 17.0		$ 17.0	$ 17.0
Accounts receivable (a)	40.0	40–50%	16.0	20.0
Inventory (b)	20.5	70–80	14.3	16.4
Property, plant, & equipment, net (c)	17.0	14–19	2.4	3.2
	$ 94.5		$ 49.7	$ 56.6
Less cash to DIP lender (d)			(10.5)	(10.5)
			$ 39.2	$ 46.1
Plus unused portion of standby L/C (d)			3.1	3.1
			$ 42.3	$ 49.2
Less Chapter 11 administrative expenses			(0.7)	(0.7)
Gross liquidation proceeds			$ 41.6	$ 48.2
Less operating expenses:				
Warehouse expense (e)			$ (1.2)	$ (1.2)
Store expense (f)			(2.6)	(2.6)
Advertising expense (g)			(4.0)	(4.0)
General & administrative expense (h)			(2.3)	(2.3)
Total operating expenses			$(10.1)	$(10.1)
Plus interest income on cash balance (i)			0.4	0.4
Net liquidation proceeds			$ 31.9	$ 38.8
Less Chapter 7 administrative costs (j)			(1.6)	(1.9)
			$ 30.3	$ 36.9
Less postpetition accrued expenses (k)			$ (9.0)	$ (9.0)
Less prepetition priority claims:				
Priority customer deposits (l)			$(10.3)	$ (9.0)
Reclamation claims			(0.5)	(0.5)
Priority lease rejection claims			(0.2)	(0.2)
Priority claims arising from WARN (m)			(2.3)	(1.8)
Priority taxes			(2.1)	(1.7)
Total prepetition priority claims			$(15.4)	$(13.2)
Net proceeds available for distribution to unsecured creditors (n)			$ 5.9	$ 14.7

Claim	Amount of Unsecured Claim	Cash Received in Liquidation		% of Equity Received in Chapter 11 Reorganization	Value of Equity Received Based on Aggregate Equity Values Of:	
		Low	High		$40	$50
Class 2 bank group claims	$153.0	$5.1	$12.8	69.56	$27.8	$34.8
Class 3 general unsecured claims	42.2	0.8	1.9	11.46	4.6	5.7
Class 4 Series A notes claims	35.9	0.0	0.0	6.29	2.5	3.1
Class 5 Series B notes claims	31.6	0.0	0.0	5.55	2.5	3.1
Class 6 C & D notes claims	17.9	0.0	0.0	3.14	1.3	1.6
Class 7 12% junior subordinated notes claims	24.3	0.0	0.0	2.08	0.8	1.0
Class 8 15% junior subordinated debentures claims	22.4	0.0	0.0	1.92	0.8	1.0
	$327.3	$5.9	$14.7	100.00%	$40.0	$50.0

TABLE 7.11. Seaman Furniture Company pro Forma Income Statement ($ in millions)

Exhibit to the Disclosure Statement
Sales / Income
Projected Income Statements

	10/1–4/30 1993		1994		1995		1996		1997	
Year Ended 4/30	$	%	$	%	$	%	$	%	$	%
Sales	106.0		190.8		200.4		220.4		246.9	
% increase		−18.6		14.0		5.0		10.0		12.0
S/F/S % increase		−0.3		14.0		5.0		10.0		12.0
Retail margin	48.0	45.3	86.1	45.1	91.2	45.5	100.3	45.5	112.3	45.5
Delivery income	5.6	5.3	10.1	5.3	10.6	5.3	11.7	5.3	13.1	5.3
Total income	53.6	50.6	96.2	50.4	101.8	50.8	112.0	50.8	125.4	50.8
Whse. & delivery	14.4	13.6	25.2	13.2	26.4	13.2	29.1	13.2	32.6	13.2
Store expense	17.8	16.8	32.7	17.1	33.4	16.7	34.8	15.8	36.5	14.8
Advertising	11.2	10.6	20.6	10.8	21.0	10.5	23.1	10.5	25.9	10.5
Gen. & admin.	10.4	9.8	18.9	9.9	19.8	9.9	20.8	9.4	21.9	8.9
Total expense	53.8	50.8	97.4	51.0	100.6	50.2	107.8	48.9	116.9	47.3
Other income	1.2	1.1	1.7	0.9	2.0	1.0	2.6	1.2	3.0	1.2
EBIT	1.0	0.9	0.6	0.3	3.1	1.5	6.8	3.1	11.5	4.7
Restruct. costs	0.0	0.0		0.0		0.0		0.0		0.0
Interest expense	1.1	1.0	1.2	0.6	1.2	0.6	1.1	0.5	1.0	0.4
Prov. for inc. tax	0.1	0.1	0.2	0.1	0.6	0.3	2.3	1.0	4.1	1.6
Gain-cap lse/ extraord. credit	0.0	0.0	0.0	0.0	0.0	0.0	0.0	0.0	0.0	0.0
Amort./goodwill	0.0	0.0	0.0	0.0	0.0	0.0	0.0	0.0	0.0	0.0
Net income	−0.2	−0.2	−0.8	−0.4	1.3	0.6	3.4	1.5	6.5	2.6
# Stores open	22		22		22		22		22	

TABLE 7.12. Seaman Furniture Company Cash Flow ($ in millions)

Exhibit to the Disclosure Statement
Cash Flow
Projected Cash Flow Statements

Years Ended 4/30	10/1–4/30 1993	1994	1995	1996	1997
Earnings before income tax & interest	1.0	0.6	3.1	6.8	11.5
Plus noncash expenses:					
Depreciation	1.4	2.8	2.8	2.8	2.8
Noncash portion of capital leases	0.2	0.4	0.4	0.4	0.4
Earnings before income tax, depreciation, and amortization	2.6	3.8	6.3	10.0	14.7
Plus (minus) operating and discretionary items:					
Capital (expenditures) sales	−0.3	−0.6	−0.7	−0.8	−2.4
Investment in capital leases					
(Incr.) decr. in accounts receivable	0.3	−5.6	−2.3	−4.7	−6.3
(Incr.) decr. in inventory (net of accounts payable)	2.3	0.1	−0.6	−1.2	−1.0
(Incr.) decr. in other working capital	−0.8	1.5	1.0	2.2	2.8
Cash flow from operations	4.1	−0.8	3.7	5.5	7.8
Restructuring costs	0.0				
Cash flow after restructuring costs	4.1	−0.8	3.7	5.5	7.8
Cash interest & dividends					
Interest income	0.3	0.4	0.4	0.4	0.5
Net sr. debt (tranche A)					
Def. sr. debt (tranche B&C)					
Old sr. debt & L/C fees	−0.3				
Old borrow. base agmt					
IRB	−0.5	−0.5	−0.5	−0.5	−0.4
Capital leases	−0.6	−1.1	−1.1	−1.0	−1.1
New KKR PIK Series A 12%					
New bank PIK Series B 12%					
KKR-Seaman PIK Series C&D 12%					
Jr. sub. 12% deb. (New)					
Jr. sub. 15% deb. (Old)					
Total cash interest expense	−1.1	−1.2	−1.2	−1.1	−1.0
Cash flow after interest expense	3.0	−2.0	2.5	4.4	6.8
Income tax refund (payment)	−0.1	−0.2	−0.6	−2.3	−4.1
Cash flow after taxes	2.9	−2.2	1.9	2.1	2.7
Borrowings (repayments) of loans	−0.3	−0.4	−0.5	−0.6	−0.7
Net cash flow	2.6	−2.6	1.4	1.4	2.0
Cash—beginning	13.4	16.0	13.4	14.8	16.2
Cash—ending	16.0	13.4	14.8	16.2	18.2

TABLE 7.13. Seaman Furniture Company pro Forma Balance Sheet ($ in millions)

Exhibit to the Disclosure Statement Balance Sheet Projected Balance Sheets						
Years Ended 4/30	Pro Forma 9/30/92	1993	1994	1995	1996	1997
Assets						
Current assets						
Cash	13.4	16.0	13.4	14.8	16.2	18.2
Net receivables	40.0	39.7	45.3	47.6	52.3	58.6
Inventory	20.5	19.0	18.9	19.9	21.9	23.5
Prepaid expenses & other	3.0	3.0	3.0	3.0	3.0	3.0
Total current assets	76.9	77.7	80.6	85.3	93.4	103.3
Net PP & E	29.7	28.6	26.4	24.2	22.2	21.8
Capital leases, net	6.6	6.4	6.0	5.6	5.2	4.8
Other assets	1.9	1.9	2.6	2.6	2.6	2.6
Goodwill	0.0	0.0	0.0	0.0	0.0	0.0
Total assets	115.1	114.6	115.5	117.7	123.4	132.5
Liabilities & Equity						
Current liabilities						
Accounts payable—prepetition–postpetition	4.9	5.7	5.7	6.1	6.9	7.5
Accrued expenses—prepetition–postpetition	12.0	12.0	13.7	14.4	15.8	17.7
Customer deposits	5.3	4.5	5.0	5.3	5.9	6.8
Total current liabilities	22.2	22.2	24.3	25.7	28.6	31.9
Long-term debt						
Bank sr. debt (tranche A)						
Def. sr. debt (tranche B&C)						
IRB	5.4	5.1	4.8	4.4	4.0	3.5
Capital leases	8.7	8.7	8.6	8.5	8.3	8.1
KKR PIK Series A 12%						
Bank PIK Series B 12%						
KKR-Seaman PIK Series C&D 12%						
Jr. sub. 21% deb. (new)						
Jr. sub 15% (old)						
Total long-term debt	14.1	13.8	13.4	12.9	12.3	11.6
Equity	78.8	78.6	77.8	79.1	82.5	89.0
Total liabilities & equity	115.1	114.6	115.5	117.7	123.4	132.5

TABLE 7.14. Seaman Furniture Company Treatment of Claims Classification and Estimation[a] of Claims and Interests

Class	Estimated Amount of Allowed Claims	% of Reorganization Stock Distributed under Plan	Amount of Cash Distributed under Plan	Eligibility to Vote on Plan	Remarks
Administrative claims	$2,075,080.62	None	$2,075,080.62	Not eligible. These claims are not classified under the plan	Claims paid in full
Priority tax claims	$1,689,062.59	None	$1,689,062.59	Not eligible. These claims are not classified under the plan	Claims paid in full
Class 1:					
IRB claims	$5,425,000.00	None	None	Not eligible—deemed to have accepted the plan	Claims reinstated
Class 2:					
Bank group claims	$153,025,229.12	69.56% (1)	None	Eligible	Entitled to any reorganization stock forfeited by holders of class 3 claims who make cash elections
Class 3:					
General unsecured claims	$26,700,000.00	11.46% (2)	$.05 cash for each dollar of general unsecured claims that makes cash elections in lieu of reorganization stock	Eligible	Holders of allowed class 3 claims may make a cash election to receive, in lieu of reorganization stock, $0.05 cash for each dollar of all, but not a part of, their general unsecured claims

TABLE 7.14. (Continued)

Class	Estimated Amount of Allowed Claims	% of Reorganization Stock Distributed under Plan	Amount of Cash Distributed under Plan	Eligibility to Vote on Plan	Remarks
Class 4: Series A senior subordinated note claims	$35,864,338.00	6.29% (3)	None	Eligible	
Class 5: Series B senior subordinated	$31,613,395.00	5.55% (3)	None	Eligible	
Class 6: Series C/D senior	$17,932,172.00	3.14% (3)(4)	None	Eligible	If class does not accept the plan, holders will not receive any distribution and be subject to cramdown
Class 7: 12% Junior subordinated note claims	$24,252,803.00	2.08% (4)(5)	None	Eligible	If class does not accept the plan, holders will not receive any distribution and be subject to cramdown

Class 8:					
15% Junior subordinated	$22,378,031.00	1.92% (4)	None	Eligible	If class does not accept the plan, holders will not receive any distribution and be subject to cramdown
Class 9:					
Old common stock interests	—	None	None	Not eligible—deemed to have rejected the plan	Receives no distribution under the plan; old common stock canceled; subject to cramdown

[a]Any estimation by the debtors of the amount of allowed claims in a class will not necessarily result in the allowance of such claims under Section 502 of the Bankruptcy Code.

(1) Does not include reorganization stock that may be forfeited by holders of class 6 claims, class 7 claims, and class 8 claims pursuant to the cramdown provisions of the plan and allocated to holders of this class. Also does not include reorganization stock that will be forfeited by holders of Class 3 general unsecured claims that make a cash election and that will be distributed to holders of class 2 claims.

(2) To the extent holders elect to make cash elections, reorganization stock that otherwise would have been distributed to such holders will be distributed to holders of class 2 bank group claims. Does not include reorganization stock that may be forfeited by holders of class 6, class 7, and class 8 claims pursuant to the cramdown provisions of the plan and allocated to holders of this class.

(3) Does not include reorganization stock that may be forfeited by holders of class 7 and class 8 claims pursuant to the cramdown provisions of the plan and allocated to holders of class 6 claims.

(4) Holders will receive no distribution under this plan if this class votes to reject the plan.

(5) Does not include reorganization stock that may be forfeited by holders of class 8 claims pursuant to the cramdown provisions of the plan and allocated to holders of class 7 claims.

CHAPTER 8

Business Process Reengineering

This chapter examines business process reengineering and provides concrete examples of how the process is implemented: rethinking, redesigning, and reward.

An Overview of Reengineering

Reengineering the Corporation (Hammer and Champy 1993) may be the most influential management book in the last half-century.[1] Reengineering, or business process reengineering (BPR) as it is also known, seeks to transform radically how business is conducted. Unlike other contemporary management fads promising incremental change and improvement, BPR seeks quantum enhancements (greater than 50 percent and as much as 2,000 percent) in worker productivity. It has achieved notable success worldwide.

Reengineering is both a philosophy and a management principle. Its adherents display messianic fervor in exhorting managers to see the weakness in two accepted management axioms:

1. work should be deconstructed into small activities assigned to individual workers
2. layers of management should oversee and direct everything

Reengineering adherents believe that these principles lead to

- higher costs
- lower quality
- reduced innovation
- lower profits

The central idea of BPR is to devise an escape from these axioms.

"How did work become so flawed?" To answer this question Hammer and Champy cite a worldview in which the development of modern business practices has followed a three-step evolutionary path.[2] First, in 1776 the renowned economist Adam Smith observed in *The Wealth of Nations* that production efficiency is gained by separating work into simple tasks and assigning different persons to accomplish each task. On the factory floor, for example, workers are responsible not for building an entire car but repetitively for screwing bolts into door frames or putting fenders on the frames. Application of Smith's "division of labor" theory yielded spectacular productivity gains throughout the Industrial Revolution. Those gains encouraged innovation in machine technology, promoting increased capital investment and higher rates of capital utilization. As a result, the worker became secondary to the machine in the production process.

Second, in the 1930s, the practice of management was itself revolutionized. At that time, corporations were attempting to monopolize industries by using economies of large-scale production to lower unit costs. With rising production, the size and complexity of companies also grew. Alfred Sloan, chairman of General Motors from 1937 to 1956, realized that management practices were impeding the goal of meeting an exploding demand for economical automobiles. He chose to reinvent management. Like Adam Smith, Sloan's breakthrough was specialization, but he focused on administrators instead of production workers.

General Motors was a sprawling company. Sloan modularized it so that each product and part was manufactured in a separate factory supervised by an engineer. A small cadre of financial managers controlled each plant using production and financial reports. Other managers, further up the pyramid, directed groups of plants and corporate functions such as marketing or product development. Sloan had created the modern corporation: a web of bureaucracies with numerous specialists in discrete areas like finance, accounting, marketing, sales, and operations. Other companies imitated Sloan's paradigm. On the positive side, this approach enabled companies to manage complex and expanding production processes. On the negative side, corporations became hierarchically organized, with senior managers detached from customers. These two innovations compartmentalized work, leaving workers to perform simple tasks and managers to oversee small activities.

The third evolutionary step created the profession of planners to coordinate far-flung enterprises. Planners employ scenarios and simulations to guide the company's future, despite their unfamiliarity with products or customers. Following this final innovation, work fit into one of three categories:

- work comprised of repetitive tasks,
- work managing a small part of a large enterprise
- work planning an organization from afar

This system flourished in the postwar decades, buoyed by worldwide supply shortages and rising product demand. Then supply and demand patterns underwent profound changes, upsetting the status quo.

The decade of the 1990s—with shortened product life cycles, maturing markets, and intensified worldwide competition—has created new challenges. Leading companies have faltered, while companies that once followed the leaders have disappeared. Corporate meltdowns are not a new phenomenon; what is new is how every company suddenly is at risk. Companies have sought panaceas from various innovations in management practices such as

- total quality management
- rightsizing
- just-in-time inventory control
- continuous product innovation
- automation
- product-customer alignment

Each idea attacks specific problems with narrow solutions. Reengineering is different; it is a total business redesign.

Companies are motivated to reengineer their processes (the multistep routine that yields a product) for many reasons, including

- falling market share or declining profit margin
- delayed credit approval causing aborted potential product sales
- weak inventory controls resulting in repeated write-offs

Regardless of what motivates a company to begin a reengineering project, the fundamental cause is the company's failure to meet the demands of the marketplace. The causes listed above are merely symptoms of a company's marketplace failure.

We start the inquiry by explaining the lexicon of BPR. The following key phrases and terms are used extensively in this chapter.

- Process—the creation of value for the customer by combining inputs in a series of interconnected steps that yields an output.
- Process redesign—changing the composition and configuration of a process.

- Value added—the profit earned in business. Value-added processes are those that induce customers to buy the product and allow the firm to raise its prices.
- Business process reengineering—a.k.a. reengineering, process redesign, core process redesign, and process innovation. Hammer and Champy (1993) define it as "the fundamental rethinking and radical redesign of business processes to achieve dramatic improvement(s) in . . . performance." Another lucid definition, by Manganelli and Klein (1994), is "the activity that analyzes the functioning and value of existing business processes and makes radical changes to dramatically improve their results, in the eye of the customer."

An Elementary Example

Compressed into just three words, BPR is rethinking, redesign, and reward. BPR is undertaken by *rethinking* what the company does for the customer and how it is done, *redesigning* the process to gain efficiency, and implementing the change only if it yields a *reward* in terms of productivity or some other performance measure. How these three words fuse into BPR is illustrated using a simple example concerning the artist Vincent van Gogh.

Van Gogh, a Dutch painter living from 1853 to 1890, painted fewer than eight hundred pictures, which today are worth as much as $50 million apiece. For purposes of illustration, imagine that van Gogh is employed by a company, Vincent van Gogh, Inc., whose business is the production and sale of postimpressionistic paintings.

The company has five employees, each of which is assigned a specific task to perform, as shown in table 8.1. This application of Adam Smith's division-of-labor principle is consistent with van Gogh, Inc.'s, corporate policy of mass production and low selling price. Each production worker has a defined, discrete task to perform repeatedly throughout the day. The first employee, van Gogh himself, is good at describing

TABLE 8.1. Vincent van Gogh, Inc.'s, Employee Plan

Employee	Responsibility
1	Conceptualizing a picture
2	Sketching the painting in charcoal
3	Mixing paints
4	Applying paints
5	Cleaning brushes

a new picture in abstract terms. The second employee is best at translating an abstract description into an outline on canvas. The third employee knows how to mix pigments to produce beautiful shades and colors. The fourth employee applies the paints in a sensuous and inspired manner. And the fifth employee cleans up at the end of the day so that the studio is immaculate.

Management compensation is based on the number of paintings shipped to retail outlets. Workers are encouraged to complete paintings quickly. The labor contract rewards workers if their combined picture output exceeds ten paintings a day. Artwork sold by Vincent van Gogh, Inc., retails for $99 a painting, but many pictures are never sold.

Profits at Vincent van Gogh, Inc., are low, and the warehouse is packed with unsold pictures. A reengineering team is asked to uncover problems and offer solutions. The team takes the rethinking and redesign approach. Discussions with the best customers reveal that they acquire aesthetically appealing paintings; price is not a primary consideration. The team evaluates the five steps in the production process (see table 8.1) to determine each step's cost and learn what is actually accomplished in each step.

Their analysis reveals that aesthetic appeal is a by-product of the activities performed in steps one through four of the production process. The team determines that the costs saved by having four employees perform these steps quickly is less than the aesthetic value lost by having too many cooks stir the pot. The team asks Vincent van Gogh to perform the four steps himself. A second employee continues to clean up after him. The three displaced workers are reassigned to sales operations in upscale malls. Paintings are now completed more slowly, but all of them sell at a higher price than before.[3] Rewards from reengineering come to Vincent van Gogh, Inc., in the form of higher profits, lower inventories, and presumably a happier workforce.[4]

Reengineering Details

Reengineering is not employee layoffs or another name for downsizing. Rather, it is a radical redesign of how business is conducted. In the Vincent van Gogh, Inc., example, the entire production process is rebuilt around one man, workers are reassigned (or let go), and the needs, wants, and desires of the customer become paramount.

Reengineering focuses on processes and not on the company, its products, or particular job functions. A process is the collection of activities completed in creating the product desired by the consumer. To the reengineer, the core of a business is process, not products. In fact, reengineers believe that in the long run corporate success is due not to good products but to good processes.

Reengineering deals with a company's operations while assuming that its strategy is right. Corporate strategy involves questions like "Is this the right business for us to be in?" If the strategy is wrong, reengineering cannot fix it (Tomasko 1993).

In reengineering a product, the reengineer views all associated activities as a process, discarding the notion that production is a collection of independent steps glued together at the end. All activities affecting the product in any way are part of the process. Reengineering abandons the idea of departments and groups within a company. Departmental structures inhibit communication and impair the process.

Preserving existing procedures and corporate structure is not a priority in reengineering. Instead, the goal is to master the existing process and to determine how to make it quicker, better, cheaper, and more appealing to the customer. Occasionally, processes are reengineered so that several parts of a job can be performed concurrently. In other cases, a process is reengineered into multiple processes: for custom and batch jobs, for simple and complex projects, or for rush and time-insensitive work. At other times, either the process is relocated to the customer's plant or vendors are invited into the company.

The two critical steps in reengineering are rethinking and redesigning. Rethinking scrutinizes the company's process; redesigning improves the process. The reengineer determines the customer's true wants and establishes how best to provide them. After reengineering, major gains should occur in performance measures such as profitability, production volume, quality, and customer satisfaction.

The reengineering effort is likely to fail without total commitment from top management, which must provide sufficient resources and adequate time if the effort is to succeed. One successful strategy creates a reengineering team led by a committed senior manager, and this team must provide top management and the company with tangible rewards.

The reengineering team's principal task in the rethinking phase is to acquire and interpret information. Information is generally available, though it may not be organized. Time and resources are required to fill the gap. Reengineering is probably the wrong strategy for a company in crisis.

Another obstacle to successful reengineering is resistance to change by existing departments and managers who want to preserve their power and influence. Resistance can be both overt and discreet. The obvious strategy of staffing the reengineering team with representatives from each department is likely to fail if their self-interests conflict. A better strategy puts in charge a strong individual who has ties to many departments and a vision of the new company.

Insights from rethinking fuel the redesign phase. The same reengineering team should manage the redesign because of its awareness of the firm's processes and its committment to reengineering. If necessary, another team could complete the redesign effort. Redesign goes beyond problem solving; it must also simplify, eliminate, and combine parts of the process. Redesign is not necessarily technical or engineering oriented; it also may be people oriented. For example, it may empower a group of people from different divisions to take responsibility for a process and thereby create organizational agility.

The Rethinking Phase

In rethinking the company's process, the reengineering team seeks four types of information:

- where customers perceive value being added by the company's products
- which activities produce value and what impedes or supports them
- the costs of value-added and non-value-added activities
- how those costs compare with historical and intra-industry data

The team employs a four-step analytical procedure to obtain this information. This procedure systematizes an otherwise disorganized search for data, and without it, reengineering is too imprecise. The four steps are

1. value-added analysis (a.k.a. activity analysis) to separate the firm's activities into those that are value and non–value adding
2. interim activity-based costing to assign costs to each activity (see chapter 11)
3. product-tracking analysis (PTA) to monitor the progress of products through the process
4. data comparison to compare activity analysis, interim activity-based costing, and PTA information to historical and competitor information

Much data is gathered, organized, and analyzed within the four analytical steps. Reengineering is costly and time consuming. The team must be careful to remain within its budget and time constraints. If budgets are inadequate, some of the analytical procedure must be sacrificed.

Value-added analysis is probably the most important step, followed by PTA, and then interim activity-based costing.

Value-Added Analysis

Value added is typically defined as the profit earned by a company,[5] but in the context of reengineering, value added refers to activities that heighten the consumer's perception of value. Activity analysis determines where, in the eyes of the customer, the company adds value. As perceived value increases, the consumer is willing to pay a higher price. Activities are either value creating or non–value adding. Companies should identify and promote value-added activities. Non-value-added activities either are nonessential or essential. Nonessential non-value-adding activities can be suspended; for example, if consumers place no value on packaging colors, these expenditures are an extravagance. On the other hand, essential non-value-added activities, such as payroll or maintenance, are necessary, though cost savings should be evaluated. Additional spending on essential non-value-added activities must pass the highest level of scrutiny (e.g., return on investment or a similar metric).

Deciding where value is added has its difficulties. For example, consider the case of a professional baseball team. Of the countless activities undertaken to get the game on the field (e.g., scouting new players, designing new uniforms, painting the park, etc.) the customer is concerned only with the result: watching the game. Yet consumers are willing to pay more for tickets to watch the game when value-adding activities are performed well. Consider these examples:

- A good scouting program generates better players, a higher league ranking, and higher ticket prices. This is a value-added activity.
- New uniforms may attract new fans but may lessen the experience for older fans. This is not a value-added activity.
- A cleaner park is more enticing and supports higher ticket prices. This is a value-added activity.

Clearly, individuals assess the value-added aspects of these activities differently, but reengineering is part science and part art. Uncertainty about what constitutes a value-added step is reduced by

- asking the customer directly "Would you pay more for . . . ?"
- evaluating competitors' product characteristics and prices
- assessing what the customer really wants

Activity analysis identifies those activities performed for the company's benefit and those satisfying customer needs. Non-value-added activities benefit the company, not the consumer. For example, why is the repair division of a new car dealership closed on weekends? The answer probably is to benefit employees. It is remarkable how many activities are in that category. Non-value-added activities are not evil or corrupt; they are merely valueless to the consumer. Companies must realize that these activities

- do not promote profitability or unit sales
- do not enable the firm to charge a higher price
- raise per unit costs
- may delay and or even hinder product delivery

In the reengineering effort, the customer is the center of attention, not the company and not its workers. Only those non-value-adding activities that are absolutely essential are preserved. The maxim that the customer is king is sacrosanct to the reengineer.

Interim ABC

Activity-based costing (ABC) is a crucial corporate renewal tool that is fully discussed in chapter 11. ABC is a procedure for allocating overhead expenses to products, customers, or regions. At many companies, overhead expenses (essentially everything except direct labor and materials) are substantial because of factory automation and may equal 40 percent of total costs. Overhead costs include indirect labor, indirect materials, depreciation, maintenance, utilities and energy, receiving, shipping and handling, design, engineering, supplies, and quality control.

There are two types of ABC analysis, universal ABC and interim ABC. Universal ABC allocates overhead expenses to individual products in a multiproduct firm, enabling price setting and decision making to reflect full product costs. In either single- or multiproduct companies, interim ABC allocates overhead expenses to activities. For multiproduct companies, overhead first is allocated to products and then to activities. Both universal and interim ABC are refinements that present costs with greater accuracy.

By creating more accurate cost information, interim ABC helps redesign the process. Consider ICC, a single-product manufacturer of ice cream cones sold to distributors. ICC's process has three stages:[6] upfront activities (e.g., receiving, R&D, and engineering), production, and back-end activities (e.g., maintenance, shipping and handling, and quality control).[7]

ICC's income statement is shown in table 8.2. Selling, general, and administrative includes marketing and corporate expenses. Direct labor is production labor, including every worker who physically interacts with the product. Direct materials are raw materials used to make the product. Both direct expense items are clearly traceable back to the product. The final item, overhead, is an aggregation of other nondirect expenses.

Interim ABC disaggregates overhead expense items into key sub-aggregates like design or shipping and then identifies at which stage in the process up-front, production, and back-end expenses occur. The outcome of interim ABC is presented in table 8.3. Note that if ICC were a multiproduct firm, the table would include three additional columns (using a three-stage production paradigm) for each additional product.

Without interim ABC, managers respond to the income statement, table 8.2. It reveals that ICC is losing money. In addition, a comparison with prior-year income statements or industry averages might disclose excessive direct labor or overhead expenses. If direct labor is too high, personnel cutbacks in production are indicated. More analysis would be required to correct excessive overhead expenses.

Interim ABC provides the reengineering team with more details about the company's expenses. It reveals that shipping is ICC's second most important expense, after direct labor expenses. Shipping expenses arise in the back-end phase of the process and are caused by a large number of small lot orders requiring special shipping arrangements. The income statement hides these expenses as indirect labor or general overhead expenses.[8] Receiving, design, and quality-control expenditures are also important. During the redesign effort, the team interprets and integrates the interim ABC and the value-added information. It might

TABLE 8.2. ICC, Inc., 1996 Income Statement ($ in thousands)

Net revenues	$1,974
Expenses	
Selling, general, and administrative	260
Direct labor	978
Direct materials	300
Overhead	715
Gross income	($279)

conclude for example, that shipping costs cannot be reduced because consumers highly value speedy delivery. It might also suggest giving consumers discounts for larger orders or for accepting slower delivery that saves the company money.

Product-Tracking Analysis

Product tracking provides detailed knowledge about where time and resources are consumed in moving from a customer's need to an order to a shipment and hopefully to a reorder.[9] It helps firms target spending reductions without affecting unit costs, delivery times, or quality. Moreover, PTA helps locate redundancies in the process. One source of redundancies is departmental efforts to defend corporate empires.

PTA systematically examines each phase in a process, giving special attention to their sequence and interdependence. Tracking analysis describes how orders progress through the process. It identifies each step performed in various departments. Done well, PTA includes actions taken to service the customer after the sale, including reselling. The principal output of PTA is an order-tracking flowchart. The flowchart reveals who is involved and for how long in completing the process. The flowchart helps the reengineering team identify sources of delay and helps determine which employees actually work together (e.g., a credit analyst and a salesperson) despite being in different corporate departments. Redesign attempts to eliminate delays and create teams that work together.

Information for PTA is gathered in two ways. First, the reengineering team contacts the company through normal channels like any customer. The reengineers may find that

TABLE 8.3. ICC, Inc., Expense Disaggregation ($ in thousands)

	Total Dollars	Up-Front Dollars	Production Dollars	Back-End Dollars
Direct labor	978		978	
Direct materials	300		300	
Overhead	715			
Design		98		
Utilities		12	60	20
Receiving		108		
Shipping				327
Quality control				90

- phone calls are put on hold indefinitely
- messages are never returned
- salespeople accept orders without trying to sell a superior product, a larger size, or an extended warranty
- the product is not shipped for weeks
- the wrong product is received
- the product does not work

Second, the team nursemaids a real customer's order and follows it as it moves through the process.

Departmental boundaries are ignored in PTA since the redesign phase is likely to propose a radical shift in the nature and form of the firm. PTA is the third information input to BPR. Coupled with knowledge gained in value-added analysis and interim ABC, PTA provides a full canvas of intelligence for the team redesigning the process.

Database Design

Information itself is valueless. Informational value results when a person collates diverse facts, understands their significance, and conceives of a strategic response. As an example of the valuelessness of unused information, consider how at the U.S. space agency technicians detected indications of defective O-rings on the space shuttle but ignored the information until a disaster occurred. Funds consumed collecting O-ring information were wasted.

The database design stage of the rethinking effort creates value from disparate pieces of information, combining the activity analysis, interim ABC, and PTA information. An efficient database is essential. It must insure that no information is dismissed summarily and that serious information is reviewed.

Each reengineering effort harvests a unique collection of facts. Nonetheless, each project should follow several common principles in database design. First, if possible, current and historical information should be compared. Although interim ABC reports may not have been run before, similar information may be found in functional departments. Second, data should be compared across firms in the same industry. Trade associations and governmental reports are good sources of comparative data, and consulting firms sell surrogate company data. Data to compare PTA across the industry may be obtained by placing orders with competitors. Comparisons identify significant differences in the company's process compared with its history or with competitors. Lucid graphs, charts, tables, or pictures provide excellent exhibits to display interim results to management.

The Redesign Phase

The redesign phase is what is generally thought of as reengineering. It is where the process is transformed into something radically new and better. However, rethinking and its constituent four analytical procedures are necessary inputs to redesign and are the source of crucial decision-making information. The redesign team might receive a report like that in table 8.4 prepared for In-Hospital Pharmacy (IHP), a pharmacy that operates in the outpatient wings of hospitals and sells only ethical prescription drugs or over-the-counter medications.

IHP has a relatively simple process consisting of just three activities. The first activity is the maintenance of store shelves, both in front of and behind the counter. If a pharmacy runs out of a particular medication, patients take their prescriptions elsewhere. Consequently, inventory control is a critical function. Customers place a high value on full shelves. Scanner technologies for inventory management are not used by IHP. Management dismissed their savings potential because federal controlled-substances laws mandate that only registered pharmacists handle certain drugs. In lieu of scanners, highly paid pharmacists, assisted by order clerks, fulfill the ordering, receiving, and inventory functions. The second activity in IHP's process consists of pharmacists interacting with customers, filling prescriptions, giving instructions, and arranging for payment. Obviously, this is a high-value activity, but it is costly since highly trained professionals fulfill both technical and menial tasks: for example, pharmacists enter new prescriptions into the computer system. Bottlenecks that frustrate other customers and reduce the productivity of

TABLE 8.4. In-Hospital Pharmacy, Inc., Redesign Inputs

Activity/Steps	Value Added	Costs	Delays Caused	Do Workers in Different Groups Actually Work Together?
Ordering, receiving, and inventory	Yes	High	Yes	Yes
Prescription filling, customer information, and billing	Yes	High	Yes	No
Record keeping and administration	No	Medium	No	No

all the pharmacists at the order desk are regularly created when pharmacists get involved in protracted discussions with customers receiving new prescriptions or customers not permitted to refill existing prescriptions. The final activity, record keeping and administration, provides no value added but is necessary in order to comply with federal drug statutes and for general corporate purposes. Computers control these costs, especially in the record-keeping area.

The redesign team's assignment is to discover how to transform the company so that it becomes significantly better by some objective measure. This might mean substantially lower unit costs, higher productivity, or quicker throughput times. Changes of at least 50 percent are envisioned; mere 5 percent or 10 percent improvements are insufficient, given the expenditures of time and money to conduct reengineering and the availability of comparable returns from incremental improvement programs such as TQM (see chap. 9) or JIT. The team pursues radical changes to how business is conducted.

The redesign team starts with the rethinking report. The report is an information catalogue, not an action plan, but it furnishes clues on how to reshape the company. For example, regarding IHP it is fairly obvious that at least the following actions are needed:

- use scanner technology to notify the pharmacist when to reorder inventory
- put hospital doctors on a computer network and encourage online prescriptions
- hire a nonpharmacist college graduate to attend to patients with new prescriptions
- outsource record keeping and accounting

The redesign team seeks further information by hunting for new technologies, proposing and evaluating a revolutionary idea at a test site, or interviewing a successful noncompetitor in the same industry in a different region or country.

Redesigners are creative. They must be visionaries who can sense gold in the hills or water in the ground. The person controlling the current process is a poor choice for the rethinking team, even though technically he/she may be the best qualified, since he/she is likely to distract the team from what is possible by constant reference to what is.

Redesigners focus on the process, not on departments. Workers involved with the same process belong in the same process division and should not be separated by artificial departmental barriers. Reengineer-

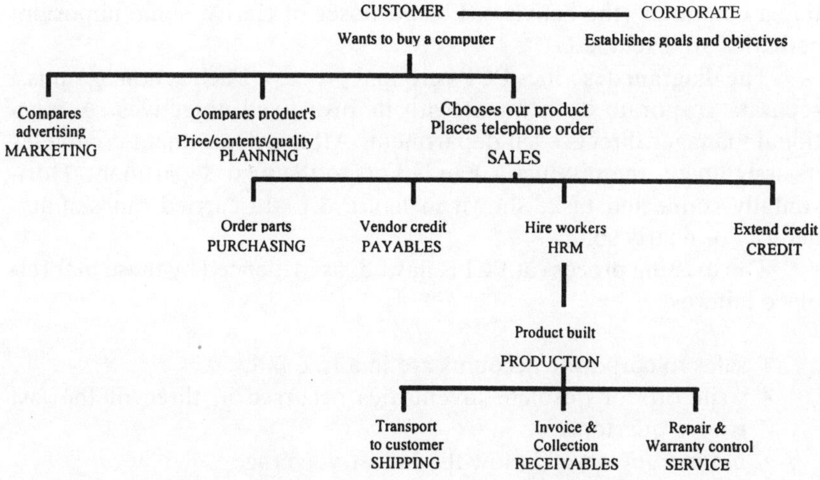

Fig. 8.1. Personal Computers, Inc., product delivery diagram

ing flattens Alfred Sloan's hierarchical corporate structure. Workers are empowered to take charge and take responsibility. In place of a boss, there is now a process unit that assigns itself tasks. Without bosses to satisfy, the customer becomes king.

Process redesign demands an increased reliance upon information technology (IT). In the IHP example, doctors' offices are wired into the pharmacy and scanners purchased to audit and maintain supply levels. Hammer and Champy say that too little IT is employed when information is sent back and forth between departments. They call this a fragmented activity. The solution is to combine those departments either physically or electronically with IT.

The reengineering process has now been described in its entirety. Even though several examples have highlighted specific critical points, there still may be uneasiness with these new ideas. This chapter's final section presents a complete example of an actual reengineering project.

A More Complete Example

Working through an example of a BPR project from beginning to end clarifies its many steps. Consider the process depicted in figure 8.1. Personal Computers, Inc. (PCI), is a PC manufacturer.[10] In the diagram, critical activities are depicted in small letters; the action agent (usually a corporate department) is indicated with capital letters. For example, at the top of the diagram, the CUSTOMER (the agent) wants to buy a computer (the activity). For purposes of clarity, some important activities are excluded.

The diagram describes PCI's original process. Each action agent is a separate corporate department with its own fixed objectives. A functional manager directs each department. After a department completes its assignment, the product is handed off to the next department. Horizontally connected tasks shown in figure 8.1 are carried out simultaneously or nearly so.

The existing process at PCI is flawed, as evidenced by these marketplace failures:

- sales to corporate accounts are in a free fall
- write-offs of obsolete inventories occurred in three of the last twelve quarters
- net margin is well below the industry average

Shareholders are distressed because the equity is lagging the performance of the overall market, and the board of directors is questioning management's ability. In response to these pressures, management tried a number of fixes; some yielded incremental gains, but overall the company remains mired. BPR is different. It abandons the old process and creates a new process. PCI has agreed to stop trying to fix what is broken and to opt instead for something new and better.

A reengineering team is formed with the senior vice president of sales at its helm. She is a twelve-year company employee with close connections to three functional areas. A consultant practiced in reengineering is hired to coach the reengineering leader. The leader selects five additional team members; she seeks knowledgeable persons with histories of being outspoken and advocating unpopular positions. During the first week, the leader and her consultant brief the team on reengineering's conceptual framework, the company's charge to them, and a rough plan of action.

The team's first step is an activity analysis to determine what are value-added, non-value-added but essential, and non-value-added, nonessential activities. Its results are presented in table 8.5. Of twenty-six activities fulfilled by twelve departments, only twelve activities, less than 50 percent, are value adding. Most of the activities in figure 8.1 create no value for the customer. Why, then, are they performed? This topic is heatedly discussed by the reengineering team. Are these activities simply performed for the company's benefit or, perish the thought, for the benefit of its workers? The team reviews which activities are essential (must be done) and which activities are nonessential. The consultant notes that essential does not mean "must be done in-house." Essential activities are carried out by internals or are outsourced. If the focus is on the customer, nonessential activities are purposeless, and the company must decide if it wants to continue them for its own benefit. The company cannot suspend all non-value-adding activities; it must have a corporate headquarters group, marketing decisions must be made, and so on. But it can closely scrutinize its investment in those activities.

Activity analysis suggests that thirteen or fourteen non-value-adding activities are essential (i.e., must be performed) (see table 8.5). The one nonessential non-value-added activity, warehousing purchasing, is categorized that way because a team member, an MBA in the operations department, insists that with JIT production, inventories are old-fashioned.

The consultant asks the team to reconsider how it classified activities as essential. "If this company is perfect," he says, "management would not have asked us to reengineer it." He remarks that companies always think that everything they do is essential. He also reminds the team that just because an activity is labeled essential does not mean that it will be performed in-house. This remark is intended to remind the team that its task is not to preserve jobs but to fix the company. Finally, he asks if the decision to outsource an activity can be based on lower costs alone.

Aroused by the consultant's words, the team revisits activity analysis to rejudge which non-value-added activities are essential. This time the question "Will the company prosper if it stops doing this?" is asked repeatedly. At first, working down the list in table 8.5, each non-value-added activity is again judged to be essential until the team gets to "buying necessary components in advance." From that point on, each activity is judged to be nonessential. The team reasons that purchasing materials in advance becomes nonessential with better IT and JIT inventories and production; getting vendor credit is nonessential if a bank credit line or some other form of credit is prearranged; human-resource management (HRM) is a nonessential function if most plant activities are outsourced; and communications with the receivables department is nonessential when an intelligent IT system monitors product sales. A revised version of table 8.5, incorporating these changes, is readied for the redesign phase.

There are alternative ways to regulate or control non-value-adding expenses and departments. Table 8.6 lists these and compares their advantages and disadvantages. The first alternative, budgeting for zero growth, is naive and not in the reengineering spirit of radically changing the company. Allowing a bleeding patient to continue bleeding at the same rate is not a cure. The final two suggestions are more practical. Although not widely used in business today, outsourcing will become especially prominent in the "virtual marketplace" created on the

Internet. Constantly reexamining vendor selection or regularly putting contracts out to bid help guarantee that the outsourced relationship provides the lowest cost and the highest quality.[11] Of course, if vendors are treated poorly and underpaid, they are likely to forsake the relationship when business picks up.

TABLE 8.5. Value-Added Assessment, Personal Computers, Inc.

Department	Action	Value Added	Essential If Non–Value Adding
Corporate	• Manages goals and budgets	No	Yes
	• Works with investment community	No	Yes
	• Makes decision to reengineer	No	Yes
Marketing	• Chooses how to position the product	No	Yes
	• Develops promotional campaign	No	Yes
Planning	• Decides what to put inside computers	No	Yes
	• Selects a base price and an add-on price for components	No	Yes
	• Sets a delivery time plan	No	Yes
Sales	• Takes business and individual inquiries	Yes	
	• Promotes the "right" product to the customer	No	Yes
	• Takes orders	Yes	
Purchasing	• Buys necessary components in advance to meet the planned delivery time objective	No	Yes
	• Warehouses purchases	No	No
Payables	• Works with vendors to get credit extended to Personal Computing, Inc.	No	Yes
HRM	• Handles employee relations, in particular hiring and firing	No	Yes
Credit	• Arranges financing for business customers and possibly some individuals	Yes	
Production	• Pulls together all the inputs to create the product purchased by the customer	Yes	
	• Tests the product for content and quality	Yes	
Shipping	• Delivers product to the customer	Yes	
	• Notifies receivables department of shipping information	No	Yes
Receivables	• Collects from credit card company for individuals	Yes	
	• Services credit accounts for customers offered credit terms	Yes	
Service	• Resolves problem issues by telephone	Yes	
	• Ships replacement parts when defects are discovered	Yes	
	• Verifies that broken parts are returned	Yes	
	• Contracts with repair vendor to service older machines	Yes	

Combining departments is a good way to eliminate a non-value-adding, nonessential group if the two linked departments can be fully integrated. Integration means that tasks are completed by the same persons. In the earlier example of a group responsible for choosing packaging colors for a product whose consumers do not value it, integration occurs when those workers join or that task is assigned to the group developing value-enhancing advertising. Just putting two groups of workers into the same building on different floors or different sides of the same floor is not integration. The PTA output helps decide which groups can be integrated.

PCI's abridged income statement for the period 1994–96 is presented in table 8.7. It reveals a steady decline in operating income, partially due to explosive growth in overhead expenses from 18 percent to 24 percent of revenues. If overhead expenses are restored to 18 percent of sales, 1996 operating income equals $16 million instead of a loss. As a single-product company, PCI's interim ABC report describes the extent to which each activity (i.e., stage) generates overhead expenses.

Figure 8.1 illustrated PCI's activities. They are also listed in table 8.8. Direct labor, direct materials, and overhead expenses are allocated to the activities in the table; PCI's overhead is split into nine constituent parts, including indirect labor, utilities, and shipping. The bottom row contains each activity's total overhead. Four activities – shipping, production, planning, and service – account for 77 percent of total overhead, or $142 million. Later in the data-comparison stage, these four activities are shown to have increased, as a percentage of overhead, from 51 percent to 77 percent in just two years.

Shipping's $46 million expenditure is the largest contributor to overhead of all activities. Shipping costs include $27 million of PCI-paid

TABLE 8.6. Advantages and Disadvantages of Methods for Dealing with Non-Value-Adding Activities

Method	Advantages	Disadvantages
Budget those departments for zero growth	Costs are fixed	Creates second-class departments
Work is outsourced	May find a vendor who performs the work better or at a lower cost than internals	Externals lack loyalty and may dump the company in periods of growth
Activities are transferred into value-adding groups as combined responsibilities	All workers are immersed in value-adding activities	Cultures may clash; performers may become nonperformers

vendor shipping bills (e.g., Federal Express and UPS), $10 million of indirect labor and materials, and $4 million of utilities and energy charges. The reengineering team is astonished; they thought that customers paid their own shipping charges. The company's advertisements promise (a) shipment within forty-eight hours for $49 or (b) for corporate accounts, shipping once credit terms are approved. However, confidential conversations on the shipping floor later confirmed by the sales force expose how PCI is unable to meet these promises. Rapid sales growth coupled with the CFO's mandate to become a JIT vendor with zero inventory have meant that fewer than 20 percent of products are shipped when promised. Angry customers are placated by shipping products overnight at a cost of $120 and charging customers just the $49 land-based shipping fee or even nothing when they are really angry. PCI pays the difference itself and charges these expenditures to overhead. Shipping includes $6 million of indirect labor charges as idle workers wait in the production area to transfer finished products to shipping before the next-day delivery service deadline. Production pays no materials charges for shipping boxes because an accounting department decision accrued them to overhead, which the interim ABC allocates to shipping.

At $38 million, production is the next largest contributor to overhead. The two major components of production overhead charges are $20 million of utilities and $12 million of depreciation. The reengineering team finds no evidence of waste, duplication, or extravagance; however, the team questions whether the company is overpaying the local gas, electric, and telephone utilities now that it has grown into a major customer. Depreciation reflects both the amount of capital equipment and the type of depreciation (e.g., straight line or double declining balance) selected by the accountants. To gauge how appropriately equipment is stocked, the team walks the production floor at various times throughout the day, recording utilization levels for various pieces of equipment. As a result of rapid product demand growth, few machines are ever idle.

TABLE 8.7. Personal Computers, Inc., 1994–96 Income Statement ($ in millions)

	1994	1995	1996
Net revenues	$201	$368	$767
Expenses			
Selling, general, and administrative	10	19	43
Direct labor	68	152	343
Direct materials	45	97	227
Overhead	36	81	184
Operating income	$42	$19	($30)

TABLE 8.8. Personal Computers, Inc., Expense Disaggregation ($ in millions)

	Total Dollars	Marketing	Planning	Sales	Purchasing	HRM	Payables	Credit	Production	Shipping	Receivables	Service
Direct labor	$343								$343			
Direct materials	$227								$227			
Overhead	$184											
Indirect labor		$3	$2	$1	$1	$1	$1	$1	$2	$6	$2	$3
Indirect materials		$2		$1						$4		$1
Utilities				$3					$20	$4		$1
Depreciation							$2	$1	$12	$1		$2
Maintenance		$1	$3	$1	$1	$1	$1	$1	$2	$1	$1	$1
Design		$4	$27	$1								
Receiving					$10			$1				
Shipping										$27		
Quality control					$2					$3		$18
Total overhead		$10	$32	$7	$14	$2	$4	$4	$38	$46	$3	$26

Planning accounts for $32 million of overhead. Most of these costs, $27 million, are incurred doing design work. Designers investigate component trade-offs (i.e., size, cost, and power), how to fit necessary components into the box, and how to improve product presentation (i.e., ergonomics and aesthetics). Component evolution and technical change have shrunk product half-lives to about eighteen months. As a result, high levels of design expenditures persist and are anticipated in the future. The reengineering team unearths several pertinent facts about the design team:

- design flaws discovered by the production department and awaiting design rework often push back schedules and raise costs
- designers lack funding to purchase competitors' machines for comparison purposes
- design has no communication channel to receive input from service/quality control

At $26 million, service activities are the last major contributor of overhead expenses. Quality control accounts for $18 million of these expenditures, including $11 million to fix working machines during their warranty period (most machines are not broken, and consumers require operating instructions), $5 million to resell machines returned by consumers within the thirty-day free return period, and $2 million fixing out-of-warranty machines for large corporate accounts. The industry standard for product repair costs is between 2 percent and 3 percent of sales. Service expenditures as a percentage of revenues remain flat at PCI. The reengineering team wonders if machines have a constant failure rate or if budgeted service dollars are spent regardless of need.

The last piece of information obtained in the rethinking phase of PCI's reengineering effort is a customer product-tracking analysis. PTA follows a customer's order through various departments, recording the actions performed, the workers involved, and the time periods when the product is being worked on, is idle, or is in transit. The analysis begins from the moment an order is received (or earlier) through when the product is shipped to the customer and ends when the customer discards the product at the end of its useful life. PTA crosses traditional boundaries between departments and activities and focuses on actions serving the customer's needs. The major output of the analysis is a table or flow diagram showing who touches the customer's order/product and for how long, what is done to the product in each step, and when the product is inactive. Table 8.9 shows a PTA for PCI that begins at the sales point. At other companies, PTA may begin at the corporate level.

TABLE 8.9. Product-Tracking Analysis for Personal Computers, Inc.

Time Clock	Location of Product/ Order	Accomplishment	Actual Work Time
Day 1 10:00–10:06 A.M.	Sales	Mr. Smith calls with ad in hand. Inquires about delivery time, warranty, and method of payment. Gives company name and phone number to agent.	6 minutes
Day 3 11:15–11:20 A.M.	Sales	Mr. Smith calls again. Orders 75 units of Model PCI 586–100. He requests financing. When he asks about delivery, he is told, "The product will be shipped 2 days after you get credit approval."	5 minutes
Day 4 9:15 A.M.– Day 5 9:15 A.M.	Credit	Mr. Smith's credit request is hand-delivered to credit department. Credit agencies are contacted via computer at 10:00 A.M. Credit is approved at 4:30 P.M. Approval is hand-delivered back to sales. Customer is contacted.	30 minutes
Day 5 9:15 A.M.– 11:45 A.M.	Scheduling	Production request is hand-delivered to scheduling.	5 minutes
Day 5 11:45 A.M.– Day 8 10:00 P.M.	Production	Parts are requisitioned from purchasing; hard disks are unavailable until tomorrow. Assembly proceeds as far as possible, then stops until Day 8 at 12:00 noon, when hard disks arrive.	10 hours
Day 8 10:00 P.M.– Day 9 9:00 A.M.	Quality control	Product burned in to test parts and assembly.	11 hours
Day 9 9:00 A.M.– Day 9 12:00 noon	Shipping	Product moved to shipping department.	10 minutes
Day 9 12:00 noon– Day 9 4:30 P.M.	Shipping	Product shipped out via overnight carrier.	1 hour
Day 10 10:00 A.M.	Customer	Product received by customer.	
Day 10 10:00 A.M.– Day 10 12:00 noon	Service	Customer has trouble networking first machines opened. He spends 60 minutes waiting in telephone queue to get to customer service. Hierarchical telephone service system requires 30 minutes to get to high-level agent. Problem quickly fixed.	30 minutes
Day 10 10:00 A.M.– 11:00 A.M.	Receivables	Notified to process invoice and start client on a payment schedule.	30 minutes
Monthly	Receivables	Customer invoiced for monthly payments.	30 minutes
Occasionally	Service	Service calls taken from 75 computer users at Mr. Smith's company. Repairs often effected over the phone, but occasionally parts are shipped out. PCI personnel on several occasions install new equipment.	1 hour/ month
In the future	Sales	No remarketing effort undertaken at this time.	

The longest interval occurs in production, where twenty-one hours are spent making and testing the product. The two exterior columns in the table are critically important: the one on the left describes how long the product is at a location, the one on the right tells how much actual work occurs during that interval. Credit work is an interesting example. The credit department takes an entire day to perform thirty minutes of work. A more time-efficient activity is receivables collection, which takes one hour to perform thirty minutes of work.

The reengineering team is now equipped with three sets of data—activity analysis, interim ABC, and PTA—upon which to base the redesign effort. Redesign is probably the least scientific reengineering step, but it is the most important. It is where the information obtained in the rethinking phase is translated into real breakthroughs. Common characteristics of redesign are

- willingness to do things differently; creativity rewarded
- inhibitions and commitments abandoned
- all alternatives considered
- employees empowered; organizational structure flattened
- cross-functional teams assembled

PCI's redesign effort produces a number of practical suggestions. These are listed below in their natural order, based on the team's discussion:

1. A number of activities are outsourced, including product servicing (other than telephone related), HRM, investor relations and shipping. Vendors are found in a competitive bidding process. Shipping is contracted out to a single major next-day and two-day delivery service that installs its personnel at PCI. Second-day shipping is the norm (i.e., PCI wins a 40 percent reduced fee) unless next-day air is approved.
2. A computerized JIT plan minimizes inventories of raw materials and finished products.
3. Product advertisements are altered to indicate a range of delivery times. Customers are given the option of next-day delivery for a reasonable fee.
4. Negotiations with a new long-distance carrier reduce telephone charges by 23 percent. The local gas and electric utilities cut rates by 5 percent.
5. A cross-functional team is created from the design staff, parts of the service department, the procurement department, and the production department and renamed the DSPP depart-

ment. DSPP employees are empowered to decrease costs, delivery times, and service issues. Authority is given to workers. Design rework is substantially reduced, and designers gain access to competitors' machines for comparison purposes. A computer system ties DSPP to sales inquiries, allowing inventories to be preordered. Only the DSPP team is empowered to sanction next-day delivery.

6. A multimedia instructional CD that clarifies how the machine works and what to do if it does not work is produced and sent with each new computer sale. Persons buying their first computer are also sent a short instructional video.
7. Persons calling to return machines within the thirty-day free return period are asked if the company can send a representative to their homes or offices to make the machine work properly.
8. Out-of-warranty repairs at major accounts are charged a service fee unless the sales team makes a specific request. Future new product sales to these accounts are offered a $99 lifetime service plan.
9. A special toll-free phone number is established for corporate buyers. Calls are assigned to individuals who follow leads.
10. Nonbusiness inquiries are answered a day after they contact the sales department using caller-ID phone numbers.
11. A computer system is established to instantaneously send (a) credit requests to the credit department, (b) orders to scheduling, (c) notifications of deliveries to the receivables department.
12. Resale efforts to old customers are instituted by quarterly delivery of a corporate promotional magazine.

PCI implemented these changes. Overall, costs fell substantially and productivity grew. Letting consumers choose next-day delivery reduced shipping costs. However, certain suggestions achieved no improvement. PCI is still having trouble with inventory ordering as sales continue to grow by 30 percent per year, compounded by an eighteen-month product life.

Process Reengineering: Summary

Companies with many processes must choose where to start reengineering. Taking on too much at one time is a recipe for failure. But where should they begin? They would like to begin with the process that confers the greatest productivity gains or some other definable goal.[12] Yet potential gains are unknown before the redesign phase. During the data-comparison phase, it may be possible to identify an area in the company that recently has deteriorated or is underperforming.

Reengineering sometimes fails.[13] Companies may discover that they have achieved only small gains; reengineering is not overly expensive, however, and they can begin again. Reengineering is far from pure science, and success is not guaranteed. Failure occurs for many reasons, some internal, some team related, and some company related.

Among the reasons for reengineering failure are

- the team lacks leadership
- the team is not supported at the highest levels
- the team is not aware of its methodology
- the team ignores people and the corporate culture
- the team tries to fix the present as opposed to finding the future
- the team ignores the process

Finally, Hammer and Champy say that the reengineering team must learn to think inductively; that is, it must first find a solution and then seek the problem.

CHAPTER 9

Deming and the Quality Revolution

In recent years, the "quality revolution" has altered the shape of American business thinking and practice. This chapter examines that revolution and its impact on corporate reengineering.

American companies, which had dominated the world's economy since the end of the Second World War, lost their advantage to Japanese companies in the 1980s. One American firm after another lost market share and reputation to innovative Japanese companies that introduced less expensive but higher quality products. The combatants and the battles are familiar names: Toyota versus General Motors, Fujitsu against IBM, Sony over Zenith, and Seiko opposite Timex, to name just a few. American companies laid off thousands of workers because they were unprepared to compete in the global business environment of the 1990s.

What precipitated this unimaginable change? In a single word, the answer is quality. Japanese firms had learned to examine regularly how and what their factories manufactured. The need to constantly improve both the production process and the product itself is ingrained into the Japanese business psyche. No doubt the total reconstruction of Japan's production platform after its annihilation under the fierce wrath of American bombers during the war also contributed to a production standard higher than that of American industry. But quality is the driving force. The irony of this parable is that the guru of quality in Japan is an American: W. Edwards Deming, an Iowa-born engineer trained at Yale.[1]

The history of quality management actually predates Deming, beginning with Walter Shewart, who pioneered the concept of statistical process control (SPC). SPC is the application of the old idea that the apple does not fall far from the tree; that is, in life, most properly functioning activities (including manufacturing) contain some degree of natural variation. An activity falling outside the normal range of variation attests to an unusual occurrence. Consider these nonproduction examples of normal ranges:

- we generally take between forty and forty-five minutes to complete our daily five-mile run
- we ordinarily consume between 2,200 and 2,700 calories a day

A high percentage of cases falls within these ranges. Observations outside the normal range are anomalies. For example, a faster run may indicate we have been in a race, while a slower run may denote our failure to stretch before running. A lower caloric intake may indicate that we have begun a diet, while a larger caloric intake may denote that we celebrated Thanksgiving Day at our parents' home.

Variety may be the spice of life, but in manufacturing it is vinegar. Although companies aspire to the goal of standardizing production, output is not uniform despite the advent of computer-controlled machinery and automation. No pair of items (such as two integrated circuits or two tires) at any factory are precisely identical. The normal range of product variation is defined by carefully reviewing a sample of outputs. Product variation occurs for different reasons within and outside the normal range, as seen in table 9.1. Basically, within-range variation is caused by ordinary circumstances that are relatively hard to modulate or control, while out-of-range variation is linked to unusual events. Within-range variation is anticipated, though not acceptable; variation outside the normal range defines an out-of-control manufacturing process that requires fixing.

Product variations produce uneven quality, expensive rework efforts, and diminished consumer product opinion. Naturally, companies want to reduce product variation, but to do so is expensive. Shewart

TABLE 9.1. Causes of Product Variation

Causal Factor	Tolerated Variations within the Normal Range	Unacceptable Variations outside the Normal Range
Labor	• Interworker variation	• New, poorly trained workers
	• Change in shifts	• Workers are overtired
Machines	• Natural tolerance	• Missed maintenance schedule
	• Different age machines	• Broken part
Material	• Uncontrollable imperfections	• New supplier
	• Difficulty removing packaging	• Materials not input
Shipping and handling	• Different size orders	• New shipper
	• Method of shipping	• Problems with containers

defined a product improvement protocol whose first target is out-of-control processes and whose second target is normal product variation. Out-of-control processes are fixed as soon as possible. Other quality problems are approached more deliberately. He envisioned a company experiencing continual improvement, what is now called the Shewart cycle. In the cycle, sequential product improvements are planned, trial tested, confirmed, and implemented. Incremental improvement in product quality is achieved with each successive enhancement.

When Deming was a graduate student at Yale, he met Shewart and became his disciple (Luecke 1994). Afterward, he taught Shewart's SPC principles to manufacturing companies and was mostly ignored in the United States. But after the war, his message of quality was warmly received in Japan, which had mediocre production methods and product quality. American companies rekindled their interest in his quality message after the resurgence of Japanese industry and an acknowledgment of Deming's contribution.

Deming articulated a universal message of absolute quality. He applied it to large and small organizations, to service and manufacturing industries, and even to corporate divisions. The ideas are neither too technical nor overly esoteric; they embody good old-fashioned common sense. At the core of the Deming system is a keen focus on achieving customer satisfaction (Deming 1982). How to accomplish this is conveyed in his fourteen-point system, reproduced in table 9.2. Shewart's

TABLE 9.2. Deming's Fourteen Quality Points

1. Improvement in product and service is a permanent goal.
2. Management must accept the new philosophy of change and must be leaders in the pursuit of change.
3. Build quality in; do not expect to achieve it by output inspection.
4. Award contracts based on minimizing total cost. Cost includes more than price. Develop a permanent trusting relationship with a single supplier.
5. Constantly decrease costs by steadily improving quality and productivity by improving production and service.
6. Advocate on-the-job training.
7. Become a leader by helping things to get done better.
8. Remove fear to create collegiality.
9. Get disparate functions working as a team to anticipate problems.
10. Remove slogans and production targets. Replace them with a better system that can raise productivity and quality.
11. Eliminate numerical quotas and goals and replace them with leadership.
12. Eliminate ratings or merit systems and institute pride in quality.
13. Encourage education.
14. Get everyone in the company to work together to achieve change.

Source: Deming (1982)

SPC contributes to these ideas. Worker/manager cooperation, education and reeducation, and trust and fellowship are other key components of his formula.

Total Quality Management

More recently, the quality movement has adopted the acronym TQM, which denotes total quality management.[2] TQM is the culmination of Shewart and Deming's doctrine that quality comes not from inspecting products for defects but from building quality products; that SPC provides a mechanism to control the process of production; and that all employees bear the responsibility for creating quality. An early corporate adherent of TQM was Martin Company[3] which in 1961 accepted the task of delivering problem-free missiles to the Pentagon. It labeled its program "zero defects." A key element in Martin's success was the marriage of management and labor behind the idea that it was better to build-in quality than to find and fix defects (Garvin 1988).

The key word in TQM is *management.* It represents a new style of management. TQM-driven managers focus on

- satisfying customer needs
- continuous improvement driven by
  - —employee teams empowered to make changes
  - —problem solving, not blame assigning
  - —a focus on the process, not the product
- forming partnerships with suppliers

First and foremost, TQM focuses managers on understanding their customers' wants and needs instead of on their earnings per share next quarter.

The word *quality* is also meaningful in TQM. There are many dimensions of quality, including performance, reliability, durability, and serviceability (Pisek 1987). Combining these dimensions, the consumer discerns the product's quality. Quality is defined not by the company but by customers. Quality products with consumer-desired features, practical design characteristics, and attractive appearance achieve winning reputations.

Quality Costs

How much does quality cost? And what benefits accrue to a company that increases the quality of its products? The first question has an exact

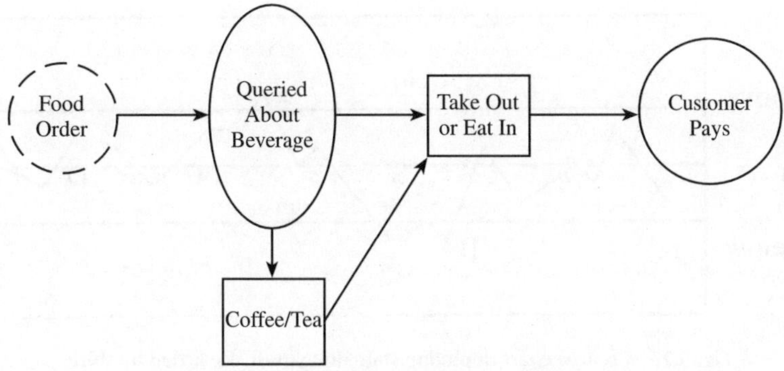

Fig. 9.1. Process flowchart for a doughnut shop

quantitative answer; the answer to the second question can be estimated. There are four types of quality costs (Juran 1951):[4]

1. Prevention costs, incurred avoiding low quality, such as quality engineers, training exercises, equipment maintenance, and supplier evaluations.
2. Inspection costs, incurred detecting low quality of inputs and outputs.
3. Failure costs, incurred from low-quality production, such as rework, warranty claims, liability claims, and insurance costs.
4. Future costs, incurred from lost sales resulting from a bad reputation caused by selling low-quality goods or services.

These costs are reported to management in detail in a quality cost report (Roth and Morse 1983). Quality costs, at most American companies, are estimated to be 15–20 percent of sales revenues (Horngren, Foster, and Datar 1994). In *Quality Is Free,* Philip Crosby (1979: 15) estimates that a TQM program can reduce these costs to 2.5 percent. Money spent on quality initiatives is an investment that should return lower costs and higher profits. Managers underestimate the cash return to quality investments because without the investment, costs are unknown.

Tools of TQM

TQM adopts an eclectic variety of techniques and methods originally applied elsewhere. For example, it uses process flowcharts to study the process of creating the product. A process flowchart describes the steps, branches, and outputs of the process. Figure 9.1 displays a process

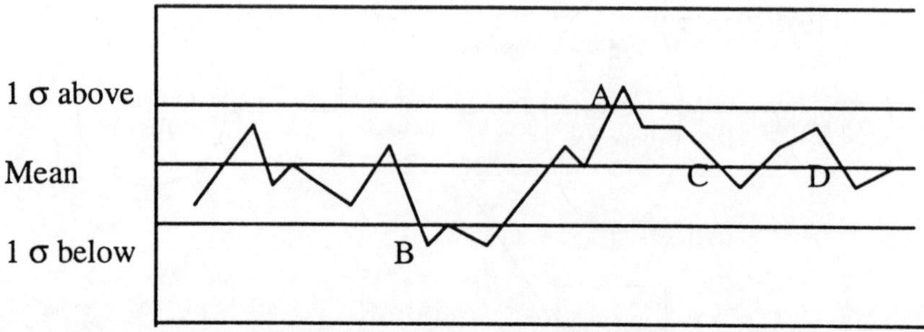

Fig. 9.2. Control chart depicting stale doughnuts discarded by shift

flowchart for a nationally known chain of doughnut shops. It shows that a customer's order progresses from a food item, to the beverage choice, to the carry-out or eat-in decision, to payment being rendered. In its full rendition, the chart highlights

- various steps in the process
- employees involved
- customers' needs at each step
- where quality is lost

Next, control charts are developed. Run charts (a.k.a. time sequence charts) depict plotted production-value statistics that show variation between units or over time; for example, the number of chips on a painted surface or the number of defective lightbulbs per shift. Time sequence charts are the primary tool of SPC. They describe mean response, statistically derived differences from the mean, like standard deviation, and actual values, as seen in figure 9.2 for the doughnut shop.

There are four decision variables in a control chart:

- sample size – number of doughnut shops
- number of samples – duration of control period
- sample frequency – measurement interval
- control limits – how many standard deviations to tolerate

The trade-offs from these variable choices influence the quality of the information. Clearly, more information is preferred, but larger samples and more observations raise costs. Quality-control specialists examine each occurrence outside the preset control limits to determine the causes of unfavorable (point A in fig. 9.2) or exceptional performance (point B in fig. 9.2). They also explore why several consecutive observations were

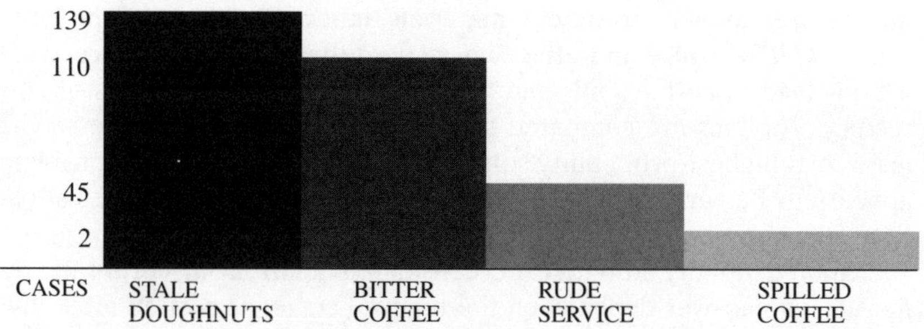

Fig. 9.3. Pareto diagram of quality failures at a doughnut chain (#s in hundreds)

above or below the central mean line (point C in fig. 9.2) or why the level abruptly changed from above the line to below the line (point D in fig. 9.2).

A third tool of TQM, a Pareto diagram, ranks a company's quality problems by frequency, as shown in figure 9.3 for the doughnut chain. The first three problems—stale doughnuts, bitter coffee, and rude service—affect future quality costs if customers shift to new purveyors as a result of poor quality; the fourth problem, spilled coffee, affects failure costs, either insurance related or liability.

Knowing the characteristics of quality failures is half the battle; learning to fix them is the other half. Cause-and-effect charts, the final TQM tool, help the doughnut chain identify sources of process variation: table 9.3 shows the source of coffee spill failures and their possible solution.[5] Any process element (see figure 9.1) may contribute to the

TABLE 9.3. Accountability Chart—Spilled Coffee

Source	Action	Remediation	Chances of Success	Cost
People	• Cups are too slippery • Drinking while eating or walking	Caution customers and monitor them	Low	Tarnishes friendly atmosphere
Material	• Cardboard is slippery when hot • Cups lack handles	Convert to ceramic cups	High	Ends carryout service (60% of trade)
Procedures	• Coffee is too hot • Cup lacks a lid	Lower heat setting	Very High	Customers may go elsewhere
Environment	• Customers pick up order at counter	Use waiters	Very High	Converts from fast food

quality breakdown: customers, materials, labor, machines, or the environment. The cause-and-effect chart describes for each source what actions lead to coffee spills and how they are fixed. Then costs of correcting problems are compared against the probability of success. The least-cost, highest-probability solution to the scalded-customer problem appears to be turning down coffee pots' temperatures. In other situations, the solution is less obvious.

Should quality initiative be considered apart from corporate renewal? The answer depends on the renewal stage, as seen in table 9.4, and on the present quality of the firm's products or services. During a crisis, there probably are insufficient time and resources to devote to quality beyond discussing the issue with employees. However, a company whose products lack quality may need to invest resources to make quality an issue, though in a crisis it is impossible to change product substance quickly enough. Employees are instructed to refocus on quality. Modest quality improvements, even in the heart of the crisis, can

- lower costs and raise productivity
- reveal to employees, suppliers, and customers the company's intention to persevere and cure past difficulties

In turnaround management, fewer constraints limit quality efforts. Developing an SPC database improves an understanding of the company's processes and provides the basis for planning a quality initiative with workers. Control charts developed from SPC data provide a framework for exploring reasons for quality success and failure. A full-blown TQM effort is possible during corporate transformation.

ISO 9000, a Worldwide Standard of Quality

The consumer/producer struggle has shifted, with the consumer gaining the upper hand. Consumers now insist on purchasing a low-cost, high-

TABLE 9.4. Applying Quality Initiatives during a Crisis

Renewal Stage	Quality Initiative
Crisis management	• Talk with employees about how the company's survival is affected by quality issues
Turnaround management	• Begin SPC effort • Get workers to participate in quality decisions
Corporate transformation	• Organize TQM teams • Develop relationships with suppliers • Begin education initiative

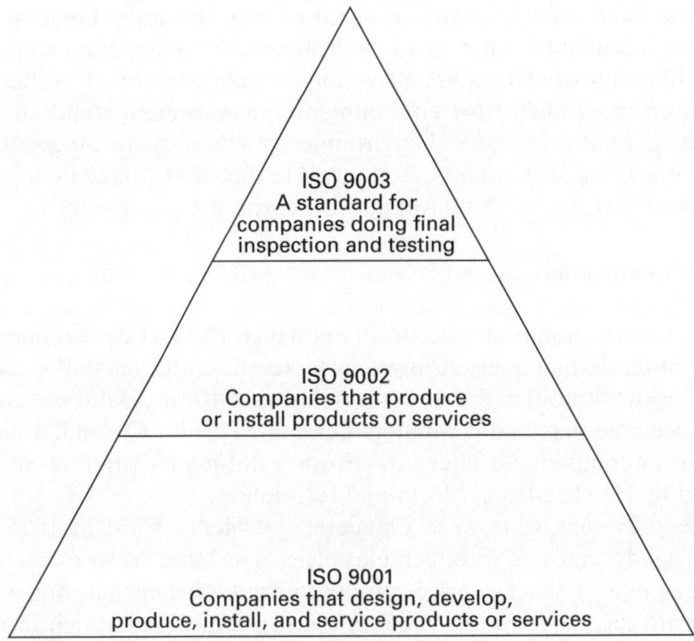

Fig. 9.4. ISO standards

quality product. Companies unable to deliver on these two conditions are shunned.

ISO 9000 has emerged as an international standard of quality systems. It pertains to both products and services. ISO 9000 compliance is frequently essential if a company want to be an approved supplier, (e.g., in the European Economic Community or to the U.S. Department of Defense). The standard ignores the quality of a company's products; instead, it evaluates the work processes and procedures used by the company to design, manufacture, market, and service its products. Intuitively, a company that meets the ISO 9000 standard should produce high-quality products, but that is no guarantee. Any one product of an ISO 9000 firm, especially new products or those using new technologies, may be of low quality.

There are three separate ISO 9000 standards, as shown in figure 9.4. Companies meeting the ISO 9001 standard are certified as capable of doing virtually every task at the highest possible standard of quality. By contrast, at ISO 9002 or 9003, a company is certified only regarding production and installation or final inspection and testing.

The International Organization for Standardization in Geneva, Switzerland, intends to turn next to environmental-management standards: ISO 1400. This would require all complying manufacturers to adhere to a minimum requirement for environmental-management standards. ISO 1400 would not replace local environmental laws; firms would still need to adhere to local standards. It is possible that ISO 1400 will appeal to consumers, while ISO 9000 will interest corporate purchasers.

Product Innovation

Product innovation is another form of quality. Product development is a constant battle that every firm wages to keep up with technological and market discontinuities that bring obsolescence to successful companies. Consider how personal computers devastated Smith Corona, a leading typewriter company, or later how Epson's dot-matrix printers were left behind by Hewlett-Packard's ink-jet technology.

Product platforms were pioneered by Henry Ford in 1925. The modern advocates of product platforms are Marc Meyer and Alvin Lehnerd (1997). Their work is premised on the belief that longevity of corporate success requires "a continuous stream of value-rich products that target growth markets. Such products form the product family (Meyer and Lehnerd 1997: ix). Meyer and Lehnerd argue that product families are planned with future generations of products in mind utilizing the same core technology. They term the core technology a product platform and define a product platform as "a set of subsystems and interfaces that form a common structure from which a stream of derivative products can be efficiently developed and produced" (x).

Meyer and Lehnerd advocate a type of corporate renewal wherein companies invest to keep their platforms current by renewing their core technologies. Intel's family of chips—the 8086, 286, 386, 486, and the Pentium processor—is an excellent example of how this strategy can succeed. Success is also found outside the high-technology arena. Swatch watches, a subsidiary of Société Micromécanique et Horlogère of Switzerland, used a product platform centered on two non-Swiss ideas: plastic and inexpensive. The platform has enabled the company to turn out 140 distinctive watch styles a year; in the decade and a half since its inception, sales have grown from $1.1 billion to $2.1 billion, and income has gone from a $124 million loss to a $286 million profit.

CHAPTER 10

Tax Considerations: Protecting Tax Attributes

This chapter turns to the consideration and concrete application of tax considerations to the process of restructuring and renewing distressed companies.

Net Operating Loss

Financial distress does not sneak up on firms; most companies slide downwards into bankruptcy over many years. Queen and Roll (1987) observe a steady erosion, for as long as five years, in the equity prices of public companies that ultimately fail. Investors react, among other things, to falling or negative net income. As a result, it is not uncommon for firms in bankruptcy or those seeking to restructure their debt obligations to have accumulated an extensive net operating loss carryforward (NOL). NOLs shield future income from taxation. Gilson (1997) observed for a sample of 111 public companies—fifty-one bankruptcies and sixty companies restructuring their debt—that the ratio of NOLs to total assets equaled 80 percent for the median firm and 1,200 percent for the average firm. He argues that this tax shield may be the most valuable asset of bankrupt and restructured firms.

Companies apply their NOLs to reduce future tax obligations. Under existing tax laws, tax loss carryforwards expire after fifteen years. Consider Stram Builders, which emerged from bankruptcy on December 31, 1996, with a $1 million NOL. If Stram's net income in 1997 equals $100,000, its tax liability equals zero after using a portion of its NOL, as seen in table 10.1. At the end of 1997, Stram's NOL is $900,000: the original $1 million less the $100,000 shielding income in 1997. Stram could earn out the entire NOL in the first year or use it up over the next fifteen years. From a present-value perspective, the NOL should be consumed expeditiously; hence, the capital structure of a company emerging from bankruptcy should avoid excessive debt in order to maximize reported income and thereby rapidly consume the NOL.

Section 382 of the Internal Revenue Code mandates a major reduction in a firm's NOL when it

- experiences a significant change in ownership
- changes its core business

A significant change in ownership occurs whenever any group of individual shareholders, each of whom owns at least 5 percent of the total equity of a company, increases its total ownership percentage by more than fifty percentage points. All less than 5 percent owners are aggregated into one 5 percent owner. Ownership changes occur for a number of reasons:

- stock-for-debt exchange
- debt composition affected by a bankruptcy plan of reorganization
- through purchase of equity

For example, suppose Stram Builders had three shareholders who each owned at least 5 percent of the equity after the reorganization was complete: person 1 began with 10 percent, person 2 with 20 percent, and person 3 with 0 percent of the original equity. Consider the three examples in table 10.2. In each case, there has been a change in control. In example 1,

TABLE 10.1 Stram Builders, Inc.: Net Income

Revenues	$12,500,000
Costs	$12,400,000
Net income	$100,000
Less the tax shield	$100,000
Taxable income	$0
Tax	$0
Net income after tax	$100,000

TABLE 10.2. Changes in Ownership of Stram Builders, Inc.

Shareholder	Original Ownership	Example 1	Example 2	Example 3
Person 1	10%	0%	0%	25%
Person 2	20%	0%	71%	60%
Person 3	0%	51%	0%	5%

a new shareholder has acquired 51 percent of the equity, which is a 51 percent (i.e., 51 percent–0 percent) increase; in example 2, an existing shareholder has increased his/her equity position by 51 percent from 20 percent to 71 percent; and in example 3, the three shareholders have increased their ownership by 60 percent (i.e., 25 percent + 60 percent + 5 percent − 10 percent − 20 percent − 0 percent). In each case, Stram Builders' tax attribute, its NOL, is reduced. Reductions in ownership are ignored because they do not balance one owner's ownership increase.

The NOL modification depends on three issues:

- whether the company is in Chapter 11 reorganization
- whether historic shareholders and creditors own at least 50 percent of the equity
- whether the company continues its historic business line

Table 10.3 summarizes the major situations. The most harmful status, version 3, is when there has been a change in both ownership and the business line: the NOL is forfeited in that case. If the firm remains in the same business but experiences an ownership change, versions 4a, 4b, and 4c, it keeps a portion of the tax attribute. In versions 4a and 4b, it retains the portion of its NOL equal to the firm's equity value just before the ownership change occurred, multiplied by the long-term federal tax-exempt bond rate. This tends to be a minimal dollar amount, since the equity value was probably depressed and the long-term tax-exempt

TABLE 10.3. Treatment of NOLs

Version	Ownership Change	Same Business	Chapter 11	Treatment of NOL
1	No	No	Yes or no	No change
2	No	Yes	Yes or no	No change
3	Yes	No	Yes or no	All removed
4a	Yes	Yes	No	Annual deduction equal to X (see below)
4b	Yes	Yes	Yes, and historic shareholders and creditors own <50%	Annual deduction equals X
4c	Yes	Yes	Yes, and historic shareholders and creditors own >50%	NOL is cut by 1/2 of debt forgiven plus deducted past interest over 4 years

Note: X = [Equity value just prior to ownership change] × [Long-term federal tax-exempt bond rate].

interest rate is generally very low. Alternately, in version 4c, if historic owners and creditors keep at least 50 percent of the equity, the NOL is reduced by one-half of any debt forgiven plus all interest on that debt deducted from taxes over for the past four years. "Historic" includes a period eighteen months prior to the bankruptcy. If there is an ownership change subsequent to bankruptcy (i.e., over the next two years), the entire NOL is lost.

Debt Forgiveness

Companies that restructure their debt or reorganize under Chapter 11 routinely decrease their indebtedness. Consider the income statement in table 10.4 for Titanium, which has total debts of $25 million at an average interest rate of 10 percent. Titanium has positive EBIT of $1 million per year, showing that its business operations cover their costs, but its net income is negative as a result of high interest payments. If depreciation and other noncash charges are assumed to be inconsequential, then Titanium's annual cash flow is approximately $1.5 million in the red. This outflow persists until Titanium's cash reserves or salable assets are exhausted or until its creditors refuse to extend additional credit.[1]

Titanium's problem is excessive debt. It should confront this issue while it has some negotiating strength, otherwise, when it has run out of unencumbered assets to sell or its creditors have refused to extend it additional credit, it must accept harsher terms. A number of alternatives are possible:

1. sell or merge company
2. liquidate
3. restructure indebtedness
4. reorganize company through bankruptcy court

The first option is the most desirable but the least likely if Titanium's problems are common knowledge. A potential buyer would realize that

TABLE 10.4. Income Statement for Titanium, Inc.

Net sales	$43,000,000
Operating costs	$42,000,000
EBIT	$1,000,000
Interest	$2,500,000
Net income	($1,500,000)

it could acquire the company for less by waiting for options 2, 3, or 4. Option 2 is probably desirable to only secured creditors. The last two options reduce the company's debt level. In a restructuring, old debt holders exchange their securities for new securities, either debt or equity.[2] If new debt, it is likely to have different interest rates, redemption years, and face amounts than the securities being replaced. If equity, the substituted shares may have a market value less than the par value of the securities being exchanged. In a bankruptcy reorganization, old debt and equity are expunged; holders of these securities receive a package of items that may contain cash, equity, debts, or even some of the firm's assets.

In either a restructuring or a bankruptcy, Titanium's $25 million of debts may be traded for:

1. shares of Titanium's stock (i.e., a stock-for-debt exchange)
2. new smaller debt issue
3. new debt issue of equal size but with lower interest rate

In the first two cases, some of Titanium's debts are forgiven; that is, creditors have released it from an obligation. The creditor claims this forgiveness as a deduction against its income, thereby reducing its income tax obligation. Correspondingly, Titanium treats the forgiven debt as income and pays a tax on this income.

Three major debt holders are banks, insurance companies, and mutual funds. Each organization has a different degree of willingness to accept equity in exchange for debt or writing down a loan amount in a restructuring. For one thing, banks are legally restricted from stock ownership: the Bank Holding Act prohibits bank holding companies from owning more than 5 percent of the voting stock of a nonbank company (the Bankruptcy Code disallows the issuance of nonvoting stock), Federal Reserve Board Regulation Y and the Glass-Steagall Act impose similar restrictions on non-holding-company banks. Equity obtained by banks in a restructuring or bankruptcy may disregard these rules for period limited to two to five years.

Loan write-downs negatively affect the calculation of capital levels for both insurance companies and banks. The amount by which assets are reduced is matched by a reduction in the institution's equity on the liability side. The bad loan problems of the 1980s led to tightened lender capital requirements. Institutions that agree to write off loans may be forced by these regulations to raise new capital, making it a less desirable strategy to the lender. Consequently, banks would prefer to receive a lower-interest-rate new loan with the same principal amount.

Mutual funds mark their assets to market daily. They may prefer a stock-for-debt exchange if they receive equity approaching the market value of their forgiven debt. In contrast, a debt write-off or acceptance of a lower-interest-rate debt instrument lowers market value and the net asset value of the mutual fund's holdings. These institutional characteristics guide the development of an offer sheet for a restructuring or a bankruptcy.

Section 61(a)(12) of the Internal Revenue Code describes "cancellation of indebtedness" (COI) income as the excess of the adjusted issue price of the canceled debt

- over the fair market value of transferred stock
- over the lowered debt level in a workout
- over the new market value of exchanged debt
- (if there is no market in the new securities) over the value of the debt instrument determined by discounting all payments of principal and interest with the discount rate set at the applicable federal rate for obligations of similar maturity

Table 10.5 describes similar calculations for Titanium. The original debt instrument is depicted in the "Original" column. If the firm replaces the debt by issuing new equity with a fair market value of $15 million, COI income equals the difference between the original face amount, $25 million, and the fair market value of the equity, $15 million. If in a workout the company's creditors agree to reduce the obligation to $20 million, then COI income equals $5 million, as seen in the "Workout" column. Finally, if a new debt instrument replaces the old security, then COI income is calculated using the market value of the new instrument, here set at $15 million because of the below-market interest rate.[3] If Titanium's securities are not traded in a market, the issue price of the security is calculated as the present value of future principal and interest payments using as the discount rate one of three federal interest rates (depending on the maturity of the security)

TABLE 10.5. Calculation of Cancellation of Indebtedness Income of Titanium, Inc. (securities that are traded in a market)

	Original	Equity	Workout	New Issue
Face value	$25,000,000		$20,000,000	$25,000,000
Interest rate	10%		10%	2%
Market value		$15,000,000		$15,000,000
Cancellation of indebtedness income		$10,000,000	$5,000,000	$10,000,000

Titanium must pay the full tax on its COI income if it is not in bankruptcy or insolvent (i.e., with book value of its liabilities exceeding the market value of its assets). With Titanium in Chapter 11, however, no taxes are due, provided that Titanium has tax attributes to reduce the COI income; they are used in the following order:

- NOLs for the current year
- NOL carryovers
- carryovers of the general business tax credit
- the minimum tax credit under the Revenue Reconciliation Act of 1993
- capital loss carryovers
- the basis of depreciable and nondepreciable assets
- passive activity loss or credit carryover
- foreign tax credit carryovers

These are reduced dollar-for-dollar except for the tax credits, which are reduced by 33 1/3 cents for every dollar of forgiven debt. Once the tax attributes are depleted, remaining COI income is taxable. Should Titanium be insolvent but not yet bankrupt, its COI income is expunged using its tax attributes only up to the amount of its insolvency.

The Stock-for-Debt Exemption

In a controversial and hotly debated decision, the Omnibus Budget Reconciliation Act of 1993 eliminated the stock-for-debt exemption in Chapter 11 cases completed after December 31, 1994, except for cases filed before December 31, 1993 (Rawden 1991). The exemption was a popular mechanism for escaping COI income taxation without losing tax attributes. It was a tax doctrine that developed judicially[4] but that Congress eventually recognized by amending the tax code three times to limit its applicability. Under the stock-for-debt exemption, COI income was not taxable if in the exchange the creditor received a material amount of the firm's equity. Materiality meant that creditors received at least 50 percent of the stock due them, and all unsecured creditors received only stock for their claims. Of course, if a creditor received 50 percent of the corporation's stock, a change in control limitation on the use of NOLs arose. The bankruptcy exception maximized the surviving NOL but was wiped out if a second ownership change occurred within two years. Efforts to reinstate the stock-for-debt exemption continue in order to strengthen companies emerging from bankruptcy.

In repealing the stock-for-debt exemption, Congress created a disincentive for distressed companies to deleverage their financial structure by issuing common shares to creditors. NOLs constitute a major asset, as illustrated by the example in table 10.6 using the company discussed in table 10.5. The enterprise value of Titanium is $28 million, assuming the existence of the stock-for-debt exemption and sufficient future earned income. In a reorganization plan creating a debt-free company, the $25 million of debt is canceled, and its holders receive new equity in the newly reorganized Titanium. If the APR is observed, the owners of the $25 million debt instrument own 25/28, or 89.3 percent, of the reorganized company, with existing shareholders receiving the balance.

Without the stock-for-debt exemption, if Titanium reorganizes as a debt-free company, it loses its NOLs, and its enterprise value shrinks to $21 million. In that case, continuing to assume that the APR holds, creditors receive 100 percent of the equity. Junior creditors and shareholders receive nothing in the reorganization plan. With management responsible for developing the new plan, it is probable that a marginally feasible reorganization plan with too much debt will be advocated.

Distressed Investing: Buying into a Troubled Situation

Distressed companies, both public and private, are vulnerable to acquisition by new investors. Public companies are susceptible to takeovers because (a) some established investors are forbidden, contractually or institutionally, from owning securities in distressed companies, and (b) other investors sell out to pursue safer investments; as a result, the debt and equity securities of distressed companies trade at significant discounts from book and historic values. In contrast, privately held distressed companies welcome new investors when they are the only source of fresh capital.

Participants in the distressed investing market include

- passive investors and mutual funds that purchase securities but do not participate in management
- active managers who gain control and institute a change program[5]

TABLE 10.6. Determination of the Enterprise Value in Chapter 11 of a Debt-Free Titanium, Inc. (in present values)

Asset	Valuation pre-1994	Valuation post-1994
Future business opportunity	$20,000,000	$20,000,000
Assets to be disposed of	$1,000,000	$1,000,000
Reduced taxation from NOLs	$7,000,000	
Total	$28,000,000	$21,000,000

This market is sizable and growing. Gilson estimates that in 1993, a nonrecession year, approximately $10 billion in distressed bank loans traded and twenty-seven investment companies[6] managed approximately $20 billion of funds devoted to the purchase of distressed securities (1995: 8).

Investors in this market target 25–35 percent annual returns on investment; some claim to have consistently earned 40 percent or more.[7] It is unclear if these returns are sufficient to compensate for the risks inherent in these investments. Academic proponents of efficient markets argue that market competition among investors achieves an equilibrium balance between risk and return (see Morse and Shaw 1988; Eberhart and Sweeney 1992). However, the efficient market may not extend beyond publicly traded securities. The private debt market is less competitive by virtue of its smaller average transaction size and its confidential nature, and it may provide canny investors with excess returns. In addition, the market for distressed securities has unusual risks independent of trading characteristics or market trends. These hazards diminish total investment returns and may lead to forfeiting the entire investment. Researchers inadequately account for these risks. Some of these perils are considered next.

The Risk of Forfeiture

The probability that a corporate renewal strategy will fail is relatively high. Turnaround managers estimate that upward of 75 percent of severely distressed companies are unsalvageable.[8] For example, reorganization is impractical if the turnaround manager is unable to ferret out a sustainable core business or identify a capable management team. In both cases, the pragmatic option is to sell or liquidate the business.

Sales of distressed businesses are problematic; sellers establish unrealistic price floors based on history, while buyers, knowing that the failed business is destined for the auction block, propose a low price ceiling. Sales do occur when parties are brought together. Many private investors hire turnaround managers to perform a due-diligence review and value estimation when they consider selling or buying distressed companies.

Liquidation is a more likely outcome. In fact, liquidations are preferred by investors with secured claims since, compared to reorganizations, they are relatively speedy and adhere strictly to the absolute priority rule (see "Lineup in Bankruptcy," chap. 2); by contrast, junior investors are likely to be wiped out in a liquidation.

Some distressed investors speculate on senior securities since that class of claims can best block a proposed plan of reorganization (see "Plan of Reorganization," chap. 2); in addition, senior creditors generally receive some payment, either in liquidation or reorganization, which reduces investment risk. More intrepid investors, on the other hand, purchase junior subordinate debentures or even common stock. If the turnaround is successful, they receive substantially greater returns as a result of their lower cost basis.[9] If the turnaround plan fails, however, these investors are likely to be wiped out.

The Risk of Hidden Liabilities

Environmental Claims

A secured note, such as a mortgage, is the least risky security in a bankruptcy, but investors in distressed debt may acquire liabilities from environmental damages under the Comprehensive Environmental Response Compensation and Liability Act (CERCLA). That act holds a lender liable for environmental cleanup costs if it forecloses on a property or becomes involved in its management.[10] The risk is compounded because a prior owner's behavior can invoke CERCLA on the current owner.

Fraudulent Conveyance Risk

One type of fraudulent conveyance occurs when a firm is made insolvent by an asset transfer for too little compensation. Some leveraged buyouts (LBOs) are examples of fraudulent conveyances. Legal action either before or after the filing of a Chapter 11 petition seeks to recover funds expended in the LBO for the benefit of the bankrupt estate. The Bankruptcy Code allows these suits for a one-year period after the LBO; state law may permit suits up to six years after the deal is completed. The defendant generally is the former stockholder who has received a cash payment in the LBO, but a suit may result in the loss of seniority to investors in distressed debt.[11]

The Risk of Contingent Claims

The balance sheet presents only the initial layer of corporate liabilities. Beneath the surface lies a second layer of contingent liabilities whose number and size are unknown until they are validated and their valuation estimated. Examples of contingent liabilities that affect the value of distressed securities include

- cigarette smoker health claims
- birth-defect claims from the children of women with IUDs

- environmental damages
- pension benefit claims
- negligence, security, and malpractice lawsuits

If a large contingent claim is accepted, the future recovery of the distressed security investor is less than originally anticipated.

The Risk of Being Outmaneuvered
Distressed security investors in a company entering Chapter 11 are at risk if another investment group acquires a controlling interest in a higher-security category in the bankruptcy-claims priority listing. The plan-blocking power of that group enables it to define the terms and conditions of the bankruptcy plan of reorganization. In that event, investors in securities lower in the hierarchy may receive less return than anticipated.[12]

CHAPTER 11

Advanced Accounting Issues

This final chapter examines advanced issues in implementing corporate turnaround and reengineering and addresses accounting issues germane to this process.

Cost, or managerial, accounting, provides detailed cost information on any cost object.[1] A cost object may be a product, a service, or even a customer. This information allows the manager to estimate the cost of making each product, delivering services, and ministering to each customer's needs. Managers use this framework to resolve critical managerial issues such as

- products
  1. where to set product prices
  2. how much floor space to allocate to each product
  3. which products to terminate, maintain, or expand
- services
  4. how to price various levels of service
  5. how much customer support to include with each service
- customers
  6. which customers to cancel because revenues are less than costs
  7. which customers should receive discounts and special promotions

But decisions are only as good as their estimated-cost information. Erroneous cost information misleads managers and results in myopic behavior, like selling products below cost or terminating lucrative customers while retaining unprofitable ones.

How can cost information be inaccurate or, more correctly, imprecise? The difficulty is that some costs are not clearly attributable to specific products, services, or customers; these are classified as indirect costs. Indirect costs exist in service, manufacturing, and merchandising businesses.

Corporate expenses bifurcate into

- direct costs—traced to particular products, services, or customers, such as materials, labor, or cost of goods sold
- indirect costs—related to those products, services, or customers for which it would be too costly to determine a precise allocation, for example, marketing, administrative, and general labor expenses

The cost accountant readily attributes direct costs to specific products; for example, silver pens cost $12 to buy or making plastic buckets requires $4.75 worth of labor. But allocating indirect costs is troublesome. Companies develop arbitrary systems to connect indirect costs such as property taxes, depreciation charges, or corporate overhead to particular products, services, or customers.

Managerial accounting uses "cost drivers" to distribute indirect costs to products, services, or customers. Cost drivers are elements that affect costs, such as labor expenses, dollar sales, or number of units produced. While the logic behind the use of cost drivers is generally clear, their allocation is imprecise. For example, a customer buying 18 percent of the units produced is assumed to be responsible for and is allocated 18 percent of indirect costs. When cost objects consume corporate resources at a rate deviating from the cost driver's presumed allocation, cost information becomes erroneous.

Table 11.1 presents a conventional cost allocation scheme for Castle Records, a retailer of CDs, cassettes, and videotapes.[2] Castle Records' direct costs, $828,000, include purchase of prerecorded CDs, cassettes, and videotapes and special shelving groupings to display products. Each of these easily is assigned to specific products. Indirect costs of $414,000 include salesperson labor, shrinkage, rent, and space conditioning. The

TABLE 11.1. Castle Records, Inc.: Operating Income ($ in thousands)

	CDs		Cassettes		Videotapes	
Sales		$764		$428		$103
Operating costs						
Direct—COGs	$480		$272		$76	
Indirect—50% of COGs	$240		$136		$38	
Operating costs		$720		$408		$114
Operating income		$44		$20		($11)

ratio of indirect to direct expenses is 50 percent. Castle Rock uses this percentage of cost of goods (COGs) to allocate indirect costs to products. This decision effectively assumes that labor time, shrinkage, and other indirect costs are generated by CDs, cassettes, and videotapes in direct proportion to COGs. Operating income of $53,000 is less than total financing costs, provoking a deficit at Castle Records.

Jason Ridgeway, a corporate renewal specialist hired by management at the behest of the lead bank worried about its loan, is listening to Susan O'Conner, Castle Records' CEO. Susan puts the product line profitability report shown in table 11.1 on her desk and says, "We'd better get out of videotape sales. I thought they would be an important new product segment for us, but I was wrong."

Jason shakes his head and replies, "I'm not sure, Susan. The problem may be with your cost information, not your strategy. Let me first compile a profitability report based on activity-based costing."

Activity-based costing (ABC) utilizes activities as its cost drivers to allocate indirect costs. Activities are events that give rise to costs, for example, when customers open up new accounts at a financial service company, when a manufacturing plant sets up a new product run, or when a merchandiser orders a shipment from the jobber. Five steps are followed in establishing an ABC cost system; these are listed on the left side of table 11.2, while the outcomes from performing the ABC analysis at Castle Records are listed on the right-hand side.

Jason visited several of Castle Records' retail stores and its small distribution center, where he talked with employees. He observed no

TABLE 11.2. Castle Records, Inc.: ABC Analysis

ABC Steps	Results at Castle Records
1. Find the activities (ask people what they do)	The major activity is helping customers search for products and providing product critiques. Shelving inventory and operating the cash register are low and proportional to COGs for each product.
2. Determine the cost of each activity	General labor expense equals $220,000.
3. Find a cost driver for each	Not every customer inquiry results in a sale, but every inquiry raises costs. The cost driver is inquiries.
4. Determine the indirect cost rate (#2 divided by #3)	Jason surveys two stores and estimates that, over one year, 110,000 inquiries occur for the chain. He estimates that inquiries cost $2 apiece.
5. Allocate costs to products	Based on Jason's survey, 70% of the inquiries concern CDs, 28% concern cassettes, and 2% relates to videos.

difference per unit between CDs, cassettes, or videos in time spent shelving, inventorying, or ringing up products. In fact, inventorying and checking out customers consumed very little time. Salespeople spent most their time helping customers making choices. CD buyers asked more questions than cassette buyers. Jason assumed that many people bought cassettes of CDs they already owned, while video buyers seemed to know what they wanted to buy and had fewer choices. Jason remarked, "If Castle Records only sold videos, each store could get by with only one full-time employee versus the current average of five."

Salespersons' salaries equal $220,000. The traditional costing system allocates these dollars proportionately with COGs; the ABC cost system allocates these dollars in proportion to their customer-inquiry activity. With 70 percent of the inquires concerning CD sales, 70 percent of indirect costs are allocated to CDs, and likewise for the other products.[3]

Jason suspected that stealing (i.e., shrinkage) varied across products. Videos are kept behind the counter and are difficult to steal, while CDs and cassettes are small and easily concealed. Aggregate bar code data reveals that two-thirds of total shrinkage, $20,000, is pilfered CDs, and the remaining one-third is stolen cassettes. With this knowledge, $30,000 of pilferage can be reassigned from the indirect to the direct cost category. Remaining indirect costs, $164,000, are allocated in proportion to COGs. Jason submitted his ABC cost system product-line profitability report, shown in table 11.3, to O'Conner.

Operating income is the same in both product-line profitability reports, $53,000; however, profit distribution is dramatically different among the three products. All three products are profitable using the ABC cost system, though their profit margins vary: 2 percent for CDs, 7 percent for cassettes, and 7 percent for videos. Susan's idea to curtail

TABLE 11.3. Castle Records, Inc.: Cost Breakdown ($ in thousands)

	CDs		Cassettes		Videotapes	
Sales		$764		$428		$103
Operating costs						
Direct						
COGs	$480		$272		$76	
Shrinkage	$20		$10		$0	
Indirect						
Salespersons	$154		$62		$4	
19.8% of COGs	$95		$54		$15	
Operating costs		$749		$398		$95
Operating income		$15		$30		$8

video sales was erroneous. Jason and Susan used the ABC report to persuade the bank that Susan's strategic plan was sound.

ABC analysis

- increases the percentage of costs attributed to cost objects
- seeks to learn more about costs by studying activities

Castle Records allocated $220,000 in labor charges to products. It also learned that many inquiries did not result in final sales: about 40 percent of CD inquiries, 20 percent of cassette inquiries, and 5 percent of video inquiries. Most nonsale CD inquiries concerned pricing; salesclerks were empowered to distribute special $3-off CD coupons to customers making a price inquiry. Further analysis might investigate profitability by type of CD, cassette, or video.

The Interview in Activity-Based Cost Systems

ABC accounting is most commonly applied in manufacturing settings, where indirect costs are a larger proportion of total costs. The gain from ABC is that more corporate resource costs are assigned to the cost object responsible for their expenditure. It is not desirable, given economic constraints, to empty the indirect cost pool and fully trace all costs. On the other hand, expensive resources, especially those where consumption varies across different cost objects, should be monitored, tracked, and assigned to particular products, services, or customers.

Accounting traditionally is viewed as a discipline with few human issues or connections. That certainly is a false impression, at least when it comes to ABC costing, where the accountant must work closely with employees throughout the enterprise. The critical first step in ABC costing is a series of interviews around the plant to determine what activities are associated with which costs. A special talent is needed to induce supervisory employees to articulate clearly what their areas do. ABC also asks the accountant to guide management actions in searching for ways to raise profits and lower costs. ABC is more than just a better scheme to develop product costs.

Consider the results, shown in table 11.4, of interviews conducted in a small midwestern manufacturing plant producing proprietary toothbrushes for grocery- and drug-store chains. Product offerings differ according to eight designs (straight or curved handles, adult or youth size, and ridged or straight bristles) and four colors. Knowing that design changes are expensive, demanding machine reconstruction and different tolerances, while color changes cost relatively less, the accountant focuses on design issues. Four principal activities are identified. Using the unit-cost estimates in table 11.4, the eight designs are charged individually for their contribution to corporate expenses from orders, machine setups, production, and shipping costs. The cost estimates describe the demands each product places on corporate resources. The analysis shows that youth-sized, curved-bristle brushes, which are ordered infrequently and in small numbers, are relatively expensive to produce, while adult-sized straight brushes with straight bristles are relatively inexpensive to produce.

Products should not be abandoned after an ABC exercise just because they are found to be more costly to produce or to yield a smaller per-unit or total profit than other products. Customers may demand the capability to purchase an entire line of product from a single manufacturer. Discontinuing unprofitable units might send customers to other vendors and lead to lower, rather than higher, profits.

Fresh-Start Accounting

Companies filing petitions under the Bankruptcy Code after December 31, 1990, and expecting to reorganize under Chapter 11 are required by the American Institute of Certified Public Accountants' Statement of Position 90–7 to use fresh-start accounting (FSA) for their financial statements.[4] Plans of reorganization and financial reports of companies newly emerged from bankruptcy contain FSA statements. Since FSA reports are asynchronous with conventional financial statements, their purpose and design is studied to avoid misinterpreting the statements and the companies they describe.

FSA rehabilitates a reorganized company's financial statements. The improvement is so profound that certain healthy companies, if allowed, would consider administering FSA. To restrict the application of FSA to companies with legitimate bankruptcy filings, two additional conditions must be satisfied before FSA is adopted:

TABLE 11.4. Manufacturing Activities

Activity	Total Cost	Allocation Measure	Unit Cost
Scheduling production	$1,000,000	Number of orders	$200 per order
Setting up machines	$5,000,000	Number of production runs	$250 per production run
Running machines	$10,000,000	Number of units produced	$0.16 per unit
Shipping and handling finished product	$3,000,000	Number of shipments	$30 per shipment

1. reorganization value of assets immediately before the date of confirmation must be less than the total of all postpetition liabilities plus allowed claims in the bankruptcy
2. holders of existing voting shares must receive less than 50 percent of new equity

Reorganization value equals the fair-market value of a reorganized company, excluding its liabilities. The first condition translates into the requirement that some prebankruptcy creditors are not fully repaid in the plan of reorganization. The second requirement means that, as a group, original shareholders own less than a majority of the new enterprise after reorganization. These conditions limit the application of FSA to companies that pressure creditors to compromise some portion of past liabilities in exchange for a greater than one-half ownership position.[5]

FSA is designed to serve the needs of financial-statement users like investors, the government, and creditors rather than those of the bankrupt company itself. Their principal need is to understand the company's financial evolution under bankruptcy. FSA achieves this clarification by distinguishing between transactions related to the reorganization and transactions conducted in the normal course of business.

The basic rules and procedures of FSA are demonstrated by example. Consider Sonic Boom, Inc. (Sonic), which filed for bankruptcy protection in February 1993.[6] Its plan of reorganization contains the financial statements mandated by FSA, which are reproduced here. The first statement, table 11.5, determines Sonic's reorganization value and compares it to the total of all postpetition liabilities. Most of the terms are self-explanatory, with the exception of the following:

TABLE 11.5. Reorganization Value of Sonic Boom, Inc.

Reorganization value	
Cash in excess of normal operating requirements	$100,000
Net realizable value of asset dispositions	$150,000
PV of cash flows of emerging entity	$1,625,000
Reorganization value	$1,875,000
Total postpetition liabilities	
Postpetition current liabilities	$625,000
Liabilities deferred pursuant to Chapter 11	$1,350,000
Total	$1,975,000
Excess of liabilities over reorganization value	$100,000

- "Cash in excess of normal operating requirements" is funds whose removal from current assets would not affect the firm's ability to operate; many companies nearing bankruptcy accumulate cash that they disburse later in reorganization
- "Net realizable value of asset dispositions" is funds secured from asset sales net of liabilities
- "Liabilities deferred pursuant to Chapter 11" is monies owed to historic creditors that are subject to compromise in the reorganization

Sonic's reorganization value is comprised of excess cash, money to be raised by selling assets, and future profits. Present value of cash flows for the emerging entity is determined using traditional valuation tools such as discounted cash flow or price-earnings ratios.

Sonic is a candidate for FSA, since its reorganization value is $100,000 less than the total of its postpetition liabilities. Liabilities include money owed before the bankruptcy (i.e., prepetition) and after the bankruptcy filing (i.e., postpetition).

Sonic's balance sheet, in table 11.6, details assets and liabilities for the firm operating in bankruptcy. The box at the bottom of the table

TABLE 11.6. Balance Sheet of the Debtor in Possession: Sonic Boom, Inc. ($ in thousands)

Assets		Liabilities	
Cash	$190	Liabilities not subject to compromise	
Accounts receivable	$423	Notes payable	$119
Inventory	$333	Accounts payable	$432
Other	$77	Other	$74
Total	$1,023	Total	$625
Net fixed assets	$666	Liabilities subject to compromise	$1,350
Goodwill	$311	Total Liabilities	$1,975
		Shareholders' deficit	
		Preferred stock	$800
		Common stock	$200
		Retained earnings	($975)
Total	$2,000	Total liabilities and deficit	$2,000

Note: Liabilities subject to compromise consist of

Secured debt secured by building	$100
Priority tax claims	$60
Senior subordinated secured	$490
Trade and other	$450
Subordinated	$250
Total	$1,350

details the components of the "liabilities subject to compromise" in Chapter 11 that are a major component of total liabilities. Claims are ranked in the hierarchical order prescribed by the Bankruptcy Code. It should be noted that since the reported $2,000,000 of total assets exceeds the emerging entity's present value of future cash flow, balance-sheet assets are overvalued. The negative retained earnings entry balances assets and liabilities but also represents the cumulative losses suffered by Sonic since inception. Negative retained earnings suggest that a substantial tax loss carryforward may survive the reorganization if this tax attribute is protected; it also warns that a plan of reorganization may dilute or extinguish the ownership of common shareholders.

A key element in crafting a plan of reorganization is to decide on a new capital structure. The split between new debt and equity depends on the needs and interests of various creditors, the earning capacity of the debtor, and on Sonic's debt capacity. The total value of liabilities and stock to be created in the plan, in table 11.7, equals the "continuing value of the enterprise" in the reorganization value table ($1,875,000 from table 11.5) less cash dispersed in the plan.

Representatives of the various classes of claims engage in fierce negotiations that culminate in a specific allocation of the continuing value of the enterprise. The topmost allocation goes to the postpetition current-liabilities category, which arises in the ordinary course of operating the business after the bankruptcy filing. This generally is protected by a superpriority lien conferred by the bankruptcy court in exchange for an agreement to lend or supply a company operating under protection of the Bankruptcy Code. Moreover, this class receives its entire undiscounted claim. A common strategy regarding postpetition liabilities, however, is to restate them and to bring them forward as continuing liabilities of the newly reorganized company. Creditors acquiesce to this arrangement because trade creditors want to continue to be the primary vendors and banks want to add a new permanent client. Sonic's remaining value ($1,875,000 less $625,000 of postpetition liabilities) is apportioned among

TABLE 11.7. Negotiated Reorganized Capital Structure ($ in thousands)

Category	Dollars	Notes
Postpetition current liabilities	$625	
Worker's compensation note	$60	
Senior debt	$120	
Subordinated debt	$525	
Common stock	$445	A plug
Total	$1,775	= 1,875 − 100 (paid out)

prebankruptcy liabilities. The Bankruptcy Code does not fix how these residual funds are split between old debtors and equity (see the discussion on the absolute priority rule in chap. 2). Generally, secured creditors are fully repaid before other creditors obtain any repayment.[7] Senior subordinated creditors are awarded more dollars than junior creditors. Equity classes have no recovery unless the estate has sufficient value. Certain creditors, such as banks, prefer nonequity securities, while other creditors, such as vulture investors, favor nondebt securities.

In Sonic's case, the capital structure outlined in table 11.7 is acceptable to all creditors. Sonic earmarks its $100,000 of excess cash to pay off the secured prepetition mortgage, which coincidentally has the same dollar value. The Worker's Compensation Note in the new capital structure balances a prepetition priority tax claim. Two classes of debt securities are created to distinguish among seniority and security differences in prior debt instruments. The value shown for the new common stock is derived as the difference between the total value of the enterprise (net of the cash payout) and the sum of other claims against the reorganized estate.

The securities envisioned in the reorganized capital structure are exchanged for the $1,350,000 in prepetition liabilities. After the exchange, the old liabilities are extinguished (wiped out). How these securities are divided among claimants is determined through guidance provided by the Bankruptcy Code, the negotiating skills of the various bankruptcy committees, and the status of the plan's proponents.[8]

All classes of claims in the Sonic bankruptcy accept the plan of reorganization proposed by the debtor in possession. The basic elements of the plan are described in table 11.8. There is enough value in Sonic

TABLE 11.8. Distribution of Reorganization Proceeds

Original Claim Category	Amount of Claim	Allocation Of: Cash	Debt	% of Equity	Dollars Received[a]	% of Claim Received
Secured debt	$100,000	$100,000			$100,000	100%
Priority tax claim	$60,000		$60,000		$60,000	100%
Senior debt	$490,000		$420,000[b]	16%	$470,000	100%
Trade claims	$450,000		$225,000	51%	$450,000	100%
Subordinated debt	$250,000			13%	$57,720	23.1%
Preferred stock	10,000 shares			7%	$31,080	N/A
Common stock	700,000 shares			13%	$57,720	N/A

[a]Equity values obtained from plug value of common stock in table 11.7 and percentage of equity received.

[b]Equaling $120,000 of senior debt and $300,000 of subordinated debt.

Boom to fully repay most of the classes of claims. The senior debt class, the first nonsecured, nonpriority class, is fully repaid with its allotment split among:

- all of new senior debt issue
- part of new subordinated debt issue
- some new equity

During negotiations, the senior debtors argued that their claim should be replaced entirely with a new senior note. However, the class agreed to the new mix, as described above, to facilitate the trade class also receiving debt securities; Sonic desperately needs the cooperation of these vendors if it is to generate sufficient cash flow to service the new debt instruments. In exchange, the senior debt holders received enough new equity, 16 percent, to bring their total recovery to 100 percent.[9] Trade creditors also are fully repaid, with half of their recovery as debt and half as equity.

Too little value remains for subordinated debt holders to recover their entire claim. Originally these claimants proposed keeping all of the remaining equity for themselves and not allocating any to the old equity classes, but they agreed to take less in order to accelerate confirmation of the bankruptcy plan.[10] Preferred and common shareholders receive 20 percent of the new equity, in part because all of the old stock was owned by management following an LBO and management is deemed essential to Sonic Boom's future.

The crux of FSA is knowing how to incorporate these reorganization transactions and related adjustments into Sonic's financial statements. These procedures are complicated. Students need to review them carefully.

The transition to FSA is presented in two parts. First, the three kinds of accounting entries that record the shift to FSA are shown in table 11.9. Second, these entries are incorporated into Sonic's balance sheet, shown in table 11.10. Instructional notes appear beneath each table to explain the steps.

Entries recording the shift to FSA in table 11.9 include

- entries to record debt discharge
- entries to record the exchange of stock for stock
- entries to record the adoption of fresh start reporting and to eliminate the deficit

"Debt discharge" refers to eliminating from the balance sheet liabilities subject to compromise (i.e., the prepetition obligations). These are

TABLE 11.9. Accounting Entries Required to Record the Plan and to Adopt Fresh-Start Accounting ($ in thousands)

Part I. Entries to Record Debt Discharge

Liabilities subject to compromise		$1,350	
	Senior debt	$120	
	Subordinated debt	$525	
	Worker's compensation note	$60	
	Cash	$100	
	Common stock (new)	$107	(80% of total)
	Additional paid in capital	$249	(80% of total)
	Gain on debt discharge	$189	plug
		$1,350	

Notes: Both sides of the "entries to record debt discharge" equal the total of prepetition liabilities, $1,350. The new common stock and paid-in-capital entries are 80% of their totals because old equity holders (preferred and common) receive 20% of the new equity. The split between common stock (new) and additional paid in capital is arbitrarily set at 30% and 70%, respectively. This is seen more clearly in Table 11.10. The gain on debt discharge is the difference between prepetition liabilities and the dollars of debt, cash, and equity awarded to those liabilities in the plan of reorganization.

Part II. Entries to Record the Exchange of Stock for Stock

Preferred stock (old)	$800		
Common stock (old)	$200		
	$1,000		
	Common stock (new)	$27	20% of total
	Additional paid in capital	$973	plug
		$1,000	

Notes: The values of old preferred and common stock are found in table 11.6. The value of new common stock equals the remaining 20% left over from part I above. Additional paid in capital equals the difference between the old preferred and common and new common stock given to old equity holders. Additional paid in capital here is not equal to one-fifth of the amount in part I; instead, the plug figure here plus the calculated additional paid in capital in part III equal 20% of total additional paid in capital.

Part III. Entries to Record the Adoption of Fresh-Start Reporting and to Eliminate the Deficit

		Notes
Inventory	$100	Written up to market value
Accounts receivable	($23)	Written down to expected recovery
Net plant	$75	Written up to market value
Reorganization value in excess of dollars allocable to identifiable assets	$34	= 1,775 − net fixed assets (new) − current assets (new)

TABLE 11.9 (Continued)

Gain on debt discharge	$189	From Part I
Additional paid in capital	$911	= (107 + 27) + (249 + 973) – 445 (to balance the total)
	$1,286	
Accounts to be set to zero		$311
Goodwill		$975
Deficit		$1,286

Notes: Asset values are reset at their market values. "Reorganization value in excess of dollars allocable to identifiable assets" represents those dollars in the "reorganization value" of the entity that cannot be attributed to specific tangible or identified intangible assets. The entry for additional paid in capital in part III equals the difference between the sum of common stock and additional paid in capital from parts I and II and the plug value of common stock in the reorganization plan. Following these adjustments, goodwill and stockholders' deficit are both set to zero.

balanced by cash paid out, debt securities issued, a portion of the new equity, and a gain on debt discharge.[11] "Stock for stock" involves the issuance of new shares of preferred or common stock to replace old stock. "Fresh start reporting and to eliminate the deficit" pertains to the revaluation of assets to market values and the elimination of goodwill and stockholders' deficit from the balance sheet.[12] The IRS does not allow firms to deduct for tax purposes any extra depreciation resulting from these changes.

The initial input to FSA is the prebankruptcy confirmation balance sheet in table 11.6. To this are added the three entries presented in table 11.9 to record debt discharge, stock exchanged for stock, and fresh start reporting and to eliminate the deficit. The end result is a reorganized balance sheet. These components and the final reorganized balance sheet are displayed in table 11.10. Notice several things about table 11.10:

1. The top and bottom of the table balance; that is, preconfirmation assets and liabilities are equal, as are the changes resulting from (a) debt discharge, (b) exchange of stock, and (c) fresh start reporting.
2. The middle three columns in table 11.10 are the separate parts of table 11.9.
3. The reorganized balance sheet is derived by adding across the table.

TABLE 11.10. Implementing Fresh-Start Accounting for Sonic Boom, Inc. ($ in thousands)

	Adjustments to Record Confirmation of Plan				
	Pre-confirmation	Debt Discharge	Exchange of Stock	Fresh Start	Reorganized Balance Sheet
Assets					
Cash	$190	($100)			$90
Accounts receivable	423			(23)	400
Inventory	333			100	433
Other	77			0	77
Total	1,023	(100)		77	1,000
Net fixed	666			75	741
Assets to be disposed of	0				0
Reorganization value in excess of amount due to identifiable assets				34	34
Goodwill	311			(311)	0
Total	2,000	(100)	0	(125)	1,775
Liabilities					
Not subject to compromise					
Notes payable	119				119
Accounts payable	432				432
Other	74				74
Total	625				625
Liabilities subject to compromise	1,350	(1,350)			
Worker's compensation note		60			60
Senior debt		120			120
Subordinated debt		525			525
Shareholders' deficit					
Preferred	800		(800)		
Common	200		(200)		
Common (new)		107	27		134
Additional paid in capital		249	973	(911)	311
Retained earnings	(975)	189		975 (189)	0
Total liabilities and deficit	2,000	(100)	0	(125)	1,775

4. Reorganized assets and liabilities are lower than preconfirmation assets and liabilities.
5. Goodwill and retained earnings both equal zero.

Statement of Operations

As Sonic Boom prepares to emerge from bankruptcy, it issues the statement of operations or income statement for the preceding period in table 11.11. The statement contains two additional sections, not in ordinary income statements, to reflect Sonic's bankrupt status: reorganization items and income tax benefits. The former includes professional fees paid in the bankruptcy, loss on the disposal of facilities, and cost of rejected executory contracts. The latter are dollars refunded from prior-year tax payments. The statement of operations is important because it is an input to the statement of cash flows, which is the key instrument to follow the cash.

Statement of Cash Flows

The task force assembled to create FSA believed that the statement of cash flows "is the most beneficial information that can be provided in the

TABLE 11.11. Statement of Operations for Sonic Boom, Inc. ($ in thousands)

Revenues	
Sales	$3,964
Cost and expenses	
Cost of goods sold	2,348
Selling, operating, and administrative	1,418
Interest	4
	3,770
Earnings before reorganization items and income tax benefit	194
Reorganization items	
Loss on disposal of facility	(55)
Professional fees	(75)
Provision for rejected executory contracts	(36)
Interest earned on accumulated cash in Chapter 11	7
	(159)
Loss before income tax benefit and discontinued operations	35
Income tax benefit	5
Loss before discontinued operations	40
Discontinued operations	
Loss from operations at discontinued segments	(116)
Net loss	(76)

financial statements of an entity in Chapter 11" (*AICPA Technical Practice Aids* 1990). The statement of cash flows for a company in Chapter 11 is analogous to that prepared for an ordinary company except for several key differences. Both statements contain

- cash flows from operating activities (normal conduct of business)
- cash flows from investing activities (purchase and sale of physical assets)
- cash flows from financing activities (raising funds)
- reconciliation of the net loss to net cash from operations (indirectly generating the cash flow from operating activities)

Investors use the statement of cash flows to identify the sources of cash inflows and outflows. Ongoing concerns are expected to have positive cash flow from operations, while their cash flows from investing and financing may either be positive or negative depending on important transactions during that period. Firms in Chapter 11 are more likely to have negative cash flow from operations[13] and may treat both cash flows from investing and financing as sources of funds.

Differences between healthy and failed firms' statements of cash flows are highlighted using Sonic Boom's statement in table 11.12. In the "cash flows from operating activities" section, the only variation from the statement for an ordinary company is the addition of an "operating cash flows from reorganization" section. Here, interest earned on the Chapter 11's cash hoard is reported, as is the cost of employing professionals to assist the bankruptcy. In the "cash flows from investing activities" section, the statement includes monies raised by the sale of assets as a result of the Chapter 11. This is likely to be a major source of funds. In the "cash flows used by financing activities" section, pre- and postpetition obligations are bifurcated.

The most dramatic changes in the statement of cash flows for a company in Chapter 11 appear in the reconciliation section at the bottom. Here, where the variance between net profit and cash flow are ordinarily reconciled, the bankrupt firm explains differences between its net loss and the net cash provided by operating activities. In addition to ordinary noncash charges, such as depreciation, from the income statement that are added back to reported net income or loss to restate it in cash terms, additional items are added back for the bankrupt firm to recapture charges such as rejected executory contracts, loss on the disposal of facilities, and loss on discontinued operations.

Benefits from FSA

FSA results in important advantages for companies emerging from Chapter 11:

- negative retained earnings are eliminated
- goodwill is eliminated
- assets are marked to market values

TABLE 11.12. Statement of Cash Flows for Sonic Boom, Inc. ($ in thousands)

Cash flows from operating activities	
Cash received from customers	$3,829[a]
Cash paid to suppliers and employees	3,617
Interest paid	(4)[b]
Net cash provided by operating activities before reorganization items	208
Operating cash flows from reorganization items:	
Interest received on cash accumulated because of Chapter 11	7
Professional fees paid for services rendered in connection with Chapter 11 proceedings	(75)
Net cash used by reorganization items	(68)
Net cash provided by operating activities	140
Cash flows from investing activities	
Capital expenditures	(12)
Proceeds from sale of facility due to Chapter 11	150
Net cash provided by investing activities	138
Cash flows used by financing activities	
Net borrowings under short-term credit facilities (postpetition)	75
Principal payments on prepetition debt authorized by court	(5)
Net cash provided by financing activities	70
Net increase in cash and cash equivalents	348
Cash and cash equivalents at beginning of year	7
Cash and cash equivalents at end of year	355
Reconciliation of net loss to net cash provided by operating activities	
Net loss	(76)
Adjustments to reconcile net loss to net cash provided by operating activities	
Depreciation	34
Loss on disposal of facility	55
Provision for rejected executory contracts	36
Loss on discontinued operations	37
Increase in postpetition payables and other liabilities	20
Increase in accounts receivable	34
Net cash provided by activities	140

[a]Cash received may be less than reported sales.

[b]Generally, interest is not paid in Chapter 11 except on secured obligations when there is sufficient cash flow and the court approves.

Doing away with the burden of prior net losses more fairly treats the emerging enterprise as a new entity. It also enables firms to be listed on stock exchanges that have positive-retained-earnings requirements. Canceling goodwill reduces future depreciation charges and increases future net income.[14] Insofar as future taxes are increased, this may not be a benefit, but many reorganized companies emerge with sizable tax loss carryforwards. Fairly valuing assets assists investors with little intimate knowledge of the firm or its industry.

Companies Ineligible to Use FSA

Companies not eligible to use FSA follow two conventions:

1. Liabilities that have been compromised are stated at present values.
2. Forgiveness of debt is reported as an extraordinary event.

Beyond these two changes, there are no changes in their financial statements.

Writing off Goodwill

When one company acquirers another at a purchase price that exceeds the value of its net assets, the acquirer's balance sheet receives an amount of goodwill equal to the overpayment. Obviously, the purchaser believes that the price is equitable, so the overpayment results for other reasons. One possibility is that some of the acquired firm's assets are understated or excluded from its balance sheet. Asset values are understated when, for example, accounting depreciation overstates market depreciation, leaving the residual value below true values, or after appreciation in equities held by the company. Assets are excluded from the balance sheet when the target company owns product brand names, valuable patents, or unexploited natural resources. Goodwill may also result when the target is worth more to the acquirer than its book value for reasons of synergy, market share, or market access.

FASB rules order companies to amortize goodwill over time, usually forty years. Companies prefer to expense (immediately deduct) these costs. Amortization, like depreciation, is a noncash charge that reduces net income. Prior to 1993, amortization provided no tax benefit since it was not deductible from federal income taxes. Despite its current deductibility, companies abhor goodwill since it

- retards reported income
- appears as a nonearning asset on the balance sheet

For most companies there is no recourse from these regulations; however, in exceptional situations, goodwill is written off

- when assets associated with the goodwill are sold, distributed to shareholders, or otherwise disposed of
- when net losses occur for several consecutive years and upcoming results are likely to be mediocre

The rationale for the first case is straightforward: if the assets are no longer owned, amortizing the goodwill is inconsistent. In the second case, it is unreasonable to fully amortize goodwill if the expense is not covered by a return on the assets.

Supermarkets General Holding Corporation (Supermarkets General) is a superb example of a company that wrote off its goodwill after informing the SEC and its accountants that its "total operating income of the next thirty-five years, the duration of the remaining goodwill, would not reach $600 million, the amount of goodwill remaining" (Feldman 1993). After-tax profits increased by $17 million a year for Supermarkets General as a result of the $600 million write-off. Applying Supermarkets General's price-earnings ratio, a $17 million a year increase in net income translates into a $200 million increase in its market value. Overall, this is a very satisfying situation for Supermarkets General.

Companies unable to write off goodwill, nonetheless, have a method to partially conceal it from investors. General Motors and USX both sold stock in subsidiaries that had assigned all their goodwill to the parent company, thereby making the new stock offerings more enticing to investors. RJR Nabisco Holdings attempted to duplicate this maneuver when it considered selling off its Nabisco subsidiary. Nabisco's after-tax profit, excluding goodwill, jumped from $179 million to $345 million in 1992, the year before the proposed offering. The SEC balked at RJR's stratagem and required it to explain why it had excised Nabisco's goodwill in any future offering statements (Randall Smith 1993).

Fudging Net Income with Inventory Overvaluation

Unscrupulous businesses manipulate their net income by deliberately or accidentally misrepresenting their inventory levels. Overestimated inventories result in an upward bias in net income, and vice versa.

Inventories are an asset represented on the balance sheet, while net income is derived on the income statement. The connection between inventories and net income is cost of goods sold, which itself is calculated as the sum of beginning-period inventories and cost of goods manufactured or purchased, less ending period inventories, as illustrated in table 11.13. If, instead of the numbers used in table 11.13, the firm overstates its ending inventories, for example putting them at $250,000, then cost of goods sold is reduced by $50,000, and net income increases by the same amount.

Numerous ruses exist to exaggerate inventory counts, including[15]

- generating fictitious paperwork, such as invalid purchase invoices
- including obsolete and scrap inventory as salable
- "bill and hold," where customers are billed early for purchases, which inflates revenues, while inventories are maintained and counted; profits rise for both reasons

Even professional accounting auditors have trouble detecting these frauds. Auditors apply two related operations to expose inflated inventories: a test for reasonableness, and observation of ending inventories.[16] The reasonableness test includes analytical procedures that provide evidence of accuracy, such as calculating financial ratios and comparing them with historic or expected values. These prudent calculations evaluate whether results differ from expectations and seek to uncover the source of these differences.

Year-end financial reports are generally audited and therefore are less likely to be overstated. In contrast, quarterly reports are unaudited and are more prone to deception. To assuage suspicions and fears, a turnaround manager should, upon accepting an engagement, immediately revalue inventories using independent agents.

Net income is also overstated if the cost of goods manufactured or purchased is underestimated. Fewer companies willfully distort these accounts.

TABLE 11.13. Deriving Cost of Goods Sold

Beginning finished-goods inventory	$125,000
Add cost of goods manufactured (or purchases for a merchandiser)	$575,000
Goods available for sale	$700,000
Less ending inventory	($200,000)
Cost of goods sold	$500,000

Conclusion

Globalization has shrunk the world and has contributed to an unprecedented extension of economic prosperity. It has also created a volatile and uncertain business climate in which the number of failing and underperforming businesses remains high by recent standards. Corporate renewal has an important role to play in such a world. It prepares businesses to master their difficulties with either statutory or nonjudicial remedies. A growing realization of this vital role spurs the movement to include corporate renewal in management education curriculum.

Corporate renewal benefits every company: those in severe distress and those with nonfatal problems as well as successful ones. Its message is often simple, though its prescriptions generally require training and preparation. Individuals with corporate renewal skills are identified and promoted within major companies, and some establish independent consulting practices. Over time, more and more persons will identify themselves as corporate renewal, turnaround, or restructuring specialists, and their skills will be highly valued.

The three parts of this book divide the structure of corporate renewal into foundation issues, basic processes, and advanced skills and knowledge. Each part discusses a variety of issues, and yet some readers will protest that the book has excluded important topics. Later editions of the book may well contain those topics. Corporate renewal is a new business discipline still defining its boundaries. Like other capstone fields, corporate renewal absorbs and assimilates important topics from every discipline.

Readers employing corporate renewal in a real-world setting must be reflective practitioners since every engagement is unique and requires its own path to be broken. For them, this book is simply the beginning of an interesting journey. Healthy travelers are flexible and ever vigilant for new opportunities. One excellent guide for the new and for the seasoned voyager is the Turnaround Management Association, which continues to grow and which offers a certificate to persons working in the corporate renewal field.

Acronyms

ABC	Activity-based costing
AFN	Additional funds needed
APR	Absolute priority rule
BJR	Business judgment rule
BPR	Business process reengineering
CBP	Cash balance pension
CEO	Chief executive officer
CERCLA	Comprehensive Environmental Response Compensation and Liability Act
COBRA	Consolidated Omnibus Budget Reconciliation Act of 1985
COG	Cost of goods
COI	Cancellation of indebtedness
D&B	Dun & Bradstreet
DBP	Defined-benefit plan
DCP	Defined-contribution plan
DFL	Degree of financial leverage
DIP	Debtor in possession
DOL	Degree of operating leverage
DSO	Days sales outstanding
DTL	Degree of total leverage
EAT	Earnings after taxes
EBIT	Earnings before interest & taxes
EBITDA	Earnings before interest & taxes + depreciation & amortization
EBT	Earnings before taxes
EOQ	Economic ordering quantity
EPS	Earnings per share
ERISA	Employee Retirement Income Security Act
EVA	Economic value added
EWS	Early warning system

FASB	Financial Accounting Standards Board
FIFO	First-in, first-out
FSA	Fresh-start accounting
GAAP	Generally accepted accounting principles
HRM	Human-resource management
IT	Information technology
JIT	Just in time
LBO	Leveraged buyout
LIFO	Last in, first out
LLC	Limited-liability company
MDA	Multiple-discriminate analysis
MVA	Market value added
NOL	Net operating loss
OEM	Original equipment manufacturer
PBGC	Pension Benefits Guarantee Corporation
POR	Plan of reorganization
PTA	Product-tracking analysis
PV	Present value
ROE	Return on equity
ROI	Return on investment
SBA	Small Business Administration
SEC	Securities and Exchange Commission
SGR	Sustainable growth rate
SPC	Statistical process control
TIE	Times interest earned
TQM	Total quality management
UCC	Uniform Commercial Code
WARN	Worker Adjustment and Retraining Notification Act of 1988

Notes

Chapter 1

1. No doubt smaller companies actively engage in corporate renewal, but less is heard about their exploits since the press focuses on larger companies.

2. The *New York Times* (1996a) titled it "A National Heartache," in its seven-consecutive-day series, "On the Battlefield, Millions of Casualties."

3. Jensen (1996:A29) argues that companies face the choice between corporate renewal and demise; the former has immediate costs but long-term benefits; the latter postpones the costs to the future and as a result magnifies their severity.

4. Triage denotes a scarce resources allocation scheme developed on the battlefield. Severe problems (beyond help) and those that are stable are ignored; only problems that respond immediately are assigned resources. Emergency medical care on the battlefield relies on the triage principle.

5. This book (Bibeault 1982) is out of print but is currently available through Top of the Hill Books at (781) 863–8639.

6. Contact the Economic Analysis Department, Dun & Bradstreet Corporation, 187 Danbury Road, Wilton, CT 06897, or call (203) 834–4711.

7. It would be more convenient to express failures in percentage terms. However, D&B adopted the failure rate convention long ago and it has stuck. The percentage of firms failing is found by dividing the failure rate by 100.

8. Personal bankruptcies are not studied to the same extent as corporate bankruptcies. The major determinant of personal bankruptcy is thought to be disposable income, which depends on the state of the economy. More attention is focused on understanding the determinants of mortgage and car loan defaults.

9. Several related research papers by the author are "The Determinants of Inter-Industry Failure," *Journal of Economics and Business* 41 (1989), and "Business Cycle Effects on State Corporate Failure Rates" (with Marjorie Platt), *Journal of Economics and Business* 46 (1994).

10. For the recent period, 1961–94, see figure 1.2. When the percentage change in gross domestic product (GDP) is directly compared with the failure rate, the correlation is −0.07; however, the correlation between these series is

0.14 and 0.19 with a one- and two-year lag on GDP, respectively. None of these correlations is statistically significant, though the 0.19 correlation is significant at the 0.15 level.

11. Judge Paul Glennon, who was chief bankruptcy judge in Worcester, Massachusetts, for twenty-six years, reports to me that this omission was frequently observed in many of the thousands of small-business failures that passed through his courtroom.

12. See Domowitz and Eovaldi 1980, and Hudson 1992. Christine Zavgren also has a fine unpublished paper looking at failure rates of industrial firms.

13. Another possible influence is the failure rate of industries. Platt 1989 suggests that bankruptcy moves systematically through the economy, affecting first one industry and then another. Also see the historical discussion of industry failure rates in appendix A of Platt 1985.

14. Unfortunately, D&B discontinued this effort in 1993.

15. D&B obtains its information from field agents. Criticism arises because gathering this information is not their principal occupation, nor are these persons trained business analysts.

16. Ineffective management is an excessively broad classification that probably includes many of the important categories in the D&B surveys.

17. Most of their responses concerned companies in the 1970s.

18. Bibeault's results would have been strengthened had he reported the percentage of all companies that are centrally organized to compare with the reported 44 percent of distressed businesses so organized.

19. Geographic decentralization remained constant pre- and postturnaround.

20. Merry Go Round, Inc., filed for Chapter 11 soon after its CEO's airplane crashed in Aspen, Colorado. Some felt that the deceased chief was irreplaceable or at least that he had not arranged for an heir apparent.

Chapter 2

The author is not a legal professional. Be advised that this and all other legal topics are discussed for the sole purpose of providing basic information and should not be construed as legal advice or counsel. Please consult an attorney on legal questions.

1. I have received considerable assistance on this section from Margaret Howard, Chris Ryan, and Sheldon L. Solow.

2. The merchant's bench is synonymous with the mercantilist period. With a bench to sell his/her wares, a person gained economic freedom from the landlords. When debts were not repaid (usually to the landlord), his troops or the sheriff would seize the merchant's goods and break his table, effectively putting him out of business.

3. Texas is a state notable for protecting a person's home against creditors, regardless of its size or worth. Similarly, Florida's homestead law exempts a resident's home and up to 160 surrounding acres of land from attachment by any creditor including the government. Laura Pedersen (1995) reports that Bowie

Kuhn, the ex-commissioner of baseball, bought a Florida mansion just before declaring personal bankruptcy to protect some of his assets.

4. Taxes are discharged in a Chapter 13 filing.

5. However, a liquidating plan can discharge past debts, creating a corporate shell with a questionable loss carryforward.

6. Mark S. Summers (1989) notes that Connecticut voted against the inclusion of bankruptcy laws in the Constitution because it did not allow the death penalty, as was then permitted in England.

7. This does not imply a dearth of failures. Some reports suggest that 5 percent of big-city adults in the late 1800s had spent some time in debtors' prisons.

8. Debt compromise and extension are generic phrases for reduction in amount and stretching of payments. For further discussion, see Platt 1984.

9. Venue is decided by the bankruptcy court judge where the case is filed.

10. Comparison shopping is especially important since the legal principle of *stare decisis,* or the rule of binding precedence, is replaced in the bankruptcy court system with a rule of persuasive precedence. With persuasive precedence, one bankruptcy judge's rulings are precedent in cases in another district, but since the two judges are equals, one cannot bind the other unless they are in a direct hierarchical relationship to each other.

11. Overall, 567,240 and 14,773 Chapter 7 and Chapter 11 petitions, respectively, were filed in 1994.

12. Chapter 13 bankruptcies are available to them.

13. Bridgeport, Connecticut, sought bankruptcy court protection, but the local bankruptcy judge refused to hear the case and instead told the city to either cut its services or raise its taxes.

14. An alternative to bankruptcy is to arrange a debt restructuring with creditors. However, credit agreements cannot be rewritten without nearly unanimous creditor consent. A smaller percentage of creditors must approve a bankruptcy plan than is required to alter the covenant on a bond issue. Creditors indicating their approval of a prepackaged plan before the Chapter 11 petition is filed are not legally bound to support the plan in bankruptcy. This and other risks may delay a prepackaged plan.

15. This rule is only significant for individuals since a corporation can never get a discharge in Chapter 7.

16. An example is the Texas International, Inc., bankruptcy, in which an examiner was appointed to act as a mediator between the creditors and management. See Platt 1994.

17. Aggregate fees paid to a Chapter 13 trustee must not exceed the federal employee's GS 16 salary level—about $80,000 in 1996.

18. Some judges have demanded time statements, believing 3 percent of distributions to be excessive payments.

19. These requirements come from Article 9 of the UCC.

20. Franks and Torous (1989) found in a majority of Chapter 11 cases studied that classes that should have been shut out of the case according to the APR actually received some repayment.

21. Sheldon L. Solow pointed out to me that "in rare cases, a court may allow a debtor to grant liens on property to secure post-petition loans ahead of a prior first lien."

22. An estate is created when a petition is filed to obtain relief under the Bankruptcy Code. It removes from the debtor all legal and equitable interest in property it possessed at the time of the filing. This is why the debtor becomes the "debtor-in-possession" and is not the owner.

23. For example, the general unsecured debt category may contain both trade creditors (vendors) and junior bond holders, or they can be separated into different classes.

24. The debtor must also file schedules of assets and liabilities and a statement of its financial affairs.

25. One reason why debtors might not want to serve on a committee is that their ability to trade securities is proscribed since the committee becomes an insider and is given access to all confidential information. Close competitors would not be eligible to serve on a committee. See Platt 1994 for a discussion of the role of a Goldman Sachs trader on the Texas International, Inc., Creditors' Committee.

26. Expenses in bankruptcy consume upwards of 5 percent of total assets (Altman 1984).

27. Thanks to Sheldon L. Solow for this detail.

28. As a result, in the LTV case, the court did not allow the company to pay medical insurance premiums for its retirees. The Retiree Benefits Bankruptcy Protection Act amended the Code to allow these payments.

29. In the WRT Energy case, the creditors' committee objected to the continued payment of officers' and directors' insurance premiums.

30. But if the debtor contests the involuntary petition, the single filing creditor must show that the debtor is generally not paying its debts as they become due.

Small businesses should probably be advised to have more than a dozen creditors.

31. The creditors who filed the petition might then be liable for damages.

32. The SEC is the sole body relaxing its rules for a distressed company. It treats distressed companies and those in bankruptcy as being "partially" discharged from SEC reporting requirements as a result of their diminished financial resources and the seriousness of the situation.

33. The entire case may center on cash collateral, particularly if the bank does not approve of the use of the cash, causing an evidentiary hearing to occur.

34. The code authorizes superpriority liens, which have unsecured status. If credit can not be obtained on that basis, a priming lien that elevates that lien above all others is authorized; however, existing secured creditors who are primed are entitled to adequate protection.

35. I appreciate the assistance given to me on this topic by Edward P. Collins at the Bank of Boston.

36. Market price is often difficult to determine so that it is not always possible to know when a fraud has occurred.

37. Again, I owe a debt to Sheldon L. Solow for this observation. See Section 548(a)(2) of the Bankruptcy Code.

38. The trustee was William Grabscheid.

39. Insiders in these cases are generally defined as corporate officers, directors, persons in control, or their relatives.

40. An agreement to repay old debts in exchange for continued shipment of inventories is less obviously a preference since something of value is received in exchange for the payment.

41. The Code invalidates certain types of claims, e.g., an excessive claim by an insider for services or an excessive penalty claim for breaking a lease. See Summers 1989: 97.

42. Sizzler, a restaurant chain, filed for bankruptcy in June 1996 primarily to shut about 150 underperforming restaurants by rejecting their leases.

43. There is a sixty-day limit for executory contracts and leases of residential real property or of personal property in Chapter 7 cases; in every chapter, a sixty-day limit applies to leases of nonresidential real property. These sixty-day limits may be extended by the court "for cause."

44. The landlord has a general unsecured claim that is limited to the greater of one year's rent or 15 percent of the remaining rent (up to three years' rent).

45. My thanks to Christopher Ryan, at Baker Hughes, Inc., a participant in over 1,100 bankruptcy cases, for this observation.

46. Most formerly bankrupt companies retain copies of their bankruptcy plans of reorganization for several years after emerging from bankruptcy. They will usually send out copies to students without charge.

47. In the LTV case, the exclusive period was extended for five years.

48. Small claims may be cashed out (i.e., fully repaid) in order to save the expenses of reproducing and mailing each participant a copy of the disclosure and plan of reorganization. Unimpaired classes are assumed to vote yes (Summers 1989: 130).

49. Trade creditors are unsecured. Some courts do not permit separate classifications.

50. This is not a matter of choice; secured claims cannot be classified with unsecured claims.

51. Banks do take equity in Chapter 11s, but they must usually sell these securities within three to five years.

52. See Platt 1994 for an example of the allocation of warrants to common stockholders.

53. I am indebted to Rick Mikels, an attorney with the Boston firm of Mintz, Levin, and Cohn, for explaining these complex relationships to me.

54. Creditors are not forestalled by law or practice from doing their own analyses. Their acquiescence to the DIP's plan may signal a willingness to cooperate and find amicable solutions.

55. Creditors may voluntarily choose to receive less in a reorganization. One motivation for doing so would be to keep a customer operating to purchase goods in the future.

56. The author is not a legal professional. Be advised that this and all other

legal topics are discussed for the sole purpose of providing basic information and should not be construed as legal advice or counsel. Please consult an attorney on legal questions.

57. Louisiana has adopted some of the UCC's articles.

58. Article 9 does not apply in real estate transactions, where proscribed by federal law, in transfer of wage claims or deposit accounts, in mechanics or artisan liens, or in the sale of accounts (such as accounts receivable) or chattel paper made to transfer a business to another for purposes of collection.

59. Chattel paper is the combination of a promissory note and a security agreement. It is writing showing that money has been paid and a security interest given or a lease made.

60. A filing is required for perfection except where excused in the UCC.

61. This may be disregarded in a Chapter 7.

62. In modern Europe corporate reorganization is regulated under companies acts, not bankruptcy acts.

63. Solvent firms needing to restructure can use any of these palliatives or may seek a scheme of arrangement with creditors with approval from 75 percent of creditors.

64. Liquidations are voluntary or compulsory. An automatic stay of creditors exist only on compulsory liquidations.

65. For fuller details, see *Turnarounds & Workouts Europe,* (1995).

66. Unlike U.S. practices, discharge takes seven years and is subject to court supervision.

67. Some totally insolvent firms choose the suspension of payments proceedings approach as an easier route to liquidation.

68. Two interesting books about the American bankruptcy process are Harlan Platt's *The First Junk Bond* (1994) and Sol Stein's *A Feast for Lawyers* (1989).

Chapter 3

1. The fourth-largest telephone company, LDDS Worldcom, uses credit scoring techniques before accepting new customers, as do credit card companies and lending institutions.

2. The market for risky debt (junk bonds), for example, cycles through interminable optimism, followed by unanticipated failures, and ending with interminable pessimism (*Wall Street Journal* 1995g: C2).

3. It is also possible using similar methods to predict successful debt restructurings, loan defaults, deleveraging of buyouts, and other related corporate actions. Credit card companies, for example, accept applications for new credit based on responses to several critical questions derived from this type of research.

4. Two additional important financial statements are the statement of retained earnings and the statement of cash flows. They are not presented here since the focus is on ratio analysis.

5. Even audited reports may be fraudulent. JWP, Inc., was charged in 1995

by the SEC with accounting fraud during the period 1991–92. The documents in question had originally been audited by Ernst & Young (*New York Times* 1995: D6).

6. The retail industry is the clearest example of this point. In 1995, factors (i.e., banks that buy in accounts receivables at a discount) announced their unwillingness to continue to accept (i.e., buy in) paper from Caldors and Bradless, two East Coast retailers. Within days following the announcements pertaining to each, the companies filed for bankruptcy. Factors react to the speed with which companies pay their existing trade debt and other circumstances. One way to get a handle on this risk is to calculate the average payables period. So as not to miss very old invoices, an aging analysis is also performed.

7. More precisely, energy and raw materials are additional inputs to the production process.

8. How long is the short run? The long run arrives when all costs are variable.

9. Operating profit is the correct measure here because the discussion does not involve the amount of debt used to finance the firm.

10. Matching failed and nonfailed firms is now a common approach in the bankruptcy literature.

11. Three zones of recognition are what most textbooks report for Altman's model; however, Altman concluded that 2.675 is the value to use when a single cutoff score is required.

12. Some analysts of public and privately held firms who want to rely on the same Altman model for all their companies despite the fact that market price data are missing for some of the companies replace market value of equity by book value of equity. Although theoretically incorrect, this idea probably works reasonably well in practice.

13. Another strategy would have been for Altman to have compiled a new sample of nonpublic companies and estimated model coefficients for them. But again, data limitations probably forestalled this approach.

14. These issues concerned the capitalization of leases, reserves, minority interests and other liabilities; captive finance companies; goodwill; capitalized R&D costs, capitalized interest, and deferred charges.

15. Sample size provides degrees of freedom and is directly related to the size of estimated standard errors.

16. Altman is aware of this problem. At one point he reestimated the original *Z*-score model without the total assets turn variable "to minimize the potential industry effect" (see Altman 1983: 124). Then in Altman and Izan 1984, he explored the industry-relative variable format.

17. See, for example, the industry data obtainable from Robert Morris and Associates.

18. This requirement of adding five to the total is a consequence of using SPSS^x in estimating the logit function.

19. Banks never recommend just one crisis manager to avoid potential liabilities that arise if the firm fails. Getting onto this short list is the best way for a crisis-management company to obtain engagements.

20. Crisis companies keep copious records of their activities to help document billing times and to aid in their defense in the event of any court actions.

21. Companies often classify all nonexecutive employees as direct costs; however, if they never lay off workers in response to fluctuations in sales, then labor is really a fixed cost or possibly a semivariable cost.

22. Credit terms of net 30 mean that a company must pay its suppliers about 12 times per year. If credit purchases amount to $1,200 per year or $100 per month, the company's accounts payable would on average equal $50 since they begin each month at $0 and end each month at $100. With net 60 terms, this same company pays its suppliers six times per year, and each check equals about $200. Accounts payable, in this case, would average about $100. Hence, as credit terms increase (more days outstanding permitted), the amount of credit available increases.

23. This method of presenting SGR is based on Eisemann 1984. He references Higgins 1977.

24. Gary Brooks first described this aphorism for me.

25. EVA is a trademark of Stern Stewart & Co., New York, NY.

26. These are referred to as positive net present value (NPV) investments.

27. Bennett Stewart (1994: 54) describes how Sloan established a 15 percent hurdle rate of return on GM's investments. In the same article, Jerold Zimmerman discussed a 1955 General Electric monograph in which they defined "residual income" as operating income less a capital charge that is fundamentally the same as EVA.

28. The next best measure, ROE, explained 30 percent (Stewart 1994: 75).

Chapter 4

1. Why companies extend new credit cards to these persons is interesting.

2. Judge Erithe Smith of the U.S. Bankruptcy Court in Los Angeles described this to me. She reports that most of the perpetrators owed sizable gambling debts and that they reported being forced to engage in these frauds.

3. Unscrupulous companies advertise that they can procure new credit cards for recently bankrupt persons, but these usually turn out to be debit cards that allow the person to charge against funds they have deposited in the bank.

4. Chapter 5 discusses accounting issues other than fraud.

5. Although not as much a guide to becoming a forensic accountant, another good book on the topic is O'Glove 1987. Also see Robertson 1993.

6. *Front Line,* the Public Broadcasting System show, has a fantastic video tape available of a program that details the scope and nature of the Phar-Mor fraud.

7. Proctor and Gamble claims that it was similarly victimized by Bankers Trust.

8. Smith and Lipin 1996 also reports that between 1991 and 1994, twenty-four of the thirty Dow Jones Industrial companies took restructuring charges amounting to $41 billion or 18 percent of their 1990 book value.

9. To say that shareholders sue is really a misnomer. Frequently, these suits are conceived by one or two shareholders who then turn the suit over to law firms noted for suing corporations.

10. In *Credit Lyonnaise Bank Nederland N.V. v. Pathe Communications Corporation,* 1991 Del. Ch. LEXIS 215, Allen C. (December 30, 1991).

11. Edelson (1995) presents a wonderful litany of directorial abuses in small businesses.

12. Regular corporations are known as C corporations. S corporations are generally small-business corporations (at least in terms of the restriction that there be fewer than thirty-six shareholders) that aid in the flowing of profit from the corporation to its stockholders.

13. At any point in time, tax rate differences may give an advantage to incorporation, but at a later time changes in tax rates may negate that superiority.

14. Wyoming was the first state to legalize LLCs, in 1977. Internationally, they have existed for some time: for example, GmbH's in Germany.

15. Going the other direction, it does create a taxable event.

16. At this time, a subsequent LLC is formed.

17. In fact, total PBGC liabilities are currently in the billions of dollars for plans that have terminated with insufficient assets. As of 1992, PBGC supervised over 1,800 terminated pension plans insuring over 335,000 participants.

18. One strategy that recently saved the pension plans of tailors was arranged by having the PBGC take over the multifirm plan that is currently underfunded by $250 million in this shrinking industry. The men's suit industry has fallen from 575 suit makers in 1986 down to 200 in 1996. If surviving firms all agreed to continue to make payments into the fund, the PBGC agreed to protect the pensions and would limit each suit maker's future liabilities.

Chapter 5

1. Finance theory (Gertner and Scharfstein 1991) notes that equity holders have little to lose from adopting risky strategies once their firms are so distressed that the value of the equity is gone. Further losses only diminish the recovery of creditors. Corporate control does not convert automatically to creditors at such times, allowing management to continue to pursue adventuresome schemes.

2. This analogue is the probably the oldest in the turnaround management/corporate renewal literature. I am unsure of its source but personally first heard it in a talk conducted by David Ferrari of Argus Management Company.

3. The wind huffed and puffed and only got the man to wrap his jacket more tightly around him. When it was the sun's turn, it shone warmly on the man's back, and he soon took off his jacket.

4. For an interesting account of his first three weeks on the job at Sunbeam, see Collins 1996.

5. Organizational development studies how change can make organizations more effective.

6. Although his original list is longer (eight steps), see Kotter 1995.

7. Rodgers, Hunter, and Rogers 1993 found strong evidence that change is more acceptable to employees when top management articulates a commitment to the change.

8. Clearly, in distressed cases there is no time for diplomacy.

Resistance may be active, such as sabotage, or passive.

9. A classic reengineering failure was an attempt by Schlitz Beer to increase its brewing capacity without building a new brewery by quickening the production time. The outcome was that more beer was brewed, but it tasted different, and consumers abandoned the brand.

10. Wyatt defines dysfunctional organizational change as "when shared values and behavior are at odds with long term health" (T. A. Stewart 1994).

11. Acs and Gerlowski (1996) call this bounded rationality.

12. Maslow's (1954) needs hierarchy is a commonly used framework for evaluating an individual's needs. His five primary needs are physiological (i.e., salary and working conditions), security (i.e., job security), belonging (i.e., teamwork), status (i.e., title and responsibility), and self-actualization (i.e., new challenges). Each person ranks differently along the Maslow five-point scale. Another model of human needs is McClelland's three-needs theory. He proposes three needs that workers strive to satisfy: the need for achievement, the need for power, and the need for affiliation.

13. Similarly, a new employee with an M.B.A. degree may enter three pay grades above a new employee with a B.A. degree.

14. Human capital, as devised by Gary Becker, describes the accumulation of knowledge after investments made in people.

15. It is important that the productivity gains more than pay for the new bonuses.

16. In 1995 IBM conducted a review of all wages. Afterward it cut some salaries by 40 percent (Hays 1995).

17. Thomas Flannery, David Hofrichter, and Paul Platten (1996) argue that gainsharing with workers yields future returns for the company that far exceed those possible with a profit-sharing contract.

18. The argument in this type of lawsuit is that the failure of a company results from the sudden and precipitous elimination of a long-standing banking relationship. Management is likely to contend that with sufficient credit its plan would have succeeded and saved the company.

19. Many large factors are subsidiaries of major banks such as Bank of America.

20. Brian Betker (1991) found in a study of seventy bankruptcy cases that unsecured creditors on average recover about 51 percent of their claims.

21. This source may be unreliable if the salespeople are commissioned or bonused based on sales and not on receipt of payment. Also, sales representatives who do not work for the company may have little incentive to share bad news with the company.

22. The company also gains in the long run if after reorganization, management remembers the willingness of the supplier to continue shipments during its crisis.

23. Pawnbrokers, who have existed throughout history, are a crude type of asset-based lender.

24. Asset-based loans are costly to administer and monitor, but the huge spread over prime is enough to more than offset these incremental costs.

25. This idea was brought to my attention by Dick Worth and explained in detail by Chris Ryan.

26. These ideas were gleaned from Edward P. Collins (1995) and are used with his permission.

27. GPA owns over 325 aircraft.

28. I appreciate the guidance of Don Margotta on this section.

29. The topic is even more urgent today as stock ownership gravitates toward mutual funds and pension accounts and when the equity ownership of managers is a small percentage of outstanding shares and of their own personal wealth. Attention to corporate control has grown since the hostile takeovers and leveraged buyouts of the 1980s.

30. Mutual funds and pension managers cast a majority vote in many companies.

31. A fiduciary is a person with a special relationship of trust or responsibility.

32. Judge Paul Glennon, a twenty-six-year veteran of the bankruptcy court, says, "The easiest mistake to fix is to keep the board of directors independent."

33. Wertheim's lucid Northeastern University working paper (1995) has guided my discussion in this section.

34. Interested students should pursue this topic with more readings, videotape lectures, and special classes. See, for example, Nierenberg 1984 and Fisher, Ury and Patton 1981.

35. Wertheim calls the former "rational decision making issues" and the latter "psychological issues."

36. The relationship is imperfect since negotiating disposition is also influenced by how powerful a party is. A high level of concern does not automatically produce a competitive disposition if the party has no strength; instead, to achieve its goals it may adopt a collaborative, helpful, or compromising disposition.

37. I have heard this comment repeatedly in conversations with Peter Stabell of Prudential Bache.

38. Some companies accomplish both types of production. For example, Stan Shih founded Acer Corporation in Taiwan as an input manufacturer to the personal computer industry. Over time he has grown his original equipment manufacturer (OEM) beyond a billion dollars in sales, at which point he integrated it upward into a final producer. Sales now exceed $5 billion a year (see *Fortune* 1995).

39. This issue is so important that most large accounting firms now have transfer-pricing departments.

40. Managerial economics textbooks discuss this issue in greater depth than is presented here.

41. Federal acquisition regulations (FAR) are long and complicated. Under one section of FAR, transfer prices, when the federal government is the final purchaser, may not be set above prices charged, for the same component,

to other customers. FAR does permit the use of "the lowest commercial price."

42. Some readers may find this presentation too brief, too quick, and with too many new definitions. They should do extra reading in a good managerial economics textbook.

43. This point is arguable. Many product differences are fanciful.

44. Solutions to the other two transfer-pricing cases are not presented here because of the amount of additional economics that would have to be added. Readers are directed to a good managerial economics textbook if they wish to pursue this topic.

45. Over 85 percent of companies engaged in some outsourcing as of 1995, while 93 percent said they anticipated doing so by 1998. See the *Management Accounting* (1995: 20) report prepared by the Economist Intelligence Unit and Arthur Andersen.

46. Some contracts allow for price escalations or reductions based on delivery volumes, volatility in raw materials markets, or the occurrence of anticipated events. If a firm requires even more certainty, the supplier may be willing to charge a slightly higher original price and in exchange give up future escalations.

47. A related issue is providing benefits that workers do not want or need. For example, if one spouse working elsewhere already receives health benefits, a worker receives little advantage from that benefit being duplicated by his or her employer. In fact, if two insurance policies exist, the worker may have to fight a bureaucratic battle to get paid by even one company.

48. Toyota is a counterexample of this. It outsources many of its designs to American design firms that have achieved a company-wide recognizable look.

49. See *Wall Street Journal* 1995a, in which Delta Airlines announces an agreement with Lockheed Martin to service L1011 aircraft.

50. Legally, the authority to issue accounting principles vests in the SEC. The SEC has transferred that power to the FASB.

51. Notes to the financial statements disclose these liabilities.

52. See *Wall Street Journal* 1995e. Caldor filed for bankruptcy despite being profitable because factors, the purchasers of Caldor's accounts receivable held by vendors, lost confidence in their ability to pay as its fixed asset rose while its working capital fell. This chain of events is becoming familiar.

53. This exposition is similar to that found in Stickney (1993: 24).

54. GAAP also permits weighted average inventory accounting, which is not mentioned in the text.

55. This reverses if the firm sells more units than it produces.

56. LIFO companies must report in the footnotes to their financial statements the amount by which their inventories would be higher had they used FIFO accounting or current costs. The difference between the two estimates is called the LIFO reserve.

57. Since the balance sheet and income statements in the financial reports are prepared using straight-line depreciation, they underreport the amount of depreciation actually taken with the IRS and thus they overstate the amount of taxes paid. The deferred tax item on the balance sheet cures this discrepancy.

Chapter 6

1. Another way to pose this question is to ask why certain companies tolerate a too large workforce? That is, why do some managers operate with more workers than are needed? Of course, some idleness is unplanned and results from bad management.

2. Two other types of industry structures, monopolistic and monopolistic competition, are excluded from discussion for simplicity's and brevity's sake.

3. It was not until Deming educated Japanese firms in how to lower their costs by analyzing production functions that American businesses understood that production functions are important to more than just theoretical economists. See chapter 8 for a further discussion on Deming.

4. Leontief's work was designed to alert the War Department during World War II to potential shortfalls in military production resulting from critical resource shortages. In the real world, most firms have "some" degree of resources adaptability; possible examples of a fixed-proportions production function include hospitals, which need at least one surgeon per operation, or trucking companies, which need at least one driver per truck.

5. Supplemental savings may result if layoffs are limited to the least productive members of the firm. Of course, who the better workers are may be unclear.

6. The EOQ formula is found by minimizing the total-cost curve. The formula is found in every financial management textbook, see for example, Ben-Horim 1987: 469.

7. Gardner Ackley, a member of President Johnson's council of economic advisors, emphasized that the aggregate labor market cannot clear with all workers employed. At best, perhaps a 2 percent unemployment rate is achievable, with these workers moving between jobs.

8. Carl Icahn acquired TWA and shortly afterward reduced the compensation of flight attendants by almost 50 percent. A strike ensued, but he hired replacement workers and imposed the new schedule on all attendants.

9. Strangely, it is socially acceptable to close down a plant in the United States and reopen it at a foreign site paying workers one-third of the American wage, but it is not acceptable to cut wages in the United States by one-third in order to maintain the domestic jobs.

10. Thomas L. Friedman (1996) argues that reactionary political movements arise in countries undergoing radical change from corporate renewal (or country renewal in the case of Eastern Europe). Reactionaries make promises that are "populist solutions that . . . defy globalization or ease its pain." Friedman contends that the Islamic regime elected to power in Turkey is an economic backlash against globalization and not a trend toward Islamic fundamentalism. The warning for other countries is that they must provide some safekeeping of the interests of the losers from corporate renewal.

11. Warnaco Group, which owns a number of successful businesses, decided to shut its Hathaway shirt business in 1996. The compensation of Linda Wachner, the CEO of Warnaco, was $16.57 million that year. According to

Stephanie Strom (1996), "half of the $16.57 million . . . would probably cover the annual payroll at Hathaway's principal factory in Waterville, Maine."

12. An example of bad downsizing is the Russian army in June 1941 as Hitler's armies invaded. Stalin had just murdered half of the officer corps and survivors were frightened and unwilling to make independent judgments. The Red Army collapsed until the fundamental issues were attacked and a new breed of officers emerged (see Figes 1996).

13. At the time, the president of General Motors was asked why his company did not make a good $10,000 car. He retorted that they did—"a three year old Buick." The company's attitude is clearly defined by this statement: the market must accommodate what GM wants to sell rather than GM producing the cars that the market demands.

14. Empirical evidence shows that managerial compensation rises as companies grow and become more complex (Platt 1987).

15. Undoubtedly, a diversified business may better weather the storm of adversity than a single product or industry company. However, the diversified business may delay taking drastic actions to fix a distressed business, thereby aggravating its difficulties.

16. Cash flow is the critical factor, not profits. But cash flow should be determined from an income statement that allocates overhead expenses using activity-based costing (see chapter 10) before individual product profits are determined.

17. Experienced turnaround managers such as Dave Ferrari of Argus Management describe the process as "peeling the onion." In the crisis-resolution phase, managers may not engage in formal rightsizing but in effect do so since they extricate the good businesses from the bad.

18. Some nonprofits supplement their revenues with transfers from endowment earnings or even from principal. Others are restricted by their charters or lack of adequate endowments from making transfers and are forced to run balanced budgets or to borrow money.

19. Rightsizing and downsizing are not procedures to please or benefit employees. They are designed to deal with the company's problems.

20. Contribution (not contribution margin) measures the number of dollars in fixed costs paid by an unprofitable business after paying its variable costs. In the short run, businesses with a positive contribution are generally kept running though in the long run they are shut down.

21. It is important that cutbacks not be pro rata: businesses that are doing well should be invested in, those doing poorly should bear the burden. However, this dictum can be violated if the failing business demonstrates unequivocally that its fortunes improve with further investment.

22. Many of these savings are produced in the next round of the rightsizing effort, where jobs to be filled are selected.

23. Combined businesses need to be oriented in the consumer's mind as providing the same support as when the businesses were discrete.

24. Todd Haines, who carried out a turnaround of a nonprofit theater, the Roundabout, in New York City, asked all fifteen employees in the subscription

department to identify the absolute minimum number of employees for their department. The answer was fifteen. Using zero-based budgeting, he ended up with three employees in that department (Wilson 1995).

25. Readers familiar with linear programming may grasp this concept as an exercise in the opposite direction of the usual LP investigation of how many more resources of each type are needed to expand output by one more unit. Here the issue is how many units of other resources are also not required if the firm lays off one unit of the prime resource.

26. Including the layoff of people and products that are linked to the initial plant layoff.

27. The Supreme Court ruled in 1996 in *O'Connor v. Consolidated Coin Caters Corporation* that the law still holds if the replacement worker is also older than forty. In the case in question, a fifty-six-year-old worker was replaced by a forty-year-old (Linda Greenhouse 1996).

28. This discussion assumes that the company's desperation index does not suggest that Chapter 11 is imminent. When a company is most desperate, ROI is an inappropriate metric for a severance program; in that case, any idea that saves the company cash is acceptable regardless of its ROI.

29. A more demanding view requires a severance program to earn a higher ROI than the program it displaces since downsizing reduces the scope of the company while regular investment grows the company.

30. Managers not familiar with present-value analysis and ROI may substitute the payback approach, which asks how long the firm must wait to fully recover dollars invested in the severance plan. The shorter the time period waiting for the invested funds to be returned to the corporation, the better the investment.

31. New hires may be offered a lower wage than retiring workers. Farmland Dairy paid experienced workers $14.50 per hour plus $8.00 per hour in benefits. It offered new hires their choice of $11.00 per hour or $8.00 per hour plus benefits (Steven Greenhouse 1996).

I am indebted to Henry Garelick for this interesting observation.

32. If 23 percent of older workers, in the example, are likely to voluntarily retire or die within a year, there are no net/net benefits from the severance program.

33. This is a useless question during a debate or argument since it precludes rational discussion.

34. Students have generally disagreed with me on this issue until they heard about the case of Malden Mills and its owner, Aaron Fuerstein. After a devastating fire that shut the facility, Fuerstein personally accepted the responsibility to continue to pay his workers until the plant could be rebuilt in about six months. Few students disagree that those workers have a higher level of ethical duty to Fuerstein.

35. I realized that there are strategic ways to fire executives after reading David Ewing's "How Bureaucrats Deal with Dissidents." I am unable to locate the original source for his work. He does cite a Department of Health, Education, and Welfare manual as the source of his ideas. The strategic approach described here is based on his work.

36. Executives at Xerox were even regimented in terms of the number of wall hangings. Each increase in executive rank allowed for one extra picture on the wall. A similar hierarchy existed at General Motors, where vice presidents were allowed one golf club membership, senior vice presidents two golf club memberships, etc.

37. The rate of return earned on invested dollars partially determines the unfunded dollar amount. As interest rates rise during the economic cycle, the unfunded component changes.

38. To fix their risk, employers are permitted to tie the promised return to the government interest rate and then to invest the funds in a government bond fund.

39. Two prior layoffs, both occurring in 1993, involved more workers: 60,000 at IBM and 50,000 at Sears, Roebuck, and Company.

40. Legislation is pending in Congress to permit the local Bell companies to offer long-distance service of their own. MCI and British Telecom are planning to merge and enter the local markets now served by the Baby Bells, on which AT&T had set its own sights.

41. Both received eight weeks' notification pay: laid-off workers must work for the eight weeks; those accepting the buyout receive the money without working.

42. When America's downsizing began in the early 1980s, companies offered even more generous benefits then these. For example, DuPont gave some of its managers as much as two years' pay to voluntarily leave.

43. © Harlan D. Platt 1996. All rights reserved.

44. A typical grocery store stocks approximately 2,500 items. Super stores may stock 4,000 or 5,000 items.

45. Mexican labor costs in 1996 were 25 percent of U.S. wages, up from 23 percent in 1995. Canadian labor costs equaled 90 percent of U.S. levels in both years.

Chapter 7

1. The disclosure statement is submitted for court approval first. There are strict legal requirements about the contents of the disclosure, but basically it "discloses" facts and details pertaining to the corporate history and the onset of the bankruptcy case. When the plan of reorganization is prepared, the disclosure is attached to its front. In rare instances, the two documents are kept separate.

2. Plans of reorganization are public documents that are obtainable either by visiting the resident bankruptcy court or by requesting a copy from the debtor.

3. Unfulfilled obligations with responsibilities on both parties.

4. A portion of the unpaid obligation becomes an unsecured claim in the bankruptcy proceedings.

5. Examples include Bradlees, Inc.

6. The first assignment is to see if the company has operating income. Without EBIT, a company cannot be reorganized, it must be liquidated.

7. By assuming away inflation and sales growth, a single year can represent all years. This technique can be followed with an actual company, but then the one year studied should not be the first year after the bankruptcy but should instead be a representative year.

8. The tax rate is assumed to equal zero for the bankrupt company since most reorganized companies have sufficient bankruptcy-related tax shields to not have to pay tax for many years (see chapter 9).

9. Equity may not have a cash cost, but it is not free. Historically, equity has earned about 6 percent more than debt. A simple scheme to estimate equity's costs adds this 6 percent to the cost of debt. A high-risk company should use a higher adjustment factor than 6 percent.

10. Senior lenders may extract an equity share to compensate them for time spent in court and for lost interest.

11. The assumption is invalid if the market perceives the reorganized company to have a high default risk, if the new debt carries a below-market interest rate, or if the debt has unusual provisions such as being payment in kind or having a long maturity period.

12. Additional value definitions include assessed value (obtained from tax rolls), value to an acquirer, going-concern value (the present value of future cash flows), and highest use value.

13. Some debt covenants mandate the repurchase of debt in the event of an acquisition.

14. Savings from shutting down an operation (salaries, rents, etc.) may be larger than the loss in asset value caused by the hurried liquidation.

15. Certain claims are identified but not quantified, such as litigation liabilities or claims arising from environmental damage.

16. See Section §361 of the Bankruptcy Code.

17. Certified Turnaround Professionals (CTPs) must demonstrate a minimum level of knowledge in bankruptcy law, Article 9 of the UCC, management, accounting, and finance.

18. A clear example is given in Stein 1989, where he describes how several expensive hourly billing attorneys argued for a protracted period of time over a $200 item.

19. Gilson (1995) reports that the bankruptcy judge even authorized Eastern to spend $200 million out of an escrow account established for unsecured creditors.

20. If they value the firm at less than $200, it may be cheaper to buy it from the new owners directly without using the warrants.

21. This purchase was actually made by a company formed by Holdings called Acquisition. It is ignored in the text for reasons of simplicity.

22. Including $12 million in accrued and unpaid interest. Note that the $327 million in long-term debt shown in the table for 1988 includes approximately $75 million of Old Debentures. Twenty-five million of this amount was a payment in kind obligation.

23. Only 80 percent or $73 million of the Old Debentures agreed to the swap; the remainder preferred to hold onto their original securities. See Platt 1994 for

a detailed discussion of reasons why security holders opt out of exchange offers and the consequences of those decisions.

24. The DIP financing is not included in this category because it is a postpetition, or after the bankruptcy, claim. The plan envisions a new bank line that will pay off the DIP lender.

25. Consider what security these banks held.

Chapter 8

1. Perhaps the earliest literature references to reengineering are Hammer (1990), and Sirkin and Stalk (1990).

2. This world view is echoed by Manganelli and Klein (1994).

3. As a historical note, during his lifetime Vincent van Gogh only sold one painting.

4. This system may not work best for all companies. For example, the noted French artist Hergé, who created the character Tin Tin, maximized his output by hiring other artists to fill in the backgrounds of his story frames while he personally drew the characters.

5. For example, a value-added tax is a tax placed on the excess of a product's selling price over its production costs.

6. The word *stages* is used here instead of *activity* to avoid confusion with activity-based costing. The reengineering lexicon uses the word *activity* to mean parts of the overall process to create a product; *activity* in ABC means a particular transaction that gives rise to overhead costs.

7. Aggregation is for simplification purposes only. In an actual reengineering exercise, the component activities in the three aggregate stages are treated separately.

8. Managerial accounting procedures allow managers to obtain detailed information for particular overhead expense items. However, in most small firms and many large firms, this detail is unavailable.

9. Products need not be physical; they include services and access.

10. For brevity's sake, Personal Computers, Inc., is treated as if it has only a single product or a single process.

11. Kingston Technology is a counterexample of this. Kingston is in second place in the highly competitive add-on memory business for personal computers, with 1994 revenues of approximately $800 million. Its policy is always to accept suppliers' prices, to pay early, and to never cancel an order. When business conditions improve and other vendors run out of supplies, Kingston always get its supplies. See *Economist* 1995.

12. Hammer and Champy argue that the first process to be reengineered should be the one in the "deepest trouble."

13. Some estimates place the reengineering failure rate between 50 and 70 percent (*Fortune* 1993). Arthur D. Little surveyed senior executives' satisfaction with reengineering: 16 percent were satisfied, 45 percent were partly satisfied, and 39 percent were unhappy (Noble 1994).

Chapter 9

1. Deming's life is documented in *Scuttle Your Ships before Advancing* by Richard Luecke (1994).

2. Related names include quality control, total quality control, and customer-driven management.

3. Later called Martin Marietta and now Lockheed Martin.

4. The earliest work on quality costs.

5. These may be represented diagrammatically but are shown here in a table in order to list solutions.

Chapter 10

1. Such a situation is not unusual in a developing field that has more potential than customers. The genetic-engineering industry in the late 1980s is one example.

2. Platt 1994 discusses the debt exchange process.

3. Before the Revenue Reconciliation Act of 1990, the face value as opposed to the market value of the new debt was used in making this calculation.

4. In the case *Capento Securities Corporation v. Commissioner,* 47 B.T.A. 691 (1942).

5. The line drawn between passive and active investors is somewhat ambiguous since certain investors adopt both strategies at different times. For example, the Fidelity Capital and Income fund is generally a passive investor in distressed securities; however, it took charge of the Macy's, El Paso Electric, and Zales bankruptcies.

6. Commonly referred to as vulture investors for their role in buying securities at a discount.

7. Based on conversations with several private investment fund managers.

8. Based on numerous discussions with some of the most widely respected turnaround managers.

9. Salomon Brothers found that junior subordinated notes of distressed businesses sold for 59 percent less than senior secured bonds (twenty-three cents on the dollar versus fifty-five cents) (Gilson 1995: 13).

10. Environmental law holds all current and prior owners liable. As a result, liability is not eradicated by selling off assets. Deep pockets, such as banks and investment funds, attract lawsuits.

11. Gilson (1995: 8) notes that these suits are generally settled for 10 cents on the dollar or less (see his footnote 20).

12. Platt 1995 discusses the drama and deceit of the plan-formulation stage.

Chapter 11

1. Accountants distinguish between job costing (custom projects) and process costing (mass-produced products) systems. Distinctions between the two categories are immaterial to the subject matter presented in this book.

2. This example is for a merchandiser and focuses on products. Most ABC applications are in the manufacturing sector.

3. CDs and cassettes require stocking and reshelving, while videos are kept behind the counter and are purchased upon request.

4. Additionally, companies that filed before January 1, 1991, but whose plans of reorganization are confirmed before June 30, 1991, must also use FSA. Prior to this opinion, companies in Chapter 11 received no specific instructions about how to modify their financial statements. Exempted from the filing requirement are companies that restructure their debt outside of Chapter 11, governmental organizations, and companies that liquidate.

5. The first condition is especially relevant. It is drawn from the Bankruptcy Code, which says that, when there is insufficient "reorganization value of assets," shareholders lose their legal right to any economic value from the entity without the consent of creditors. This is the absolute priority doctrine.

6. This example draws upon the *AICPA Technical Practice Aids* (1990), Section 10,460, Statement of Position 90–7, 19, 281.

7. This assumes that there is sufficient value in the assets securing the obligations.

8. In most instances, management (the DIP) has the exclusive right to formulate a plan of reorganization. However, if management fails to deliver a plan after sufficient time has transpired (the definition of what is sufficient varies by court and bankruptcy), the exclusive period lapses, and any group may propose its own plan. Competing plans are allowed with claims voting to accept any and all plans (as opposed to voting for one plan against another).

9. Actual recovery depends on the accuracy of the reorganization value calculation and on the market for the new security.

10. The cramdown procedure is a mechanism to gain plan approval. The Code says that to be approved, all classes must approve a plan. In situations where certain classes receive nothing, they are presumed to vote against the plan.

See Franks and Torous 1993, who report an abundance of cases of violation of the absolute priority rule, which results in some allocation to old equity holders.

11. The gain on debt discharge is found as the difference between the liabilities subject to compromise and the sum of cash, debt, and equity paid out to those creditors.

12. These adjustments are required to balance the increase in value created by the fictitious sale in the Chapter 11 plan of the company at the reorganization value level.

13. The corporate renewal specialist decides whether the firm can be saved with reference to its cash flow from operations.

14. Goodwill arises from an acquisition that paid more than book value.

15. Professor Michael Cottrill in Northeastern University's accounting department provided me with these insights.

16. Numerous frauds have been perpetrated even with auditors observing ending inventories. In one case, where large oil tanks were separated by great distances for safety reasons, a company pumped oil from one tank (already inspected by the auditors) to the next while the auditor was delayed and misled.

Glossary

Absolute priority rule (APR)—Arises in a cramdown when, to achieve fairness and equity, unsecured classes must receive their claim in full, or if they receive less than that amount, creditors junior to them must receive nothing at all. In a cramdown, equity classes receive nothing.

Administrative claim—Expenses associated with professionals hired to administer the bankruptcy case—including a trustee, an examiner, and attorneys or other professionals approved by the court—costs of preserving the estate, and some taxes. Section 507(a)(1) of the Code gives these claims first priority.

Allowed claim—A court-approved claim, debt or equity, that must be satisfied in some way in the plan of reorganization.

Automatic stay—A court order that takes effect coincident with the bankruptcy petition filing that prohibits collection actions by creditors. There are exceptions to the application of the order. It keeps one creditor from seizing an asset before other creditors are aware of the firm's financial difficulties.

Balance of equities test—Invoked in bankruptcy cases in which the debtor seeks to invalidate a labor contract. The Bankruptcy Amendment Act of 1984 requires management to demonstrate that all parties in the case suffer proportionately and that pain is not disproportionately affecting workers.

Bankruptcy—The acknowledgment of inability to pay one's creditors, resulting from a variety of causes, including financial, operational, legal, and strategic. It implies the state of being insolvent.

Bankruptcy Code—The current federal law, Bankruptcy Reform Act of 1978, governing issues pertaining to bankruptcy, effective as of October 1, 1979, with amendments.

Bankruptcy judges—Appointed by the president of the United States to fourteen-year terms, bankruptcy judges serve in one of ninety-four local federal districts. Each court has a chief judge and several associate justices. Officially the bankruptcy judge is a special assistant to the federal district court judge; in fact, in bankruptcy cases, the judge's authority is virtually absolute.

Bankruptcy petition—A document filed with the bankruptcy court that initiates the processes and procedures spelled out in the Bankruptcy Code. It automatically initiates protection of debtors through the automatic stay.

Bankrupt estate—The assets of the debtor, which include off-balance-sheet items such as intellectual property and settlements from lawsuits, that are subject to the jurisdiction of the bankruptcy court.

Bar date—The last date to file a proof of claim.

Best-interest-of-creditors test—Also known as fairness in a plan of reorganization; can be established by showing that every impaired class of claims receives no less than it would receive in a liquidation.

Cash collateral—Liquid funds or monies soon to be received by the bankrupt firm that are subject to creditor liens.

Chapter 7 liquidation—A trustee-supervised liquidation of a business or an individual. May be either voluntary or involuntary. Adheres to rules and guidelines promulgated in Chapter 7 of the Bankruptcy Code.

Chapter 9 municipal bankruptcy—The reorganization of a municipality following rules and guidelines established in Chapter 9 of the Bankruptcy Code.

Chapter 11 corporate reorganization—The reorganization of a business or an individual using procedures in Chapter 11 of the Bankruptcy Code. Old debts are discharged and a new capital structure is created following completion of the court-supervised reorganization.

Chapter 12 family farm bankruptcies—Family farm bankruptcies conforming to rules in Chapter 12 of the Bankruptcy Code.

Chapter 13 individual bankruptcies—Bankruptcies of persons limited to those with a regular income and secured debts of less than $350,000 and unsecured debts less than $100,000. Follows Chapter 13 in the Bankruptcy Code.

Chapter 22—A company that has filed Chapter 11 twice.

Collection laws—Laws determining which creditors may seize the assets of a debtor. They generally permit a first-come, first-served allocation of assets to creditors.

Confirmation—Bankruptcy court approval of a plan of reorganization. Requires both creditor and court approval. A confirmation hearing determines that claims are properly classified and that the plan is fair and feasible.

Consensual plan—A plan supported by all the participants in the bankruptcy. Normally this includes the debtor, secured creditors, unsecured creditors, and the equity class.

Consummation—Attests to the completion of all the commitments laid out in a plan of reorganization. See Effective date.

Corporate renewal—The comprehensive classification for all activities directed at the improvement of a company's condition. The subclassifications are corporate transformation, turnaround management, and crisis management.

Corporate transformation—The reassessment by a healthy company of its policies, procedures, and methods in an effort to improve its performance.

Cramdown—Court approval given to a plan of reorganization that has not received the consent of all classes of claims. Requires one class to approve the plan. Invokes the absolute priority rule in its application, since a junior class may not receive any payment in a cramdown unless all classes senior to it are fully repaid.

Creditors—Entities owed money by the debtor.

Creditors' committees—A committee appointed by the U.S. trustee to represent all creditors. Usually includes representatives of the seven largest creditors.

Crisis management—The implementation of actions designed to save a troubled company nearing extinction. In the worst case, it anticipates the firm's demise and seeks to maximize the recovery from liquidation or acquisition.

Debt discharge—The permanent elimination and removal of past debts by means of a court order. Depending on the type of entity filing for court protection and the chapter of the bankruptcy code used, discharge may or may not result. For example, companies liquidating under Chapter 7 are not discharged from their debts.

Debtor—The entity that has borrowed money, leased property, or accepted goods on credit.

Debtor in possession (DIP)—An entity filing for bankruptcy protection using Chapter 11 that continues to operate without the administration of a trustee.

Debtor reorganization—The notion of reorganizing a company by discharging past debts and allowing the firm to remain in existence.

Default—Failure to make a scheduled interest or principal payment. An act of default not remedied may precipitate an involuntary bankruptcy filing after a specified number of days.

Deprizio decisions—A court decision to expand the ninety-day preference period to one year in the case of an insider who benefits as a result of payments to a creditor on a debt that the insider had guaranteed personally. Arising from the VN Deprizio Construction Company case in the Northern District of Illinois in 1988.

Discharge—See Debt discharge.

Disclosure statement—A document accompanying the plan of reorganization in a Chapter 11 case. The disclosure must describe the causes of the firm's distress, the firm's current and historical financial condition, and the plan of reorganization.

Dissenting classes—Any class of claims rejecting the plan of reorganization. Equity classes not receiving any distribution from a plan of reorganization are presumed to vote no. Votes are counted according to two measures: two-thirds in dollar amount and one-half in number. Each class's votes are counted separately, and approval must be obtained from each class.

Downsizing—The purposeful reduction in the number of people, products, and plants in order to regain or sharpen a competitive edge.

Effective date—Date that a plan of reorganization is implemented; also called the consummation date.

Enterprise value—The postbankruptcy value of the firm as a going concern. The DIP is the usual source of this estimate. Also called the going concern value.

Equity classes—Holders of common or preferred stock.

Equity committee—A committee representing the interests of equity holders. Usually comprised of the largest shareholders or their representatives.

Examiners—A person appointed by the U.S. trustee to investigate and explore issues pertaining to the management of the bankrupt firm. Does not have operating authority, as would a trustee.

Exclusive period—A 120-day period of time during which management has the exclusive right to prepare and distribute a plan of reorganization. Acceptance of the plan must be carried out within 180 days. Courts generally increase the period when requested.

Executory contract—A contract that has not been fulfilled by both parties. Examples include leases and materials contracts. During a bankruptcy, they may be assumed, assigned, or rejected.

Fairness—Means that in a plan of reorganization, every impaired class of claims receives no less than it would receive in a liquidation. The class may receive less than it is owed, and the plan may deviate from the APR. Also called the best-interest-of-creditors test.

Fast-track bankruptcies—Created by the Bankruptcy Reform Act for small businesses whose total secured and unsecured debts do not exceed $2 million and who are not primarily in the real estate business. Cases are accelerated by not necessarily creating a creditors' committee, limiting the debtors' exclusive period to file a plan to one hundred days, requiring all plans to be filed within 160 days, and authorizing a "conditionally approved" disclosure and holding a combined disclosure and plan confirmation hearing.

Feasibility—A plan is feasible if the company is not expected to return to bankruptcy court soon (usually at least three years). Factors considered in determining feasibility include the prospective capital structure, expected cash flow, management's strengths and weaknesses, and the availability of credit.

Fraudulent conveyance—May be intentional or constructive. An intentional fraudulent conveyance involves a sale or transfer of an asset within one year of bankruptcy that was designed to hinder, delay, or defraud creditors. A constructive fraudulent conveyance occurs when an insolvent debtor receives less than a fair value in a transfer. The latter are used to rescind leveraged buyouts.

Fresh-start accounting (FSA)—Accounting rules pertaining to companies filing for bankruptcy after January 1991 or emerging after June 1991. Mandated use when the firm distributes 50 percent of its equity to new owners. Wipes out goodwill and negative retained earnings and values assets at market.

Going concern value—Value of a company if it continues to operate. Also called enterprise value.

Impaired class—A class of creditors whose legal or contractual rights are impinged by a plan of reorganization. Examples include classes receiving less than what they are owed, receiving what they are owed later than was expected, or receiving a lower rate of interest than had originally been contracted for.

Insolvent—

a) Technical insolvency—when a firm violates an indenture covenant
b) Insolvent in a bankrupt sense—negative net worth
c) Economic insolvency—the present value of future cash flows is less than debts

d) Equitably insolvent—too little capital to conduct its business (used in fraudulent conveyance actions designed to recover monies lent to LBOs).

Involuntary bankruptcy—A firm with more than a dozen creditors may face an involuntary bankruptcy petition from any three creditors who in the aggregate are owed at least $10,000 more than any lien they hold on the debtor's property. If there are fewer than a dozen creditors, the company need be in arrears to only one.

Leveraged buyout (LBO)—A transaction wherein a company's assets are used to secure loans used to acquire the company. Also called highly leveraged transactions, or HLT.

Liquidation, a.k.a. straight bankruptcy—The orderly sale of a firm's assets with the proceeds distributed to creditors. It is one of two possible outcomes from a bankruptcy filing.

Liquidation analysis—Performed during a Chapter 11 in accordance with the best-interest-of-creditors test to determine what a creditor would receive in a liquidation.

Motion to lift stay—Motion filed in bankruptcy court by a secured creditor who is attempting to foreclose against an asset upon which it holds a lien in contradiction to the automatic stay provision.

New value—The infusion of money, usually by the equity class or an outside group, into a bankruptcy case in exchange for a large share of the ownership of the emerging company. Results in a contradiction of the absolute priority rule.

Plan of reorganization—A document prepared by any of a number of parties describing the treatment proposed to resolve prior indebtedness by the issuance of new securities, sale of assets, or the infusion of new value. To be approved, each class of claims that are impaired must vote for the plan.

Preference—A transfer to a creditor in the ninety days preceding a bankruptcy filing (one year for an insider), not in the ordinary course of business, that results in the creditor receiving more than it would have received in a liquidation.

Prepackaged bankruptcies—Plans that obtain necessary creditor approval before the company has filed a bankruptcy petition. It is easier to change debt indentures in bankruptcy than out of court.

Priority claim—A class of claims designated by the Bankruptcy Code that includes administrative expenses and back wages, which are paid in a reorganization after secured claims.

Reengineering, a.k.a. business process reengineering or process reengineering—The reevaluation and assessment of the components of a business process to determine the value of each step and to prepare a redesign that substantially improves its outputs, such as costs or productivity.

Reorganization—Another word for a restructuring. It also describes a bankruptcy reorganization in which a failed company sheds its old obligations and issues new securities and emerges as a new company.

Restructuring—The transformation of a corporation's divisions into a different structure, generally performed in order to reduce costs or simplify the line of control. A financial restructuring exchanges new securities (i.e., bonds with lower interest rates, payment in kind, or longer maturity or equity) for existing debt securities or negotiates improved payment terms.

Secured creditor—A creditor with a lien or collateral protecting its debt.

Single-asset case—A bankruptcy case in which the debtor has a single asset, usually a piece of real estate.

Substantive consolidation—Combining the estates of two or more debtors before devising a scheme to repay their creditors. Some parties may argue for it with parent and subsidiary companies.

Superpriority liens—The highest category of claims described in the Bankruptcy Code, including new creditors who provide the bankrupt firm with money or supplies to continue doing business.

341 meeting—A meeting called by the U.S. trustee early in the bankruptcy to allow creditors and shareholders to question the DIP regarding the detection of assets, disputed claims, and the debtor's financial condition.

Trade claims—Claims arising from the ordinary purchase of goods and materials by the debtor.

Trustees—Persons appointed by the U.S. trustee to liquidate or manage the debtor's assets. They are appointed in some Chapter 11s and all Chapter 7s and 13s. Names are drawn from a pool of eligible persons.

Turnaround management—The process of discovering what ails a company and the design and implementation of activities to ameliorate major issues.

Uniform Commercial Code (UCC)—The Uniform Commercial Code is law in every state except Louisiana. It establishes law governing commercial transactions. Article 9 governs consensual liens commonly called security interests.

Unimpaired class—A class of claims that has been fully paid out or that has received new securities that in no way infringe on the class's legal or contractual rights.

Unsecured creditors—Creditors whose debts are not secured or collateralized by any assets.

U.S. trustee—Appointed by the U.S. attorney general, one for each of twenty-one geographic regions subdividing the country. They initiate the bankruptcy proceedings and may appoint a trustee to supervise a case.

Voluntary bankruptcy—A bankruptcy petition filed by an individual, corporation, municipality, or partnership of and by its own volition.

Voting rules in bankruptcy—To be approved, a plan of reorganization must receive from each class of claims an affirmative vote from at least two-thirds of each class in dollar amount and one-half in number. Only votes that are cast are counted. The equity class's votes are counted only in terms of number.

Vulture investors—Persons buying up securities of bankrupt or distressed companies at low prices. Vultures may seek to gain control of companies by blocking plan approval by using the voting rules of bankruptcy.

References

ABI Bankruptcy Reform Study Project. 1995. "The Professional Turnaround Manager's Case for Exclusivity." ABI National Symposia Series, *Exclusivity and DIP Management: Too Much Debtor Control,* October 17.

Acs, Zoltan, and Daniel Gerlowski. 1996. *Managerial Economics and Organization.* Upper Saddle River, NJ: Prentice Hall.

AICPA Technical Practice Aids. 1990. "Financial Reporting by Entities in Reorganization under the Bankruptcy Code." Chicago: Commerce Clearing House.

Altman, Edward I. 1995. *Corporate Financial Distress.* New York: Wiley.

———. 1984. "A Further Empirical Investigation of the Bankruptcy Cost Question." *Journal of Finance* 39 (4), 1067–89.

———. 1983. *Corporate Financial Distress: A Complete Guide to Predicting, Avoiding, and Dealing with Bankruptcy.* New York: Wiley.

———. 1977. "Predicting Performance in the Savings and Loan Association Industry." *Journal of Monetary Economics* 3 (4), 443–66.

———. 1968. "Financial Ratios, Discriminant Analysis, and the Prediction of Corporate Bankruptcy." *Journal of Finance* 23 (4), 589–609.

Altman, Edward I., Robert Haldeman, and P. Narayanan. 1977. "Zeta Analysis: A New Model to Identify Bankruptcy Risk of Corporations." *Journal of Banking and Finance* 1 (1), 29–54.

Altman, Edward I., and H. Izan. 1984. "Identifying Corporate Distress in Australia: An Industry Relative Analysis." Working Paper, New York University, New York.

Altman, Edward, and H. Izan. 1982. "Identifying Corporate Distress in Australia." Australian Graduate School of Management, Sydney.

Altman, Edward I., and James La Fleur. 1981. "Managing a Return to Financial Health." *Journal of Business Strategy* (Summer), 31–38.

Argenti, J. 1976. *Corporate Collapse: The Causes and Symptoms.* New York: Wiley.

Aszodi, Ilona. 1995. "Liquidation and Bankruptcy: An Overview of Regulations." *Turnarounds & Workouts Europe,* September 1, 4 (5), 1.-1, Washington, DC: Beard Group.

Bailey, Henry J., III, and Richard B. Hagedorn. 1988. *Secured Transactions: In a Nut Shell.* Eagan, MN: West Publishing.

Baumol, William J. 1952. "The Transactions Demand for Cash: An Inventory Theoretic Approach." *Quarterly Journal of Economics* 65 (November), 545–56.

Beaver, William. 1977. "Financial Ratio as Predictors of Failure." *Journal of Accounting Research* 4 (suppl.), 71–111.

Ben-Horim, Moshe. 1987. *Essentials of Corporate Finance.* Newton, MA: Allyn and Bacon.

Berle, Adolf, and Gardner Means. 1932. *The Modern Corporation and Private Property.* New York: Harcourt Brace World.

Berton, Lee. 1996. "Many Firms Cut Staff in Accounts Payable and Pay a Steep Price." *Wall Street Journal,* September 5, A1.

——. 1994. "Tech Concerns Fudge Figures to Buoy Stocks." *Wall Street Journal,* May 19, B1.

Best Practices in Corporate Renewal: Wyatt's 1993 Survey of Corporate Renewal. 1993. Chicago: Wyatt Company.

Betker, Brian. 1991. "Risk and Return of Securities of Financially Distressed Firms." Working Paper, Ohio State University, Columbus.

Beyer, William G. 1993. "Pension Plans and Pension Benefit Guaranty Corporation." In *The 1993 Bankruptcy Yearbook and Almanac,* ed. George Putnam. Boston, MA: New Generation.

Bibeault, D. B. 1982. *Corporate Turnaround: How Managers Turn Losers into Winners.* New York: McGraw-Hill. Reprint, Top of the Hill Books, 1996.

Black, Pam. 1994. "Limited Liability: A Safer Strategy for Small Business," *Business Week,* July 18, 47.

Blumenstein, Rebecca, and Nichole M. Christian. 1996. "Parts Dispute to Remain Despite GM-UAW Accord." *Wall Street Journal,* March 25, A5.

Blumenstein. Rebecca, and Gabriella Stern. 1996. "GM's Parts Purchasing Fuel Labor Strife." *Wall Street Journal,* October 1, A2.

Bradshaw, Keith. 1996. "New Union Contract Lets GM Trim Labor Costs." *New York Times,* November 3, A29.

Branch, Ben, and Hugh Ray. 1992. *Bankruptcy Investing: How to Profit from Distressed Companies.* Chicago: Dearborn Trade.

Buchholz, Barbara B. 1996. "The Bonus Isn't Reserved for Big Shots Anymore." *New York Times,* October 27, 5A, 10.

Bulkeley, William M. 1993. "Kendall Square Demotes 3 Top Officials, Restates Its Revenue Sharply Downward." *Wall Street Journal,* December 2, A3.

Cainzos, Jose Antonio, and Enrique Valera. 1995. "Insolvency under Spanish Law." *Turnarounds & Workouts Europe,* May 1, 4 (3), 1. Washington, DC: Beard Group.

——. 1995. "Suspension of Payment Issues." *Turnarounds & Workouts Europe.* September 1, 4 (5), 1. Washington, DC: Beard Group.

Carlton, J. 1996a. "Apple Posts Record $740 Million Loss, More Than Doubles Planned Layoffs." *Wall Street Journal,* April 18, B6.

——. 1996b. "Apple's Losses to Stretch into 2nd Period." *Wall Street Journal,* January 18, B7.

Collins, Edward P. 1995. Comments presented at a seminar at Northeastern University, Boston, MA, April 27.

Collins, G. 1996. "For a Struggling Sunbeam, Shock Therapy." *New York Times,* August 11, C1.

Cork Report. 1982. "Insolvency Law and Practice Report of the Review Committee." London: HMSO, CMND 8558.

Crosby, Philip B. 1979. *Quality Is Free.* New York: McGraw Hill.

Current Legal Issues Facing Massachusetts Based Companies in 1993. 1993. "Fiduciary Duties of Directors of Financially Troubled Corporations." Boston: Skadden Arps Slate Meagher & Flom, June, 39–56.

Damato, Karen. 1995. "Retire with the Biggest Pension Check You Can Get." *Wall Street Journal,* April 14, C1.

Data Disk. 1996. Cambridge, MA: Cambridge Planning and Analytics.

Davis, Bob. 1995. "G-7 Summit Expected to Boost Support for Proposals to Help Insolvent Nations." *Wall Street Journal,* June 13, A4.

Deming, W. Edwards. 1982. *Out of Crises.* Cambridge, MA: MIT University Press.

Domowitz, I., and T. L. Eovaldi. 1980. "The Impact of the Bankruptcy Reform Act of 1978 on Consumer Bankruptcy," *Journal of Law and Economics* 4, 803–35.

Drucker, Peter. 1993. "The Five Deadly Business Sins." *Wall Street Journal,* October 21, A32.

Dun & Bradstreet Corporation. 1995. *1994 Business Failure Record.* New York: Dun and Bradstreet.

——. 1994. *Business Failure Record.* New York: Dun and Bradstreet.

——. 1993. *Business Failure Record.* New York: Dun and Bradstreet.

——. 1984. *Business Failure Record.* New York: Dun and Bradstreet.

——. 1965. *Business Failure Record.* New York: Dun and Bradstreet.

Eberhart, Alan C., and Richard J. Sweeney. 1992. "Does the Bond Market Predict Bankruptcy Settlements?" *Journal of Finance* 47 (3) (July), 943–80.

Economist. 1996. "DIY in Germany," March 2, 60.

——. 1995. May 20, 64.

Edelson, Harry. 1995. "Dispatch from the Boardroom Trenches." *Wall Street Journal,* February 6, A26.

Eisemann, Peter C. 1984. "Another Look at Sustainable Growth." *Journal of Commercial Bank Lending,* (October), 47–51.

Epstein, David G. 1995. *Bankruptcy and Other Debtor Creditor Laws.* Eagan, MN: West Publishing.

Ewing, David. "How Bureaucrats Deal with Dissidents."

Faltermayer, Edmund. 1992. "Is This Layoff Necessary?" *Fortune,* June 1, 71–86.

Feldman, Amy. 1993. "Goodwill Games." *Forbes,* September 13, 58.

Ferrari, David. 1995. Argus Management Company. A talk presented at Northeastern University, Boston, MA.

Figes, Orlando. 1996. "The Eastern Front." *New York Times Book Review,* February 18, 1.

Fisher, Roger, William Ury, and Bruce Patton. 1981. *Getting to Yes.* Boston: Houghton Mifflin.

Flannery, Thomas, David Hofrichter, and Paul Platten. 1996. *People, Performance, and Pay.* New York: Free Press.

Fortune. 1995. October 30, 187–204.

——. 1993. "Debunking the Failure Fallacy." September 6, 21.

Franks, Julian R., and Walter N. Torous. 1993. "A Comparison of the U.K. and U.S. Bankruptcy Codes." *Journal of Applied Corporate Finance* 6 (1), 95–103.

——. 1989. "An Empirical Investigation of U.S. Firms in Reorganization." *Journal of Finance* 44 (3), 747–70.

"Fraud Awareness Auditing," 1993. In *Auditing,* ed. T. Robertson. Burr Ridge, IL: Irwin.

Friedman, Thomas L. 1996. Foreign Affairs Column. *New York Times,* July 17, A23.

Front Line (Public Broadcasting System). 1992. "How to Steal $500 Million." PBS Video.

Garvin, David A. 1988. *Managing Quality: The Strategic and Competitive Edge.* New York: Free Press.

Gertner, Robert, and David Scharfstein. 1991. "A Theory of Workouts and the Effects of Reorganization Law." *Journal of Finance* 46, 1189–1222.

Gilson, Stuart. 1997. "Transactions Costs and Capital Structure Choice: Evidence from Financially Distressed Firms." *Journal of Finance* 52 (1) (March), 161–96.

——. 1995. "Investing in Distressed Situations: A Market Survey." *Financial Analysts Journal* 51 (6) (November–December), 8–27.

——. 1989. "Management Turnover and Financial Distress." *Journal of Financial Economics* 25 (2), 241–62.

Gilson, Stuart C., and Michael R. Vetsuypens. 1993. "CEO Compensation in Financially Distressed Firms." *Journal of Finance* 48 (2), 425–58.

Gomes, Lee. 1996. "Herein Lies the Worm: Apple's Shipments Still Decline." *Wall Street Journal,* October 18, B4.

Greenhouse, Linda. 1996. "Justices Say Age Bias Can Occur Even When One Over-40 Worker Replaces Another." *New York Times,* April 2, A14.

Greenhouse, Steven. 1996. "A Startling Ad Campaign Highlights the Bitterness of a Strike at a Dairy." *New York Times,* March 4, D5.

A Guide to Limited Liability Companies. 1994. Chicago: Commerce Clearing House.

Hambrick, D. C., and S. M. Schecter. 1983. "Turnaround Strategies for Mature Industrial-Product Business Units." *Academy of Management Journal* 26 (2), 232–49.

Hammer, Michael. 1990. "Re-engineering Work: Don't Automate, Obliterate." *Harvard Business Review* 68 (4) (July–August), 104–12.

Hammer, Michael, and James Champy. 1993. *Reengineering the Corporation.* New York: Harper Business.

Hamstreet, Clyde. 1995. "Going beyond the Numbers." Presented at Turnaround Management Association Meeting, Atlanta, GA, October.

Hanley, Robert. 1996a. "Employees Anxious as Layoffs Loom." *New York Times,* January 4, C2.

——. 1996b. "Today 2,000 Fewer AT&T Employees." *New York Times,* January 17, C2.

Hays, Laurie. 1995. "IBM Plans to Slash Secretaries' Salaries in Sweeping Review." *Wall Street Journal,* May 18, B1.

Higgins, Robert C. 1995. *Analysis for Financial Management.* 4th ed. Burr Ridge, IL: Irwin.

——. 1977. "Sustainable Growth: New Tool in Bank Lending." *Journal of Commercial Bank Lending* (June), 48–58.

Hofer, C. W. 1980. "Turnaround Strategies." *Journal of Business Strategy* 1 (1) (Summer), 19–31.

——. 1975. "Toward a Contingency Theory of Business Strategy." *Academy of Management Journal* 18 (4), 1–17.

Hofer, C. W., and M. J. Davoust. 1977. *Successful Strategic Management.* Chicago: A. T. Kearney.

Hoffman, R. C. 1989. "Strategies for Corporate Turnarounds: What Do We Know about Them?" *Journal of General Management* 14 (3), 46–66.

Holden, Benjamin A. 1996. "It's Named PacifiCorp, but the Atlantic Is Beckoning." *Wall Street Journal,* March 26, B8.

Horngren, Charles T., George Foster, and Srikant M. Datar. 1994. *Cost Accounting: A Managerial Emphasis.* 8th ed. Upper Saddle River, NJ: Prentice Hall.

Hudson, J. 1992. "The Impact of the New Bankruptcy Code upon the Average Liability of Bankrupt Firms." *Journal of Banking and Finance* 16, 351–72.

Jensen, Michael C. 1996. "Capitalism Isn't Broken." *Wall Street Journal,* April 1, A29.

——. 1993. "The Modern Industrial Revolution, Exit and the Failure of Internal Controls Systems." *Journal of Finance* 48 (3) (July), 831–80.

Jensen, Michael C., and Kevin J. Murphy. 1990. "Performance Pay and Top-Management Incentives." *Journal of Political Economy* 98 (2), 225–64.

Johnston, David Cay. 1996. "A Hybrid Pension Plan Gains Ground." *New York Times,* February 25, B11.

Juran, Joseph. 1951. *Quality Control Handbook.* New York: McGraw Hill.

Keller, John. 1996a. "AT&T Posts Loss of $2.68 Billion." *Wall Street Journal,* January 26, A3.

——. 1996b. "AT&T Will Eliminate 40,000 Jobs and Take a Charge of $4 Billion." *Wall Street Journal,* January 3, A3.

Kim, T., and T. Mauborgne. 1995. "Trust in Me." *Economist,* December 16, 100.

Koopmans, Henk A. 1994. "Financial Insolvency: Three Approaches Are Available." *Turnarounds & Workouts Europe,* November 1, 3 (4), 1-1. Washington DC: Beard Group.

Kotter, John P. 1995. "Leading Change: Why Transformation Efforts Fail." *Harvard Business Review* 73 (2) (March–April), 59–67.

Leavitt, Harold. 1987. "Applied Organizational Changes in Industry: Structural, Technological and Humanistic Approaches." In *Handbook of Organizations,* ed. James G. March. New York: Garland.

Lewin, Kurt. 1951. *Field Theory in Social Science.* New York: Harper and Row.

Lipkin, Alan J. 1994. "Legal Framework for Bankruptcy and Reorganization Proceedings in International Emerging Markets." Merrill Lynch Extra Credit, September–October, 39–49. New York: Merrill Lynch.

Little, Arthur D. 1993. "Re-engineering the Hot New Managing Tool." *Fortune,* August 23, 41–45.

Lowenstein, Roger. 1996. "Riklis Plays McCrory Creditors Perfectly." *Wall Street Journal,* March 14, C1.

Lucheux, Jean-Michel, and Remi Passemard. 1995. "International Bankruptcy Proceedings in the European Union." *Turnarounds & Workouts Europe.* July 1, 4 (4), 7–8. Washington, DC: Beard Group.

Luecke, Richard. 1994. *Scuttle Your Ships before Advancing.* New York: Oxford University Press.

Management Accounting. 1995. "New Directions in Finance: Strategic Outsourcing," report prepared by the Economist Intelligence Unit and Arthur Andersen, December.

Manganelli, Raymond, and Mark Klein. 1994. *The Re-engineering Handbook: A Step by Step Guide to Business Transformation.* New York: AMACOM.

Maslow, Abraham. 1954. *Motivation and Personality.* New York: Harper and Row.

Mazzei, Agnese. 1995. "Bankruptcy Proceedings in Italy." *Turnarounds & Workouts Europe,* September 1, 4 (5), 1-1. Washington, DC: Beard Group.

McCartney, Scott. 1995. "How to Make an Airline Run on Schedule." *Wall Street Journal,* December 22, B1.

Meyer, Marc, and Alvin Lehnerd. 1997. *The Power of Product Platforms.* New York: Free Press.

Michel, A., and I. Shaked. 1990. "The LBO Nightmare: Fraudulent Conveyance Risk." *Financial Analyst Journal* 46 (March–April), 41–50.

Mikels, Rick. 1994. "Creditor/Debtor Power." Lecture, Northeastern University, Boston, MA.

Milbank, Dana. 1993. "F&C International Fires Its Chairman, Discloses Discrepancies in Inventory." *Wall Street Journal,* April 5, A13.

Morse, Dale, and Wayne Shaw. 1988. "Investing in Bankrupt Firms." *Journal of Finance* 43 (5) (December), 1193–1206.

Murray, M. 1996. "Massive Restructuring at Scotts to Include Cuts in Spending, Staff." *Wall Street Journal,* April 3, B4.

Narisetti, Raju. 1994. "Gibson Greetings to Restate 1993 Profit, Reduce It by 20%; Stock Tumbles 14%." *Wall Street Journal,* July 5.

Nelson, Emily. 1996. "Danka to Market Kodak Copier Line as Part of Sale." *Wall Street Journal,* September 10, A4.

New York Times. 1996a. "On the Battlefield, Millions of Casualties." March 3–10, A1.

———. 1996b. "Paid by the Widget and Proud." June 16, D1.

———. 1995. "Fraud Can Occur at a Company Even with Auditors Checking." September 22, D6.

———. 1993a. Article on research by John Addison and McKinley Blackburn, August 3, D1–2.

———. 1993b. "Critics of Bankruptcy Law See Inefficiency and Waste." April 12, D1.

Nierenberg, Gerard. 1984. *The Art of Negotiations.* New York: Pocket Books.

1995 Bankruptcy Yearbook & Almanac. 1995. Boston, MA: George Putnam New Generation Research Inc.

Noble, Barbara Presley. 1994. "Questioning Productivity Beliefs." *New York Times,* July 10, 21.

Nolo's Little Law Book. 1996. Berkeley, CA: Nolo Press.

O'Brien, Timothy L. 1997. "Wesco Finds Strange Answer to Losing Money: Spend More." *Wall Street Journal Interactive Edition,* April 10, 1–5.

O'Glove, Thornton. 1987. *Quality of Earnings: The Investor's Guide to How Much Money a Company Is Really Making.* New York: Wiley.

Pantalone, Coleen, and Marjorie Platt. 1987a. "Predicting Commercial Bank Failure since Deregulation." *Federal Reserve Bank New England—Economic Review* 4, 37–47.

———. 1987b. "Predicting Failure of Savings and Loan Associations." *Journal of American Real Estate and Urban Economics Association* 15 (2), 46–64.

Pearl, Daniel. 1992. "Judge Orders Removal of Two Cascade Officials." *Wall Street Journal,* June 1, A14.

Pedersen, Laura. 1995. "One Florida Attraction Not in the Brochures." *New York Times,* July 9, C3.

Pereira, Joseph. 1995. "Bradless Seeks Bankruptcy Protection, but Denies It Is Facing Liquidity Crisis." *Wall Street Journal,* June 26, A10.

Petzinger, Thomas, Jr. 1996. "Lisa Zankman Solved Her Staffing Woes with a Wacky Plan." *Wall Street Journal,* June 21, B1.

Phillips, Michael M. 1996. "Vickrey and Mirlees Win Nobel." *Wall Street Journal,* October 9, A1.

Pisek, Paul E. 1987. "Defining Quality at the Marketing/Development Interface." *Quality Progress* 22 (6) (June), 28–36.

Platt, Harlan. 1995. "A Note on Identifying Likely IPO Bankruptcies: A Symphonic Paradox." *Journal of Accounting, Auditing, and Finance* 10 (1) (Winter), 71–80.

———. 1994. *The First Junk Bond.* Armonk, NY: M. E. Sharpe.

———. 1993-94. "Measuring the Cost of Loan Workout." *Journal of Retail Banking* 15 (4) (Winter), 39–44.

———. 1991. "The LBO Executive: Risk Today, Gone Tomorrow?" In *A Business Perspective.* Boston, MA: Northeastern University College of Business Administration.

———. 1989. "The Determinants of Inter-Industry Failure." *Journal of Economics and Business* 41, 1–19.

———. 1987. "Determinants of Executive Compensation: The Neoclassical Model versus Concept Formation." *Journal of Economic Psychology* 8, 255–72.

———. 1985. *Why Companies Fail.* Lexington, MA: Lexington Books.

Platt, Harlan, Guangli Chen, and Marjorie Platt. 1995. "Sustainable Growth Rate of Firms in Financial Distress." *Journal of Economics and Finance* 19 (2) (Summer), 147–51.

Platt, Harlan, and Marjorie Platt. 1997. "Excessive Debt or Inefficiency? Evidence on the Causes of Leveraged Buyout Failure." Working Paper, Northeastern University, Boston, MA.

———. 1994. "Business Cycle Effects on State Corporate Failure Rates." *Journal of Economics and Business* 46 (2), 113–27.

———. 1991a. "Eluding Business Failure: Capital Structure Planning Using a Bankruptcy Model." *Turnarounds & Workouts: Survey Crisis Management* 1 (1), July 15, 3–4.

———. 1991b. "A Note on the Use of Industry-Relative Ratios in Bankruptcy Prediction." *Journal of Banking and Finance* 15 (6), 1183–94.

———. 1990. "Development of a Stable Class of Predictive Variables: The Case of Bankruptcy Prediction." *Journal of Business Finance and Accounting* 17 (1), 31–53.

Platt, Harlan, Marjorie Platt, and Jon Pedersen. 1994. "Bankruptcy Discrimination with Real Variables." *Journal of Business Finance and Accounting* 21 (4), 491–510.

Queen, Maggie, and Richard Roll. 1987. "Firm Mortality: Using Market Indicator to Predict Survival." *Financial Analysts Journal* (May–June), 9–26.

Rawden, David. 1991. "Understanding the Stock for Debt Exception." *Distressed Business and Real Estate Newsletter* 5 (4) (October–November), 245–47.

Rexer, Christian, and Timothy Sheehan. 1994. "Organizing the Firm: Choosing the Right Business Entity." *Journal of Applied Corporate Finance* 7 (1) (Spring), 59–65.

Robertson, T. 1993. "Fraud Awareness Auditing." In *Auditing.* New York: Irwin.

Rodgers, R., J. E. Hunter, and D. L. Rogers. 1993. "Influence of Top Management Commitment on Management Program Success." *Journal of Applied Psychology* 78 (1) (February), 151–55.

Roth, Harold, and Wayne Morse. 1983. "Let's Help Measure and Report Quality Costs." *Management Accounting* (August), 27–29.

Rowland, Mary. 1995. "If the Tax Man Says, I'll Be Seeing You." *New York Times,* February 26, B2.

Rundle, Rhonda L. 1996. "Sunrise, Restating Net Lower, Claims Faked Data." *Wall Street Journal,* January 5, A18.

Rutberg, Sidney. 1994. *The History of Asset Based Lending.* New York: Commercial Finance Association.

Sampson, Anthony. 1995. *Company Man: The Rise and Fall of Corporate Life.* New York: HarperCollins.

Sandler, Linda. 1996. "Marvel Investors Find the Perils in Perelman's Superhero Plan." *Wall Street Journal,* November 18, C1.

Schendel, D. E., R. Patten, and J. Riggs. 1975. "Corporate Turnaround Strategies." Working Paper 486. Krannert Graduate School of Industrial Administration, Purdue University, West Lafayette, IN.

Schifrin, Matthew. 1994. "Bust-outs and Bleed-outs." *Forbes,* November 7, 51.

Schilit, Howard M. 1993. *Financial Shenanigans: How to Detect Accounting Gimmicks and Fraud in Financial Reports.* New York: McGraw-Hill.

Scully, J. 1987, *Odyssey: Pepsi to Apple—A Journey of Adventure.* New York: Harper and Row.

Shuchman, Matthew L., and Jerry S. White. 1995. *The Art of the Turnaround.* New York: AMACOM.

Sinkey, Joseph. 1975. "A Multivariate Statistical Analysis of the Characteristics of Problem Banks." *Journal of Finance* 30 (1), 21–36.

Sirkin, Harold, and George Stalk. 1990. "Fix the Process, Not the Problem." *Harvard Business Review* 68 (4) (July–August), 26–33.

Skadden Arps Meagher & Flom. 1993. "Fiduciary Duties of Directors of Financially Troubled Corporations." In *Current Legal Issues Facing Massachusetts Based Companies in 1993,* 39–56.

Smith, Adam. 1776. *The Wealth of Nations.* Reprint, 1994, New York: Modern Library.

Smith, Randall. 1993. "RJR Nabisco's Use of Accounting Technique Dealing with Goodwill Is Getting a Hard Look." *Wall Street Journal,* April 14, C2.

Smith, Randall, and Steven Lipin. 1996. "Are Companies Using Restructuring Costs to Fudge the Figures?" *Wall Street Journal,* January 30, A1.

Standard & Poor's Compustat™. 1996. New York, Standard & Poor's.

Stein, Sol. 1989. *A Feast for Lawyers: Inside Chapter 11—An Exposé.* New York: M. Evans.

"Stern Stewart Performance 1,000." 1995. *Journal of Applied Corporate Finance* (Winter) 111–38.

Stewart, Bennett. 1994. "Stern Stewart EVA Roundtable." *Journal of Applied Corporate Finance* 7 (2) (Summer), 54–59.

Stewart, T. A. 1994. "Rate Your Readiness to Change." *Fortune,* February 7, 106–10.

Stickney, Clyde P. 1993. *Financial Statement Analysis: A Strategic Perspective.* 2d ed. New York: Dryden.

Strom, Stephanie. 1996. "Double Trouble at Linda Wachner's Twin Companies." *New York Times,* August 4, D3-1.

Summers, Mark S. 1989. *Bankruptcy Explained.* New York: Wiley.

Tomasko, Robert M. 1993. *Rethinking the Corporation: The Architecture of Change.* New York: AMACOM.

Turnarounds & Workouts Europe. 1995a. "The New German Insolvency Law." July 1, 4 (4), 1-1. Washington: Beard Group.

———. 1995b. "Revisions to the Swiss Bankruptcy Code." *Turnarounds & Workouts Europe.* November 1, 4 (6), 1-1. Washington: Beard Group.

Uniform Commercial Code. 1991. The American Law Institute and the National Conference of Commissioners on Uniform State Laws.

United States Small Business Association. 1990. *Small Business Success Guide.* Washington, DC: USSBA.

Wall Street Journal. 1996a. "America West Awards Pact for Aircraft Maintenance." January 22, B8.

——. 1996b. "Asset Backed Securities." March 14, C20.

——. 1996c. "Call it Dumbsizing: Why Some Companies Regret Cost-Cutting." May 14, A1.

——. 1996d. "A Rich Benefits Plan Gives GM Competitors Cost Edge." March 21, B1.

——. 1995a. "Alliance with Lockheed Planned for Maintenance." December 6, B4.

——. 1995b. "Denver Sues Continental over Airport Lease Pact." April 12, A3.

——. 1995c. "How Low-Key Style Let a Con Man Steal Millions from Bosses." December 4, B1.

——. 1995d. "Kmart Advertises Jobs, but Posts Are Closed to Former Employees." February 27.

——. 1995e. "Lenders' Stampede Tramples Caldor." October 26, C1.

——. 1995f. "Retailer to Close 375 Stores in '96; Chess King to Cease." November 14, B4.

——. 1995g. "Spate of Sudden Junk-Bond Crashes Awakens Investors, Analysts to Companies' Tough Times." August 28, C2.

Wertheim, Edward. 1995. "Negotiations and Resolving Conflicts: A Guide." Working Paper, Northeastern University, Boston, MA, April 24.

Whitman, Martin J., and Stanley J. Garstka. 1992. "Bankruptcy: Reforming a Flawed Process." *Yale Management* (Fall), 2–15.

Wilson, Edwin. 1995. "The Wonder Kid of Broadway." *Wall Street Journal,* September 20, A33.

Woo, Junda, and Daniel Pearl. 1992. "Former Cascade International Officials Are Charged with Corruption, Larceny." *Wall Street Journal,* November 13, A16.

Zachary, G. Pascal. 1996. "More Public Workers Lose Well-Paying Jobs as Outsourcing Grows." *Wall Street Journal,* August 6, A1.

Zavgren, Christine. 1988. Unpublished paper.

Zimmerman, Jerold. 1994. "Stern Stewart EVA Roundtable." *Journal of Applied Corporate Finance* 7 (2) (Summer), 54.

Index